Constitutional Remedies

Recent Titles in Reference Guides to the United States Constitution
Jack Stark, Series Editor

The Right to the Assistance of Counsel
James J. Tomkovicz

Prohibited Government Acts
Jack Stark

State Sovereign Immunity
Melvyn R. Durchslag

Constitutional Remedies

A Reference Guide to the United States Constitution

Michael L. Wells and
Thomas A. Eaton

Foreword by Marshall S. Shapo

REFERENCE GUIDES TO THE
UNITED STATES CONSTITUTION, NUMBER 4
Jack Stark, *Series Editor*

PRAEGER

Westport, Connecticut
London

Library of Congress Cataloging-in-Publication Data

Wells, Michael L.
Constitutional remedies : a reference guide to the United States Constitution / Michael L. Wells and Thomas A. Eaton ; foreword by Marshall S. Shapo.
p. cm.—(Reference guides to the United States Constitution, ISSN 1539-8986 ; no. 4)
Includes bibliographical references and index.
ISBN 0-313-31449-7 (alk. paper)
1. Constitutional law—United States. 2. Remedies (Law)—United States. 3. Procedure (Law)—United States. I. Eaton, Thomas A., 1950- II. Title. III. Series.
KF4550.W45 2002
342.73'02—dc21 2002067783

British Library Cataloguing in Publication Data is available.

Library of Congress Catalog Card Number: 2002067783
ISBN: 0-313-31449-7
ISSN: 1539-8986

First published in 2002

Praeger Publishers, 88 Post Road West, Westport, CT 06881
An imprint of Greenwood Publishing Group, Inc.
www.praeger.com

Printed in the United States of America

The paper used in this book complies with the Permanent Paper Standard issued by the National Information Standards Organization (Z39.48–1984)

10 9 8 7 6 5 4 3 2 1

We would like to dedicate this book to the Honorable John D. Butzner and Robert R. Merhige, Jr., who taught us about law, the Constitution, and the pursuit of justice, and whose careers exemplify the highest aspirations of our profession.

The very essence of civil liberty certainly consists in the right of every individual to claim the protection of the laws, whenever he receives an injury.

—Chief Justice John Marshall, *Marbury v. Madison*,
1 Cranch 137 (1803)

Contents

Series Foreword

JACK STARK

One can conceive of the United States Constitution in many ways. For example, noting the reverence in which it has been held, one can think of it as equivalent to a sacred text. Unfortunately, most of its devotees have had less knowledge and even less understanding of the document than they have had reverence for it. Sometimes it is treated as primarily a political document and on that basis has been subjected to analysis, such as Charles Beard's *An Economic Interpretation of the Constitution of the United States*. One can plausibly argue that the Constitution seems most astounding when seen in light of the intellectual effort that has been associated with it. Three brief but highly intense bursts of intellectual energy produced, and established as organic law, most of the Constitution as it now exists. Two of those efforts, sustained over a long period of time, have enabled us to better understand the document.

The first burst of energy occurred at the Constitutional Convention. Although some of the delegates' business, such as the struggle between populous and nonpopulous states about their representation in Congress, was political, much of it was about fundamental issues of political theory. A few of the delegates had or later achieved international eminence for their intellects. Among them were Benjamin Franklin, Alexander Hamilton, and James Madison. Others, although less well known, had first-rate minds. That group includes George Mason and George Wythe. Many of the delegates contributed intelligently. Although the Convention's records are less than satisfactory, they indicate clearly enough that the delegates worked mightily to constitute not merely a polity but a rational polity—one that would rise to the standards envisioned by the delegates' intellectual ancestors. Their product, though brief, is amazing. William Gladstone called it "the most wonderful work ever struck off."

Despite the delegates' eminence and the Constitution's excellence as seen from our place in history, its ratification was far from certain. That state of affairs necessitated the second burst of intellectual energy associated with that document: the debate over ratification. Soon after the convention adjourned, articles and speeches—some supporting the Constitution and some attacking it—began to proliferate. A national debate commenced—not only about the document itself but also about the nature of the polity that ought to exist in this country. Both sides included many writers and speakers who were verbally adroit and steeped in the relevant political and philosophical literature. The result was an accumulation of material that is remarkable for both its quantity and its quality. At its apex is the *Federalist Papers*, a production of Alexander Hamilton, James Madison, and John Jay that deserves a place among the great books of Western culture.

Another burst, although not as impressive as the first two but highly respectable, occurred when the Bill of Rights was proposed. Some delegates to the Constitutional Convention had vigorously asserted that such guarantees should be included in the original document. George Mason, the principal drafter of the Virginia Declaration of Rights, so held, and he walked out of the convention when he failed to achieve his purpose. Even those who had argued that the rights in question were implicit recognized the value of adding protection of them to the Constitution. The debate was thus focused on the rights that were to be explicitly granted, not on whether any rights ought to be explicitly granted. Again many writers and speakers entered the fray, and again the debate was solidly grounded in theory and was conducted on a high intellectual level.

Thus, within a few years a statement of organic law and a vital coda to it had been produced. However, the meaning and effect of many of that document's provisions were far from certain; the debates on ratification of the Constitution and the Bill of Rights had demonstrated that. In addition, the document existed in a vacuum, because statutes and actions had not been assessed by its standards. The attempt to resolve these problems began after Chief Justice John Marshall, in Marbury v. Madison, asserted the right of the U.S. Supreme Court to interpret and apply the Constitution. Judicial interpretation and application of the Constitution, beginning with the first constitutional case and persisting until the most recent, is one of the sustained exertions of intellectual energy associated with the Constitution. The framers would be surprised by some of the results of these activities. References in the document to "due process," which seems to refer only to procedures, have been held also to have a substantive dimension. A right to privacy has been found lurking among the penumbras of various parts of the text. A requirement that states grant the same "privileges and immunities" to citizens of other states that they granted to their own citizens, which seemed to guarantee important rights, was not held to be particularly important. The corpus of judicial interpretations of the Constitution is now as voluminous as that document is terse.

As judicial interpretations multiplied, another layer—interpretations of interpretations—appeared, and also multiplied. This layer, the other sustained intellectual effort associated with the Constitution, consists of articles, most of them published in law reviews, and books on the Constitution. This material varies in quality and significance. Some of these works of scholarship result from meticulous examination and incisive thought. Others repeat earlier work, or apply a fine-tooth comb to matters that are too minute even for such a comb. Somewhere in that welter of tertiary material is the answer to almost every question that one could ask about constitutional law. The problem is finding the answer that one wants. The difficulty of locating useful guidance is exacerbated by the bifurcation of most constitutional scholarship into two kinds. In "Two Styles of Social Science Research," C. Wright Mills delineates macroscopic and molecular research. The former deals with huge issues, the latter with tiny issues. Virtually all of the scholarship on the Constitution is of one of those two types. Little of it is macroscopic, but that category does include some first-rate syntheses such as Jack Rakove's *Original Meanings*. Most constitutional scholarship is molecular and, again, some fine work is included in that category.

In his essay, Mills bemoans the inability of social scientists to combine the two kinds of research that he describes to create a third category that will be more generally useful. This series of books is an attempt to do for constitutional law the intellectual work that Mills proposed for social science. The author of each book has dealt carefully and at reasonable length with a topic that lies in the middle range of generality. Upon completion, this series will consist of thirty-seven books, each on a constitutional law topic. Some of the books, such as the book on freedom of the press, explicate one portion of the Constitution's text. Others, such as the volume on federalism, treat a topic that has several anchors in the Constitution. The books, on constitutional history and constitutional interpretation range over the entire document, but each does so from a single perspective. Except for a very few of the books the special circumstances of which dictate minor changes in format, each book includes the same components—a brief history of the topic, a lengthy and sophisticated analysis of the current state of the law on that topic, a bibliographical essay that organizes and evaluates scholarly material in order to facilitate further research, a table of cases, and an index. The books are intellectually rigorous—in fact, authorities have written them—but, due to their clarity and to brief definitions of terms that are unfamiliar to laypersons, each is comprehensible and useful to a wide audience, one that ranges from other experts on the book's subject to intelligent non-lawyers.

In short, this series provides an extremely valuable service to the legal community and to others who are interested in constitutional law, as every citizen should be. Each book is a map of part of the U.S. Constitution. When this series is complete, each book will be a third kind of scholarly work that combines the macroscopic and the molecular. Together they will explicate all of the important constitutional topics. Anyone who wants assistance in understanding either a topic in constitutional law or the Constitution as a whole can easily find it in these books.

Foreword

Marshall S. Shapo

Led by the Supreme Court, American courts have built a fascinating body of law on a combination of the United States Constitution and federal statutes. At a time in which concerns about official abuse of power remain intense and perhaps even gain in intensity, constitutional remedies are of interest to every American.

As Professors Wells and Eaton explain in this excellent study, the jurisprudence of constitutional remedies effectively defines the rights of injured citizens at their point of contact with power. They provide chapter and verse on both the theory and practice of the law governing alleged violations of constitutional rights by officials and sometimes governments.

In this volume Wells and Eaton have done a service to both the legal profession and the public. On the technical side, their work will be a great aid to lawyers who desire a comprehensive summary of the law. As a chronicle, it provides a useful description of the law for historians as well as laypersons who wish to understand it.

Particularly noteworthy in the work of Wells and Eaton, each distinguished for long-term scholarship in the area, are their careful analyses of discrete areas of the law and their subtle explorations of the relationships among them. Just one illustration of such probing is the section on the relationship between qualified immunity and substantive constitutional rights.

The history of the so-called "constitutional tort" in our law is a unique one. This theory emerged from the aftermath, or Reconstruction, of our great internal cataclysm, the Civil War. The Ku Klux Act, enacted in 1871, became the statutory foundation for an all-purpose set of remedies built on the Constitution itself.

Wells and Eaton present a detailed accounting of how courts developed the abstract language of both statute and Constitution to meet a changing culture and an evolving set of expectations about the vocation of the law and the role of courts. But if scholarly virtue lies partly in the details, it also manifests itself in the broad sweep of history the authors present as a frame for their analysis of specific topics.

The authors set out to describe the law, and in this they succeed admirably. But beyond that, they offer measured criticisms, their power deriving from their care and restraint. Exemplary is their critique of the Supreme Court's difficulty in establishing a consistent vocabulary of due process. They also provide a measured and useful balancing of arguments in the controversy about affirmative constitutional duties.

Besides their careful examination of the law and its theory, Wells and Eaton dig into the practical considerations that confront litigating lawyers. Analyzing specific remedies in detail, they range along a spectrum of trench-level considerations and include a detailed section on attorney's fees.

When all the details are rehearsed, however, the great story is the tale of how American courts have shaped, and sometimes reshaped, the remedies of constitutional rights. The straight police brutality case—graphically emblematic of abuse of power—has been a staple of constitutional tort litigation. Beyond that, however, courts have applied these remedies concerning some of the heaviest topics in our political and legal lives: reapportionment, desegregation, abortion.

It is a story that is intellectually challenging, always fascinating, and sometimes downright inspiring. Professors Wells and Eaton have organized it clearly and told it straight.

Acknowledgments

We would like to thank Marshall Shapo for writing the foreword to this book. We also wish to express our gratitude to Frank Beacham for his research assistance and to Cindy Wentworth and Sylvia Stogden for their preparation of the manuscript. Finally, we thank Jack Stark for his role in organizing and giving us the opportunity to participate in this project.

Introduction: Remedies and the Constitution

This introduction addresses three basic issues that relate to the entire field of constitutional remedies and that therefore cannot be treated adequately in discussions of aspects of the doctrine. One of these is the relationship between rights and remedies. We show that one cannot understand constitutional rights without also studying the remedial law. Then we describe the types of constitutional remedies and note the ways in which those remedies may be used to enforce particular rights. Finally, we discuss the general aims of constitutional remedies.

RELATIONS BETWEEN CONSTITUTIONAL RIGHTS AND REMEDIES

Other books in this series examine the entire range of constitutional rights, such as freedom of speech, freedom from unjustified searches, the right to due process and equal protection of the law, and the right against cruel and unusual punishment. The emphasis in those books is on the substantive rules that forbid the state and national governments from arbitrarily discriminating against people, that keep governments from intruding in one way or another on the private lives of individuals, or that limit governmental powers in other ways. This book has a different focus. Although it contains some discussion of substantive rights, it mainly assumes that someone has suffered violation of a constitutional right and turns its attention to the types of relief that may be available to the victim of the violation. The book describes the law of constitutional remedies and, in particular, the use of awards of money damages and injunctions (ordering officers to stop doing something the court has determined is illegal, or ordering them to do something the law requires of them) as means of redressing constitutional violations. In the private law system, suits to recover damages for physical or emotional harm sustained in the past are called "common law torts" ("torts" because these cases involve wrongs done to the plaintiff, typically in a noncontractual setting; "common law" because most of the law in the area is made by judges, and this is the term courts use to denote judge-made, as opposed to statutory or constitutional, law).

In focusing on remedial issues, this book differs in certain ways from most of the other volumes in this series. The law of constitutional remedies is not grounded in the constitutional text, for the Constitution contains very few remedial provisions. Two themes dominate the text of the United States Constitution. One is governmental structure. This is the central concern of the original document, ratified in 1788. Most of its provisions address the division of power between the national and state governments and among the legislative (article 1), executive (article 2), and judicial (article 3) branches of the national government. The second major constitutional theme is the relation between the state and the people. The main aim here is to guarantee citizens certain rights so as to thwart abuses of power. Though the original Constitution contains few individual rights, the omission was a source of concern to many citizens of the new nation and was quickly corrected. To this end, the Bill of Rights, enacted in 1791, and the Thirteenth, Fourteenth, and Fifteenth Amendments, ratified after the Civil War, set forth constitutional rights that limit the scope of governmental power over persons. For example, the First Amendment guarantees freedom of speech and religion; the Fourth Amendment restricts the power of government to search persons and property; the Eighth forbids cruel and unusual punishment; and the Fourteenth obliges states to accord everyone equal protection of the law and prevents states from depriving anyone of life, liberty, or property without due process of law. Nowhere in the document or the amendments does one find any effort to guarantee adequate remedies for violations of constitutional rights, apart from provisions in the post–Civil War amendments authorizing Congress to enact "appropriate legislation" to enforce them. The consequence of this lack of attention to remedies in the Constitution itself is that, as noted earlier, most offensive constitutional remedies have, at least superficially, a statutory or common law "pedigree."

Another difference between this book and analyses of other constitutional topics is that the policy considerations bearing on what remedies should be available may be quite different from the matters of principle that determine the outcome of disputes over the scope of constitutional rights. Many leading constitutional theorists share the views of Peter Schuck. Addressing specifically the constitutional tort context, Schuck maintains that "rights and remedies are utterly different legal phenomena—products of distinct reasoning processes employing distinct sources, methodology, and decision criteria."[1] Ronald Dworkin argues that

> the best interpretations of the most important rights-bearing clauses of the Constitution show these clauses to embody principles of political morality that are abstract in the sense that they require fresh moral judgment to apply to particular circumstances . . . [J]udges must

engage in moral reasoning at two levels. They must try to identify and formulate the abstract principle that best expresses the content of a constitutional provision, properly understood, and they must also decide whether that principle, so understood, has been violated in the case at hand.[2]

Remedies, on the other hand, are "sensitive to consequence."[3] Owen Fiss claims that remedies are "subsidiary, . . . strategic, . . . [and] instrumental" and operate "in the world of practical reality."[4] Unlike rights, remedies are not immune to "incursions by prudence, compromise, and utility."[5]

Granting these differences between constitutional rights and constitutional remedies, it is impossible to understand the former without studying the latter as well. Even the most rigorous constitutional theorist would likely agree that, as a practical matter, rights and remedies go hand in hand. The reason people assert constitutional rights in the course of litigation is in the hope of obtaining some remedy for the violation of those rights. As a result, constitutional rights and remedies interact constantly. Many modern constitutional rights can hardly be enforced at all without offensive remedies. These include the free speech rights of public employees, the right against the use of excessive force by the police, the Eighth Amendment right of prisoners to be housed in humane conditions, and such equal protection rights as desegregated schools and equally apportioned legislative districts. What these disparate rights have in common is the kind of action by which the state may threaten them. When the state encroaches upon these rights, it does not use the judicial process. It merely apportions districts, or assigns students to public schools, or fires employees, or houses prisoners, or treats suspects as state officers see fit. As a result, injured persons cannot enforce these rights by raising them defensively as a shield against an enforcement action brought by the state or someone else. The aggrieved party must have recourse to an offensive remedy for an injunction or damages. In order to understand the practical scope of these rights in the real world, how they operate, and whether lawyers and judges can enforce them effectively, one must understand the relevant remedial doctrine. This is so even if remedies themselves do not have a constitutional pedigree and even if the considerations relevant to remedial issues differ sharply from those that inform substantive constitutional decisions.

For example, one cannot grasp the true significance of the school desegregation right without knowing that certain remedies are permissible and others are not. In particular, students may not be bused to a different school district without a showing that the receiving district has practiced government-mandated ("de jure") segregation (Milliken v. Bradley, 1974). Nor can one understand the real-world value of public employee speech rights without understanding the remedial context in which those rights are enforced. In the Supreme Court's opinions on public employee speech, the rights seem to be stronger than they are in practice. The problem is that they usually have to be vindicated in suits for damages, and the plaintiff faces a host of difficulties in such suits.[6]

Furthermore, the premises of "rights essentialism" (as the views of scholars such as Dworkin, Fiss, and Schuck have been called) are not necessarily valid in any event. Consider the proposition that rights and remedies must be kept separate because they are governed by fundamentally different considerations. The Court's actual practice is at odds with any such sharp distinction between the two domains. Whether or not a right exists in a given situation may depend on the remedy sought by the person asserting the right. Perhaps an illustration will help to make this point. We shall see later in the book that a public employee does not commit a constitutional tort when he makes defamatory statements against another citizen, even if the speaker knows the statements are false and acts with malice, intending to destroy his victim's reputation (Paul v. Davis, 1976; Siegert v. Gilley, 1991). (Statements of this kind would expose the speaker to liability under widely accepted principles of defamation law if uttered by a private person.) From the perspective of abstract constitutional principle, the Supreme Court's refusal to impose constitutional tort liability is hard to justify, because the malicious official who uses words to harm another can hardly be distinguished from the similarly motivated official who uses a gun or a nightstick to accomplish the same purpose. Yet the latter may be charged with a constitutional violation, while the former cannot. The likely explanation for the outcomes in the defamation cases is that the Court feared the remedial consequences of recognizing a constitutional claim. The Court in *Paul* declared that ruling for the plaintiff "would make of the Fourteenth Amendment a font of tort law to be superimposed upon whatever systems may already be administered by the States." Thus, Daryl Levinson has asserted that "[i]n all likelihood, *Paul* would have come out differently if the only available remedy had been an injunction."[7] Levinson goes on to discuss other examples of a process he calls "shrinking rights to avoid expansive remedies."[8] He also shows that rights are sometimes defined more broadly than they otherwise would be, in order to provide effective protection for the underlying substantive constitutional values at stake.[9] The available remedies often determine the real-world value of the substantive right.[10]

Finally, one may question the validity of the proposition that the sole sources of constitutional remedies are statutory and common law rules. The Constitution itself demands the availability of certain remedies, perhaps including some of the offensive ones. No one disputes that someone who is the target of an enforcement proceeding must, as a matter of constitutional right, be allowed to raise constitutional objections to the imposition of criminal or civil liability. Even in this context, the task of making remedial law is shared by the Supreme Court and Congress. Thus, the legislature may choose the vehicle by which such a challenge may be brought. For example, in World War II Congress enacted price control legislation to be enforced by criminal penalties. The legislation provided that certain constitutional challenges to the validity of the regulations must be brought before engaging in the regulated activity rather than as a defense to the enforcement action, and the Supreme Court upheld this arrangement. (Lockerty v. Phillips, 1943).

When the litigant comes to court in an offensive rather than a defensive posture, a host of new issues arise. The most fundamental of these is that it is uncertain whether and in what circumstances the Constitution itself is an appropriate source of remedial law. The Supreme Court's cases are equivocal as to whether there is a constitutional right to an offensive remedy, or whether the availability of such remedies turns on legislative and judicial discretion.[11]

An important reason for the lack of certainty as to the constitutional status of offensive remedies is that the Court has rarely had to face the issue. The Court has found two other means by which to recognize offensive remedies. One of these is a federal statute, § 1983. The other is an outgrowth of the power possessed by courts generally to fashion rules of law in areas not governed by statutes. This authority to make common law traditionally extends not only to substantive rules, like the law of torts, property, and contracts, but also to the power to create appropriate remedies for violations of rights. The Supreme Court has used this common law remedial power to create federal causes of action for both prospective relief (Ex Parte Young, 1908) and damages (Bivens v. Six Unknown Named Federal Narcotics Agents, 1971). A consequence of the existence of these statutory and common law remedies is that the Court rarely needs to face the question of whether, in their absence, the Constitution itself would require an offensive remedy.

The Supreme Court decisions do contain reasoning that bears on the issue of whether, and in what circumstances, offensive remedies may be constitutionally required, but they send conflicting signals. Some of them suggest that there is a constitutional right to an offensive remedy, while others point in the opposite direction. Support for the latter view may be found in cases that refuse to hear certain constitutional claims on the ground that they present nonjusticiable "political questions," or because special circumstances, such as the need to avoid judicial interference in the affairs of the military, make it unwise to recognize a cause of action (e.g., United States v. Stanley, 1987). In other situations, sovereign immunity prevents litigants from recovering damages from state governments (e.g., Alden v. Maine, 1999; Seminole Tribe of Florida v. Florida, 1996). Suing an official can also prove fruitless, on account of the doctrine of official immunity (e.g., Wilson v. Layne, 1999).

Other rulings support the position that there is indeed a constitutional right to an offensive remedy. When the Court encounters statutes that seem to deny such a remedy by omitting any mention of one, it typically construes the statute in the plaintiff's favor, finding that it provides access to the courts in spite of the lack of explicit textual support for a cause of action (Webster v. Doe, 1988). In most cases that deny a remedy, the Court takes pains to point out the availability of some other source of redress (e.g., Schweiker v. Chilicky, 1988). One case declares outright that, as a matter of federal constitutional law, governments must provide a remedy for takings of private property for public use (First Evangelical Lutheran Church of Glendale v. County of Los Angeles, 1987). In another recent case the Court held that, in connection with tax collection, a state may choose to provide a pre-collection challenge to the constitutional validity of taxes, or it may prefer to deny such review, collect the taxes, and permit a suit for refund, in which the constitutionality of the tax collection could be challenged. But it could not validly deny both. Nor could it hold out the promise of a post-collection action, collect the taxes, and then take away the remedy it had earlier promised (Reich v. Collins, 1994).

Given the inconsistencies among the cases, one cannot confidently answer the question of whether there is a constitutional right to an offensive remedy. There seems to be no ironclad rule requiring effective redress for all constitutional violations. Instead, the cases reflect a general principle favoring redress, both to vindicate rights and to "keep government generally within the bounds of law."[12] Most of the cases are consistent with the following propositions: (a) such a remedy must presumptively be available, unless some good reason stands in the way; (b) one such reason is the need to protect official discretion to act in compliance with what an official believes is valid state law, without fear of being sued in the event that his or her understanding turns out to be wrong; (c) in some circumstances, especially the tax context, governments may choose between allowing suits for prospective relief and requiring compliance with the law and then permitting a suit for damages later.

TYPES OF CONSTITUTIONAL REMEDIES

In order to more fully describe the scope of this book, it will be useful to distinguish between two kinds of constitutional remedies. A person charging a violation of constitutional rights may, depending on the circumstances, wield the Constitution offensively or defensively, as a "sword" or as a "shield".[13] Which type of remedy is appropriate depends on the way in which the government has violated the individual's rights.

Defensive, "shield-like" remedies are employed when the holder of the right is a defendant in a criminal or civil proceeding. In these cases, the individual is the target of an effort by the government (or in some cases another private individual) to enforce a statute or other legal rule (an "enforcement proceeding"). The defendant charges that the law being enforced is itself invalid, or that it is being enforced in an impermissible way on account of the overriding command of the Constitution. An example of the use of a defensive remedy is a criminal defendant on trial for distributing child pornography, who asserts that the statute under which he is being prosecuted violates his First Amendment right to freedom of speech (e.g., New York v. Ferber, 1982). Though remedies of this kind are not specified in the Constitution, the Supreme Court has always recognized that one can assert one's constitutional rights as a defense to an enforcement proceeding. It is a basic constitutional principle that when a court convicts someone of a crime, or awards civil damages against someone, it must rely on law that is compatible with the Constitution. Most of these defensive remedies raise few legal issues and, apart from their bearing on the availability of offensive remedies, will receive little attention in this book.

If the government proceeds against someone by using the judicial process, resort to these defensive remedies may effectively vindicate constitutional rights (though we will see that this is not always true). The main problem with defensive remedies is that the government's enforcement of the criminal and civil law is only one of the contexts in which it may violate constitutional rights. Whenever government officials interact with persons, across the spectrum of government activities, there is a danger that government officers will trample on constitutional rights in one way or another. Suppose government fires an employee who speaks out on an issue of public concern (e.g., Pickering v. Board of Education, 1968). In cases of this kind, citizens' constitutional rights may be violated, yet government has made no use of the judicial process. Consequently, there is no judicial proceeding in which a defendant may raise constitutional rights as a shield. One must become a plaintiff, and use the Constitution as a sword in order to vindicate one's rights.

We are concerned with the legal problems raised by offensive remedies. Here a further distinction will prove useful. Offensive remedies can be divided into two groups, depending on the circumstances of a given constitutional violation. Someone may seek either prospective relief that looks to the future and obliges the government to cease a current violation or forbids it to take unconstitutional action in the future. Alternatively, the violation may be entirely in the past, so that the only practicable remedy is money damages. Sometimes both remedies may be available. If the violation took place in the past and continues into the present, it may be appropriate to award both damages and prospective relief. Some illustrations will show how the appropriate relief depends on the circumstances. Suppose the legislature enacts a statute that requires prayer in the public schools. The statute may be challenged before it ever goes into effect, and the relief requested will be an injunction (an order forbidding state officials from enforcing the statute) or a declaratory judgment (a statement from the court that the statute is unconstitutional, which may then form the basis for a later injunction in the event state officials ignore it).[14] On the other hand, suppose the plaintiff is someone who was beaten by the police in a random incident in the course of a traffic stop. In such a case, the violation is in the past and the appropriate relief would be damages. Finally, a typical case in which both prospective and retrospective relief may be available is when a government employee is fired for speech protected by the First Amendment. The violation occurred in the past and has already produced damages in the form of lost salary and emotional distress, thereby justifying a retrospective remedy. At the same time, the employee may have a right to be reinstated to the post so that he can obtain an injunction ordering the government to rehire him.

Offensive remedies—the focus of this book—are far more important in connection with certain constitutional rights than are others. Some constitutional rights virtually always arise in the context of an enforcement proceeding. We have already noted one example: raising the Constitution as a substantive defense to conviction for a crime, as in the example of the pornographer. The most obvious examples are the rights we have as criminal defendants, such as the right to counsel, the right to confront one's accusers, the right to a speedy trial, and the right to an impartial jury of one's peers. Certain rights are nearly always raised as defenses to private law civil suits. The best example is the free speech right to make certain defamatory statements about others, which one typically raises as a defense to a tort suit brought by a defamed person seeking recovery for libel or slander (e.g., New York Times v. Sullivan, 1964).

Other rights almost always need to be litigated with the putative right-holder on the plaintiff's side of the case seeking an offensive, "sword-like" remedy. Besides the example of firing a public employee for constitutionally impermissible reasons, cited previously to distinguish offensive from defensive remedies, there are many other contexts in which rights must be raised offensively. These include situations in which the state (a) maintains a segregated school system, (b) draws legislative districts so that some contain many more voters than do others, (c) regulates property so heavily that it becomes worthless, (d) runs a prison or a mental hospital in which the inmates nearly starve, are beaten by the guards, and lack access to medical care, (e) refuses to grant a permit for a parade or a demonstration, or (f) the police use excessive force in arresting a suspect. These basic fact patterns give rise to the great majority of constitutional litigation seeking offensive remedies.

Some rights may be enforced by either offensive or defensive remedies or by both, depending on the circumstances. For example, the state may have a criminal statute that forbids certain kinds of speech, such as hate speech or speech tending to incite people to overthrow the government. One may challenge this statute by violating it, submitting to a criminal prosecution, and raising the First Amendment as a defense. But this is a risky strategy. Many people would rather not risk being wrong about the constitutionality of such a statute if they could wind up in prison as a result of the error. They would prefer to take the role of a plaintiff suing the state's attorney, charge that the statute violates freedom of speech, and seek the offensive remedy of an injunction forbidding the state from enforcing the statute. Whether a prospective challenger will be permitted to bring such a suit depends on the answers to two questions. First, is the challenger already a defendant in a criminal case? If so, he or she will probably be obligated to raise the constitutional issue there (Younger v. Harris, 1971). If not, the second question must be addressed: Is there a real threat that the statute in the future will be enforced against the challenger? If not, the case is not "ripe" for judicial consideration. But if others have been prosecuted, or if the challenger has been threatened with prosecution, there is a good chance the case will be ripe (Steffel v. Thompson, 1974). (See "Prospective Relief" for a more detailed treatment of the hurdles one must overcome in order to pursue an offensive remedy in this kind of case).

Many courts and commentators, looking for a way to describe the distinctive cause of action such a case presents, have developed the habit of combining the tort analogy with the distinctively constitutional aspect of the case. Thus, they use the label "constitutional tort" to describe lawsuits in which someone seeks to obtain damages for a constitutional violation, and we will follow that usage here. "Constitutional remedies" is a broader term, covering not only suits for damages but also requests for injunctive and other forward-looking ("prospective") relief. Suits for damages and injunctive relief demand most of our attention, as they present especially complex problems of constitutional principle and remedial policy.

AIMS OF THE LAW OF CONSTITUTIONAL REMEDIES

In order to resolve issues related to constitutional remedies, courts need to identify the goals they seek to achieve in this area of the law. In this way, a court can evaluate the alternatives by asking which of them will better achieve the policies at stake. Not surprisingly, one finds both in the cases and in the scholarly literature much analysis of the goals of constitutional remedies and how best to achieve them. A noteworthy feature of these debates is that they are largely limited to just one of the remedies discussed previously. The focus is on suits for damages rather than defensive remedies or injunctions. Our understanding of the law of constitutional remedies can be enhanced by asking why this is so.

The answer lies in the costs and benefits of remedies. Remedies always have a benefit, in that they enforce constitutional values. Remedies that have few costs will be imposed routinely, while those with significant costs will be limited in some way. When someone raises the constitution defensively, as a shield against criminal conviction or civil damages, no issue arises as to why he or she is allowed to do so; no legitimate cost is inflicted by such a remedy. In our legal culture, it is universally agreed that a court may not impose penalties unless the law authorizes them. A statute or common law rule that violates the Constitution is invalid and cannot be invoked as authority for any sanction, so long as the defendant raises the constitutional objection at the proper time and place. The same is true of the imposition of penalties by the use of procedures that fail to meet constitutional requirements, so long as the error is not so trivial as to fall within the "harmless error" doctrine.

Nor is there much discussion in the cases of the goals served by prospective relief. Once the state's current or threatened action is found to be unconstitutional, the general view is that the conduct ought to be stopped, absent special circumstances. By "special circumstances" we mean that sometimes there will be significant costs associated with such a remedy that need to be taken into account. If an injunction would be especially disruptive of legitimate state goals—as in the case of an employee being fired and whose reinstatement would produce turmoil in the office—the injunction may be denied. Even then, the plaintiff may be entitled to a substitute in the form of "front pay" (i.e., a portion of the salary he or she would have received in the future, but for the unjust firing). More often, the cost of prospective relief will merely be that the state cannot pursue its unconstitutional objectives and that this kind of cost does not count, just as it counts for nothing in the defensive context. In both areas, the benefits of the remedy are great and the legitimate costs are small. Given this relationship between costs and benefits, courts naturally conclude that the appropriate level of constitutional violations is zero or close to it.

Suits for damages present a more complicated set of issues, because one cannot be so confident that the costs of the remedy are generally far less than the benefits. Unlike defensive and prospective remedies, we cannot in any event prevent the constitutional violation itself; it has already taken place. Obliging the defendant to pay money may make up for some harm done, but it cannot wipe out the constitutional violation. Already, then, the benefit of the remedy seems to be less than in those other contexts. As for costs, officers are not merely told what to do now and in the future. The imposition of such a remedy means that officers may be told, after the fact, that what they have done is illegal, and that they must pay damages out of their own pockets. This, in turn, may lead them to be especially cautious in going about their work, failing to take bold and decisive action because they fear making an error that will cost them money.[15] Passivity may not be in the public interest, but it will protect the timid official. By reducing the effectiveness of government in achieving its legitimate ends, damage remedies may generate far greater costs than defensive or prospective remedies. This is the problem of "overdeterrence," and we will see that it carries great weight in some areas of constitutional tort doctrine. In some contexts, the opposite problem may arise: Officials may benefit so much from their constitutional violations that the prospect of being sued will not serve to deter them. In these circumstances, the imposition of damages may accomplish little or nothing.

For these reasons, the Supreme Court has decided that it cannot make the damages remedy generally available, simply for the sake of enforcing the Constitution. Beginning from the premise that the benefits of a damage remedy do not necessarily outweigh the costs, the Court instead has sought to specify more precisely the goals served by damages, as well as to identify the situations in which the costs of liability may not be worth the benefits. The Court has identified two main policies served by awarding damages to the victims of constitutional violations. First, damages vindicate constitutional values and compensate plaintiffs for the lost wages, medical expenses, emotional harm, and other losses caused by the violation. Second, they deter governments and their officers from committing constitutional violations in the future (Carey v. Piphus, 1978).

On the other hand, the important policy serving as a restraint on the imposition of damages is one we adverted to earlier in distinguishing damages from other remedies. Since damage awards result from after-the-fact evaluation by a court of the constitutionality of an officer's action, the Court worries that officers may not merely be deterred from violating the Constitution. There is a problem of overdeterrence of beneficial actions by government (Harlow v. Fitzgerald, 1982). In much of constitutional tort law, the Court seems to perceive its task as being one of determining how much vindication and deterrence can safely be achieved without going too far and overdeterring officers. For example, the "official immunity" doctrine is an effort to minimize the risk of overdeterrence by shielding officers from liability for damages in certain circumstances. We shall see that immunity is rarely an obstacle to obtaining prospective relief, because the justification for the doctrine is not so strong in that context.

NOTES

1. Peter Schuck, *Suing Government for Official Wrongs* (New Haven, Conn.: Yale Univ. Press, 1983) 26.
2. Ronald Dworkin, Reply, 29 Ariz. St. L. J. (1997) 431, 449.
3. Ronald Dworkin, *Law's Empire* (Cambridge, Mass.: Harvard Univ. Press, 1986) 389–92.
4. Owen Fiss, "The Forms of Justice," 93 *Harv. L. Rev.* (1979) 1, 51–52.
5. Schuck, *Suing Government for Official Wrongs* 26–28.
6. Michael L. Wells, "Section 1983, The First Amendment, and Public Employee Speech: Shaping the Right to Fit the Remedy (and Vice Versa)," 35 *Ga. L. Rev.* (2001) 939.
7. Daryl J. Levinson, "Rights Essentialism and Remedial Equilibration," 99 *Colum. L. Rev.* (1999) 857, 893.
8. Id, 894–99.
9. Id., 899–904.
10. Id. 904–11.
11. Richard Fallon, Daniel Meltzer, & David Shapiro, *Hart & Wechsler's The Federal Courts and the Federal System* (Westbury, N.Y.: Fountain Press, 4th ed. 1996) 849–57.
12. Richard Fallon & Daniel Meltzer, "New Law, Non-Retroactivity, and Constitutional Remedies," 104 *Harv. L. Rev.* (1991) 1731, 1779.
13. This metaphor is borrowed from Walter Dellinger, "Of Rights and Remedies: The Constitution as a Sword," 85 *Harv. L. Rev.* (1972) 1532.
14. The federal "declaratory judgment" statute is codified in 28 U.S.C. §§ 2201–02.
15. Shuck, *Suing Government for Official Wrongs* 59–81.

Part I

A History of Constitutional Remedies

If there is a historical pattern in the law of constitutional remedies, it is that the growth of remedial doctrines has responded to the expansion of substantive rights. Early in our history, the Supreme Court recognized few constitutional rights, and the remedial doctrine consisted mainly of the possibility of bringing suit under the traditional common law. As new rights were recognized, pressure grew for remedial doctrines that would effectively enforce those rights. Congress and the Supreme Court responded to the call by authorizing lawsuits for prospective relief and for damages. This discussion traces, in broad strokes, the history of these developments. It is organized by topic, dealing first with sovereign immunity, then with remedies against officers and local governments.

SOVEREIGN IMMUNITY

From the beginning of our history as a nation, the central obstacle to an effective system of constitutional remedies has been the doctrine of "sovereign immunity": that is, the principle that the government may not be sued without its consent. This is not an obstacle to raising the Constitution as a shield, but it immediately becomes a problem whenever someone would like to use the Constitution as a sword, naming the government as the defendant. (This distinction between "sword" and "shield" is described in the Introduction.) In a sense, all of the law of offensive remedies is a study of exceptions to sovereign immunity, for sovereign immunity is a constraint within which all the remedies discussed in succeeding sections have been developed. Therefore, a good place to begin our history is by examining this obstacle that must be overcome if there are to be any offensive remedies at all, and by describing the inroads that have been made upon it.

ENGLAND AND EARLY AMERICA

Throughout this history, and indeed throughout the book, we refer to the "common law." The phrase has several meanings. First, it refers to the source of a legal rule. If a rule is based on a constitutional provision, it is of course called a constitutional rule. If it is found in a statute enacted by the legislature, it is a statutory rule. If it is made by judges, without any clear authorization by Congress or the Constitution, it is common law. But the term has another side to it as well, one that is more relevant to the history of constitutional remedies. It refers to the body of law made by judges in England, beginning after the Norman Conquest in 1066 and continuing into the present. The American colonists brought this body of law with them and, after the American Revolution, legislatures and judges adopted it (with suitable modifications) as the basic framework of the American legal system. Many provisions of the Constitution are based on the common law.

In England and in early America, an important area of common law was (and remains to this day) tort law, which is the body of law dealing with physical and other harms inflicted upon the plaintiff by a stranger, (i.e., a harm produced outside the scope of a contractual relationship). Examples of acts that may give rise to tort suits are a punch in the nose, a car accident, or false claims about the plaintiff in a newspaper story. People may suffer such injuries at the hands of governments and their officers, and one aspect of the common law of England was a body of rules governing such suits. The central point regarding this doctrine is that, going back into the distant past, the rules governing these tort suits were different from those governing suits between private individuals. In general, the rules were tilted in favor of the government and its officers, notably by the doctrine of sovereign immunity.

As long ago as the thirteenth century, the English monarchy successfully asserted sovereign immunity in tort suits brought to recover damages for injuries committed by government officers. It was in the nature of sovereignty, the English courts ruled, that the sovereign may not be sued without his or her consent. Thus, no matter how egregious the king or queen's conduct or how severe the injury inflicted, the victim may have been unable to obtain any redress. In this way, sovereign immunity became part of the common law of England.

A cynic may regard this exception for the monarch as an exercise of naked political power. There is no doubt that English kings and queens were powerful individuals, and judges surely knew their careers would be better served by accepting monarchial immunity than by standing up to royal power. A second factor likely also played a role in the establishment of sovereign immunity. Government then, as today, had greater responsibilities than a private individual and, unlike a private actor, could not easily delimit the scope of its activities. Often it had to act in ways that displeased at least one interested party. Government was, as a result, more vulnerable to being sued and more in need of a special shield against those suits. This provision for government is, if anything, even more relevant today and will be discussed in greater detail in our discussion of modern constitutional remedies (see "Absolute Immunities" and "Qualified Immunity").

Whether the need for special treatment justifies an all-encompassing exemption from defending lawsuits is a separate question. In England, sovereign immunity did not mean that a person injured by official action had no remedy at all. It meant only that he could not sue the king or queen directly. Although one could not bring suit for certain harms, there were royal officers to whom the injured person could, in some circumstances, make an appeal for reimbursement. And the evidence suggests that most persons felt they were treated fairly by these agents of the king. In other circumstances one could bring suit against an officer, either to recover damages for a past injury or to obtain a judicial order forbidding illegal acts in the present or the future. Special defenses were available to royal officers in these suits, but these obstacles did not generally interfere with the overall goal of seeing to it that their activities were subject to judicial oversight.[1]

So long as the Americans were British colonists, they were of course subjects of the Crown and were governed by the British rules of sovereign immunity. When they declared their independence, however, they could have chosen to renounce the English doctrine. One might have expected them to do so. After all, one reason for the Revolution was to rid themselves of the monarchy, with all its privileges and its abuses of power. With the monarchy gone, the spirit behind this goal would have been served by doing away with a doctrine based on the king's prerogatives. But the newly independent American states did no such thing. On the contrary, many of them vigorously asserted that they, too, were sovereign, and that, like the English Crown, they were entitled to assert immunity in their own courts. It appears that some states did not even adopt the measures that had tended to significantly soften the impact of immunity in Britain.[2] Whether one state's assertion of immunity would be respected in the courts of another state is less clear.

ARTICLE 3, CHISHOLM V. GEORGIA, AND THE ELEVENTH AMENDMENT

Upon winning their independence, the states were a loose confederation with a weak central government. Widespread dissatisfaction with this arrangement led to the Philadelphia convention of 1787, which produced a new Constitution. Under the new system, the national government would be stronger than before, with its power separated among three branches. Article 3 dealt with the federal judiciary. Section 1 of that article provided for a Supreme Court and left the creation of lower federal courts to Congress. Section 2 listed the potential jurisdiction of federal courts. On the list were "controversies" between a state and citizens of another state and "between a state and foreign states, citizens or subjects." Foes of the proposed Constitution, sensitive to encroachments on the states, charged in the ratification debates that these provisions would deprive the states of sovereign immunity. Many proponents of the new document answered that the mention of suits involving states merely referred to the possibility that they may be plaintiffs in federal court suits, or that they may consent to suit, though at least one prominent champion of the Constitution—James Wilson—asserted that the states would indeed give up immunity.[3]

After ratification one of the first cases litigated in the Supreme Court was Chisholm v. Georgia (1793). A South Carolina citizen, Chisholm, had sold goods on credit to the state of Georgia during the Revolution and had not been paid. After his death, Chisholm's estate brought suit in the United States Supreme Court to recover the debt, and the state asserted sovereign immunity as a defense to paying it. In a decision that many found shocking, the Court ruled that, whatever may have been the practice under the Articles of Confederation, and whatever may have been said in the ratification debates, the states did not enjoy sovereign immunity in the federal courts. James Wilson was one of the Justices at the time. Not surprisingly, he strongly supported this outcome.

Chisholm provoked a storm of protest. Soon after the case was decided, Congress and the states set about reversing it by amending the Constitution. The Eleventh Amendment, clearly drafted with the aim of nullifying the *Chisholm* decision, provides that "[t]he judicial power of the United States shall not be construed to extend to any suit in law or equity, commenced or prosecuted against one of the United States by citizens of another state, or by citizens or subjects of any foreign state." Thus, the Eleventh Amendment restores the immunity that *Chisholm* had taken away. The amendment deals only with suits against state governments. The Constitution says nothing so far as the national government is concerned, but as we shall see, the Supreme Court has always taken the position that the United States may not be sued without its consent.

With regard to the states, adoption of the Eleventh Amendment did not by any means put the matter to rest. It remained to be determined just how much protection sovereign immunity afforded state governments. Between 1798, when the Eleventh Amendment was ratified, and the Civil War, there were few cases involving sovereign immunity. In one case the Supreme Court seemed to say that a plaintiff could avoid any difficulty merely by taking care to name an official, rather than the state, as the defendant (Osborn v. Bank of the United States, 1824). Other cases suggested that this technique would not always suffice to defeat immunity (Governor of Georgia v. Madrazo, 1828). One explanation for the different outcomes is that an important issue of federal government power vis-à-vis the states was at stake in *Osborn*. Facing the immunity issue would have diverted attention from that issue. Also, the Supreme Court may have felt no pressing need to resolve the immunity issue definitively, since it seemed to come up only rarely.

POST–CIVIL WAR DEVELOPMENTS: THE FOURTEENTH AMENDMENT, *HANS,* AND *EX PARTE YOUNG*

Two developments in the second half of the nineteenth century revived interest in the Eleventh Amendment and sovereign immunity. First, many Southern states went deeply into debt during and after the Civil War and balked at paying their creditors. When their bondholders sued, the states asserted sovereign immunity as a defense. It became necessary for the Supreme Court to focus again on the proper scope of sovereign immunity. Second, the Thirteenth, Fourteenth and Fifteenth amendments were enacted after the war to forbid slavery, guarantee equal citizenship to freed slaves, and assure them the right to vote. In particular, the Fourteenth Amendment imposed significant new obligations on the state governments, including the duty not to deprive any person of life, liberty, or property without due process of law, and the obligation not to deny to any person the equal protection of the laws. In addition, § 5 of the Fourteenth Amendment granted Congress the power to enact legislation to enforce the substantive provisions. Armed with these new rights against state governments, litigants brought their complaints to the federal courts, seeking to use the Constitution as a sword to obtain relief. In resolving their claims, the Supreme Court once again had to determine the scope of sovereign immunity.

Hans v. Louisiana: The Nature and Scope of State Sovereign Immunity

In Hans v. Louisiana (1890) a bondholder sued the state for reneging on its promise to pay interest. The bondholder, Hans, was a citizen of Louisiana who argued that the Eleventh Amendment did not bar the lawsuit because the explicit language of the amendment applies only to suits brought by "citizens of another state." His substantive argument for liability was that Louisiana's conduct violated the "contracts clause" (article I, section 10, clause 1), a constitutional provision that forbids states from jeopardizing contractual obligations. The Supreme Court rejected Hans' argument. In a landmark sovereign immunity case, the Court clarified the nature and scope of state sovereign immunity. It located the source of the immunity not in the Eleventh Amendment but in the original Constitution (though there is nothing about it in the text of that document). It ruled that the immunity extends not only to suits asserting common law rights, such as an ordinary breach of contract or common law tort, but also to suits brought to recover for constitutional violations (such as the contracts clause claim that was at issue in *Hans* itself). It followed that immunity would also be available in suits brought under the new rights granted against states by the Fourteenth Amendment. On the other hand, in a case decided on the same day as *Hans*, the Court also ruled that the immunity did not protect local governments (Lincoln County v. Luning, 1890). The rationale for this distinction was that, as a matter of history, local governments began their existence as private associations that gradually took on the functions of governments. States did not treat them as sovereign partners with whom power was shared. Consequently, they did not enjoy the immunity that accompanies sovereignty.

Hans "marked a critical turning point," because "ever since, the Court has not adhered to a 'literal' reading of the amendment in determining its effect on federal jurisdiction."[4] In the decades after *Hans*, the Supreme Court relied on the principle of sovereign immunity rather than on the language of the Eleventh Amendment to resolve disputes about the scope of state immunity. For example, it held that states are immune from suits by foreign governments, though the Eleventh Amendment does not so provide (Monaco v. Mississippi, 1934). Suits "in admiralty" (involving maritime matters) are barred, though the amendment does not mention this kind of litigation (Ex Parte New York, 1921). By contrast, suits by other states are ordinarily not barred (Kansas v. Colorado, 1907), unless the state is simply a front for ordinary persons who are trying to evade the immunity doctrine by this subterfuge (New Hampshire v. Louisiana, 1883). An especially important limit on the immunity is that it does not forbid suits by the United States against a state (United States v. Mississippi, 1965). Thus, it does not necessarily hamper efforts by the national government to compel a state to comply with federal law. It simply interferes with litigation by private persons, even when they rely on federal law. From the standpoint of enforcing federal rights, the problem is that the time and other resources of the national government are limited. It obviously would be helpful to be able to enlist private litigants in efforts to enforce federal law without the obstacles posed by the sovereign immunity doctrine.

Prospective Relief: *Ex Parte Young*

Hans considerably extended the scope of sovereign immunity, but taken alone, the case would give a misleading picture of the Court's post–Civil War immunity decisions. *Ex Parte Young* (1908), for example, carved out a big exception to sovereign immunity. The Minnesota legislature had enacted a ceiling on the rates railroads could charge farmers. Railroads objected to these limits, claiming they were in violation of the Fourteenth Amendment by being so low as to amount to a deprivation of property without due process of law. The railroads brought suit in federal court, naming Young, the state attorney general (the chief legal officer of the state), as the defendant, and asked that he be forbidden from enforcing the rate statute. Young defended on the ground that the suit really was against the state and was therefore forbidden by the Eleventh Amendment. Relying on the distinction between suits against an officer and suits against the state, which began centuries ago in England and had surfaced in early–nineteenth-century American cases, the Supreme Court allowed the suit to go forward. It ruled that when the officer violated the Constitution, he was "stripped of his official or representative character and is subjected in his person to the consequences of his individual conduct. The State has no power to impart to him any immunity from responsibility to the supreme authority of the United States."

Later cases fleshed out the scope of this exception to the immunity doctrine. *Young* was solely a request for prospective relief. The point of the lawsuit was to change the government's behavior going forward, not to redress any past injuries. There appears to be only one situation in which a litigant may not use *Young* as a vehicle for obtaining prospective relief for a constitutional violation. Idaho v. Coeur d'Alene Tribe of Idaho (1997) arose from a dispute over whether the tribe or the state owned a tract of submerged land. The tribe sued state officials, claiming that the officers' activities related to the land amounted to a violation of the Constitution. The Court was badly fragmented, with some Justices favoring broad limits on *Young* and others preferring to make no exceptions at all. The Court ruled that *Young* does not apply to this rather peculiar kind of lawsuit. The case probably stands for the proposition stated in Justice O'Connor's opinion for three Justices, that in the narrow context over a dispute of this kind, "[w]here a plaintiff seeks to divest the state of all regulatory power over submerged lands . . . it simply cannot be said that the suit is not a suit against the state."

In Edelman v. Jordan (1974) the plaintiff sought to obtain an award of money from the state by using the same strategy of suing an official. The Supreme Court rejected this effort to widen the exception. It distinguished between retrospective and prospective relief, and held that only prospective relief could be obtained in a suit within the *Young* doctrine. In Pennhurst State School and Hospital v. Halderman (1984) the plaintiff sought prospective relief (thus avoiding the *Edelman* rule) but under state law rather than federal constitutional law. He reasoned that if, under *Young*'s reasoning, an official's violation of the Constitution "strip[s]" the official of his representative character, then a violation of state law does the same. But the Court held otherwise, and in the course of the opinion set forth the modern rationale for the *Young* doctrine. It explained that the purpose of the *Young* exception is to provide what we have called an "offensive" mechanism for enforcing constitutional rights against state governments. It allows people to use the Constitution as a sword and not merely as a shield. The Court reasoned that when the source of the right is state law, the rationale for an exception to immunity is no longer applicable. Thus, *Young* should not be used by federal courts to give relief for violations of state law.

Within this framework the Supreme Court and Congress have worked out an elaborate body of law governing access to federal court for suits seeking prospective relief. State governments, unhappy with the decision in *Young*, looked for ways to limit the scope of the federal cause of action that case had created. Congress soon enacted the "three judge court" statute, which mandated that federal court rulings striking down state statutes must be done by a court consisting of three judges, not the usual single judge.[5] Though that statute has since largely been repealed, other statutory limits on the use of *Ex Parte Young* remain in force. In the 1930s Congress prohibited federal courts from interfering with state tax collection (the Tax Injunction Act) and state utility rate orders (the Johnson Act), so long as state courts were available to hear constitutional complaints about those matters.[6] In the 1940s the Supreme Court ruled that federal courts must defer to state courts ("abstain") in spite of *Ex Parte Young*, if the case presented unsettled issues of state law and if resolution of those issues obviated the need to face a difficult constitutional question (Railroad Commission v. Pullman Co., 1941). Other cases of that era held that abstention was required if a matter of peculiarly local concern were at issue (Burford v. Sun Oil Co., 1943) or if the issues could be resolved in a state proceeding already underway (Douglas v. City of Jeannette, 1943) (see "Federalism and Constitutional Torts"). Despite these limits, *Ex Parte Young* remains to this day a powerful tool for challenging government action on constitutional grounds, so long as the relief one seeks is forward-looking rather than retrospective.

SOVEREIGN IMMUNITY IN THE LATE TWENTIETH CENTURY

The six decades or so following *Ex Parte Young* saw few changes in the basic structure of sovereign immunity law. In the late 1960s pressure began to build for new ways to obtain relief from state governments. No doubt the main factors behind the renewed interest in immunity law were the growth of government and its interference in people's lives after World War II, the expansion of constitutional rights under the Warren Court, and the resulting increase in situations in which someone would consider himself wronged by the government and would have access to a plausible legal theory for obtaining relief. The *Edelman* decision (noted previously), in which the Supreme Court declined to broaden the *Young* exception to the Eleventh Amendment, signaled the beginning of yet another period of Supreme Court activism in this area of the law. Some decisions, like *Edelman*, narrowed the availability of constitutional remedies, whereas others recognized new theories on which to sue governments and their officers.

Shortly after *Edelman* the Supreme Court decided Fitzpatrick v. Bitzer (1976) and opened the door to a new means of overcoming sovereign immunity. The plaintiffs in that case challenged Connecticut's treatment of employees, charging that the state discriminated on the basis of gender in violation of the equal protection clause of the Fourteenth Amendment and federal statutory prohibitions on employment discrimination. They took advantage of Congress' decision, a few years earlier, to explicitly extend the coverage of the statute to include state governments. They sought retroactive benefits, a form of relief that would not ordinarily be appropriate under the *Edelman* doctrine. Yet they prevailed, for this case was different from earlier cases; here Congress had enacted a statute that authorized the lawsuit and abrogated the immunity. Section 5 of the Fourteenth Amendment authorizes Congress to enforce the substantive provisions of that amendment by "appropriate legislation." The Court concluded that this is what Congress had done in subjecting states to suit under the employment discrimination statute. It explained that "the Eleventh Amendment, and the principle of state sovereignty which it embodies, are necessarily limited by the enforcement provisions of § 5 of the Fourteenth Amendment." It held that "Congress may, in determining what is 'appropriate legislation' for the purpose of enforcing the provisions of the Fourteenth

Amendment, provide for suits against States or state officials which are constitutionally impermissible in other contexts."

Fitzpatrick led to further questions regarding the scope of Congress' power to abrogate state sovereign immunity. One issue was whether Congress could take away state immunity not only under its § 5 power, but under its more general Article 1 powers, such as the power to regulate interstate commerce (a source of authority that the Supreme Court has, over the years, construed broadly). For most of the 1980s the Court avoided deciding this question, though it came up in several cases. Instead, the Court made a "clear statement" rule, instructing Congress that, whatever the scope of the power to abrogate immunity, Congress must state its intention to do so explicitly (Atascadero State Hospital v. Scanlon, 1985). In the late 1980s, the Court finally confronted the abrogation issue directly, holding by a vote of 5–4 that Congress may indeed deprive states of immunity from suit in federal court when acting under its Article 1 powers (Pennsylvania v. Union Gas, 1989). The victory for foes of immunity was short-lived, however, for the composition of the Court soon changed. Seven years later a different 5–4 majority overruled *Union Gas* and held that immunity could be abrogated only when Congress was enforcing constitutional rights under its § 5 power (Seminole Tribe of Florida v. Florida, 1996). The most recent chapter in this saga is Alden v. Maine (1999), in which a litigant tried to escape the Seminole Tribe decision by suing in state court. The plaintiffs thought they may be able to avoid the bar because the Eleventh Amendment by its terms only applies to federal courts. Echoing *Hans*, the Court explained that the principle of sovereign immunity is not limited by the terms of the amendment; it applies in state court as well. As for the future, it is noteworthy that, like *Union Gas* and *Seminole Tribe*, *Alden* was a 5–4 decision, and the losing side has never seemed to be reconciled to any of the outcomes. One may safely predict that the issue is not yet put to rest.

Another question left unresolved by *Fitzpatrick* is the scope of Congress' § 5 authority. This issue is, of course, all the more crucial in view of *Seminole Tribe* and *Alden*, for everything now turns on whether Congress has enacted valid § 5 legislation. In the twenty-five years following *Fitzpatrick* the Court tended to take a narrow view of Congress' § 5 power. It began by applying the clear statement rule to this kind of legislation. One consequence is that 42 U.S.C. § 1983, the main statute under which constitutional claims are brought, does not permit suits against state governments but only local governments and officials (Quern v. Jordan, 1979). More recently the Court has ruled that Congress may not expand the substantive scope of constitutional rights under its § 5 power to provide appropriate remedies for the violation of those rights (City of Boerne v. Flores, 1997). A few years later, it ruled that even when Congress merely provides a remedy for a right the Court itself has established, the legislation will be upheld only if Congress has documented a pressing need for action (Florida Prepaid Post-Secondary Education Plan v. College Savings Bank, 1999).

Another recent development in sovereign immunity law is quite separate from the congressional authorization theme. In a few cases the Supreme Court has suggested that state governments cannot use their sovereign immunity to completely shield themselves from accountability for constitutional violations. This has occurred in two areas. One concerns "takings" of private property for public use. Suppose, for example, the state tears down someone's house to build a highway, or forbids the owner from using his or her property in any economically valuable way. The Fifth Amendment then requires the government to pay "just compensation" for the value of the property. The Supreme Court has held that the just compensation clause "dictates the remedy for interference with property rights amounting to a taking." It is "the compensation remedy," which means that governments may not invoke sovereign immunity against such suits (First Evangelical Lutheran Church of Glendale v. County of Los Angeles, 1987).

The other line of cases concerns constitutional challenges to state taxes. This is a distinctive area of the law of constitutional remedies because of the Tax Injunction Act, the federal statute that forbids access to federal court if a state remedy is available. The Supreme Court has held that the state remedy may take the form of the opportunity for a pre-payment challenge to the taxes or a post-payment refund action. In Reich v. Collins (1994) the state of Georgia tried to avoid constitutional scrutiny in the following way: At the time the taxes were due, Georgia provided a post-taxation refund action. But when the taxpayer paid and then sought a refund on the ground that the tax was unconstitutional, Georgia took away the refund action. The Supreme Court told Georgia it could not behave in this way:

> [D]ue process requires a clear and certain remedy for taxes collected in violation of federal law. A State has the flexibility to provide that remedy before the disputed taxes are paid (predeprivation), after they are paid (postdeprivation), or both. But what it may not do, and what Georgia did here, is hold out what plainly appears to be a clear and certain postdeprivation remedy and then declare, only after the disputed taxes have been paid, that no such remedy exists.

Later in the opinion the Court quoted a case decided seven decades ago in support of the proposition that "a denial by a state court of a recovery of taxes exacted in violation of the laws or Constitution of the United States by compulsion is itself in contravention of the Fourteenth Amendment" (Carpenter v. Shaw, 1930). In view of the Court's reasoning, the premise of the decision requiring Georgia to grant a refund seems to be that the states are, at least in some circumstances, constitutionally obliged to open their courts to suits for retrospective relief brought against the states themselves. While the scope of this rule must await further development, it may be a significant step toward weaker immunity in constitutional cases.

THE SOVEREIGN IMMUNITY OF THE UNITED STATES

Most of the foregoing discussion has focused on state government immunity, because that is the issue that has produced a complex history with a great deal of litigation. The history of sovereign immunity of the national government is more straightforward. The Supreme Court has always assumed that the United States enjoys sovereign immunity, so that it may not be sued without its consent. Over the years, Congress has chosen to give up much of this immunity. In 1855, Congress created the Court of Claims to hear such suits. In 1887 it enacted the Tucker Act, which authorized the Court of Claims to hear breach of contract claims, among other matters. The Federal Tort Claims Act, enacted in 1946, authorizes suit for many ordinary torts. With regard to constitutional claims, however, there has never been any general consent to suit, though the *First Evangelical Lutheran Church* and *Reich* decisions, noted previously, presumably apply to the federal government as well as to state governments. The main avenue for challenging federal government action on constitutional grounds is once again *Ex Parte Young*. Ever since that case was decided, the Supreme Court has read it broadly. Though the case itself involved an effort to sue a state official, its scope is not limited to activities of state governments and their officers. Rather, the Court has treated its holding as a basis for an exception to the federal government's sovereign immunity as well (e.g., Shields v. Utah Idaho Central R.R., 1938). Today, however, there is another ground besides *Young* for escaping immunity. In 1976 Congress enacted a statute that waives the government's sovereign immunity in any suit for prospective relief.[7] There remain significant gaps in the government's amenability to suits for damages.

REMEDIES AGAINST OFFICERS AND LOCAL GOVERNMENTS

Though the national government and the state governments may assert sovereign immunity, that immunity does not extend to their officials. Nor does it protect local governments. Thus, we can describe the history of constitutional remedies against such actors without being distracted by sovereign immunity. Even so, that history shows that the plaintiff has often had a hard time in constitutional litigation, for a number of other obstacles have always stood in the way of obtaining relief.

THE COMMON LAW BACKGROUND OF CONSTITUTIONAL REMEDIES

The Constitution itself contains few remedial provisions, probably because the framers assumed that persons seeking offensive remedies for constitutional wrongs would bring ordinary lawsuits using the remedies available in the common law against any defendant who inflicted injury on another.[8] If the government took something belonging to an individual, the common law action of "replevin" would be available, just as if the wrongdoer were a private individual. "Ejectment" was the remedy for disputes about the ownership of land. Personal injuries, deprivations of liberty, and harm to property could be remedied by a suit for "trespass." In any of these types of litigation, the successful plaintiff could obtain damages from the wrongdoer. When the defendant in such a suit was a government officer, the litigation would be more complicated than usual, because the officer would probably assert a special defense based on his official role. But if the plaintiff could show that the officer acted unconstitutionally, the defense potentially could be overridden, at least if the officer acted egregiously.

Besides these common law remedies, available for use against private actors as well as officials, certain remedies had been developed in England for the kinds of harms that only government officers could commit. These included, for example, "mandamus" (an order telling an official to perform a specific act he is obliged by law to do and over which he has no discretion), "habeas corpus" (an order requiring an official in charge of a prisoner to justify the imprisonment), and "prohibition" (forbidding a judicial or quasijudicial body from exceeding its authority.)[9] One could also seek an "injunction" against an officer (an order telling him to stop doing an illegal activity or telling him to do something the law requires). Of all the old remedies, this along with suits to recover damages are those that modern litigants find most useful. An injunction suit is similar in principle to mandamus, but it has the advantage of being more flexible. This is so because it is available even in cases where the officer has authority to exercise discretion, provided one can show that he or she has exceeded or threatens to exceed the scope of that discretion.

All these remedies were created in spite of sovereign immunity. As discussed earlier, the rationale for authorizing aggrieved persons to sue officials using these mechanisms was that the sovereign and the officer were not one and the same. Since the officer was not the sovereign, he required not the sovereign's privileges. Therefore, the officer may not have availed himself of the sovereign's immunity. These remedies were all imported into our law, where they became available for all kinds of illegal acts performed by officials. Thus, a suit for damages or an injunction could be maintained in the event the official violated a common law duty (like a trespass), a statutory duty, or a constitutional duty.

Throughout the nineteenth century litigants with complaints about unconstitutional government action used this common law framework in order to obtain offensive remedies, such as damages or orders commanding officials to change their behavior prospectively. Notice, however, that the Constitution was not, strictly speaking, the source of the remedial doctrine. Instead, plaintiffs relied on the common law, and the Constitution entered the case only as one of several possible reasons why the official should be obliged to pay damages or to alter his conduct. For a long time, the Constitution was not an especially important factor in this kind of litigation, because persons held few constitutional rights against state governments until the enactment of the post–Civil War amendments. Even in the early period, of course, one could invoke constitutional rights against federal government officials. Yet many of these rights received little attention from the Supreme Court before the Civil War, and may have been of little use to most plaintiffs. Given these features of the legal landscape, it is easy to see why litigants looked to the common law for relief, and not particularly to the Constitution. The passage of the Fourteenth Amendment changed the situation by granting people the rights to due process and equal protection against state governments. The need for a scheme of distinctively constitutional remedies, separate from and independent of the common law, soon became apparent. In the late nineteenth century and early twentieth century the Supreme Court responded to that need.

EX PARTE YOUNG AND *HOME TELEPHONE*: THE ORIGINS OF CONSTITUTIONAL REMEDIES

As constitutional rights began to figure more prominently in litigation seeking offensive remedies from government officers, courts gradually shifted their focus from conceiving of these lawsuits as common law cases that contained some constitutional issues. Instead, courts began to place the constitutional dimension in the forefront. Sometimes they would ignore features of the common law that would obstruct the enforcement of constitutional rights, or they would make special rules for constitutional cases.[10] Eventually, the common law shell fell away and a new cause of action emerged, with the Constitution at its core.

This process culminated in *Ex Parte Young* (1908). Though we have already discussed this case in connection with its "prospective relief against an officer" exception to sovereign immunity, it is equally important for its contribution to the law of constitutional remedies. Recall that the case was provoked by a Minnesota statute that set ceilings on the prices railroads could charge farmers. Shareholders of the railroads sued the Minnesota Attorney General, seeking to stop him from enforcing the rates by bringing criminal prosecutions against railroad employees who violated them. They charged that the rates were confiscatory, so that enforcing them would deprive the railroads of property without due process of law. This is a classic example of offensive constitutional litigation.

Earlier cases of this general type had involved efforts to compel states to pay interest on their bonds. In those cases plaintiffs relied on common law tort and contract principles. For example, some important cases grew out of Virginia's dealings with its bondholders. Lacking funds with which to pay bondholders the interest due them on its bonds, Virginia initially had allowed bondholders to pay their state income taxes with interest coupons from the bonds. The state then repudiated this arrangement, and a group of bondholders and taxpayers refused to pay taxes. State officials then seized or threatened to seize their property to satisfy the taxes. The bondholders sued for common law trespass. Though the officials' invasion of the plaintiffs' property ordinarily would have been justified under state law, the plaintiffs maintained that here it was not, because the state had violated their constitutional rights. The Supreme Court upheld an award of restitution, damages, and injunctive relief against the officers (Poindexter v. Greenhow, 1885; White v. Greenhow, 1885).

Notice a critical difference between these cases and *Ex Parte Young*. In *Young* the railroads could not easily rely on any common law tort or contract principles, for "Attorney General Young's announced readiness to prosecute for conduct in violation of state law [charging rates above the statutory ceiling] was probably not tortious under traditional common law concepts."[11] By allowing the lawsuit, the Court made a leap from common law causes of action to a new type of lawsuit. What the Court did, in effect, was to recognize a cause of action, unknown to the common law, under which persons were allowed to sue for violations of constitutional rights even if they could not show that the violation took place in a manner constituting a common law tort or breach of contract. The Court did not explicitly state this was its holding, yet the ruling cannot be justified in any other way, and the case has come to stand for that proposition.[12] There may be earlier cases that reach similar results,[13] but the historical dispute about the precise origins of doctrine is not especially important today. For whatever reason, *Young* captured the attention of lawyers and judges better than had any previous case.

The full significance of *Ex Parte Young* should now be clear. The case not only eliminated sovereign immunity as a concern in suits against officials to enforce compliance with the Constitution, but also authorized a federal cause of action, independent of the common law, by which suits to enforce the Constitution could be brought. In the early part of this century *Young* was the vehicle by which business enterprises challenged social legislation fixing prices (such as the railroad rates in *Young* itself) or setting maximum hours of work or minimum wages. In the latter half of the century, notably under Chief Justice Earl Warren, but even in the more conservative era that followed, the focus of substantive constitutional law changed from setting limits on social legislation to enforcing principles of equality and setting limits on state power. During that period, *Young* again served as the remedial vehicle for litigation challenging school segregation, malapportioned districts, prison conditions, restrictions on free speech, denials of equal protection, and, in short, the whole array of newly recognized constitutional rights. However, we shall see that a later Supreme Court decision, Monroe v. Pape (1961), made it unnecessary, as a technical matter, to rely on the *Ex Parte Young* "cause of action" for suits against state officers.

Another doctrinal development, crucial to the modern law of constitutional remedies, occurred five years after *Young*. Following passage of the Fourteenth Amendment in 1868, a question arose as to the proper interpretation of the due process clause of that amendment. That provision forbids the states from "depriv[ing] any person of life, liberty, or property, without due process of law." The issue was how to identify the precise point at which a constitutional violation takes place: Is it at the time an official acts, or is it at the time his action is condoned or affirmed by the state government through its courts? One view was that the constitutional violation is complete when the official has acted. The other view stressed that the due process clause is expressly addressed to the states, not to the officials who act under state authority. No matter what an official does, his act standing alone cannot be a due process violation under this interpretation of the Fourteenth Amendment, because the official is not the state and only the state can violate the due process clause. Only when someone challenges his act in the state courts, and the state courts refuse to grant relief, can a due process violation occur. The implication of this reasoning is that someone seeking to challenge official action may not go to federal court with a constitutional claim. He must litigate in the state courts instead. Cases like Barney v. City of New York (1904) seemed to follow the latter approach.

The view taken in *Barney* did not ultimately prevail. The Court ruled in Home Telephone and Telegraph Co. v. City of Los Angeles (1913) that state law remedies need not be pursued. The structure of this case was similar to that of *Young*. A phone company brought a due process challenge against the city's decision limiting the rates it would be allowed to charge. A key feature of the litigation is that, as in *Young*, the plaintiff sued in federal court. Drawing on *Barney* for support, the city argued that no violation could occur until the state courts had upheld its rates. Accordingly, the federal suit must be dismissed and any litigation should take place in the state courts. But the Supreme Court disagreed. In effect, the Court overruled *Barney*. It said that state remedies were simply irrelevant to whether a constitutional violation had taken place. "To the contrary, the provisions of the [Fourteenth] Amendment . . . are addressed, of course, to the states, but also to every person . . . who is the repository of state power." It did not matter whether the officer violated state law or not, for "the Amendment contemplates the possibility of state officers abusing the powers lawfully conferred upon them by doing wrongs prohibited by the Amendment."

It is easy to take this result for granted today, because we are accustomed to the remedial regime the Supreme Court constructed in *Home Telephone*. And perhaps the issue seems rather technical. But notice what a difference it would have made if *Barney* had survived. If *Barney* is pushed to its logical end, no one seeking an offensive remedy would be able to go to federal court for it. Everyone would be obliged initially to argue their cases in the state courts. Litigants may have found themselves bound by the outcomes in state court litigation and, in any event, would have faced extra hurdles before seeking relief in the federal courts. One need not cast aspersions on the fairness or competence of state courts to understand that persons who wish to challenge the conduct of state officers on federal constitutional grounds would prefer not to have to litigate in the courts of the very government with whom they are quarreling.[14] Together with *Ex Parte Young*, the *Home Telephone* rule forms the foundation of the modern law of constitutional remedies.

SECTION 1983: BEFORE MONROE V. PAPE

From the standpoint of constitutional remedies, the post–Civil War transformation in constitutional law produced two milestones. *Ex Parte Young* is one of them. The other is a federal statute enacted six years after the war and three years after passage of the Fourteenth Amendment. The Civil Rights Act of 1871, part of which is now codified as 42 U.S.C. § 1983, provides:

> Every person who, under color of any statute, ordinance, regulation, custom, or usage, of any State . . . subjects, or causes to be subjected, any . . . person . . . to the deprivation of any rights, privileges, or immunities secured by the Constitution . . . shall be liable to the party injured in an action at law, suit in equity, or other proper proceeding for redress.

Today this statute, called simply "section 1983" in the jargon of constitutional remedies, provides the cause of action used by virtually anyone who seeks damages or injunctions against state officials and local governments for constitutional violations. But it was not always so. Before the 1960s the statute was rarely used. Until the Court's decision in Monroe v. Pape (1961), most constitutional litigation proceeded under the cause of action recognized in *Young*. This section describes the historical context in which § 1983 was enacted and explains why the statute remained largely dormant for ninety years after its passage.[15]

After the war, the South was in turmoil. Many Southern whites remained unwilling to extend basic civil rights to the newly freed slaves. The Ku Klux Klan terrorized both blacks and their white supporters, by burning their houses, destroying their property, beating and killing them. Local law enforcement officers often did little or nothing to protect the victims. Passage of the Fourteenth Amendment in 1868 seemed to have little impact. One Congressman declared that "[t]he whole South . . . [was] rapidly drifting into a state of anarchy and bloodshed," where there was "no security for life, liberty, person, or property," and "[s]tate authorities and local courts [were] unwilling or unable to check the evil or punish the criminals."[16]

In 1871 the Republicans, who had ardently supported the war and who still controlled the 42nd Congress, concluded that something must be done. This state of affairs "require[d] extraordinary legislation for its suppression."[17] The Civil Rights Act of 1871 had four sections. Section 1, which is currently codified as § 1983, provided a civil remedy for constitutional violations committed under color of state law, § 2 created new federal criminal provisions aimed at combating Ku Klux Klan–style terrorism; § 3 permitted the president to use the armed forces to suppress outbreaks of Klan violence; and § 4 permitted the president to suspend the writ of habeas corpus in some circumstances.

Section 1 received little attention in the debates. Most of the discussion over this legislation focused on "conditions in the South. The breakdown of law and order, the acquiescence of Southern authorities, Klan terrorism against blacks and Republicans, and the consequent need for federal action."[18] Opponents questioned the accounts of Southern lawlessness and doubted the need for the legislation, claiming that crimes were committed everywhere and that the bill was motivated by partisan political considerations. Republicans responded that the Klan was a tool of the Democratic party, and Democrats claimed that the South's main problem was

Republican interference in its affairs.[19] Most discussion of the substance of the legislation focused on the provisions that would empower the President to use the army and to suspend the writ of habeas corpus,[20] (article 1, section 9, clause 2), probably because "southerners were more frightened of the United States army than they were of the federal courts."[21]

Though § 1 was not discussed much in the debates, its basic purpose is not hard to discern. The bill's supporters were clearly committed to preserving the gains won for blacks in the Civil War. They maintained that the privileges and immunities and equal protection clauses of the Fourteenth Amendment prohibited discrimination against blacks with respect to the rights of citizenship and enforcement of the law. Section 1 would provide a federal remedy for violations of these rights. Given the focus on private lawlessness as a justification for the measure, it is likely the Republicans intended that the statute be applied to the Klan's activities as well as to the actions of officials. Beyond protecting the rights of blacks to equal citizenship, one cannot fairly ascribe any specific aim to the framers of the legislation. The statute enforced the Fourteenth Amendment, but that amendment had been enacted just three years before. Though people generally agreed that the amendment granted equal citizenship to blacks, there was much disagreement as to what else it did. Some thought that the Fourteenth Amendment incorporated all of the Bill of Rights, applying them to the states. (This is the view that, a hundred years later, more or less prevailed.) But others construed it more narrowly, and some frankly professed not to know what it meant.[22]

Though the 42nd Congress had high hopes for its legislation, the statute soon fell into disuse, along with the rest of the civil rights legislation enacted after the Civil War.[23] One reason is that the Supreme Court gave the Fourteenth Amendment a narrow reading. In the Slaughterhouse Cases (1873), the Court ruled that the provision that "[n]o State shall make or enforce any law which shall abridge the privileges or immunities of citizens of the United States" was not a broad grant of civil rights. It "included only those few rights which were beyond the possible reach of state citizenship and which grew out of 'the relationship between the citizen and the national government.'"[24]

Later cases imposed another crucial limit on the scope of constitutional and statutory protection of civil rights. In Virginia v. Rives (1880) the Court distinguished between governments and individuals, ruling that "[t]he provisions of the Fourteenth Amendment . . . all have reference to State action exclusively, and not to any action of private individuals." In addition, the Court used this "state action" doctrine to strike down § 2 of the 1871 statute. That section had imposed criminal penalties on persons who conspired to deny others their rights. But the Court found it invalid on the ground that Congress had attempted to use the Constitution as a basis for regulating private action.[25] The Civil Rights Cases (1883) held that Congress could not, under its power to enforce the Fourteenth Amendment, forbid discrimination against blacks by private persons.[26] (The modern contours of the state action doctrine are described in the section on "State Action.") For now, the important point is that the Court had plainly disappointed the drafters of the Fourteenth Amendment and the expectations of the Reconstruction Congress. They considered the Ku Klux Klan and other private actors to be a major part of the problem, but the Court told them the amendment did not extend to private conduct and that the statutes they enacted to enforce it could not be so applied. Over the years, some of the legislation the Court left standing was repealed by unsympathetic Congresses.[27]

Section 1 of the 1871 statute, however, remained on the books. Though it could not be applied to private actors, it extended to the whole of the Fourteenth Amendment. Thus, the *Slaughterhouse Cases*' narrow reading of "privileges and immunities" would not affect its use to enforce the rights of due process and equal protection. Given the statute's broad wording, we need to look further for an explanation for why it lay largely dormant for ninety years.

At least three factors seem to have played a role in limiting the use of the statute. First, where injunctive relief was sought, people could bring the type of lawsuit that originated in common law principles and eventually became a federal cause of action by the time of *Young*. There was no need to worry about being tripped up by the chance that some judge would interpret the statute in a restrictive way. *Young* did not apply to suits for damages, but these suits were hard to maintain against officials anyway because of the official immunity doctrine. (Modern immunity doctrine is discussed in the section on "Absolute Immunity" and "Qualified Immunity.")

A second reason has to do with the way courts read the statutory requirement that the challenged act take place "under color of" state law. For many years lower courts took a narrow view of this term. They held that an official acted under color of state law only when state law authorized the act or provided no remedy for the violation.[28] (This is a statutory variant of the reading of the Constitution that was rejected in the *Home Telephone* case, discussed in the preceding section.) For example, if a police officer beat someone up but the act was illegal under state law and the state had a private tort remedy, courts would rule that the officer did not act under color of state law and the injured person could not sue under § 1983. Whatever its merits as a matter of policy, this interpretation of "under color of" may be faithful to the intent of the framers of the statute, given their concern with the absence of effective law enforcement in the South,[29] though some scholars argue strongly to the contrary.[30] In any event, this reading of the statute interfered with using it as a general remedy for constitutional violations, because plaintiffs would always have to worry about the possibility of being told they must instead use state remedies.[31]

The third factor that limited the utility of the statute is that, for most of the period between 1871 and 1961, there were not many constitutional rights for which it could be used. The *Slaughterhouse Cases* had severely undercut the potential range of the "privileges and immunities" clause of the Fourteenth Amendment. In the late nineteenth and early twentieth centuries, the Court used the Due Process Clause mainly as a means of protecting freedom of contract and other economic rights, and even this "economic due process" doctrine was largely abandoned in the 1930s. The Court treated the equal protection clause as a guarantee that, whatever the laws may be, they would be applied equally to everyone. There was no constitutional requirement that in making laws the legislature could not make arbitrary distinctions. The Court also refused during this period to take more than a few tentative steps toward using the Fourteenth Amendment as a mechanism for applying the Bill of Rights to the states.[32] In view of all of these factors, it is hardly surprising that § 1 of the 1871 statute was used mainly as a means of vindicating the right to vote, and little else.[33]

REVIVING SECTION 1983: *MONROE* AND ITS PROGENY

In the 1960s, under Chief Justice Earl Warren, the Supreme Court transformed both constitutional law and constitutional remedies. One product of the Court's work, and hardly the least important one, was a reinvigorated § 1983. In the landmark case Monroe v. Pape (1961), the Court resurrected the statute and made it the main weapon for pursuing offensive remedies for constitutional violations. The complaint in *Monroe* asserted that thirteen Chicago police officers invaded the plaintiffs' home at 5:45 A.M. on October 29, 1958, "routed them from bed, made them stand naked in the living room, and ransacked every room, emptying drawers and ripping mattress covers." Lower courts had ruled that the plaintiffs could not sue under § 1983, by relying on official immunity as well as the prevailing view that acts unauthorized by the state were not committed under color of state law.

Writing for the Court, Justice Douglas delved into the legislative history of the statute. He noted that "[t]he debates are replete with references to the lawless conditions existing in the South in 1871," contained in a Senate report "nearly 600 pages in length, dealing with the activities of the Klan and the inability of the state governments to cope with it." Justice Douglas found that § 1983 "had three main aims." One of these was to "override certain kinds of state laws," namely, those that violated the constitutional rights of the freedmen and their supporters. Second, the statute "provided a remedy where state law was inadequate." The third aim "was to provide a federal remedy where the state remedy, though adequate in theory, was not available in practice." Supporters of the bill stressed that it was needed because state remedies were not adequate, while opponents questioned the need for the legislation and charged that it would unnecessarily displace state law. In view of the aims of the 42nd Congress in enacting the statute and of the state of the law in the lower courts, the Court might have ruled that the lower courts had correctly interpreted it. The Court might have reasoned that since § 1983 was enacted to deal with situations where state remedies were unavailable or inadequate, it should not be applied in circumstances where those remedies were adequate. The existence of a state tort remedy for the police officers' conduct in *Monroe* would presumably be such a state remedy, unless the plaintiffs could show that it was not really effective.

The Court, however, broke with the past and took a radically different view. After discussing the aims of the legislation, Justice Douglas chose to give more weight to the broad language of the statute rather than to the specific aims of the 42nd Congress. He said:

> Although the legislation was enacted because of the conditions that existed in the South at that time, it is cast in general language and is as applicable to Illinois as it is to the States whose names were mentioned over and again in the debates. It is no answer that the State has a law which if enforced would give relief. The federal remedy is supplementary to the state remedy, and the latter need not be first sought and refused before the federal one is invoked. Hence the fact that Illinois by its Constitution and laws outlaws unreasonable searches and seizures is no barrier to the present suit in the federal court.

In his concurring opinion, Justice Harlan offered another, perhaps more pragmatic, reason for the new interpretation of § 1983. He noted that the old view, if it is taken seriously, requires an awkward and potentially time-consuming inquiry into the fairness and effectiveness of state remedies in each case. A broad rule that anything the officer does in the course of his work is under color of law avoids the need for such an investigation and the potential for federal–state friction that would accompany it.

Justice Frankfurter stood alone in dissent. Apart from relying heavily on the post–Civil War background in which the statute was enacted, he emphasized considerations of federalism. Justice Frankfurter quite correctly understood that *Monroe* presented "not merely a mine-run statutory question involving a narrow compass of individual rights and duties." He perceived that "[t]he issue . . . concerns directly a basic problem in American federalism: the relation of the Nation to the States in the critically important sphere of municipal law administration." The impact of *Monroe* is to displace state courts and state law with a federal cause of action under § 1983. Justice Frankfurter thought that primary authority over these matters ought to remain with the states.

In order to appreciate the importance of *Monroe*, one must keep in mind that it was not an isolated ruling but part of the Warren Court's general program of expanding the scope of constitutional protection against state governments. Making § 1983 a more effective tool for vindicating constitutional rights would have been a big step. Yet it would have had comparatively few real-world implications so long as the Constitution contained few rights against the actions of state officials. Contemporaneously with *Monroe*, and continuing throughout the 1960s, the Warren Court also expanded the scope of substantive constitutional rights. Brown v. Board of Education (1954), in which the Court ruled that racially segregated school systems violate the equal protection clause of the Fourteenth Amendment, signaled a new and expanded right of equal protection. Later cases established that equal protection means not only impartial application of laws on the books, but also concerns the substance of those laws. Under the Warren Court's doctrine, classifications based on race are always suspect, and other kinds of distinctions also require searching scrutiny. Some rights are fundamental and for that reason alone demand equal protection review. In another line of cases the Court accelerated the process, begun years before, of incorporating nearly all the provisions of the Bill of Rights into the Due Process Clause of the Fourteenth Amendment, so that for the first time they constrained state governments as well as the national government. It broadened the scope of the First Amendment's protection of free speech, ruling that public employees may not be fired at will on account of speech (Pickering v. Board of Education, 1968) and that public school students have free speech rights as well (Tinker v. Des Moines Independent Community School District, 1969). The Court expanded the constitutional rights of public employees and those receiving governments in other ways as well, ruling that those benefits may be "property" entitled to due process protection (e.g., Board of Regents v. Roth, 1972; Goldberg v. Kelly, 1970). Though the Court grew more conservative in the 1970s, the expansion of constitutional guarantees continued, not only with high-profile decisions like Roe v. Wade (1973), protecting the right to an abortion, but also in rulings that for the first time imposed significant constitutional limits on government treatment of prisoners and mental patients (e.g., Procunier v. Martinez, 1974; O'Connor v. Donaldson, 1975).

No doubt one of the reasons the Court revived § 1983 was to assure that effective remedies were available in the federal courts for violations of these newly recognized rights. In order to obtain the common law tort remedy that § 1983 displaced, one typically had to sue in state court. We must distinguish here between (a) the substantive rules governing relations between government and ordinary citizens and (b) the forum in which disputes about the content and application of such rules will be litigated. As for (a), the substantive law bearing on the constitutional tort cause of action may be different from the common law of torts, though in some respects (as discussed below) the Supreme Court actually requires courts in § 1983 cases to refer to the common law. But an equally important aspect of the new remedy was (b): Now the suit routinely could be brought in federal court rather than state court. Litigants with complaints about state officers seem to think they are better off if they can have their claims decided by federal judges rather than state judges.[34]

The recognition of new federal rights, along with the availability of a federal forum in which to raise them, gave rise to more litigation under the statute and increased pressure for a more effective remedy. Before *Monroe* it appeared that the opportunity to seek damages may be worth little even if "under color of" were not an obstacle, because officials could assert an absolute immunity from paying damages. That was the holding in a pre-*Monroe* case involving a suit against state legislators (Tenney v. Brandhove, 1951). But a few years after *Monroe* the Supreme Court distinguished that case and said that police officers receive only a limited immunity, dependent on whether they acted in good faith and in accordance with what they reasonably thought the law to allow (Pierson v. Ray, 1967). Later cases extended this rule to all executive officers of government, up to and including the governor (Scheuer v. Rhodes, 1974). As the law evolved over time, only judges, legislators, witnesses, prosecutors, and a few other defendants were awarded absolute immunity from damages liability. A few Warren Court cases went so far as to hint that even sovereign immunity could be finessed, by suing an official while hoping that an award of money would come from the state. At this point, however, the Court of the 1970s called a halt. As described earlier, Edelman v. Jordan (1974) thwarted this strategy on Eleventh Amendment grounds, and the sequel formed a new chapter in the law of sovereign immunity.

Beginning with *Monroe*, the Supreme Court has over the past four decades built a considerable body of constitutional tort doctrine. Besides immunity, another noteworthy development relates to rules about remedies. In Carey v. Piphus (1978) the Court said that the framers of the statute intended that damages be based on a common law tort model. The Court relied on *Monroe* itself, where Justice Douglas had directed that § 1983 "should be read against the background of tort liability that makes a man responsible for the natural consequences of his actions." Whatever he may have meant by this observation, the Court in *Carey* and other cases has taken it to mean that one looks to the common law, either as it stood in 1871 or as it has evolved since then, as a source of answers to constitutional tort issues. (The current law on remedies is addressed in detail in the section entitled "Remedies, Damages, Injunctions, Declaratory Relief, and Attorney's Fees.") References to history are sometimes, though less often, found in the immunity cases as well. It appears that the Supreme Court refers to history on a selective basis, depending on whether a historical analysis helps to bolster the outcome it has chosen on other grounds.[35] Whether the Court ought to try to resolve constitutional tort issues by looking into history is a separate issue. Since the current use of the statute is so far removed from the circumstances that led to its passage, it has been argued that it is better to ask how best to achieve the modern policies of deterrence, avoiding overdeterrence, and vindicating constitutional rights (see "Aims of the Law of Constitutional Remedies") and that inquiries into history are counterproductive.[36]

On one important issue, whether municipal governments may be sued under § 1983, the post-*Monroe* Court actually departed from *Monroe*. The city of Chicago was a defendant in *Monroe*, but in contrast to the expansive reading of "under color of," the Court was reluctant to allow suit against local governments. Relying on an episode in the legislative history, it held that the "persons" subject to suit under § 1983 did not include local governments. That episode involved the so-called "Sherman Amendment," which would have made local governments liable for private violence they did not prevent. Congress rejected this amendment. Writing for the Court in *Monroe*, Justice Douglas said that Congress was "so antagonistic" to this proposal that "we cannot believe that the word 'person' was used in this particular Act to include [municipalities.]"

Seventeen years later, the Court changed its mind. In Monell v. Department of Social Services (1978) it reconsidered the Sherman Amendment episode and this time chose to focus on the specific objection raised by the 1871 Congress to that proposal. Congressmen had complained that the Sherman Amendment would impose liability for harms that could not fairly be attributed to the municipality. In *Monell* the Court reasoned that this objection had nothing to do with the propriety of a rule that would make the municipal government liable for its own conduct, and not the actions of private persons who may be beyond its control. Therefore, *Monell* overruled *Monroe* on the liability of local governments, holding that they are liable for constitutional violations caused by their unconstitutional "official policies" and "customs." A couple of years later the Court ruled, to the surprise of many, that local governments have absolutely no immunity from liability for damages (Owen v. City of Independence, 1980).

But *Monell* also set an important limit on the scope of municipal liability, one that has presented vexing problems for the Court ever since. Local governments (cities and counties) are not liable for all the constitutional violations committed by their employees in the course of their employment. Ironically, this is a rejection of the common law, for in the common law of torts the employer is responsible for all the employee's on-the-job conduct, whether or not the employer authorized the act in question. *Monell*'s ruling that municipal liability in § 1983 cases depends on tracing the injury to an unconstitutional policy or custom is a stricter test for the plaintiff to meet. Moreover, the ruling has obliged the Court to address, time and again, the question of whether a given act by an employee represents the "official policy" of the municipality. The Court has not yet arrived at a coherent approach to the problem of determining whether a given constitutional tort is a product of official policy. (The complex and difficult body of case law on this topic is examined in "The Liability of Local Governments").

THE CIVIL RIGHTS ATTORNEY'S FEES ACT OF 1976

Besides the judicial development of § 1983 law in *Monroe* and later cases, an important statute was enacted in 1976. The "American Rule" on attorney's fees is that each party is responsible for paying his or her own lawyer, regardless of who wins. This means that people who may have good claims but who cannot afford legal counsel often have no way to vindicate their rights. The Civil Rights Attorney's Fees Award Act was an effort to improve their chances of obtaining counsel, at least when they make claims under § 1983 and other civil rights statutes.

As interpreted by the Supreme Court, the statute provides that the plaintiff in a § 1983 case, in the event he or she is a "prevailing party" in the litigation, may obtain his or her attorney's fees as part of the award from the defendant. In the ensuing twenty-five years, the Court has faced such issues as determining when the plaintiff is a prevailing party and has set forth principles for calculating the fee award. (See "Attorney's Fees" for a detailed description of the doctrine on these and other issues raised by the statute). For present purposes, what is important is that this statute contributes in an important way to the general theme of expanded access to offensive remedies, which began in *Monroe*. By enacting the statute, Congress sought to facilitate the Court's agenda of enhancing the offensive remedies available to victims of constitutional violations.

SUING FEDERAL OFFICERS: BIVENS V. SIX UNKNOWN NAMED FEDERAL NARCOTICS AGENTS

Section 1983, as construed in *Monroe* and *Monell*, is a powerful tool for seeking offensive remedies, but it applies only to local governments and to persons acting under color of state law. It does not apply to the federal government or to federal officers (unless they happen to be working under the control of state officers at the time). Another strand of doctrine, dating back thirty years, sometimes authorizes suits against federal officers for constitutional violations, without any statutory grounding. The facts of Bivens v. Six Unknown Named Federal Narcotics Agents (1971) resemble those of *Monroe*, except that the defendants were federal officers rather than Chicago police officers. Charging that the federal agents invaded his property in violation of his Fourth Amendment right against unreasonable search and seizure, *Bivens* sought relief in a federal suit for damages. His theory was that a cause of action should be implied from the constitutional provision itself. Objecting to this proposal, the government attempted to revive the old common law approach to constitutional remedies. It said that the appropriate remedy was a common law suit for trespass, in which the Fourth Amendment would not be the source of the plaintiff's rights but would be relevant only to the issue of whether the officers were justified in making their entry.

The Supreme Court took the plaintiff's side of this debate. In so doing the Court definitively rejected the old notion that common law remedies are sufficient to protect constitutional rights. The problem with the government's argument was that it sought "to treat the relationship between a citizen and a federal agent unconstitutionally exercising his authority as no different from the relationship between two private parties." In fact, "[a]n agent acting—albeit unconstitutionally—in the name of the United States possesses a far greater capacity for harm than an individual trespasser exercising no authority other than his own." In addition, "[t]he interests protected by state laws regulating trespass and invasion of privacy, and those protected by the Fourth Amendment's guarantee against unreasonable searches and seizures, may be inconsistent or even hostile." For example, one cannot be expected to deny entry to an officer who requests it. Yet the common law of trespass would hold that consent is a defense to the tort in that situation. In his concurring opinion, Justice Harlan pointed out that the cases granting prospective relief with no statutory foundation, which date back at least to *Young*, furnish ample authority for permitting suits for damages as well.

Chief Justice Burger and Justice Black dissented, arguing that the creation of remedies was a task for Congress, a body that represents the will of the people, and not for the unelected federal judiciary. The root of their argument was that this case was very different from *Monroe*, for here the Court could not frame its decision as an interpretation of a statute enacted by Congress. Justice Harlan, concurring in the Court's judgment, wrote a response to these arguments. He stressed the *constitutional* pedigree of the rights *Bivens* asserted in his suit, reasoning that since constitutional rights are "intended to vindicate the interests of the individual in the face of the popular will as expressed in legislative majorities," it would not be appropriate to leave the provision of effective remedies entirely in the hands of the legislature.

In *Bivens* the Court limited its holding to the Fourth Amendment. It did not lay down a general rule that a cause of action may be "implied" from the Constitution for every kind of constitutional violation. In fact, the Court said that other contexts may contain "special factors counseling hesitation" in recognizing such lawsuits, especially if Congress had enacted legislation in the area. Yet two cases decided in the 1970s suggested that this notion may not be much of a barrier after all. In one of them the Court allowed a former legislative aide, who had been fired on account of her gender, to sue the Congressman for a Fifth Amendment due process violation, even though Congress had explicitly exempted itself from the federal statutes that authorize such suits against other persons (Davis v. Passman, 1979). The other allowed a federal prisoner to sue prison doctors for an Eighth Amendment cruel and unusual punishment violation on account of inadequate medical care, even though suit could also have been brought under the Federal Tort Claims Act, a federal statute allowing people to sue the government for ordinary torts such as medical negligence (Carlson v. Green, 1980).

In the 1980s, the Supreme Court's attitude changed. When military personnel (for whom there are no statutorily authorized offensive remedies) tried to use the "implied cause of action" theory to challenge the military's actions on constitutional grounds, the Court rebuffed them, explaining that the military environment, and in particular the need to maintain military discipline, are special factors counseling hesitation in this area (Chappell v. Wallace, 1983; United States v. Stanley, 1987). In another case, a civil service employee tried to challenge his treatment on the ground that his superiors were motivated by a desire to retaliate against him for speaking out on matters of public concern. The Court pointed out that the employee had available to him another means to assert his rights, specifically, civil service remedies enacted by Congress as a way to protect the rights of federal employees. In these circumstances, the Court ruled, the judiciary should not interfere by creating yet another remedy (Bush v. Lucas, 1983). Similarly, in Schweiker v. Chilicky (1988) the Court denied an implied cause of action to Social Security recipients who charged that they were unconstitutionally denied benefits. As the Supreme Court saw the case, they had an adequate remedy within the Social Security system itself, so the courts should not intervene. The most recent case in this line holds that *Bivens* actions may be brought only against officers and not against the United States or its agencies (FDIC v. Meyer, 1994).

CONCLUSION

The overall picture that emerges from this historical survey is that the law of constitutional remedies has tracked developments in substantive constitutional law. Before the Supreme Court recognized many substantive constitutional rights, the law of constitutional remedies also received little attention. Over the years the Court has tended to create new remedies in tandem with its creation of new rights. Recently, however, the Court has cut back on certain constitutional remedies, perhaps because it is not entirely sympathetic to the underlying rights at stake in particular kinds of constitutional litigation. It may be influenced by a sense that prudence is a virtue and that modifying remedial law is a less drastic step than repudiating previously established rights.

NOTES

1. Clyde E. Jacobs, *The Eleventh Amendment and Sovereign Immunity* (Westport, Conn.: Greenwood Press, 1972) 4–8.
2. Id. 8–9.
3. Citations to the various positions may be found in Atascadero State Hospital v. Scanlon, 473 U.S. 234, 263–80 (1985) (Brennan, J., dissenting).
4. Richard Fallon Daniel Meltzer, & David Shapiro, *Hart & Wechsler's The Federal Courts and the Federal System* (Westbury, N.Y.: Foundation Press, 4th ed., 1996) 1051.
5. Id., 1212–13.
6. Id., 1215–22.
7. Id., 1036.
8. Id., 849–50, 995–96.
9. Id., 996.
10. Ann Woolhandler, "The Common Law Origins of Constitutionally Compelled Remedies," 107 *Yale L. J.* (1997) 77.
11. Fallon et al., *Hart & Wechsler's The Federal Courts and the Federal System* 1065.
12. John C. Jeffries, Jr., Pamela S. Karlan, Peter W. Low, & George A. Rutherglen, *Civil Rights Actions: Enforcing the Constitution* (Westbury, N.Y.: Foundation Press, 2000) 11–12.
13. Woolhandler, "The Common Law Origins of Constitutionally Compelled Remedies."

14. Burt Neuborne, "The Myth of Parity," 90 *Harv. L. Rev.* (1977) 1105.

15. This section draws heavily on Michael Wells, "The Past and the Future of Constitutional Torts," 19 *Conn. L. Rev.* (1986) 53.

16. *Cong. Globe,* 42d Cong., 1st Sess. 321 (1871) (Rep. Stoughton).

17. Id., 322 (Rep. Stoughton).

18. Wells, "The Past and the Future of Constitutional Torts," 66.

19. Id., 66–67 n.90.

20. Id., 67 n. 91.

21. Id., 67.

22. Id., 67 nn. 93–94.

23. Eugene Gressman, "The Unhappy History of Civil Rights Legislation," 50 *Mich. L. Rev.* (1952) 1323.

24. Id., 1338.

25. Id., 1340.

26. Id., 1340–41.

27. Id., 1342–43.

28. Jeffries et al., *Civil Rights Actions* (2000) 37.

29. Eric Zagrans, "Under Color of What Law: A Reconstructed Model of Section 1983 Liability," 71 *Va. L. Rev.* (1985) 499; Wells,"The Past and the Future of Constitutional Torts," 61.

30. David Achtenberg, "A 'Milder Measure of Villainy': The Unknown History of 42 U.S.C. § 1983 and the Meaning of 'Under Color of' Law," 1999 *Utah L. Rev.* 1; Steven Winter, "The Meaning of 'Under Color of' Law," 91 *Mich. L. Rev.* (1991) 323.

31. Marshall Shapo, "Constitutional Tort: *Monroe v. Pape* and the Frontiers Beyond," 60 *Nw. U. L. Rev.* (1965) 277, 279–87.

32. Louise Weinberg, "The *Monroe* Mystery Solved: Beyond the 'Unhappy History' Theory of Civil Rights Litigation," 1991 *B.Y.U. L. Rev.* 737.

33. Jeffries et al., *Civil Rights Actions* 36.

34. Neuborne, "The Myth of Parity."

35. Jack M. Beermann, "A Critical Approach to Section 1983 with Special Attention to Sources of Law," 42 *Stan. L. Rev.* (1989) 51; Wells, "The Past and the Future of Constitutional Torts," 53.

36. Michael Wells, "Constitutional Remedies, Section 1983, and the Common Law," 68 *Miss. L. J.* (1998) 157.

Part II

Constitutional Remedies and Commentary

STATE ACTION

The Constitution is aimed primarily at regulating the conduct of government. This means that, for the most part, the constitutional rights contained in the first nine amendments and the Fourteenth and Fifteenth Amendments are held solely against governments and their officers. The main exception is the Thirteenth Amendment, which prohibits "involuntary servitude." The Supreme Court has held that this provision forbids both states and private persons from practicing slavery. It is a constitutional violation for a private citizen to enslave another whether or not the state has authorized slavery. In most instances, the actions of private individuals with no state involvement do not violate anyone's constitutional rights. The rule is that, in the absence of some act by a government or its officers, no constitutional violation takes place. In the jargon of constitutional law, this is called the "state action" requirement.

This rule is easy to apply in cases where the government acts directly to injure someone and in cases where an ordinary person acts alone. In the former situation a court may find a constitutional violation, while in the latter it may not (though of course private actors are always subject to other legal requirements). But the circumstances are not always so clear. Here we address situations in which the plaintiff complains of an injury that was produced by some interaction between the state and a private individual. We deliberately choose the vague word "interaction" to describe the cases because there are many variations on the general theme and no precise rule for separating those arrangements that must satisfy constitutional requirements from those that do not.

In cases featuring some kind of private–government interaction, courts must decide just how much and what kinds of state participation will trigger constitutional protections so that the injured person may sue either governments, officials, or private persons on constitutional grounds. State action is an especially confusing area of constitutional law. One scholar has even referred to it as "a conceptual disaster area."[1] The Court identifies a number of factors that matter, but, as we shall see, it does not necessarily apply those factors in a consistent way to the cases it decides.

Whether state action is present in a given case is a constitutional issue. But it is closely linked to an important statutory limitation on the scope of the cause of action authorized by § 1983, the main vehicle for bringing constitutional claims for damages and prospective relief. That statute authorizes lawsuits only against persons acting under color of state law. The Supreme Court interprets this language as the equivalent of the constitutional state action requirement, except that the state action rule is satisfied by either state or federal governmental involvement, while the "under color of" rule is met only by the actions of state officials (Lugar v. Edmondson Oil Co., 1982). For this purpose, local government officials are treated as state officials, though for other purposes they are not. After discussing state action in general, we briefly address the special restrictions imposed on the scope of § 1983 by the "under color of" requirement.

GENERAL CONSIDERATIONS

Common Fact Patterns Giving Rise to "State Action" and "Under Color Of" Issues

State action issues may be present in a variety of situations. Though there are some general principles that apply to all of them, each has produced its own body of law. This discussion first identifies and distinguishes among these fact patterns. Next we discuss the policy considerations that bear on the area as a whole, and, in the final part of this discussion, we examine the Court's decisions related to each of the typical fact patterns.

One common fact situation is the use of "self-help" remedies (e.g., Flagg Bros., Inc. v. Brooks, 1978). Self-help remedies are legal rules that permit private persons to take action on their own to secure legal rights against other private persons. For example, a bank "B" "may lend money to a debtor, "D," for the purpose of buying a car. If D fails to make payments on the loan, state law may authorize B to take the car, without necessarily going through any legal process in which D would have a chance to explain or justify the failure to make payments at a hearing before a judge. D may then bring a § 1983 suit against B, claiming that B violated D's Fourteenth Amendment right not to be deprived of property (the car) without due process of law. The state action issue is whether B's repossession of the car, under authority of a state law that allows private persons to resolve legal disputes on their own, amounts to an action by the state that is subject to Fourteenth Amendment limitations. As we shall see, the answer may depend on the details of the state self-help repossession law.

A more amorphous category of cases concerns various kinds of cooperation between state governments and private persons. Instead of hiring workers and setting up or expanding government departments to achieve their goals, states sometimes contract out tasks to private individuals or firms. Instead of hiring doctors to attend to all the medical needs of inmates at a prison, the state may pay a private doctor to handle certain cases (e.g., West v. Atkins, 1988). Instead of funding a school for students with behavioral problems, the state may send such students to a private school (e.g., Rendell-Baker v. Kohn, 1982). When the state builds a parking garage, it may rent some of the space to private businesses to defray the costs of construction and maintenance (e.g., Burton v. Wilmington Parking Authority, 1961). In deciding whether the private entity involved in one of these arrangements is a state actor, the Supreme Court considers such factors as the nature of the job that is contracted out, the substantive constitutional right at issue in the case, and the amount of control the state exercises over the activities of the private entity (Brentwood Academy v. Tennessee Secondary School Athletic Association, 2001).

In the third group of cases, a public official and a private party agree to do something that violates someone's constitutional rights. Suppose, for example, one party to a lawsuit pays the judge a bribe in exchange for a favorable ruling. This violates the other party's right to due process of law by denying him or her a fair hearing on the merits of the lawsuit. He or she may sue not only the judge, (which would probably be thwarted by the doctrine of judicial immunity (see "Absolute Immunity"), but also the litigant who conspired with the judge (e.g., Dennis v. Sparks, 1980). In a variant of this fact pattern, a public agency has done something illegal because of pressure from a private entity, and the issue is whether the private entity can be held responsible for the public agency's constitutional violation. The resolution of these "conspiracy" cases usually turns on whether the plaintiff has sufficient evidence that the judge and the private party have made an agreement and not simply pursued similar objectives independently.

A fourth broad category of cases features a public employee who engages in conduct outside the normal scope of his or her official duties and an injured plaintiff who seeks to sue for a constitutional violation. For example, a police officer may shoot someone with his police department revolver in the course of a personal quarrel either on or off the job. And the question then arises whether the use of police equipment is enough to trigger the Constitution, whether the action must take place while on the job, or whether the personal motive is sufficient to put this case outside the realm of state action.

These four categories capture most of the fact patterns that give rise to state action issues, especially those that come up in suits seeking offensive remedies. In addition, they provide a means for imposing some order on an otherwise unruly area of the law. The Supreme Court tends to use different doctrinal formulations depending on which of these fact patterns it is addressing. But the four categories are not mutually exclusive; some cases may fall within more than one of them. And because certain state action issues do not fit into any of them, the categories are also not exhaustive. In the course of describing the Supreme Court's doctrine, we will also discuss some of these other state action problems.

Policy Considerations Bearing on the State Action Issue

Before discussing the Supreme Court's doctrine bearing on each of these fact patterns, we need to identify the broad issues of constitutional policy that the Court must consider in drawing lines between cases in which the level of state involvement is sufficiently high to justify the imposition of constitutional limits on a person's conduct, and cases in which the level of state involvement is not high enough to warrant those limits. A problem with this area of the law is that the term "state action," which the Supreme Court routinely uses to describe the doctrine, is itself misleading. It is easy to mistakenly think that state action has to do with whether the state is involved; however, one finds that the state is alway*s* involved in any private dispute, if only by furnishing the legal rules and the judicial machinery by which the dispute is resolved. Yet no one would maintain that the Constitution applies to every interaction between private persons. So the resolution of a state action issue is not furthered by asking whether there is state involvement. The real question is not whether the state is involved but what kind of state involvement is necessary to trigger constitutional guarantees. The best starting point for answering this question is to identify the costs and benefits of ruling that state action either is or is not present in a given case. State action or its absence is best understood as the outcome of an evaluation of those costs and benefits (Brentwood Academy v. Tennessee Secondary School Athletic Association, 2001).[2]

The consequence of finding state action is that the scope of constitutional guarantees is expanded, simply because those guarantees would apply to a broader rather than a narrower range of disputes. It follows that, in any given case, the policy furthered by a finding of state action is the value underlying the particular constitutional right that would be vindicated by such a finding. An example will help to make the point. Suppose the state contracts out the education of children with disabilities to a private school; a teacher at the school writes a letter to the newspaper criticizing the government's allocation of funds and is fired by his or her supervisor. The teacher sues, charging violation of First Amendment rights. In deciding whether the supervisor's act was state action, the value that would be served by ruling for the plaintiff is the value of freedom of speech. Or suppose a state contracts with a private prison to house inmates; an inmate is beaten by other inmates and brings suit against guards who failed to protect him. Finding state action in this case would promote the values underlying the Eighth Amendment's prohibition of cruel and unusual punishment.

Since constitutional rights are our basic guarantees against arbitrary and unfair exercises of state power, there would seem to be a strong case for an expansive state action doctrine. We may return to the possibility of a limitless state action doctrine, mentioned earlier as an unthinkable alternative. What, one may wonder, would be wrong with applying the Constitution to every private transaction? The problem with going so far is that constitutional values are not absolutes that trump every competing consideration in every conceivable situation. Restricting the scope of state action also serves important constitutional values. The Supreme Court has said that

> Careful adherence to the "state action" requirement preserves an area of individual freedom by limiting the reach of federal law and federal judicial power. It also avoids imposing on the State, its agencies or officials, responsibility for conduct for which they cannot fairly be blamed (Lugar v. Edmondson Oil Co., 1982).

Notice that this passage mentions two constitutional values that are furthered by a finding of no state action. One is individual liberty to do as one pleases without interference by the courts through the application of constitutional rules restricting one's actions. The other is protecting the states from unfair regulation by the courts in circumstances in which the state really is not responsible. The link between them is that judicial power can be as dangerous as any other kind of state power. A narrow state action doctrine limits the range of cases in which judges may interfere, therefore serving as a restraint on judicial power: "[A] fundamental fact of our political order," said the Court in *Lugar*, is that "courts [must] . . . respect the limits of their own power as directed as against state governments and private interests."

These competing policy considerations are very broad. It would be unwise to try simply to choose between them either by adopting an expansive or a narrow state action rule, and the Supreme Court has not tried to do so. The strength of the competing policies varies significantly depending on the circumstances, and the cost of making a sweeping rule would be to ignore those variations. A better approach, and the one the Supreme Court has in fact adopted, is to break the state action problem down into a number of narrower problems that arise in cases with similar fact pattens. These typical fact patterns are identified in "Common Fact Patterns Giving Rise to 'State Action' and 'Under Color Of' Issues." In resolving state action cases, the Supreme Court often stresses the distinctive features of the particular fact pattern at hand.

SELF-HELP REMEDIES

Two cases, decided four years apart, illustrate the Supreme Court's doctrine on self-help remedies and state action. The first is Flagg Brothers, Inc. v. Brooks (1978). When Brooks was evicted from her apartment, she agreed to have her belongings put in storage at Flagg Brothers' warehouse. A dispute arose as to payment for the storage, and Flagg Brothers threatened to sell the property under a state law that permits a warehouse to sell property entrusted to it in order to obtain outstanding fees. Brooks then brought a § 1983 suit, charging that the sale would violate the Constitution by depriving her of property without due process of law. She sought an injunction to stop the sale (see "Prospective Relief" for a general discussion of injunctions). Though no state officer would participate in the threatened sale, she relied on earlier cases that had found state action in situations where the state had confided to a private party a function it traditionally exercised itself, this doctrine is called the "public function" doctrine. Brooks' main argument was that resolving disputes about money owed one person by another was such a function, and that the state had given the power to resolve that issue to the warehouse owners (i.e., to Flagg Brothers).

The Supreme Court examined the "public function" cases she relied upon and rejected her argument. It said that Brooks had "read too much into the language of [the] prior cases." For the doctrine to apply, it is not enough that the function be one the state has traditionally performed. It must be one that has been "exclusively reserved to the State." For example, the Court has held that when states grant to private organizations the conduct of elections, the acts of that private group are state action.[3] When a private company owns a whole town and performs all the municipal functions, its actions are state action. By contrast, "the settlement of disputes between debtors and creditors is not traditionally an exclusive public function." Since our system contains many self-help remedies, the Court reasoned, it would be wrong to conclude that dispute resolution is traditionally an area over which the state exercises exclusive control.

Brooks also argued that "Flagg Brothers' proposed action is properly attributable to the State because the State has authorized and encouraged it" by enacting the statute that permitted the sale. The Court, however, drew a distinction between situations in which the state acts and situations in which the state merely permits private action. The Court said it had "never held that a State's mere acquiescence in a private action converts that action into that of the State." For example, in one earlier case it had refused to rule that a private club's policy of excluding blacks from membership could be attributed to the state just because the state permitted race discrimination (Moose Lodge No. 107 v. Irvis, 1972).

Four years later, in Lugar v. Edmondson Oil Co. (1982) the Court returned to the "self-help" issue in a somewhat different factual context. Lugar owed money to Edmondson Oil. Edmondson brought a suit in state court to recover the debt, and had some of Lugar's property "attached" while the suit proceeded. In order to understand this case, we need to make a brief detour into the law of attachment.

"Attachment" is a process by which the person in possession of the property is prohibited from disposing of it. The purpose of attaching the debtor's property is to make sure he does not sell the property and then flee with the cash or otherwise thwart the creditor's rights. The statute at issue in this case allowed the creditor, Edmondson, to go before a court clerk without notifying the debtor. (The process by which one may obtain relief from a judicial officer without providing notice to the opponent or holding an adversary hearing is called an "ex parte" procedure.) The statute allowed the clerk to tell the sheriff to attach the property if the creditor stated his belief that the debtor might dispose of the property in a way that would harm creditors.

Lugar then brought a separate lawsuit under § 1983 in federal court, challenging the state law that authorized the attachment on the ground that the ex parte attachment procedure permitted Edmondson to deprive him of property without due process of law. Edmondson claimed, on the authority of *Flagg Brothers*, that the statute raised no constitutional issue because no state action was present in the case. This time, however, the Supreme Court sided with the debtor, Lugar. The Court used a rather different approach than it had in *Flagg Brothers*. The issue in state action cases, the Court said, was whether "the conduct allegedly causing the deprivation of a federal right [could] be fairly attributable to the State." In resolving this issue, the Court employed a two-part test:

> First, the deprivation must be caused by the exercise of some right or privilege created by the State or by a rule of conduct imposed by the State or by a person for whom the State is responsible. . . . Second, the party charged with the deprivation must be a person who may fairly be said to be a state actor. This may be because he is a state official, because he has acted together with or obtained significant aid from state officials, or because his conduct is otherwise chargeable to the State.

The first of these criteria was satisfied by the state's attachment law. Had he merely argued that Edmondson misused the state process, this requirement would not be met, because then the complaint would focus solely on the private actor's conduct and not anything fairly attributable to the state. But Lugar challenged the state's procedure itself as "defective under the Fourteenth Amendment." The second prong of the test was also met, because "a private party's joint participation with state officials in the seizure of disputed property is sufficient to characterize that party as a 'state actor' for purposes of the Fourteenth Amendment." Here, Edmondson had acted together with the clerk of court and the sheriff in obtaining and carrying out the attachment order. The difference between this case and *Flagg Brothers* was that the private warehouse owner in *Flagg Brothers* did not seek the aid of state officers. The state law allowing him to sell the stored property did not require him to do so.

To put the two cases in perspective, note that most statutes that allow self-help are more like the one at issue in *Lugar* than the one in *Flagg Brothers*. For the most part, private actors must make some sort of appeal to public officials in order to attach property or take other action to protect their rights as creditors. Thus, the state action requirement will usually be satisfied in cases falling within this fact pattern. Moreover, some have argued that *Flagg Brothers* is not only an unusual case but a wrongly decided one. Viewed as a matter of policy, the benefits of extending the Constitution to the fact pattern presented in *Flagg Brothers* seem to be at least as strong as the benefits in *Lugar*, for the state law at issue in *Flagg Brothers* puts no constraints at all on the warehouse owner. The possibility of unfairness to the debtor (and hence the need for judicial supervision) seems at least as strong in such a case as in *Lugar*, where the creditor at least was obliged to take his complaint to the clerk of court in order to obtain the attachment.[4]

Contracts Between the State And Private Actors

Situations in which the state has dealings of one kind or another with a private party present a range of issues, depending on the nature of the relationship. Typically, some public function is contracted out to a private entity, or public property is leased to a private entity. Not surprisingly, Supreme Court rulings on state action have varied widely from case to case, depending on the circumstances. It would be difficult, and probably impossible, to state a general principle to explain all the results in these cases. A better approach is simply to describe a number of major Supreme Court decisions in a variety of fact patterns and identify the factors that seem to influence their outcomes.

Symbiotic Relationships

One influential case, decided thirty years ago but still relied on by lower courts, is Burton v. Wilmington Parking Authority (1961). As a government body, the Wilmington Parking Authority built a parking garage in downtown Wilmington, Delaware. In order to make the project financially feasible, the Authority leased a portion of the space to private tenants, including a restaurant called the Eagle Coffee Shoppe. The case arose when Burton, an African-American, parked his car in the garage, entered the Eagle Coffee Shoppe, and was refused service. In a challenge to this practice of racial discrimination, Burton sued the Authority for violating his Fourteenth Amendment right to equal protection of the law by allowing its tenant, Eagle, to exclude African-Americans. The Authority defended on the ground that Eagle was a private business and that it bore no responsibility for its conduct.

The Supreme Court ruled that state action was present in this case. As in the self-help cases, the test is whether the action "may fairly be said to be that of the State." But here the Court did not use the two-part test it adopted in *Lugar*. Instead it engaged in an intensive review of the facts of this particular case, declaring that "only by sifting facts and weighing circumstances can the nonobvious involvement of the State in private conduct be attributed its true significance." In this case, the "land and building were publicly owned," and the restaurant was "a physically and financially integral and, indeed, indispensable part of the State's plan to operate its project as a self-sustaining unit." Taken together, the "variety of mutual benefits" that accompanied the relationship between the restaurant and the parking authority established "that degree of state participation and involvement in discriminatory action which it was the design of the Fourteenth Amendment to condemn." But the Court warned that its holding did not mean the state is responsible for the actions of anyone who leases property from it. Whether a given arrangement triggers constitutional protections "can be determined only in the framework of the peculiar facts or circumstances present." The factor that may distinguish *Burton* from many leasing arrangements is that here the Authority had "so far insinuated itself into a position of interdependence with Eagle that it must be recognized as a joint participant in the challenged activity." Most situations where the state leases property to private entities probably would not meet this test.

The "Nexus" Requirement

Though the Supreme Court has never repudiated *Burton*, more recent cases involving symbiotic relationships have used a different test, and may be hard to square with *Burton*. In these cases, the Court says that "the inquiry must be whether there is a sufficiently close nexus between the State and the challenged action of the regulated entity so that the action of the latter may be fairly treated as that of the State itself" (American Manufacturers Mutual Insurance Co. v. Sullivan, 1999; Jackson v. Metropolitan Edison Co., 1974). (The term "nexus" evidently signifies a link or connection.) In *Jackson*, for example, a utility cut off service without giving the plaintiff any procedural protections. The mere fact that a utility company was heavily regulated by the state did not suffice to establish that this was state action subject to due process standards, because there was no particular connection between the state's regulation and the decision to terminate service.

In a later case the Court explained why it requires a connection between state involvement and the challenged action:

> The purpose of this [nexus] requirement is to assure that constitutional standards are invoked only where it can be said that the State is *responsible* for the specific conduct of which the plaintiff complains. The importance of this assurance is evident when, as in this case, the complaining party seeks to hold the State liable for the actions of private parties (Blum v. Yaretsky, 1982).

In *Blum* a suit was brought against state officials to challenge the decision by a private nursing home to move patients out of facilities offering more intensive, and more expensive, care and into less expensive facilities. The nursing home depended on the state for funds, was subjected to extensive state regulation, and performed a function the state was legally obligated to carry out. Nonetheless, the Court held that none of these factors had any connection with the transfer decision, which was based on "nothing more than a medical judgment."

In *Blum* the requirement of a connection was applied to a case in which the suit was brought against government officials. A variation on the same theme comes up when private individuals are sued. On the day it decided *Blum*, the Court also handed down Rendell-Baker v. Kohn (1982). In that case, the defendant was a private school that specialized in "dealing with students who have experienced difficulty completing public high schools" on account of "drug, alcohol, or behavioral problems, or other special needs." The plaintiffs were former teachers at the school who had been fired because they disagreed with school authorities and spoke out about the policy. They sued the school under § 1983, claiming that the dismissals violated their First Amendment rights to freedom of speech. The Supreme Court dismissed their suits for lack of state action. The reasoning tracked the *Blum* decision: In this case, as in *Blum*, the school received most of its funding from the state, was subject to extensive regulation by the state, and carried out a function (in this case, education) the state was obligated by statute to perform. But the state regulation did not focus on the treatment of employees, so the Supreme Court concluded that the state action nexus was missing. The Court explained that "the decisions to discharge the . . . [teachers] were not compelled or even influenced by any state regulation. Indeed, in contrast to the extensive regulation of the school generally, the various regulators showed relatively little interest in the school's personnel matters." One may infer that the result could be different if the plaintiffs were students and the complaint had to do with action taken to comply with a state regulation.

Special Circumstances

In some state action cases, the result seems to turn on the particular set of circumstances rather than on any general principle. Two Supreme Court cases, both involving prisons, illustrate this theme. In Polk County v. Dodson (1981), a prisoner sought to sue his lawyer, Martha Shepard, for failing to represent him adequately. Shepard was a public defender, a state employee who was paid a salary to represent impoverished criminal defendants who could not afford to hire lawyers of their own. States are required to provide such assistance under the Sixth Amendment right to counsel in criminal trials. Dodson sued the lawyer under § 1983, charging that the ineffective assistance he received was itself a violation of that Sixth Amendment right. (He also sued the county that employed Shepard.) Even though Shepard was a state employee, carrying out the state's constitutional obligation to provide counsel to indigent criminal defendants, the Supreme Court ruled that the state action requirement was not met.

The Court distinguished between Shepard's employment relationship with the state and the duties of her job, saying that the latter was the determining factor in the state action inquiry. In America we have an "adversary" system of criminal justice, in which the role of the defense attorney, no matter who pays him or her, is to "oppose the designated representatives of the State." The premise of that system is that "a defense lawyer best serves the public, not by acting on behalf of the State or in concert with it, but rather by advancing the undivided interests of his client." The Court characterized this as "essentially a private function" even if, in the circumstances, the lawyer is a state employee. On the other hand, the Court stressed that some of the actions of a public defender are indeed state action. In any given case, the key is the function being exercised. For example, the Court reaffirmed an earlier case in which it had ruled that a public defender acts for the state when he or she hires or fires a subordinate (Branti v. Finkel, 1980).

Dodson may be compared with West v. Atkins (1988), also brought by a prisoner. In this case the defendant, Atkins, was a private doctor, an orthopedist who provided medical services to state prisoners. Under a contract with the state, he operated two clinics a week at a state prison. Atkins treated West for an ankle injury, but West, unsatisfied with the results, brought suit under § 1983 on the theory that the treatment was so bad as to amount to cruel and unusual punishment in violation of the Eighth Amendment. In this opinion the Court did not reach the substantive issue of whether this treatment actually fell short of constitutional requirements. It considered only the question of whether the doctor's conduct was state action, thus subjecting him to the possibility of being held liable for an Eighth Amendment violation.

In spite of the ruling in *Dodson*, the Court held that Atkins was a state actor. The Court explained that *Dodson* depended on the particular circumstances of that case, the "decisive factor" being "the adversarial role the defense lawyer plays in our criminal justice system." In this case, by contrast, Atkins' "professional and ethical obligation to make independent medical judgments did not set him in conflict with the State and other prison authorities." Moreover, "[i]t is only those physicians authorized by the State to whom the inmate may turn." Nor did it matter that Atkins was not a state employee:

> It is the physician's function within the state system, not the precise terms of his employment, that determines whether his actions can fairly be attributed to the State. . . . Contracting out prison medical care does not relieve the State of its constitutional duty to provide adequate medical treatment to those in its custody, and it does not deprive the State's prisoners of the means to vindicate their Eighth Amendment rights.

In recent years some states have contracted with private firms to run prisons. The ruling in *West* very likely means that the on-the-job behavior of employees of these institutions is state action. On the other hand, a lower court ruled that the conduct of a private bus driver who allegedly molested children he transported to school pursuant to a contract with the state is not state action (Black v. Indiana Area School District, 1993). Perhaps the difference between this case and *West* is that children are not legally obligated to ride the bus. Or perhaps the decisive factor is that the state has no constitutional obligation to provide transportation to school.

Cooperation between Public Officers and Private Actors

The preceeding discussion examined cases in which governments contracted with private firms or individuals to do public business. Sometimes the relationship is more informal than that. We next discuss a group of cases in which the distinctive feature is some sort of joint action by a private actor and a public official. One case illustrating this theme is National Collegiate Athletic Association v. Tarkanian (1988), in which the issue was whether the NCAA, a private group, was responsible for actions taken by the University of Nevada at Las Vegas (UNLV), a public school. The NCAA had charged Tarkanian (a basketball coach) with violating its recruiting regulations, and, under pressure from the NCAA, UNLV had suspended him. In the Supreme Court the issue was whether Tarkanian could sue the NCAA under § 1983, by asserting a violation of his right to due process. He argued that

> [T]he NCAA was a state actor because it misused power that it possessed by virtue of state law. He claim[ed] specifically that UNLV delegated its own functions to the NCAA, clothing the Association with authority both to adopt rules governing UNLV's athletic programs and to enforce those rules on behalf of UNLV.

The Court acknowledged that UNLV was influenced by the NCAA in deciding to suspend Tarkanian. But this was not enough to make the NCAA a state actor. The key question was "whether UNLV's actions in compliance with the NCAA rules and recommendations turned the NCAA's conduct into state action." No government had conferred any power on the NCAA. Its members were public and private schools all over the country. No government or private group forced UNLV to become a member of the NCAA. Nor did UNLV cooperate with the NCAA in a plan that violated Tarkanian's rights. On the contrary, UNLV was "diametrically opposed" to the NCAA's efforts to impose sanctions on Tarkanian. Even if the NCAA were so powerful that UNLV had no choice but to comply with its demands, the Court reasoned that "it does not follow that such a private party is acting under color of state law." Instead of finding that the NCAA's role in the affair was state action, "[i]t would be more appropriate to conclude that UNLV has conducted its athletic program under color of the policies adopted by the NCAA, rather than that those policies were developed and enforced under color of Nevada law."

In *Tarkanian* the Court noted that a far different case would be presented if all its members were from the same state and if many of them were public, such as an association of high schools. The Supreme Court recently heard just such a case. In Brentwood Academy v. Tennessee Secondary School Athletic Association (2001) the TSSAA had imposed sanctions on Brentwood, a private school and member of TSSAA, for sending letters to prospective athletes. Brentwood sued TSSAA under § 1983, charging that the sanctions violated its First Amendment right of free speech. TSSAA objected to the lawsuit, claiming that it was a private actor and therefore not subject to free speech constraints in disciplining its members. The Court rejected this argument, agreeing with Brentwood that the suit could go forward. (The Court did not reach the merits of the free speech claim.) On the state action issue, the Court distinguished *Tarkanian* using the reasoning of *Tarkanian* itself. *Brentwood* differed from *Tarkanian* because in *Brentwood* 80 percent of the member schools of TSSAA were public schools located in Tennessee. Each of them acted under the authority of Tennessee law, and together they controlled the TSSAA. Therefore, the TSSAA's actions could fairly be attributed to the state of Tennessee. A harder case would be presented if substantially more of the association members were private schools. The Court's reasoning leaves unresolved just how many state schools need to be involved for the association to qualify as a state actor.

Another type of § 1983 "cooperation" case is illustrated by Dennis v. Sparks (1980). At the request of certain private persons, a state judge had ordered the plaintiffs not to produce oil from fields on which they held leases. Though the order was reversed on appeal, two years of production were lost. The leaseholders sued the judge and the persons who had obtained the initial order, asserting that the legal proceeding that produced the order was a sham; the judge and the private actors had acted pursuant to a corrupt agreement among themselves, with the judge accepting a bribe in exchange for issuing an order that would deprive the leaseholders of property without due process of law. The Supreme Court did not reach the merits of the case. But it did make an important ruling on the state action issue. It held that, assuming the leaseholders could prove that the judge's order "was the product of a corrupt conspiracy involving bribery of the judge . . . the private parties conspiring with the judge were acting under color of state law."

Cases of this kind, in which the claim is that the public officer and a private party have engaged in a conspiracy to achieve some illegal end, come up more often than cases like *Tarkanian* and *Brentwood.* Yet they have not received much attention from the Supreme Court. In particular, the Court has not yet addressed the issue of just what kind of evidence is necessary to establish the existence of a conspiracy between a public official and a private party. One lower court case states that the plaintiff "must allege, at the very least, that there was a mutual understanding, or a meeting of the minds, between the private party and the state actor." Merely showing that there were contacts between them, and that the official would in some way stand to gain from such a plot, would not be sufficient (Mershon v. Beasley, 1993).

At the same time, it would probably not be necessary to show that words were exchanged if the circumstances strongly indicate that an implicit agreement was reached. Suppose, for example, that a group of peaceful political activists ("group

A") are exercising their First Amendment rights by staging a demonstration in a public park. Because another group ("group B") vigorously opposes the views of the activists, the police are present to handle any conflict that might arise. Members of group B do arrive at the park, and police officers are seen exchanging looks and nods with members of that group. Clearly the police are not planning to interfere in the event group B attacks group A. In such a case, there may well be sufficient evidence of a conspiracy even though nothing was said by either side, much less written down.[5]

Public Officials' Private Conduct

Sometimes public officials are sued for actions they have taken that are outside their assigned tasks yet somehow connected to their official status. In Monroe v. Pape (1961) the Supreme Court ruled that an officer's conduct may violate the Constitution even if it also violated state law. One consequence of this ruling is that the scope of state action is broader than the official activities of an officer. Even if the officer is acting outside the scope of official duties when he or she injures the plaintiff, the conduct may still be state action and the officer may be liable for a constitutional tort. At the same time, it is clear that the Constitution does not apply to every single action taken by a state officer, no matter how unconnected to his or her official duties. A high school principal would not be subject to constitutional tort liability for punching his neighbor in the nose in an argument over a loud party. Courts must draw lines between the purely private aspects of officials' lives and those actions that have sufficient connection to their public duties to trigger constitutional limits on their actions.

The Supreme Court has taken little interest in cases of this kind. In the lower courts most of the cases involve police or other law enforcement officers. Judges have identified several factors that bear on whether, in a given set of circumstances, the officer's conduct amounts to state action, thus subjecting him or her to constitutional standards. These factors include (1) whether the conduct took place on the job, (2) whether it concerned official business, and (3) whether police equipment was used in committing the injury. If the conduct took place on the job in the course of official business and involved government equipment, courts generally find that state action is present even if the officer had a private motive. For example, suppose a police officer has a grudge against a neighbor for not cutting the grass often enough. If the officer uses his or her badge and police car to intimidate the neighbor while on duty, on the pretext that someone has made a legitimate complaint against the neighbor, he or she would act under color of state law. By contrast, if the officer visits his neighbor after work, does not claim he or she is enforcing the law, and does not use police equipment, there is no state action.

Other situations are not so clear, and, in the absence of guidance from the Supreme Court, it is impossible to state a general rule for these cases. When the officer is on duty but pursuing private ends, some courts say there is no state action. An on-duty policeman who assaulted his sister-in-law did not engage in state action when the impetus for the attack was a family and political dispute and the plaintiff was not threatened with arrest (Delcambre v. Delcambre, 1981). Others say state action may be present in similar circumstances. In one case, for example, a county jailor brandished a gun and threatened to kill the executive director of the jail on jail premises; the court said he acted under color of state law (Cassady v. Tackett, 1991). The mere fact that police equipment was used by a suspended police officer was insufficient to trigger a finding of state action in Gibson v. City of Chicago (1990). Here the officer had been suspended as mentally unfit for duty and had been stripped of his authority to act as a police officer but was permitted to keep his gun and ammunition. By contrast, courts have found state action in cases where police officers take second jobs as security guards and then identify themselves as police officers when arresting people.[6]

State Action and "Under Color of" State Law: The Scope of Section 1983

Section 1983, the vehicle by which most litigation seeking offensive constitutional remedies is brought, is a statute enacted by Congress. It authorizes liability only for actions taken under color of state law. In this section we discuss the relation between that statutory requirement and the constitutional requirement of state action. Three points need to be made. First, if a given act by an officia*l* meets the "under color of" requirement, then it also meets the state action requirement (Lugar v. Edmondson Oil Co., 1982). In other words, it is impossible for an officer to act under color of state law without also engaging in state action.

Second, it does not follow that any act satisfying the state action requirement necessarily meets the "under color of" state law requirement. A potential source of confusion is that the term "state" means different things in these two phrases. "State action" refers to any act for which any government or official, whether state or federal, may be held responsible as a matter of constitutional law. The reference in § 1983 to acts under color of state law refers to acts for which state and local governments and their officers may be sued under the statute. The phrase "under color of" is more complex than "state action." It refers not merely to the existence of governmental conduct, but also to the specific source of authority—state rather than federal—under which an officer has acted. The distinction between "state action" and "under color of" is important because sometimes state and local government officers actually act under color of federal law, as they do when they administer a federal program. In such a case they cannot be sued under § 1983 even though their conduct is undoubtedly state action in the constitutional sense (Rosas v. Brooks, 1987). Conversely, federal officers sometimes act under color of state law, as when they have collaborated with state officers in a project for which state officers are responsible. In Hampton v. Hanrahan (1979), for example, federal officers joined with state officers in a state law enforcement effort.

Third, in cases involving private actors, the "under color of" requirement may be satisfied even though the state action requirement is not. As we have seen, the act of a private person may be authorized by state law, such as the warehouse owner's sale in *Flagg Brothers*, yet it was found not to be state action. Usually (as in *Flagg Brothers*) the absence of state action will defeat a § 1983 suit. But this is not always so, and two possibilities should be noted. One is that there are a few constitutional rights that do not require state action, notably the Thirteenth Amendment's prohibition on slavery. Presumably one could sue a private slaveholder under the statute if the violation was authorized by state law, even if the conduct does not amount to state action. In addition, § 1983 authorizes suits to enforce certain federal laws as well as the Constitution. It may be possible to use § 1983 to sue private actors for injuries committed through acts authorized by state law in violation of federal laws (Lugar v. Edmondson Oil Co., 1982).

DUE PROCESS AND OTHER CONSTITUTIONAL RIGHTS

The focus of this book is on the remedies available for violations of constitutional rights. In order to appreciate the utility of these remedies, one needs to understand the rights to which they apply. Other books in this series examine in some detail the content of constitutional rights. However, certain constitutional rights—because they are usually enforced in § 1983 litigation and have some distinctive features setting them apart from other constitutional claims—need to be examined here. This discussion identifies the kinds of constitutional claims that are typically litigated under § 1983 and addresses some issues that arise in constitutional tort suits. Our starting point is the distinction between (a) the constitutional rights that are set out explicitly in the first eight amendments and (b) the rights that may be available under the Due Process Clause of the Fifth and Fourteenth Amendments. The former category includes, among others, the First Amendment right to freedom of speech, the Fourth Amendment prohibition on unreasonable search and seizure, and the Eighth Amendment right against being subjected to cruel and unusual punishment.

The discussion here deals mainly with rights in category (b), which are arguably more complex than those in category (a). For example, the Bill of Rights gives specific rules for dealing with a comparatively narrow range of the activities of state governments. The Due Process Clause, by contrast, with its directive that states may not "deprive any person of life, liberty, or property without due process of law," is a broadly worded prohibition containing at least three potentially expansive terms: "due process," "liberty," and "property." "Due process" may be defined in nonlegal language as "basic fairness," but this definition only emphasizes the open-endedness of the term. "Liberty" and "property" also may seem to be straightforward concepts, but we shall see that, for lawyers, these are nuanced terms are capable of far-reaching significance. Nor is this all; defining the terms "deprive" and "without" can also present challenges.

Since "liberty," "property," and "due process" are not easily cabined, they may be defined so broadly that any injury suffered at the hands of a state officer will be treated as a constitutional violation. In the Supreme Court's view, this would intrude too far into the domain traditionally reserved to the state governments. One theme in cases dealing with constitutional remedies has been to guard against this possibility by obliging plaintiffs to avail themselves of state remedies rather than of trying to fit their claims into the constitutional mold. The Court's main tool for accomplishing this aim has been the language of the Due Process Clause, which does not forbid states from depriving people of life, liberty, and property. It demands only that people be accorded due process of law in connection with these deprivations. If state remedies provide the process that is due, the Court can deny access to any further constitutional remedy.

One task in this discussion is to separate the contexts in which an injured person must seek relief by available state remedies from those in which he or she may bring a § 1983 suit. In so doing, we will see that the Supreme Court has found, within the language of the Due Process Clause, two quite distinct doctrines: "procedural" and "substantive." The former denotes the principle that the state may take one's life, liberty, or property so long as it follows proper procedures. For example, it may imprison or even execute a person if proper criminal procedures are employed in the process. By contrast, substantive due process is a principle that, in some circumstances, the government simply may not inflict certain harms on a person no matter what process is followed. For example, the rule that pre-viability abortion may not be criminalized at all is based on substantive due process (Planned Parenthood of Southeastern Pennsylvania v. Casey, 1992). The relevance of this distinction to the law of constitutional remedies is that when the Court wishes to send a plaintiff to state court, it may characterize his claim as one of "procedural due process" and find that state remedies provide the process that is due. When the Court wishes to allow access to federal court, it will more likely find that the case falls within the domain of substantive due process so that the existence of state remedies is not determinative. Cases involving the distinction between substantive and procedural due process have given rise to a complex and confusing body of law.

Another source of potential confusion is that the Due Process Clause is found in both the Fifth (ratified in 1791) and the Fourteenth (ratified in 1868) Amendments to the Constitution. The reason the same language appears twice is that the Supreme Court held long ago that this and other provisions of the first nine amendments only applies to the national government and not to the states (Barron v. Mayor and City Council of Baltimore, 1833). After the Civil War, however, state power was diminished and states were subjected to new constitutional obligations. Thus the Fourteenth Amendment, enacted in 1868, explicitly requires state governments to respect due process.

But the due process clause is only one of several sources of constitutional rights that may be litigated in constitutional tort suits. For example, after guaranteeing due process, the Fourteenth Amendment adds that no state may "deny to any person within its jurisdiction the equal protection of the laws." Though the Fifth Amendment contains no equal protection clause, the Supreme Court has held that Fifth Amendment due process includes an equal protection obligation as well (Bolling v. Sharpe, 1954). And, of course, one may in proper circumstances seek an offensive remedy for violations of any of the specific rights contained in the first eight amendments. Though the Bill of Rights initially only applied to the national government and not to the states, the Supreme Court has held that nearly all of those rights were incorporated into the Due Process Clause of the Fourteenth Amendment, which applies them to the state governments as well.[7] In a sense, then, these rights are indeed applications of the Due Process Clause, though the Supreme Court rarely characterizes them in that way. The Court has even held that a state's violation of the commerce clause, which forbids states from interfering in certain ways with interstate commerce, may be redressed in a § 1983 suit.[8]

We will begin with the role of due process in constitutional tort law, then discuss other constitutional rights and the relationship between those rights and the due process doctrine.

The Due Process Clause

We now turn to the role of the Due Process Clause in constitutional tort law (one aspect of that role is addressed in the section entitled "Affirmative Constitutional Duties.") This constitutional provision is the source of many of the substantive rights asserted by plaintiffs in § 1983 litigation. Though this book is mainly concerned with the remedial side of constitutional litigation, the Due Process Clause deserves attention here because substantive and remedial law are closely intertwined in this area. Sometimes the role of the Due Process Clause is not so much to create a substantive right as to require that the state provide a remedy of some kind for harms that closely resemble common law torts. Sometimes litigants are foreclosed from asserting a violation of due process due to the existence of another, more specific constitutional (or common law) right that may apply in the circumstances. The doctrine is often murky, and one cannot hope to present it with any clarity unless substantive and remedial issues are addressed together.

Substantive Due Process and Procedural Due Process

We begin with the distinction between "substantive due process" and "procedural due process." "Substance" and "procedure" are distinct aspects of any regime of law. Substantive rules tell people what their rights and duties are; giving directions as to what is forbidden and what is not. For example, the criminal law forbidding murder, the rule that persons are legally responsible for negligent conduct, and the free speech right against liability for true but defamatory speech are all matters of substantive law. When disputes arise as to these substantive obligations, people resort to courts to resolve them. There we encounter procedural law. Procedural rules are mainly of interest to lawyers, judges, and other participants in the judicial process and, taken as a body, form the mechanism by which disputes are resolved. For example, in criminal prosecutions some illustrations of procedural rules are the requirements that a criminal defendant (a) be informed of the charges against him, (b) be given an opportunity to respond, and (c) be permitted to confront adverse witnesses.

Governments act to deprive people of life, liberty, or property in a number of different contexts, ranging from the criminal process to the firing of public employees. The Supreme Court has ruled that the requirements of due process vary according to the context of a particular deprivation. The Court stated its general approach in Matthews v. Eldridge (1976):

> [I]dentification of the specific dictates of due process generally requires consideration of three distinct factors: First, the private interest that will be affected by the official action; second, the risk of an erroneous deprivation of such interest through the procedures used, and the probable value, if any, of additional or substitute procedural safeguards; and finally, the Government's interest, including the function involved and the fiscal and administrative burdens that the additional or substitute procedural requirement would entail.

The term "procedural due process" seems to be redundant, because "procedure" and "process" both refer to the same dimension of the legal system. By contrast, "substantive due process" appears to be an oxymoron because "substance" and "process" denote different aspects of law. Indeed, some judges and scholars argue that substantive due process should be banished from Fourteenth Amendment doctrine. Professor John Hart Ely, a distinguished constitutional scholar, derides substantive due process as "a contradiction in terms—sort of like 'green pastel redness.'"[9] Certainly, the term "substantive due process" lacks elegance. As a matter of policy, clearly there are arguments on either side of the controversy as to whether substantive due process ought to exist. But this controversy should not distract our attention from the fact that the Supreme Court has not chosen to eliminate substantive due process. The Court does sometimes use the Due Process Clause as the ground for substantive rules limiting government power in some way. A prominent example is Roe v. Wade (1973), where the Court held that the Due Process Clause forbids government from making it a crime to perform an abortion in the first trimester of pregnancy. It said that the right to have an abortion is part of the "liberty" guaranteed by the Fourteenth Amendment and that the state simply may not interfere with that liberty at an early stage of a pregnancy. For purposes of distinguishing substantive due process from procedural due process, the central point of *Roe* is that the state's procedures are beside the point; whatever procedures are followed, the state may not forbid certain abortions. This is a substantive limit on state power. Because the Court invokes the Due Process Clause as authority for invoking this substantive limit, the doctrine is called "substantive due process."

Thus we can see that, rather than an oxymoron, what is involved is a dispute about the proper scope of the Due Process Clause. Opponents of substantive Due Process Clause claim that the doctrine represents a judicial power grab that illegitimately takes decision-making authority away from the democratically accountable branches of government. The merits of substantive due process are taken up in another book in this series, and will not be debated here. Our focus will be on the role of substantive due process in constitutional tort litigation. But before addressing that matter, we need first to return to the procedural due process cases.

Two Kinds of Procedural Due Process Cases

Whatever one thinks of substantive due process, the explanation for the seemingly redundant phrase "procedural due process" should now be evident. Given the existence of cases that use the Due Process Clause as the basis for substantive limits on government, one needs a term to identify the procedural dimension of due process if only for the sake of avoiding confusion. With regard to constitutional tort law, it is especially important to keep separate these two strands of due process doctrine because they receive very different treatment in § 1983 litigation. As we explain below, a plaintiff who comes to federal court with a complaint that the state has denied procedural due process may be obliged to take his or her case to the state courts and seek state law remedies. Substantive due process claims brought to federal court apparently may remain there, even if state law remedies are available to the plaintiff.

The rule with regard to procedural due process is that the plaintiff may proceed in federal court if the state could reasonably have provided due process before the deprivation but did not do so. However, the plaintiff must seek state law remedies in the event the denial of procedural rights was due to a "random and unauthorized" act of a state officer (Zinermon v. Burch, 1990). Suppose a prison guard thinks an inmate has committed some infraction of the rules of the prison. Without authorization from his or her superiors, the guard withholds the inmate's mail as punishment for breaking the rule without giving the inmate an opportunity to contest the charge. Now suppose the inmate brings a § 1983 suit against the guard, claiming that the right to receive mail is an aspect of Fourteenth Amendment liberty and that the guard violated due process by summarily depriving him or her of that right. This is a procedural, rather than substantive, due process claim because the inmate must (under settled principles of law) concede that prison officials may validly punish him or her in this way so long as proper procedures are followed. The claim is that, since the guard acted unilaterally, the proper procedures were not followed in this instance. In such a case the inmate may well be told to first pursue state remedies, if they are available, because the guard's violation was a random and unauthorized action. If, on the other hand, the prison has a general policy of summary punishment without procedural safeguards, the policy and its application to this inmate could be examined in a § 1983 suit in federal court. Such a case may arise, for example, if the guard acts in this fashion on a regular basis, his superiors know about the practice, and they do nothing to stop it.

In order to understand this doctrine, we need to distinguish between two kinds of cases in which procedural due process violations may take place: those that result from established practices by state agencies and those that are the product of random and unauthorized acts by state employees. An example of the former kind of case would be a state that enacts a law authorizing officials to confine people to mental institutions without giving them a chance to contest the grounds for confinement. No deference to state remedies is required in such a case. By contrast, in the latter type of case, the state has adequate procedural safeguards, but officials simply do not follow them.

The reasoning behind deferring to state remedies in the latter kind of case is that the procedural dimension of the Due Process Clause does not broadly protect one from deprivations of liberty. It only protects one against deprivations of liberty that are effectuated without due process of law. As the Court put the matter in *Zinermon*, in procedural due process cases "[t]he constitutional violation actionable under § 1983 is not complete when the deprivation occurs; it is not complete unless and until the State fails to provide due process." Ordinarily, due process should be afforded before the deprivation. If there were a general policy within the prison as to punishments for infractions, the state could easily modify that policy to comply with the demands of the Due Process Clause. Its failure to do so, coupled with the ensuing deprivation of liberty, complete the Fourteenth Amendment violation. Upon showing these things, the inmate is entitled to relief in federal court. But it is not always feasible to provide due process before the deprivation. Suppose there is good reason to suspect that a slaughterhouse is selling contaminated beef. Safeguarding the public health may take precedence over the rights of the slaughterhouse owner, so that it will be appropriate to seize the meat first and afford the owner a hearing on the justification for the seizure later.

Returning to the inmate mail case, one could suppose the guard's act is random and unauthorized. The Supreme Court reasons that in a case of this kind it would be impossible for the state to foresee such actions by guards and provide pre-deprivation process; post-deprivation process is all that is required. The plaintiff who brings such a case to federal court before applying for relief under state law does not state a good constitutional claim, as his procedural due process claim is not complete until he is denied due process. Critics of this reasoning claim that the

Court draws an illusory distinction when it separates "random and unauthorized" acts of officers from other denials of due process. Circuit Judge Frank Easterbrook, for example, points out that "it is always foreseeable that there will be some errors in the implementation of any administrative system, and it is never foreseeable which occasions will give rise to those errors"(Easter House v. Felder, 1990). To the extent Judge Easterbrook is right, it will be impossible to determine what cases should fall into the "random and unauthorized" category and be relegated to the state courts and which cases should receive the attention of the federal courts. Experience with the *Zinermon* test suggests that, in many situations, lower courts are able to distinguish situations in which a pre-deprivation hearing is called for from those in which the state can be expected to provide only post-deprivation remedies.

For example, in a case in which the agency had a process in place that officials in charge did not follow, the plaintiff was required to go to state court (Caine v. Hardy, 1991). By contrast, in a case in which the city paid medical benefits to a disabled former employee then abruptly cut them off, the court ruled that there was no reason why a pre-deprivation hearing would not have been feasible (Cushing v. City of Chicago, 1993). Though the Supreme Court has not spoken directly to this issue in the years since *Zinermon*, it will no doubt return to it in the future as cases with this general fact pattern continue to arise.

Federalism and Rights

There are reasons why one might care whether a case is litigated in state court, with a state law remedy as the source of relief, or in federal court, with § 1983 as the ground for recovery. One reason is that the state remedy may not be as accommodating to the plaintiff as § 1983. We shall see, in the section entitled "Attorney's Fees," that the victorious plaintiff in a § 1983 suit may obtain attorney's fees but that such fees are typically not available under state tort law. Nor is there any pre-set statutory ceiling on the amount of the damages award in a § 1983 case. Depending on the state, there may well be such a ceiling on the damages award under state law. Litigants who must rely on state law in their suits against state officers and governments may face other obstacles to recovery, such as a very short time period in which to file suit (e.g., Felder v. Casey, 1988). Beyond these differences, many people, and certainly many lawyers, hold the view that federal judges are, broadly speaking, more sympathetic than state judges to plaintiffs with claims against government.[10] Whether or not this judgment is fair, it is an important feature of the background of constitutional litigation. That state judges are often subject to reelection and may feel primary loyalty to the government that employs them are factors underlying the general preference of plaintiffs for federal court. The problem is especially acute because constitutional rights often protect unpopular and politically powerless groups, such as prison inmates, criminal suspects, racial minorities, and members of fringe religious and political groups. For these reasons both plaintiffs and the officials and governments they sue care whether the case will be decided under federal constitutional law or under state tort law. In addition, they are often keenly interested in whether a given controversy will be litigated in federal or state court.

Though choice of substantive law and choice of forum are separate topics, both implicate some of the same policies, and the Supreme Court has sometimes blurred the line between them. The broad issue is the value of federalism in constitutional tort law and the extent to which that value ought to give way before constitutional claims. There are good reasons for allowing constitutional claimants into federal court. Besides the fact that § 1983 by its terms authorizes a federal cause of action, and other federal statutes explicitly give federal courts the power to hear these offensive constitutional challenges, the distinctive role of the federal courts includes deciding federal questions and vindicating constitutional rights. The expertise and sympathy for federal rights that are said to characterize the federal judiciary seem especially important in this kind of case. Also, having federal courts decide constitutional tort cases may produce more uniformity of decision, because the cases are decided in one court system rather than fifty. These policies are reflected in the doctrine on constitutional remedies. Over the broad range of constitutional tort litigation, the Supreme Court has erected relatively few barriers to obtaining access to federal court, and, not surprisingly, most constitutional tort suits are litigated in the federal courts.

One area in which the Court has not been so accommodating to plaintiffs is in cases arising under the Due Process Clause. The policies described in the preceding paragraph are in tension with an important theme of the contemporary Supreme Court, namely, respect for the autonomy and independence of the states. In pursuit of this latter set of values, the Court has strengthened the states' immunity from suit (see the section entitled "Sovereign Immunity in the Late Twentieth Century") and has even placed limits on the scope of congressional power to regulate the states. In the constitutional tort context the Court is sensitive to the danger that due process claims will displace state tort law. To see why, it is important to remember that the range of interests protected by the Due Process Clause—life, liberty (including personal security from physical and emotional injury), and property—closely resemble the interests traditionally occupying the domain of state tort law. Like the Due Process Clause, that body of law gives one recourse for a variety of harms to person and property.

Time and again the Court has invoked the need to avoid trampling on state tort law as a ground for not extending the reach of the Due Process Clause. In Paul v. Davis (1976) the plaintiff had been erroneously identified by the police as a suspected shoplifter and sought to sue for a due process violation. The Court, however, said the case was best left to the common law tort of defamation. To hold otherwise "would make of the Fourteenth Amendment a font of tort law to be superimposed upon whatever systems may already be administered by the States." The

Court repeated this admonition when it refused to allow a federal suit by a prisoner who claimed that guards had lost his hobby materials (Parratt v. Taylor, 1981).

Other cases decided in the late 1970s revealed similar resistance to allowing constitutional tort suits for harms that resemble common law torts. In Baker v. McCollan (1979) the Court refused to recognize a constitutional claim of liberty deprivation brought by a plaintiff who had been mistakenly imprisoned for three days. The Court was probably influenced by the fact that the case resembles a common law "false imprisonment" claim. In another case the Court held that junior high school students who had been paddled for misbehavior could not bring a procedural due process claim under § 1983 because state tort remedies provided adequate procedural protections (Ingraham v. Wright, 1977). Later, rejecting the notion that an inmate could bring a constitutional tort case for slipping on the floor of a jail, the Court stressed that the Constitution "does not purport to supplant traditional tort law in laying down rules of conduct to regulate liability for injuries that attend living together in society" (Daniels v. Williams, 1986). Rejecting the notion that a city could be liable for a constitutional tort for exposing employees to unsafe working conditions, the Court repeated these admonitions and added that "state law, rather than the Federal Constitution, generally governs the substance of the employment relationship" (Collins v. City of Harker Heights, 1992). As we shall see in a later section, the Due Process Clause is reserved for especially abusive acts by government officers. Ordinary accidents are left to the common law of torts.

Distinguishing Substantive from Procedural Due Process in Constitutional Tort

Roe v. Wade (1973) is a typical substantive due process case. Historically courts have relied on the doctrine as a ground for judicial invalidation of legislation that, in the Court's view, either interferes too much with one's ability to make certain fundamental decisions or interferes too much with property rights, thereby depriving one of the liberty and property safeguarded by the Fourteenth Amendment.[11] Constitutional tort seems far removed from that context; the target of the litigation here is not a statute enacted by the state legislature but rather the isolated act of some official. The plaintiff's grounds for relief ordinarily have nothing to do with limits on the state's regulatory power. Instead, the plaintiff's theory of recovery typically is that physical liberty (from confinement), as well as personal security from physical or emotional harm and other personal interests, are all part of Fourteenth Amendment liberty. The plaintiff's argument is that substantive due process forbids certain acts by state officers that injure these interests, no matter what procedure the officer may have followed. Of course, there are many situations in which it is perfectly acceptable, at least as a matter of constitutional law, for the government to inflict injuries of various kinds on individuals. Once substantive due process is recognized as a viable theory of recovery in constitutional tort, as it has been, the problem is to determine which cases fall within its ambit. A subsequent discussion will identify the factors that bear on whether a given instance of state-caused harm raises a substantive due process issue.

For now the important point is that there are two branches of due process in constitutional tort litigation: substantive and procedural. In Daniels v. Williams (1986) the Court identified the common roots of the two branches. "[T]he Due Process Clause, like its forebear in the Magna Carta, was 'intended to secure the individual from the arbitrary exercise of the powers of government.'" The Court then distinguished procedural due process from substantive due process, beginning with procedure: "By requiring the government to follow appropriate procedures when its agents decide to 'deprive any person of life, liberty or property,' the Due Process Clause promotes fairness in such decisions." As for substance, "by barring certain government actions regardless of the fairness of the procedures used to implement them, . . . [the Due Process Clause] serves to prevent governmental power from being 'used for purposes of oppression.'"

Sometimes both substantive and procedural due process claims can arise from the same facts. For example, a student who is paddled for misbehavior may claim both that the procedures followed in determining the punishment was justified were inadequate and that the physical force employed was uncalled for, no matter how impeccable the procedure may have been. In some cases the distinction between substantive due process and procedural due process in the constitutional tort context is a more subtle one. Consider the facts of an important Supreme Court case, Zinermon v. Burch (1990). The plaintiff had been admitted to the Florida State Hospital, a mental hospital, as a voluntary patient. As such he did not receive the procedural safeguards (such as notice and a hearing) that involuntarily admitted patients receive before being confined. He therefore argued that he was deprived of liberty without due process of law, reasoning that, on account of his mental condition, he was incompetent to grant the consent he gave and so the consent was invalid. The plaintiff claimed that the state ought to have procedures in place to prevent admission by invalid consent, though this would not necessarily mean one could be validly admitted involuntarily. So long as one does not pose a danger to oneself or others, it is possible to be incompetent to give consent to admission while being sufficiently competent to avoid involuntary admission. Zinermon framed his case as a procedural due process claim, and the Court treated it as one. Thus the plaintiff conceded that he may have been committable.

The Court ruled in Zinermon's favor, finding that the hospital's procedures for admitting him did not meet constitutional standards. Those procedures were not adequate to commit him involuntarily, and there was evidence that he might not have understood what he was doing. In light of this the procedures were not sufficient to commit him as a voluntary patient. The Court went on to hold that this set of circumstances did not fall within the "random and unauthorized" rule discussed in the section entitled "Two Kinds of Procedural Due Process Cases." In the Court's view Florida could have instituted pre-deprivation safeguards against this kind of allegedly improper admission. Therefore the constitutional violation was complete without the need for recourse to state processes. But note that the facts of *Zinermon* could have formed the basis for a substantive due process claim. Suppose Zinermon had framed his case differently, arguing not only that his consent was invalid but also that he did not pose a danger to himself or others. In that event he would be "claiming a deprivation of substantive due process, namely, that Florida and its officials had no sufficient reason *in fact* to commit him to a mental hospital."[12]

Another difference between the judicial treatment of procedural due process and substantive due process should be noticed. We have seen that the distinction between random and unauthorized conduct and actions taken pursuant to standard state procedures is a critical one in the law of procedural due process. When the issue is substantive due process, the distinction between random and unauthorized conduct and actions taken pursuant to state procedures evidently has no role to play. One may bring a § 1983 suit in federal court even for isolated incidents that are not authorized by state law. The case that establishes this proposition is not a modern constitutional tort case but an historical substantive due process case, Home Telephone and Telegraph Co. v. City of Los Angeles (1913). *Home Telephone* is from an era when state economic regulation often gave rise to substantive due process issues. The phone company challenged the city's ceilings on the rates it could charge on the ground that the ceilings were so low as to amount to a confiscation of property without due process of law. The city responded with an argument that the constitutional violation was not complete unless the state not only deprived the plaintiff of property but did so without according due process of law. The state, it argued, does not act until it has ratified the conduct of the alleged wrongdoer. Since state remedies were available for confiscatory rates, the phone company should have been obliged first to take its claim to the state courts. The Supreme Court rejected the city's argument, declaring that "the provisions of the [Fourteenth] Amendment . . . are generic in their terms, are addressed, of course, to the states, but also to every person, whether natural or juridical, who is a repository of state power." Further, "the Amendment contemplates the possibility of state officers abusing the powers lawfully conferred upon them by doing wrongs prohibited by the Amendment."

For purposes of substantive due process, then, the distinction discussed in the procedural due process context between "random and unauthorized" acts and other acts of state officials simply does not matter. That is, someone harmed by an unauthorized constitutional violation may sue in federal court on a constitutional claim, just like the litigant harmed by an authorized violation, at least so long as *Home Telephone* remains good law and its scope is not narrowed. But there are indications in the case law that at least some members of the Court may not be stalwart supporters of the *Home Telephone* rule. In the next section we consider the possibility that the Court may weaken the force of that case and oblige litigants with substantive due process claims to proceed in state court.

The Instability of the Court's Doctrine

In the foregoing discussion we deliberately separated the Court's doctrine on the role of state remedies in procedural due process from that in substantive due process cases. The reason for separate treatment is that, with regard to random and unauthorized acts by state officers, the issue appears to come out differently in the two contexts. The litigant who raises a procedural due process claim arising out of random and unauthorized action must resort to state remedies, whereas the one who asserts substantive due process is not obliged to do so. Most of the cases are consistent with the foregoing account of the doctrine, but the Supreme Court does not always speak clearly in this area. Certain aspects of the Court's doctrine suggest that this distinction may be mistaken and that the Court may not be wholly faithful to the *Home Telephone* rule. Some of the Court's statements seem to suggest that at least some substantive due process claims, along with procedural ones, ought to be relegated to the state courts. A thorough treatment of constitutional tort law requires that these pieces of the doctrine be examined as well.

One troubling case is Parratt v. Taylor (1981), whose ruling introduced the distinction between "random and unauthorized" acts and "established state procedure" into § 1983 law. The analysis will seem familiar to an attentive reader, but it is worth revisiting because of the factual context in which the Court used that distinction. Taylor was a prison inmate who had ordered hobby materials that, because of negligence of prison employees, never reached him. In response he brought a § 1983 suit against prison officials, claiming they had deprived him of property without due process of law. The Supreme Court acknowledged that the hobby kit was property and that the inmate had been deprived of it but said that the Fourteenth Amendment only protects against deprivations of property that occur "without due process of law." In this case, the plaintiff had not shown a lack of due process.

The Court explained that in some situations due process requires a pre-deprivation hearing before the state may interfere with property rights. But in others a pre-deprivation hearing is inappropriate, for example, because of the need for rapid action to protect the public health. Thus "either the necessity of quick action by the State or the impracticability of providing any meaningful predeprivation process, when coupled with the availability of some meaningful means by which to assess the propriety of the State's action at some time after the initial taking, can satisfy the requirements of procedural due process." In this case the random and unauthorized nature of the prison employee's act in losing the hobby kit was sufficient justification for allowing a post-deprivation remedy to satisfy due process. The Court explained that "[i]n such a case, the loss is not a result of some established state procedure and the State cannot predict precisely when the loss will occur." In such circumstances "[i]t is difficult to conceive of how the State could provide a meaningful hearing before the deprivation takes place." Applying these principles to Taylor's case, the Court ruled that he must pursue state tort law remedies that were available to him.

This reason why the *Parratt* holding may be at odds with the procedural due process/substantive due process distinction is that Taylor's claim seems, in fact, to be a substantive due process claim. Although the Court in *Parratt* uses the vocabulary of procedural due process and cites procedural due process cases as authority for its holding, it is implausible to suppose that the plaintiff here meant to be making a procedural claim. Recall that procedural due process applies to situations in which the state is substantively authorized to inflict some injury to life, liberty, or property, but in which it must follow fair procedures that aim at assuring the accuracy and fairness of the decision. Applying that doctrine to the facts of *Parratt*, one would have to suppose that the state could legitimately "lose" Taylor's hobby materials (as a form of punishment, say), so long as proper procedures had been followed in deciding to do so. But these are not the facts of the case. The officers did not deprive Taylor of his hobby kit as a sanction for something Taylor had done. With no justification or excuse whatsoever, they simply misplaced the kit. Taylor was making a substantive claim, asserting that he should, as a matter of constitutional law, be compensated for the loss of his property at the hands of state officers.[13] (Whether his substantive claim is sound is a separate question that is discussed in the section entitled "State of Mind." We shall see that the Court later held that negligence of the kind alleged in *Parratt* is not a sufficiently serious form of misconduct to amount to a constitutional violation.)

Since *Parratt*, on its facts, is better viewed as a substantive rather than as a procedural due process case, there is always a possibility that the Court will one day cite the case as grounds for applying the "random and unauthorized" principle to substantive due process cases. One case decided after *Parratt* seems aimed at limiting *Parratt* to the procedural due process context. On the other hand, another recent case revives the possibility that *Parratt* will be expanded to substantive due process. Each of these decisions deserves our attention.

The case that tries to give *Parratt* a narrow reading is Zinermon v. Burch (1990), which we have already described. For present purposes, the important aspect of *Zinermon* is that the Court explicitly distinguished procedural due process from substantive due process. It said that in substantive due process cases, "the constitutional violation actionable under § 1983 is complete when the wrongful action is taken. A plaintiff . . . may invoke § 1983 regardless of any state-tort remedy that might be available to compensate him for the deprivation of these rights." With regard to procedural due process, however, "[t]he constitutional violation actionable under § 1983 is not complete when the deprivation occurs; it is not complete unless and until the State fails to provide due process." The Court then went on to treat *Parratt* as a procedural due process case. Whether *Parratt* really is procedural due process or not, the *Zinermon* Court seemed determined to make it one, probably in order to avoid the expansion of the "random and unauthorized" principle into substantive due process, where it would threaten the continued validity of the *Home Telephone* rule.

If the *Zinermon* Court tried to cabin the "random and unauthorized" principle to procedural due process, a more recent case once again blurs the distinction between substantive and procedural due process. The case is Florida Prepaid Postsecondary Education Expense Plan v. College Savings Bank (1999). The issue in this case was whether Congress had acted in compliance with the Constitution when, in a statute called the Patent Remedy Act, it authorized the holders of patents to bring suits for damages against state governments for patent infringement. Congress has the power, under § 5 of the Fourteenth Amendment, "to enforce, by appropriate legislation" the rights granted by the amendment, including the right not to be deprived of property without due process of law. But Congress may act only where there is a sufficient need for intervention. A patent is a type of property, protected by the Due Process Clause. Yet the Court struck down the statute, in part because there was an insufficient showing of a need for legislation to address the problem of states infringing of patents. It said that "a State's infringement of a patent, though interfering with a patent owner's right to exclude others, does not by itself violate the Constitution." Citing *Parratt* as authority, the Court continued: "Instead, only where the State provides no remedy, or only inadequate remedies, to injured patent owners for its infringement of their patent could a deprivation of property without due process result." Here, "Congress . . . barely considered the availability of state remedies." Hence, the case for authorizing private suits for damages had not been made.

The noteworthy aspect of this reasoning, for purposes of its impact on the *Parratt/Zinermon* doctrine, is that the due process claim underlying the infringement suit is substantive rather than procedural. What the state of Florida did was not to impose a sanction on the College Savings Bank, in circumstances that may or may not have complied with fair procedure. What it did was to use College Savings Bank's patent without authorization. College Savings Bank's objection was that this is simply not permissible. Procedure had nothing to do with it. By suggesting that the availability of state remedies was relevant to whether College Savings Bank could show a constitutional violation, the Court has once again called the *Home Telephone* rule into question.[14] The reasoning in *Florida Prepaid* revives the possibility that at least some people with substantive due process claims will be obliged to pursue available state remedies rather than litigating their claims in federal court. (For another, narrower way to read the case, see the section entitled "The Special Problem of Takings")

For now we put aside the possibility that some substantive due process cases will be routed to the state courts in the event there are state remedies available. Under current Supreme Court precedent, substantive due process claims may be brought in federal court. In the sections that follow, we take up the question of what a plaintiff must prove to prevail with a substantive due process claim.

"Property" and "Liberty"

Due process, whether substantive or procedural, protects "life," "liberty," and "property," terms that were imported into the constitution from the English common law in the late eighteenth century. They cover some, but not all, of the kinds of harms for which judges have permitted plaintiffs to bring suit over the past several centuries. Our first task in working through the scope of substantive due process rights is to describe the interests encompassed by these terms. We are not concerned with a comprehensive treatment, however. Our inquiry is limited to the constitutional tort setting.

"Life," of course, has its ordinary meaning. If a person is killed by government action, his estate may assert an injury to a constitutionally protected interest (e.g., Sacramento v. Lewis, 1998). "Liberty" and "property" present more complex problems. First, constitutional tort covers injuries that fall within the ordinary meanings of these terms. A person confined without good reason may assert a deprivation of liberty. If government officers injure one's personal belongings, land, or house, the owner has a suit for a deprivation of property. But, like many legal terms, "liberty" and "property" have been interpreted by courts in constitutional cases to cover interests that are hardly obvious to the ordinary person. The Court interprets "liberty" to include personal security from physical and emotional harm (Ingraham v. Wright, 1977). It should be noted that some of the historical material bearing on how the terms "liberty" and "property" were understood by the framers of the Constitution suggest that harm of this kind should have been protected as an aspect of "life."[15] Be that as it may, the error seems to have no practical significance. The general conclusion to draw from the legal meaning of "life, liberty, and property" is that constitutional tort liability may arise from injury to a wide range of personal interests.

There is an important exception to the general rule that one may bring a constitutional tort suit for harm to personal injuries. Defamation is a common law tort that protects a person's interest in his reputation. When a newspaper or anyone else makes false comments that harm one's standing in the community or affect the willingness of people to deal with him or her, the injured person may sue for damages. Now suppose the speaker is a government official, and the injured person wishes to sue for a constitutional tort, claiming that reputation, like personal security from physical harm, is a component of the liberty guaranteed by the Fourteenth Amendment. The Supreme Court has held that defamation, standing alone, is not a constitutional tort. The Court's major ruling on this subject came in Paul v. Davis (1976). In this case the defendant was a police official who distributed to merchants a list of "active shoplifters," along with their pictures. The plaintiff whose name and picture were included, claimed the charge was untrue and he sought to sue under § 1983. Relying largely on the value of federalism the Supreme Court rejected his claim. Accepting the plaintiff's view of constitutional torts, the Court feared, "would seem almost necessarily to result in every legally cognizable injury which may have been inflicted by a state official . . . establishing a violation of the Fourteenth Amendment." Believing the Constitution should not become "a font of tort law to be superimposed on [state] systems," the Court said that the proper remedy was a suit for defamation governed by state tort law. From the injured person's perspective, the problem with this solution is that the state tort rules may not permit a substantial recovery against the officer, as they apparently did not in this case.[16]

Paul did not state a blanket rule forbidding constitutional tort suits brought to recover for defamation by government officials. It left open two possibilities for giving constitutional stature to some defamation cases. First, the reasoning in *Paul* did not focus on the officer's motivation. Would it make a difference if the plaintiff could show that the officer did not have a legitimate public purpose (as the police officer did in *Paul*) but acted with the intent of hurting him, knowing the information was false? In Siegert v. Gilley (1991) the Court held that the officer's motive makes no difference. It declared that "[d]efamation, by itself, is a tort actionable under the laws of most States, but not a constitutional deprivation."

Nonetheless, certain defamation victims may sue for constitutional tort. The Court's rule is that defamation by itself is not a constitutional violation. But in cases in which the defamation is accompanied by some other harm, such as loss of a government job or loss of the right to buy liquor, one may sue for a deprivation of liberty(Wisconsin v. Constantineau, 1971; Board of Regents v. Roth 1972). To illustrate this "stigma plus" doctrine, suppose a city government fires an employee and officials, and in the course of defending the dismissal, make defamatory statements about the employee. In that event, the employee would have a constitutional right to a "name-clearing hearing" and, presumably, could recover damages if the firing, coupled with the defamation, made it harder to find another job and if the name-clearing hearing establishes that the charges were unjustified. Note here that it is not sufficient for the fired employee to rely on the dismissal alone. Nor is it enough that an official has made defamatory comments about the plaintiff. In order to succeed with a stigma plus claim, the plaintiff must meet both these requirements.

Besides the potential deprivation of liberty, loss of government employment may also give rise to a claim that one has been deprived of property without due process of law. In Board of Regents v. Roth (1972) the Court said that "the property interests protected by procedural due process extend well beyond actual ownership of real estate, chattels, or money." Due process is "a safeguard of the security of interests that a person has already acquired in certain benefits" derived from government, such as welfare payments and employment. Here it is necessary to distinguish between two kinds of government jobs. A government job may be a kind of "property" if, but only if, state law accords the plaintiff a "legitimate claim" that some procedure be followed before termination and that one may be fired only for certain reasons. For example, a tenured professor at a state university probably has a property interest in the post he or she holds, whereas an aide to the governor surely does not. If an employee does have a property interest in his or her government job, due process requires that relevant procedure be followed. In the event an employee is fired for reasons other than those specified by state law, he or she could bring a § 1983 suit to recover for a violation of property rights, and, perhaps, for reinstatement in the position.

State of Mind

Throughout tort law, a critical question is what showing the plaintiff must make as to the defendant's mental attitude in order to win the case. As background for examining the special problems that arise in constitutional tort, it will be useful briefly to consider how this issue is handled in ordinary tort law. In any tort case the basic situation is that harm has occurred on account of the defendant's conduct, and now the injured party seeks to recover damages. One problem faced by courts in tort law is to decide where the loss should fairly lie. Some theorists maintain that, as between the innocent plaintiff and the defendant who has caused harm, fairness always requires that the person who has caused harm should pay for it, no matter how careful the defendant was. In tort jargon, they think there should be "strict liability."[17] Others argue that there is no moral difference between the person who innocently causes harm and one who innocently suffers it, so that causation alone is no argument on grounds of fairness for shifting the loss to the defendant. Only where the defendant is at fault should he be liable.[18] In most contexts, the latter view has carried the day. Though there are pockets of strict liability, the general rule is that a plaintiff must show "negligence" or "fault" in order to win a common law tort case. Negligence and fault are synonymous termstypically defined as a failure to exercise the care of a reasonable person in the circumstances.

Moving to the constitutional context, the Fourteenth Amendment resembles tort law in that it protects life, liberty, and property. Recall that personal security against physical and emotional harm is, for constitutional purposes, one aspect of liberty. The "state of mind" issue is whether a given injury to those personal interests, inflicted by someone acting under color of state law, is a constitutional violation. One possibility is to simply transplant the common law rule into constitutional tort. Early in the Supreme Court's development of constitutional tort law, the Court appeared to take that approach. In Parratt v. Taylor (1981) the Court said that the negligent loss of the plaintiff's hobby kit could be a deprivation of property, thus raising Fourteenth Amendment concerns. In support of its ruling that negligently caused harms could be due process violations, the Court merely pointed out that "the alleged loss, even though negligently caused, amounted to a deprivation." It devoted somewhat more attention to the issue of whether one could sue for such a negligently caused deprivation under § 1983, concluding that "[n]othing in the language of § 1983 or its legislative history limits the statute solely to intentional deprivations of constitutional rights." Accordingly, neither the Constitution nor the statute stood in the way of recovery for a negligent deprivation. It was only because of the availability of state remedies that the plaintiff lost.

A few years after *Parratt* the Court backed away from the proposition that negligent harms may be violations of substantive due process. In Daniels v. Williams (1986) the plaintiff was yet again an inmate, who claimed that he slipped on a pillow negligently left on the stairs of the city jail by a guard. Citing *Parratt*, and asserting that no state remedy was available to him, Daniels sought relief in a § 1983 suit for deprivation of liberty. Occasionally the Supreme Court squarely repudiates one of its prior rulings, and that is what it did here. The Court "overrule[d] *Parratt* to the extent it states that mere lack of due care by a state official may 'deprive' an individual of life, liberty, or property under the Fourteenth Amendment." The Court reasoned that the point of due process in general is to protect people from the arbitrary exercise of government power, and the purpose of substantive due process in particular is "to prevent governmental power from being 'used for purposes of oppression.'" But "the actions of prison custodians in leaving a pillow on the prison stairs, or mislaying an inmate's property, are quite remote from [these] concerns." Rather, "lack of due care suggests no more than a failure to measure up to the conduct of a reasonable person. To hold that injury caused by such conduct is a deprivation within the meaning of the Fourteenth Amendment would trivialize the centuries-old principle of due process of law."

We think the Court was right to reject a blanket rule that government negligence will trigger constitutional tort liability. Constitutional law is inflexible and intrusive. It overrides the judgments of officers and legislators who are closer to the problem at hand and who are politically accountable for what they do. It may be overridden only by a later Supreme Court decision or a constitutional amendment. For these reasons, constitutional rules ought to be used only in situations where there is an especially compelling case for judicial intervention. Constitutional torts ought to be reserved for especially serious breaches of care, with less serious ones left to the ordinary workings of the legislative process and the common law. Negligence does not typically rise to the level of an especially serious breach. Negligence "does not imply a moral judgment of blameworthiness [or] denote ill will or subjective lack of concern for the plaintiff's welfare."[19] Keeping in mind that constitutional rulings are immune from reversal through the normal legislative process, it would intrude too far on the principle of majority rule for courts to constitutionalize a general negligence principle.

But this does not mean that negligence should never be sufficient for liability; the Court might have limited its rejection of negligence to the facts of *Daniels* and cases like it. The accident that gave rise to this case was no different from a garden-variety common law tort, except for the fact that it occurred in prison, and the prison context seems to be merely a coincidence. As far as we can tell, there was nothing about the prison making it more likely that a pillow would be left in a dangerous place or that someone would slip on it. The Court might have made a different rule for cases in which an officer's negligence was more closely connected to the exercise of government power. But in Davidson v. Cannon (1986), a case decided the same day as *Daniels*, the Court rejected that limitation on its ruling. The plaintiff in *Davidson* was also a prison inmate who after having been threatened by another prisoner, wrote a note to Cannon and James (two prison officials) informing them of the threat and seeking special protection. On account of official negligence nothing was done, and the inmate was attacked. Davidson sued the officials who failed to take action. Applying the standard it had set forth in *Daniels*, the Court denied recovery "Far from abusing governmental power, or employing it as an instrument of oppression, . . . Cannon mistakenly believed that the situation was not particularly serious, and respondent James simply forgot about the note. The guarantee of due process has never been understood to mean that the State must guarantee due care on the part of its officials."

Writing in dissent, Justice Blackmun took issue with the Court's sweeping holding as to negligence. In contrast to the situation presented in *Daniels*, the negligence in this case was not the kind of thing that happens anywhere and that merely coincidentally happened in a prison. Here "the State assume[d] sole responsibility for [Davidson's] physical security," by "tak[ing] away [his] means of protecting himself from other inmates." Justice Blackman argued in vain for a rule that negligence may be sufficient for liability "where the State renders a person vulnerable and strips him of his ability to defend himself, " since "an injury that results from a state official's negligence in performing his duty is peculiarly related to the governmental function."

Daniels and *Davidson* are substantive due process cases. The principle they stand for is that officials do not violate substantive due process when they are merely negligent in causing harm to life, liberty, or property. Procedural due process requires separate treatment. The opinion in *Davidson* concludes with the sweeping pronouncement that "the protections of the Due Process Clause, whether procedural or substantive, are just not triggered by lack of due care by prison officials." This statement suggests that procedural due process rights are not violated unless officials act carelessly. For reasons explained by Professor Richard Fallon, it is probably an error:

> Appellate courts routinely reverse trial courts for errors of procedural due process, many of which presumably are attributable to negligence but are due process violations nonetheless. I would similarly suppose that school officials who negligently suspend a student without providing the constitutionally required hearing would violate the Constitution by doing so and that the suspension could be challenged successfully.[20]

Professor Fallon is right to chastise the Court on this point. But he, too, may fall into error. If Fallon means to suggest that negligence is required for a procedural due process violation, he seems to suffer from a lesser form of the same misapprehension that produced the Court's dubious assertion in *Davidson*. Even where officers quite reasonably believe they are following proper procedures, they can be deemed to have committed procedural due process violations later. In fact, this can happen even if they have rigorously followed the rules in place at the time, for the Supreme Court may always decide to change the rules of procedural due process and to use the case at hand as the vehicle for changing them. For example, in Owen v. City of Independence (1980) the city council fired the police chief at a time when, under prevailing law, they had no obligation to provide any procedural protections. Shortly after the termination, the Supreme Court, in a separate piece of litigation, imposed procedural due process requirements in this situation. Later, when *Owen* itself reached the Supreme Court, the Court took it for granted that a procedural due process violation had occurred, even though the officials had no reason to know they were violating the due process clause at the time they acted.

Another significant limit on the scope of the *Davidson/Daniels* rule should also be noted. Recall that in *Parratt* the Supreme Court made two distinct rulings on the role of negligence: (a) that § 1983 contains no state-of-mind requirement, and (b) that the due process clause contains no state-of-mind requirement. The court in these cases overruled only the second aspect of *Parratt*, leaving the first intact. Section 1983 is the vehicle for raising in offensive mode the whole range of constitutional rights. Some of those rights are violated only where the officer acts with a particular state of mind. Besides the Due Process Clause, another example is the right to equal protection of the laws. (We will discuss this clause more in a later section entitled "Arbitrary Acts and Equal Protection.") An officer violates equal protection only by intentionally or knowingly treating the plaintiff differently from others, not simply because the effects of his act is to leave the plaintiff in a different position from that of others (Washington v. Davis, 1976). On the other hand, there is generally no state-of-mind requirement for First Amendment violations. An officer who denies freedom of speech would be liable in constitutional tort (though he may not be obliged to pay damages, for reasons discussed in the section entitled "Qualified Immunity) even if he reasonably believed he was acting properly. When the issue is whether an officer has violated the Fourth Amendment's prohibition on unreasonable searches and seizures, negligence is indeed the state of mind required for a constitutional violation, because the very language of the Fourth Amendment directs that "reasonableness" is the touchstone. The general point here is that in any given constitutional tort suit, the presence or absence of a state-of-mind requirement will depend on the constitutional claim at issue in the case. All that *Daniels* and *Davidson* stand for is that something more than negligence is necessary for a substantive due process violation.

If negligence is not enough to make a substantive due process case, then the next issue is what state of mind will be sufficient. The Court in *Daniels* explicitly reserved this issue for later cases, noting that "this case affords us no occasion to consider whether something less than intentional conduct, such as recklessness or 'gross negligence,' is enough to trigger the protections of the Due Process Clause." Once again the Court employs the common law of torts as its starting point for analysis. Before proceeding, we need to introduce the terms the Court refers to in this passage. In torts and in criminal law, courts have identified degrees of culpability that are more serious than negligence, and they have imposed one kind of liability or another depending on how blameworthy a given act is. We can conceive of blameworthiness as a spectrum, with "reasonable care" at or near one end (perhaps coming after "extraordinary care"). Negligence would come next in order of blameworthiness. The next point on the spectrum would be "gross negligence," which we may define adequately, for present purposes, as especially egregious lack of care. For example, a driver who simply exceeds the speed limit may be negligent, while a someone who drives with a blood alcohol level of .2 would surely be grossly negligent. When someone is consciously aware of a serious risk of harm to others (which may not be the case with regard to the drunk driver), the conduct will be deemed "reckless." A person who knows that harm will occur (or who intends that harm should occur)as a result of his or her act, is at the far end of the blameworthiness spectrum. (At least in tort law, courts rarely distinguish between knowing and intentional harm or, for that matter, between reckless and intentional harm.)

As to which of these degrees of culpability is appropriate for constitutional tort, there is no short answer. In the cases decided after *Daniels,* the Court has chosen not to state a single principle governing all due process cases, much less all constitutional cases. Instead it has identified a number of different contexts in which due process cases (and similar cases involving other constitutional rights) may arise and has devised different rules for each context. The result is a complex body of law, which we describe next. We begin with cases in which due process plays a predominant role and then move to situations in which other constitutional rights are more important.

Abuse of Power and the "Shocks the Conscience" Test

After *Daniels* the Court might have rejected substantive due process altogether, on the ground that the doctrine is illegitimate in general or that personal injury litigation should be left exclusively to state tort law. Alternatively, it might have set forth a general standard of gross negligence to govern these cases. In Collins v. City of Harker Heights (1992) the Court rejected both these alternatives. The plaintiff was the widow of a man who, as an employee of the city's sanitation department,suffocated after entering a manhole to unstop a sewer line. His widow did not claim that anyone intended the death or knew it would occur; her claim was simply that the city had a constitutional obligation to provide a reasonably safe work environment.

Yet the Court rejected the argument, explaining that the aim of due process was to protect against abuses of government power and that a city's failure to provide a safe place to work does not constitute such an abuse. Some earlier cases had described the substantive due process standard as one that is met if the government's act "shocks the conscience" (e.g., Rochin v. California, 1952). The Court was "not persuaded that the city's alleged failure to train its employees, or to warn them about known risks of harm, was an omission that can properly be characterized as arbitrary, or conscience-shocking, in a constitutional sense." Instead, the case was "analogous to a fairly typical state law tort claim" involving unsafe working conditions. State law, not the Constitution, "generally governs the substance of the employment relationship."

Collins stands for the proposition that constitutional tort liability is unavailable even for serious departures from reasonable care toward government employees. In County of Sacramento v. Lewis (1998) the Court returned to this theme, extending its rule beyond the employee context to include other plaintiffs as well. The case arose from a high-speed police chase of a motorcyclist who refused to stop when directed to do so. The chase ended when the motorcyclist lost control and crashed. The plaintiff, a passenger on the motorcycle, was hit by the police car and killed. His estate claimed that the police were liable for a substantive due process violation on the ground that the police officer's conduct showed reckless disregard for the plaintiff's life and personal security. The Supreme Court rejected this standard. It held that, even when the plaintiff is not a government employee, the appropriate substantive due process standard is whether the officer committed an abuse of power or engaged in conduct that shocks the conscience. With regard to police chases, this test would be met only if the officer meant to cause harm. The problem with imposing liability on a lesser showing of culpability is that "the police on an occasion calling for fast action have obligations that tend to tug against each other." They are supposed to "restore and maintain lawful order, while not exacerbating disorder more than necessary to do their jobs." Thus, the Court held that "high-speed chases with no intent to harm suspects physically or to worsen their legal plight do not give rise to liability under the Fourteenth Amendment, redressable by an action under § 1983."

Collins and *Lewis* do not govern the whole range of injuries due to government inattention to safety. The Court was careful to distinguish these cases from situations in which the plaintiff is a person confined by the state, such as a prisoner or a mental patient, making the issue whether he is constitutionally entitled to some minimal level of medical care or protection from other inmates. The victim in *Collins* was an employee who was free to leave his job. In *Lewis*, the policeman had to make quick decisions about how to react to danger. When the plaintiff is confined, the case for liability is stronger and the standard ought to give more weight to the plaintiff's interests. In such a case the government has deprived the inmate of the means to care for himself. In addition, *Lewis* noted that prison officials have "time to make unhurried judgments" about such matters as medical care and protection from other inmates. In the custodial situation, "the 'process' that the Constitution guarantees in connection with any deprivation of liberty . . . includes a continuing obligation to satisfy certain minimal custodial standards." As we shall see, in the custodial setting the liability standard for medical care and protection cases is "deliberate indifference" to the inmates's needs—an easier test for plaintiffs to meet than the "purpose to harm" rule of *Lewis*.

With regard to quelling disturbances inside the prison, however, prison officials have more latitude. The most important case is Whitley v. Albers (1986). There the Court acknowledged that one must consider the risk of harm to the prisoner against whom force is used. But prison officials also "must take into account the very real threats . . . [that] unrest presents to inmates and prison officials alike . . . . In this setting, a deliberate indifference standard does not adequately capture the importance of such competing obligations." Nor does it give sufficient regard to the need to make quick decisions. Thus, the Court held that liability in such circumstances should turn on "whether force was applied in a good faith effort to maintain or restore discipline or maliciously and sadistically for the very purpose of causing harm." The key to liability therefore is the defendant's motive, and not whether the plaintiff actually suffered serious harm (Hudson v. McMillian, 1992). It is noteworthy that the Court in *Lewis* relied on *Whitley*'s reasoning, maintaining that a policeman faced with a dangerous motorist was like the prison guard faced with a riot, because both had to make difficult choices and delicately balance competing interests without much time for reflection. Like the prison guard, the policeman should be liable only if his purpose was to cause harm.

Collins and *Lewis* do not altogether foreclose constitutional tort liability for physical harm inflicted by government officers on ordinary citizens and state employees. If such a plaintiff can prove an abuse of power or conduct that shocks the conscience, he or she will succeed in showing a substantive due process violation. The problem in *Collins* and *Lewis* was that unsafe working conditions and high-speed chases do not, at least in the Court's view, meet those standards. Surely a supervisor would commit a substantive due process violation if he or she told the plaintiff employee to enter an unsafe environment intending or knowing that the employee would be harmed. Lower court cases hold that a student paddled for misbehavior may recover if the punishment is far out of proportion to the need for discipline. Echoing *Whitley*, one court described the standard governing corporal punishment as one that considers

> such factors as the need for application of force, the relationship between the need and the amount of force that was used, the extent of injury inflicted, and whether force was applied in a good faith effort to maintain or restore discipline or maliciously and sadistically, for the very purpose of causing harm. (Metzger v. Osbeck, 1988)

Of course, certain kinds of official wrongdoing, no matter how malicious, may never be redressed in constitutional tort suits. Surely it would be an abuse of power and a shock to the conscience for an official to use his position to ruin the plaintiff's reputation. Yet we know from our earlier discussion of Siegert v. Gilley (1991) that this particular type of abuse of power does not amount to a constitutional violation. Defamation is just not actionable in a § 1983 case unless the "stigma plus" doctrine is satisfied, as where the defamation occurs in connection with firing someone from a government job. (See the section entitled "Property and Liberty.") In this respect *Siegert* seems to be at odds with *Lewis* and *Collins*.

Other Constitutional Rights

Due process is, of course, not the only constitutional right that gives rise to § 1983 suits. On the contrary, more suits are brought under other constitutional provisions than under due process. We have examined due process issues at length because some of the issues presented in due process cases are especially difficult and are distinctive to the constitutional tort context. Next, we address other substantive rights that are often litigated in constitutional tort suits. We are especially concerned with the relation between these substantive rights and the problems that arise in suits seeking to recover damages. And we do not leave due process entirely behind. We shall see that when someone suffers physical injury one determination to make is whether a given case should be adjudicated under substantive due process or another constitutional provision.

Unreasonable Searches and Seizures and the Fourth Amendment

The Fourth Amendment states that "[t]he right of the people to be secure in their persons, houses, papers, and effects, against unreasonable searches and seizures, shall not be violated." The police search persons, cars, and houses on a daily basis, and not surprisingly, constitutional tort suits are routinely brought by people who claim that a search of their person or property was unreasonable. But a suit for damages is not the only remedy for an illegal search. Another remedy should be mentioned as well. When police find evidence of a crime, the evidence will often be used as the basis for bringing a criminal prosecution against the target of the search. In that event the defendant may seek to raise the Fourth Amendment as a shield, asking that the evidence be excluded from the trial because it was obtained unconstitutionally. The Supreme Court calls this the "exclusionary rule." It is different from most shield-like remedies in that the defendant does not have a constitutional right to keep the evidence out of the trial. The primary justification for withholding it is to deter the police from gathering evidence by unconstitutional means (Stone v. Powell, 1976).

Whether the Fourth Amendment is raised in a suit for damages or as grounds for excluding evidence from the criminal trial, its reasonableness standard is the same. The substantive law as to what makes a given search unreasonable is discussed in another book in this series and need not be repeated here. There seem to be no special features of constitutional tort suits such that courts would produce distinctive substantive rules for Fourth Amendment issues in this kind of litigation. Some observers suggest that the victim of the search will likely have a greater chance of success in such a suit, as the focus is on the illegal search rather on than the criminal activity with which he or she is charged. One further point is relevant to the relations between the two remedies: If the criminal defendant raises the Fourth Amendment as grounds for excluding evidence and fails, he will probably be precluded from later bringing a constitutional tort suit to recover damages. Having lost once, he will be bound by that determination and may not reopen the issue of the legality of the search (Allen v. McCurry, 1980). See section "Issue and Claim Preclusion" for further discussion of this issue.

A different kind of constitutional tort suit arises when the police injure someone in the course of an arrest. Graham v. Connor (1989) illustrates the sort of encounter that produces such suits. Graham, the plaintiff, was a diabetic who claimed that one evening he felt the onset of an insulin reaction and asked a friend to drive him to a convenience store for some orange juice to counteract the reaction. Unfortunately, there was a long line at the register. Wanting to avoid the delay, Graham left the store quickly and asked his friend to drive him to another friend's nearby house. The defendant, Connor, was a police officer who saw Graham enter and leave the store in haste. This raised his suspicions that Graham may have been involved in some crime. He stopped the car carrying Graham and told the occupants to wait while he investigated the events at the convenience store. Graham, in the middle of the insulin reaction, "got out of the car, ran around it twice, and finally sat down on the curb, where he passed out briefly." Other police officers arrived and handcuffed Graham, thinking he was drunk. Graham regained consciousness and told them he was diabetic. The Supreme Court described his allegations:

> In response, one of the officers told him to "shut up" and shoved his face down against the hood of the car. Four officers grabbed Graham and threw him headfirst into the police car. A friend of Graham's brought some orange juice to the car, but the officers refused to let him have it. Finally, Officer Connor received a report that Graham had done nothing wrong at the convenience store, and the officers drove him home and released him. At some point during his encounter with the police, Graham sustained a broken foot, cuts on his wrists, a bruised forehead, and an injured shoulder; he also claims to have developed a loud ringing in his right ear that continues to this day.

Lower courts had said that the plaintiff could not win even if he could prove the facts he alleged. So, for the purpose of reviewing the lower court decision, the Supreme Court assumed the facts were as the plaintiff recounted them in his complaint.

Graham's § 1983 suit claimed that the officers used excessive force in their treatment of him and sought damages for the injuries he suffered. One problem presented by the case was to identify just what constitutional provision furnished the substantive law governing Graham's rights. Lower courts, including the lower court in this case, had used substantive due process principles to resolve such cases. The Supreme Court ruled that this was an error. Cases involving excessive force by the police in stopping someone for an investigation or arrest ought to be adjudicated under the Fourth Amendment's rule prohibiting unreasonable seizures. The Court explained that the vague substantive due process right should be avoided when a nonspecific constitutional provision is available.

This Fourth Amendment reasonableness test is not limited to the fact patterns of *Graham*, where the police are engaged in an investigation or making an arrest. It also applies to the use of deadly force to stop a fleeing suspect (Tennessee v. Garner, 1984). A somewhat different fact pattern was presented in Albright v. Oliver (1994). After being prosecuted and acquitted of a crime, the plaintiff sought to sue for a constitutional tort on the ground that the prosecution was unjustified. Citing *Graham* as authority, the Court agreed that one has a right to be free from prosecution if there is no good reason to think he or she is guilty of a crime. It also ruled that because a prosecution is a kind of "seizure" of the person, the proper test for applying constitutional scrutiny to the decision to prosecute was Fourth Amendment reasonableness.

After ruling that the Fourth Amendment governs excessive force cases, the Court in *Graham* gave lower courts some guidance as to the substantive Fourth Amendment principles they should apply in such cases. A noteworthy feature of the law here is that the standard resembles a negligence test. Though the Court rejected negligence as the substantive due process test in Daniels v. Williams (1986), the Fourth Amendment's use of the term "unreasonable" to identify actions that cross the constitutional line seems to bring negligence back into the constitutional tort arena. The distinction between reasonable and unreasonable conduct is at the core of negligence law. As in such law, the reasonableness test under the Fourth Amendment is external to the actor, focusing on what people generally would find appropriate rather than on their own beliefs and purposes. Whereas the substantive due process standard relies heavily on the defendant's motive, requiring an abuse of power or conduct that shocks the conscience, the Court in *Graham* said that the Fourth Amendment "inquiry in an excessive force case is an objective one: the question is whether the officers' actions are 'objectively reasonable' in light of the facts and circumstances confronting them, without regard to their underlying intent or motivation." Thus, motives do not matter either way: "An officer's evil intentions will not make a Fourth Amendment violation out of an objectively reasonable use of force; nor will an officer's good intentions make an objectively unreasonable use of force constitutional."

There are no fixed rules for determining whether the amount of force used on a given occasion is reasonable or not. That inquiry, according to *Graham*, "requires a careful balancing of 'the nature and quality of the intrusion on the individual's Fourth Amendment interests against the countervailing governmental interests at stake." Among other things, the court should consider "the severity of the crime at issue, whether the suspect poses an immediate threat to the safety of the officers or others, and whether he is actively resisting arrest or attempting to evade arrest by flight." Reasonableness is determined not by hindsight but "from the perspective of a reasonable officer on the scene." The decision "must embody allowance for the fact that police officers are often forced to make split-second judgments . . . about the amount of force that is necessary in a particular situation."

Even after *Graham*, *Garner*, and *Albright*, some encounters between citizens and the police are outside the scope of the Fourth Amendment, and are covered by substantive due process. The continuing vitality of substantive due process in this area was established by Sacramento v. Lewis (1998), a case we discussed for its contribution to substantive due process doctrine in the section entitled "Abuse of Power and the'Shocks the Conscience' Test." But we have not yet addressed the issue of why substantive due process is the appropriate standard in a high-speed chase case, whereas reasonableness is the test in an arrest, investigatory stop, pursuit of a suspect, or decision-to-prosecute case. The Court in *Lewis* explained that "the Fourth Amendment covers only searches and seizures, neither of which is present here." A seizure occurs "only when there is a governmental termination of freedom of movement through means intentionally applied." The force used in dealing with the diabetic plaintiff in *Graham* was intentional, as was the prosecution in *Albright* and the bullet used to kill the fleeing suspect in *Garner*. But the police did not intend the collision that killed the motorcycle passenger in *Lewis*. That was an accident and therefore not a "seizure" covered by the Fourth Amendment.

Arbitrary Acts and Equal Protection

Under the equal protection clause of the Fourteenth Amendment, a state is forbidden from "deny[ing] to any person within its jurisdiction the equal protection of the laws." Early in our history the Supreme Court treated this as merely a guarantee that "government must not impose differences in treatment except upon some reasonable differentiation fairly related to the object of regulation."[21] In the 1950s and 1960s, under Chief Justice Earl Warren, the Supreme Court developed a new approach to the clause, ruling that legislatures may violate equal protection when they make certain kinds of distinctions in the absence of very strong justification. In particular, distinctions based on race are suspect and will only be upheld when the state can demonstrate a compelling state interest in using them (Brown v. Board of Education, 1954). Also, certain rights, such as the right to vote, are fundamental. Hence, distinctions that give one person's vote more weight than that of another, such as grossly disproportionate legislative districts, may offend the equal protection clause (Reynolds v. Sims, 1964).[22] These decisions gave rise to much litigation under § 1983 chiefly seeking prospective relief from such practices as state-sponsored racial segregation, malapportioned electoral districts, and other state legislative policies that discriminated against racial and other minorities. In the 1970s the Supreme Court limited the range of the equal protection clause by requiring the plaintiff to show that the government intended to discriminate (Washington v. Davis, 1976). This means that one cannot win an equal protection case simply by showing that members of the suspect class end up worse off than others. It is necessary to show that the government's purpose was to disadvantage the suspect class.

Just recently, the Supreme Court identified a rather different way in which a person may employ the equal protection clause as the basis for a constitutional tort suit. Every day, across a broad range of interactions with citizens, government officers treat some people differently from others. Consider the case of a person who is denied a zoning variance or a building permit, for example, in circumstances in which other applicants have received what they wanted. The disappointed applicant brings suit under section 1983, asserting that the official's ruling against him is a constitutional violation. Lower courts have sometimes treated such claims as substantive due process cases, allowing recovery if the plaintiff could show that the decision was arbitrary or badly motivated. In Willowbrook v. Olech (2000) the Supreme Court adopted an equal protection approach.

According to the plaintiff, she sought to have her property connected to the village's water supply, but was told that the connection would be made only if she granted the village a thirty-three-foot easement (i.e., permission to use thirty-three feet of her property for the village's purposes). Other applicants had received a connection upon granting a fifteen-foot-foot easement. Though the village eventually relented, Olech brought suit under § 1983 for the initial refusal. The Supreme Court ruled that these facts asserted a good claim under the equal protection clause. Quoting earlier cases, the Court explained that the purpose of the equal protection clause "is to secure every person within the State's jurisdiction against intentional and arbitrary discrimination." Though much of equal protection law deals with discrimination against classes of people on such grounds as race or gender, the Court stressed that its prior "cases have recognized successful equal protection claims brought by a 'class of one,' where the plaintiff alleges that she has been intentionally treated differently from others similarly situated and that there is no rational basis for the difference in treatment." If the plaintiff could prove the allegations in this case regarding the city's standard practice and the departure from it, she should prevail under these equal protection principles.

Olech is a recent case, so it remains to be seen just how much litigation it will spawn or what new issues will be resolved in working out the details of this equal protection right. One further aspect of the case should be noted, however. Olech claimed that the city's demand for a thirty-three-foot easement was "motivated by ill will resulting from the Olechs' previous filing of an unrelated, successful lawsuit against the Village." The Court explicitly reserved judgment one way or another on this "theory of 'subjective ill will.'" One implication of the Court's recognizing a good equal protection claim in such a case (while refusing to determine whether liability could also be based on a bad motive) is that the plaintiff need not show a bad motive in order to win on the equal protection theory adopted by the Court. He or she need only show intentional and arbitrary discrimination to her detriment, without regard to the motive behind the discrimination.

Deliberate Indifference and the Eighth Amendment Rights of Prisoners

This section considers issues that arise when the plaintiff is confined in a state prison and suffers some physical injury for which he seeks to hold an officer liable. Two situations must be distinguished. First, the injury may arise out of the officer's efforts to keep order in the prison. The leading case dealing with this fact pattern is Whitley v. Albers (1986), which is discussed in the section entitled "Abuse of Power and the 'Shocks the Conscience' Test." Recall that the key to liability in cases of this type is whether the guard acted with a bad motive. Second, the prisoner may be injured by inadequate medical care or by another prisoner. This section analyzes cases of this sort. The state of mind that can trigger constitutional tort liability in these cases is deliberate indifference by the defendant officer to the plaintiff's constitutional rights. "Deliberate indifference" is relevant to several distinct theories of recovery and, since the content of the term differs depending on the context, we will first sort out the various fact patterns in which the term is used.

At the outset, it is necessary to introduce the Eighth Amendment right against "cruel and unusual punishments." In the preceding, we have been mainly concerned with (a) the right not to be deprived of life, liberty, or property without due process of law, (b) the Fourth Amendment, and (c) the equal protection clause. The Eighth Amendment right against cruel and unusual punishments introduces constitutional values we have not yet examined closely. Historically, the right against cruel and unusual punishments was used to regulate the kinds of punishments a state may deliberately inflict. Its specific aim was to ensure that certain English practices, such as drawing and quartering (in which the prisoner's body would be torn into four parts) would not be employed in the United States. The history and general scope of the Eighth Amendment is discussed in another book in this series. We are concerned here only with its application in § 1983 suits.

In the 1960s and 1970s, courts began to increase the scope of the Eighth Amendment right against cruel and unusual punishments, using that right as the ground for regulating the conditions under which prisoners were kept. Two extensions of the Eighth Amendment are relevant to the role of deliberate indifference in constitutional tort law. One arises when a prisoner falls ill and receives grossly inadequate treatment. The Supreme Court held in Estelle v. Gamble (1976) that this could amount to cruel and unusual punishment even though no one at the prison intended for the prisoner to suffer harm. A somewhat different set of circumstances was present in Farmer v. Brennan (1994). The prisoner was a male transvestite who was sexually attacked by another prisoner who sued prison officials for cruel and unusual punishment. The Court ruled that officials could be liable for an Eighth Amendment violation in the event their protection of the plaintiff was so lax as to amount to deliberate indifference to his personal security. Though both cases used the term "deliberate indifference" to describe the standard of liability, there are differences between the doctrine governing the "medical treatment" fact pattern and the "protection from other prisoners" fact pattern.

With regard to medical treatment the leading case is *Estelle*, in which the prisoner suffered a back injury, received medical care he found unsatisfactory, and sued under § 1983 for cruel and unusual punishment. Though the Court found the care given him to be constitutionally adequate, the importance of the case lies in the Court's recognition that prisoners do have a constitutional right, under the Eighth Amendment, to some minimal level of care. The Court reasoned that "[a]n inmate must rely on prison authorities to treat his medical needs; . . . denial of medical care may result in [death or] in pain and suffering which no one suggests would serve any penological purpose." Since "infliction of such unnecessary suffering is inconsistent with contemporary standards of decency," the Court concluded that "deliberate indifference to serious medical needs of prisoners constitutes the unnecessary and wanton infliction of pain proscribed by the Eighth Amendment."

Deliberate indifference seems to be akin to common law recklessness, in that liability is appropriate only if there is a high degree of knowledge on the part of the defendant. In the context of medical care, *Estelle* said that deliberate indifference "does not mean . . . that every claim by a prisoner that he has not received adequate medical treatment states a violation of the Eighth Amendment." In particular, negligence "in diagnosing or treating a medical condition does not state a valid claim of medical mistreatment under the Eighth Amendment." In the years since *Estelle* the Supreme Court has not elaborated on the meaning of "deliberate indifference" in the medical care context, apart from ruling that prison authorities may be liable for exposing a healthy inmate to heavy doses of cigarette smoke from a cellmate who smoked five packs a day. This case establishes that deliberate indifference may be found in situations in which the threat to health lies in the potential for development of health problems in the future (Helling v. McKinney, 1993). Lower federal courts have faced the issue routinely, and several general principles have emerged. First, the inmate must show that the defendant was aware of the inmate's serious medical needs; second, he or she must show that the defendant deliberately failed to respond to those needs. As a result, refusing to provide prescribed medical treatment or denying access to doctors and others qualified to evaluate the problem can be considered deliberate indifference. On the other hand, disagreements as to diagnosis or treatment do not give grounds for a constitutional tort suit.[23] Nor, of course, does mere failure to meet the standard of the medical profession (the main test in ordinary tort law for whether a doctor has committed malpractice).

Farmer v. Brennan (1994) addresses the constitutional right of a prisoner to receive protection from assault by other prisoners. In this case, too, the Court held that "deliberate indifference" is the proper standard. Yet the term is defined differently in cases of this kind. The problem of protection from others is quite different from medical care and requires different standards, even if the category "deliberate indifference" is applied to both of them. The common thread linking *Farmer*'s use of the term to *Estelle*'s medical care standard is that, in both situations, liability is imposed only if the defendant has a high degree of knowledge of danger and does nothing to respond. In the prisoner protection context, *Farmer* ruled that a prison official is liable if he or she "knows of and disregards an excessive risk to inmate health and safety; the official must both be aware of facts from which the inference could be drawn that a substantial risk of serious harm exists, and he must also draw the inference."

In order to give a comprehensive account of the rights of persons confined by government, we must leave the Eighth Amendment and turn again to substantive due process. Though the Supreme Court has expanded the meaning of cruel and unusual punishment in cases like *Estelle* and *Farmer*, it has continued to apply the Eighth Amendment primarily to persons convicted of crimes and punished by the state. (We will call these inmates "prisoners" to distinguish them from other persons confined by the state.) Someone who is arrested and confined prior to trial (a "pre-trial detainee") may not use the Eighth Amendment as the basis for suing his guards or doctors. The same is true of someone kept in a state mental hospital without having been convicted of a crime. Yet persons subjected to these types of confinement, like those who are imprisoned upon conviction, may also suffer inadequate medical care or brutality from other inmates. The Supreme Court's solution to the problem is to recognize a substantive due process right on the part of these plaintiffs (Youngberg v. Romeo, 1982; Revere v. Massachusetts General Hospital, 1983).

The scope of this right remains unclear. Some of the Supreme Court's statements in *Youngberg* and *Revere* suggest that these plaintiffs may receive a higher level of protection than prisoners. For example, in *Revere* the Court said that "the due process rights of a [person injured while being apprehended by the police] are at least as great as the Eighth Amendment protections available to a convicted prisoner." The plaintiff in *Youngberg* was confined in a state mental hospital; about such cases the Court said that "[p]ersons who have been involuntarily committed are entitled to more considerate treatment and conditions of confinement than criminals whose conditions of confinement are designed to punish." But in these cases the Court did not specify the scope of the right to medical treatment or of the right to be protected from other inmates, and it has not returned to the issue since these cases were decided. Lower courts have reached varying results. Some treat these plaintiffs like prisoners, whereas others give them more constitutional protection.[24] Only the Supreme Court can give a definitive answer to the question.

Having discussed the Fourth Amendment, the Eighth Amendment, and substantive due process, we are now in a position to notice a peculiarity of the legal doctrine regarding the rights of persons in custody against officers who injure them. The point is that the doctrine bearing on a given claim depends on the moment at which the injury occurs: (a) If the plaintiff is injured by the police but not in the context of an arrest (e.g., an innocent bystander who is harmed incidentally in the course of a police chase), he or she would have to sue under the "shocks the conscience" test of *Lewis*; (b) someone who is beaten by the police in the course of an arrest would sue under the Fourth Amendment and its reasonableness standard; (c) once he or she is confined, pending trial, the plaintiff would be classified as a pretrial detainee, and any injury he suffers would be litigated under principles of substantive due process; (d) if the constitutional tort plaintiff has been convicted of a crime and imprisoned, his rights would be secured under the Eighth Amendment's cruel and unusual punishment clause. In situations (c) and (d) the legal standard seems to depend not on the label by which the right is identified but on the circumstances giving rise to the injury. With regard to medical care and protection from other inmates, the test is deliberate indifference, whether the suit is litigated under the Eighth or Fourteenth Amendment. As for the use of force by guards to put down disturbances, under Whitley the plaintiff probably needs to show a malicious and sadistic purpose to cause harm whether the source of the right is the Eighth Amendment or the Fourteenth Amendment.

The Special Problem of Takings

The Fifth Amendment forbids the national government from taking private property for public use without just compensation, and the Supreme Court has held that the Fourteenth Amendment applies the same restriction to state and local governments. When the government wants to build a highway, for example, it must pay people for the land taken for the project. Though another book in this series analyzes at length this clause of the Constitution, one feature of just compensation law is especially important in § 1983 suits. Ordinarily, a state or local government seeking to take private property for its own use will initiate a proceeding in the state courts for the purpose of determining how much it must pay for the property. However, there is a class of takings, called "inverse condemnation," in which the government "takes" the property by using it without paying ahead of time or by regulating it so heavily that it becomes worthless. In these cases no judicial proceeding occurs before the taking; nonetheless, the Constitution requires that the government pay for the loss of value.

The issue then arises of whether the property owner may bring a § 1983 suit in federal court to recover the damages, or whether he or she instead must proceed in state court. The Supreme Court has held that the property owner must first pursue state remedies, and only if they are inadequate may he or she then bring a § 1983 suit (Williamson County Regional Planning Commisson v. Hamilton Bank, 1985). The Court in *Williamson County* reasoned that "a property owner has not suffered a violation of the Just Compensation Clause until the owner has unsuccessfully attempted to obtain just compensation through the procedures provided by the State for obtaining such compensation." This ruling is hard to reconcile with the longstanding principle of the *Home Telephone* case, that a constitutional violation is complete when an official acts unconstitutionally, regardless of the availability of state remedies. *Williamson County* is probably best understood as a narrow exception to that general rule, applicable only to takings claims, and justified by the text of the Fifth Amendment, which authorizes the government to take property for public use so long as it gives just compensation. One can plausibly read that language to mean that no constitutional violation occurs until the state, through its courts, has denied just compensation.

Recently the Court ruled that Congress may not authorize suits against state governments in federal court to recover for patent infringement (Florida Prepaid v. College Savings Bank, 1999). *Florida Prepaid* is discussed in the section entitled "The Instability of the Court's Doctrine." Because a patent is a form of property and infringement is a taking of property, that decision may simply be an application of the *Williamson County* rule that one must employ available state remedies rather than bring an immediate federal cause of action in "takings" cases.[25]

Freedom of Speech and Public Employees

One frequently recurring fact pattern in § 1983 litigation arises when supervisors fire or otherwise retaliate against an employee on account of something the employee has said or written. The dismissed employee then brings a constitutional tort suit seeking reinstatement and damages for lost wages. The main issues in such cases are (a) whether the speech in question is constitutionally protected and, if so, (b) whether the firing was motivated by the protected speech. The second issue is dealt with in the section entitled "Causation." It seems appropriate here to give a brief summary of the substantive law bearing on whether the speech is protected, because cases of this kind are frequently litigated and almost always arise in these offensive § 1983 suits. The reason for the latter feature, of course, is that the state simply fires the employee. It does not try to bring a civil or criminal proceeding against him or her, in which the employee might raise the Constitution as a defense.

Public employees have a right of free speech under the First Amendment, as does everyone else. But the Supreme Court has held that the need for order in the workplace gives the government more leeway in controlling their speech than in the general regulation of speech. Whether a given instance of public employee speech is protected depends on the answer to two questions. First, a court must ask whether the subject matter of the speech bears on a matter of public concern (Pickering v. Board of Education, 1968). The purpose of protecting speech of public employees is that employees may make particularly valuable contributions to our understanding of government. We need that information in order to evaluate the work of public officials. If the employee's speech relates only to the internal affairs of the agency for which he or she works—for example, if the comments deal with the personal opinions of workers toward their supervisors—then the speech has little value to the public and will not be protected (Connick v. Myers, 1983). But if the speech addresses a topic about which the general public needs information, such as the policy choices made by a school board, then it passes the "public concern" hurdle.

Assuming the speech does relate to a matter of public concern, another question must be addressed. In *Connick* the Court made it clear that the value of the speech has to be balanced against its potential for disruption of the public workplace. Thus, speech by a high-level employee will likely receive less protection than speech by a low-level employee, because public disagreements among high-level employees are more likely to cause disruption. Speech by a police officer is less likely to be protected than speech by other officers, because discipline within the police force is thought to be especially important to its effective functioning, and small disruptions are thought to be comparatively less tolerable. Both the "public concern" and the "balancing" prongs of the test turn on a careful evaluation of the circumstances of individual cases.[26] In some situations these "retaliation" claims can be brought not only by government employees but also by people who contract with the government in one way or another (Board of County Commissioners v. Umbehr, 1996).

AFFIRMATIVE CONSTITUTIONAL DUTIES

Most of the claims considered in the preceding discussion concerned positive actions taken by government officials that injured the plaintiffs. We now turn to claims in which the plaintiff suffers an injury at the hands of someone other than the government official named as the defendant. The defendant government official is allegedly responsible for this injury either because he or she did something to make the plaintiff more vulnerable to the injury or because he or she did not take precautions to prevent it. Examples of these types of claims are found in suits filed against police officers who arrest the driver of a car and leave its passengers in a position of danger, or against social workers who fail to place a child in protective custody in the face of evidence of abuse.[27]

The broad issue presented in these cases is whether the defendant has a constitutional duty to protect the plaintiff from the threatened danger even when the source of the danger is a private actor. Plaintiffs frequently, but not always, base their claims on the Due Process Clause of the Fourteenth Amendment. They maintain that the government official deprived them of liberty without due process by not protecting them from the threatened danger. In more general terms, such claims raise the question of whether the Constitution acts only as a limitation on the exercise of governmental power vis-à-vis individuals, or whether it sometimes imposes affirmative duties on government officials to protect individuals from dangers posed by third parties.

Before addressing the key affirmative duty cases, we touch briefly on a related body of law. When the person who actively injures the plaintiff is a private party, the affirmative duty issue sometimes becomes confused with the issues discussed in the section entitled "State Action." Consider, for example, a claim brought on behalf of a child against a municipal social worker who did not protect her from an abusive parent. Some courts have denied liability in that situation on the grounds that the active wrongdoer (e.g., the parent) was not a state official, so that the injury was not the product of state action. State action, however, is only marginally relevant to the affirmative duty issue. On a superficial level, both lines of cases raise the question of whether the state bears any responsibility for the conduct of a nominally private actor. On closer examination, the two lines of cases address distinctly different concerns. The affirmative duty cases raise the question of whether a state official has an obligation to protect the plaintiff from some peril, not whether the peril itself can be said to be that of the state. In the typical affirmative duty case, the defendant is a government official (e.g., a state social worker) whose conduct constitutes state action. Liability depends on whether the state actor had any constitutional obligation (i.e., affirmative duty) to protect the plaintiff.

DeShaney v. Winnebago County Dept. of Social Services (1989)

The facts giving rise to this 1989 case were, in the words of the Court, "undeniably tragic." Joshua DeShaney was the victim of repeated acts of physical abuse inflicted by his father. Pursuant to state law, emergency room personnel reported the suspected abuse to the Winnebago County Department of Social Services (DSS) on at least three occasions. When neighbors informed the police they had seen or heard physical beatings, the police brought these reports to the attention of DSS. The caseworker assigned to Joshua's case personally "observed a number of suspicious injuries . . . dutifully recorded these incidents in her files . . . but she did nothing more." Two years after the first report of suspected abuse, four-year-old Joshua was beaten into a life-threatening coma by his father.

Suit was brought on Joshua's behalf against various social workers and the DSS, alleging that they deprived Joshua of liberty without due process by failing to protect him against his father's violence. The claim was grounded in substantive rather than procedural due process. That is, Joshua did not complain that the defendants failed to invoke appropriate procedural safeguards but that they were categorically obligated to protect him under the circumstances. The Court rejected this claim. (The difference between substantive and procedural due process was discussed in the section entitled "Distinguishing Substantive from Procedural Due Process in Constitutional Tort.")

In an opinion written by Chief Justice Rehnquist, the Court held that "[a]s a general matter . . . a State's failure to protect an individual against private violence simply does not constitute a violation of the Due Process Clause." This conclusion was based on the language of the Due Process Clause, its history, and prior cases ("precedent"). The Court stressed that "[t]he Clause is phrased as a limitation on the State's power to act, not as a guarantee of certain minimal levels of safety and security." As for history, the Court found that the Due Process Clause "was intended to prevent government from abusing [its] power, or employing it as an instrument of oppression." Its "purpose was to protect the people from the State, not to ensure that the State protected them from each other." Finally, the Court relied on prior decisions, which had held that the State has no constitutional obligation to pay for abortions or other medical procedures (Harris v. McRae, 1980) or to provide adequate housing for the poor (Lindsey v. Normet, 1972). These cases indicated that "the Due Process Clauses generally confer no affirmative right to governmental aid, even where such aid may be necessary to secure life, liberty, or property interests. . . ."

The Court acknowledged that under "certain limited circumstances" government officials may have a constitutional obligation to protect a person. These circumstances arise most often when the state "takes a person into its custody and holds him there against his will," as when a person is arrested, is imprisoned after having been convicted of a crime, or is involuntarily committed to a mental hospital. These exceptions did not apply in *DeShaney*, according to the Court, because "the harms Joshua suffered did not occur while he was in the State's custody, but while he was in the custody of his natural father. . . . While the State may have been aware of the dangers that Joshua faced, . . . it played no part in their creation, nor did it do anything to render him any more vulnerable to them."

Justices Brennan, Marshall, and Blackmun dissented. The dissenting justices did not disagree so much with the general framework of the majority opinion as with its application to the facts of the case. Justice Brennan agreed that the Due Process Clause does not create a "general right to basic governmental services" but argued that the extent of the state's involvement in Joshua's life warranted the recognition of an affirmative duty in this case. Specifically, Justice Brennan emphasized the actions taken by the state—not its inaction—that contributed to Joshua's peril. "Through its welfare program . . . the State of Wisconsin has relieved ordinary citizens and governmental bodies other than [DSS] of any sense of obligation to do anything more than report their suspicions of child abuse to DSS." Inaction in this context, he concluded, "can be every bit as abusive of power as action." Writing separately, Justice Blackmun asserted that the Fourteenth Amendment precedents could be read broadly or narrowly to suit the desired end. "A moral ambition," he declared, should have led the Court to recognize an affirmative duty toward Joshua.

Keep in mind that the majority's ruling in *DeShaney* is just a refusal to find constitutional tort liability. The decision does not mean that someone in Joshua's situation could not bring any kind of tort suit; it remains possible to sue under state law. The problem is that, absent a constitutional duty, the states are free to do as they please. They may allow a tort suit against the state or its officers, but they may equally choose to foreclose such suits. What many states do is to allow the state law tort suit but limit the amount of damages the plaintiff may recover. For example, Joshua's representative could have sued under Wisconsin law, but the recovery would have been limited to $50,000 against a governmental unit.[28]

The Indeterminancy of Language, History, and Precedent

DeShaney has produced voluminous and largely critical academic commentary.[29] These scholars (ourselves included) generally take the view that the majority opinion places more weight on the language of the Due Process Clause, its history, and precedent than those sources of law can reasonably bear. That is, each of these sources provides at least as much support for arguments favoring liability as they do for the antiliability arguments the Court advances. Even a staunch defender of the result in *DeShaney* seems to agree that "as a purely linguistic matter," a person can be "deprived" of liberty through governmental inaction as well as by action.[30] The critical issue is not whether the governmental conduct is characterized as action or inaction but whether there was an initial legal entitlement.

Furthermore, there is historical evidence that the drafters of the Fourteenth Amendment believed it included an obligation for a state to protect its citizens from harm. The privileges and immunities clause of the Fourteenth Amendment provides that "[n]o State shall . . . abridge the privileges and immunities of citizens of the United States." This clause was inspired by and patterned after the privileges and immunities clause of the Fifth Amendment. During the debates over the Fourteenth Amendment, proponents explained the intended meaning of this provision by quoting from Justice Bushrod Washington's 1823 opinion in Corfield v. Coryell. In *Corfield*, Justice Washington identified several privileges and immunities of citizenship under the Fifth Amendment. The very first right he identified as a privilege of citizenship was the right to "[p]rotection by government." Senators Trumbull and Howard quoted this passage from *Corfield* with approval when explaining their understanding of the privileges and immunities that states could not abridge under the Fourteenth Amendment. Although this history pertains to the privileges and immunities clause rather than to due process, it certainly indicates that some framers of the Fourteenth Amendment envisioned it as something more than a negative limitation on governmental power.

The majority opinion in *DeShaney* recognized that prior Supreme Court decisions had held that state officials have a constitutional obligation to provide medical care and protection to those the state has taken into custody. However, the majority opinion pays no attention to other Supreme Court decisions that may impose affirmative constitutional duties in other contexts as well. For example, there is no discussion of Boddie v. Connecticut (1971). The issue in that case was the constitutional validity of a state law that required people seeking divorce to pay a fee even if they were too poor to afford to pay. The Court held that due process "does prohibit a State from denying, solely because of inability to pay, access to its courts to individuals who seek judicial dissolution of their marriage." Essentially, Boddie found that due process obligates states to affirmatively assist the poor to obtain divorces by waiving the normal fees. More directly relevant to *DeShaney* is the 1921 decision in Truax v. Corrigan involving the availability of injunctions in labor disputes. An Arizona statute prohibited state courts from issuing injunctions to stop picketing during labor disputes. The employer contended that this statute deprived it of property without due process since it would allow the picketers to damage its business. The Court agreed and struck down the Arizona law under the Due Process Clause. In effect, the Court said that the Due Process Clause obliged the state to protect the employer from harmful acts of private parties.

The point here is not that the language of the Due Process Clause, its history, or precedent compel a different result in *DeShaney*, only that they do not preclude it. These traditional tools of legal analysis are simply too indeterminate to offer a concrete answer to the affirmative duty issue. The key to *DeShaney* lies more in policy considerations than in constitutional language, history, or case law.

Policy Considerations

The argument for recognizing a governmental duty to aid its citizens has both straightforward and subtle components. The most obvious justification for such a rule is to encourage government officials to protect those in danger, thereby reducing the number and extent of injuries. In addition, a duty to protect would reinforce widely shared understandings and expectations about the proper role of government. Under the Court's sharp distinction between active and passive misconduct, the outcome in *DeShaney* would be the same even if the social worker (or a police officer) watched passively as the father beat Joshua into a coma. Most, if not all, people would consider it wrong for the police officer or social worker to fail to respond under these circumstances and, perhaps, would be surprised to learn that states may, if they choose, deny recourse to the injured person or limit the damages he or she may recover. Imposing a constitutional affirmative duty in such cases would vindicate societal expectations of protection and provide a means for redressing a wrong.

A more subtle point concerns the role of the state in modern life. Critics of *DeShaney* point out that government plays a big role in virtually every aspect of daily life. This being so, it is naive to give decisive weight to the difference between the active and passive defaults of government. According to this view, the Winnebago DSS was not a detached stranger that passively observed the plight of Joshua DeShaney, but an active participant in a system that encouraged potential rescuers to defer to DSS. This perspective builds on Justice Brennan's dissenting opinion and reformulates the legal issue in terms that emphasize the active role of DSS in Joshua's life. As stated by Professor Tribe, "[t]he majority's question in *DeShaney* was simply: did the State of Wisconsin beat up that child? and not 'did the law of Wisconsin, taken in its entirety, warp the legal landscape so that it in effect deflected the assistance otherwise available to Joshua DeShaney?'"[31]

We do not mean to say that all the arguments point in the same direction. Other policy considerations argue against broad affirmative constitutional duties.[32] These begin with a concern about the discretionary allocation of scarce public resources. Government is a complex enterprise in which hard choices must be made as how to best deploy limited funds. Money spent to improve child welfare services, police protection, or fire fighting services may come at the expense of schools, public hospitals, or recreation programs. Since there is no single right answer to such budgetary issues, they are more properly resolved through political processes than litigation. As a matter of democratic theory, the more politically responsive branches of government (i.e., the legislative and executive branches) should decide the proper mix of public expenditures. Judicial intervention through the imposition of constitutional tort liability would disrupt the balance of competing interests achieved through the democratic political process.

This is more than a matter of democratic theory, however. There is also the related question of institutional competence. A court adjudicates individual cases by applying rules of law to facts presented to it by the parties. Courts are therefore limited to the facts and information made available to them in this way. Legislatures, on the other hand, have access to a wider variety of sources of information. They can investigate, conduct hearings, commission studies, and receive input from a variety of competing points of view. For these reasons, the legislative process is thought to be better suited than adjudication for resolving multidimensional issues such as how best to allocate limited resources among virtually infinite demands.

There is nothing distinctively constitutional about the preceding arguments against affirmative constitutional duties. They would apply with equal force whether the asserted affirmative duty is grounded in state common law or the federal Constitution. Constitutional considerations raise two additional points, however. The first point is the relatively inflexible nature of constitutional rules. If a court recognizes an affirmative duty as a matter of state common law, the legislature can modify or reverse that rule through legislation. For example, the legislatures in several states responded to court decisions recognizing a duty to protect by passing statutes that created an immunity for particular protective services. However, congressional and state legislative power to alter or reverse a rule recognized as a matter of constitutional law is much more limited. The "very purpose" of constitutional rights is "to withdraw certain subjects from the vicissitudes of political controversy, to place them beyond the reach of majorities and officials and to establish them as legal principles to be applied by the courts" (West Virginia State Board of Education v. Barnette, 1943). An example from the constitutional tort context is Martinez v. California (1980), in which the Supreme Court ruled that the California legislature could not immunize state parole officials from liability under 42 U.S.C. § 1983 for claims based on alleged violations of the Constitution. The inflexibility of constitutional rules is a virtue, of course, in that it shields these rights from the pressures of the legislative process. Yet that same inflexibility heightens concerns about discretionary allocation of resources, as any missteps cannot easily be corrected in the political arena.

The second constitutional consideration concerns the liberty of third parties. Often the government cannot protect one person without interfering with another person's freedom. In order to protect Joshua, the Winnebago County social workers almost certainly would have had to risk violating the constitutionally protected rights of his father by closer surveillance or by taking Joshua away. This possibility creates the danger of state officials being sued no matter what they do. The majority in *DeShaney* acknowledged this when it commented, "Had [the social workers] moved too soon to take custody of the son away from his father, they would likely have been met with charges of improperly intruding into the parent–child relationship, charges based on the same Due Process Clause that form the basis for the present charge of failure to provide adequate protection." While interference with the father's liberty may have been warranted under the facts alleged in *DeShaney*, a general affirmative duty rule would inevitably lead to governmental disruption of the parent–child relation when, in hindsight, it was not justified. Those who support the outcome in *DeShaney* fear that affirmative constitutional duties would lead to an overall increase in governmental interference with individual liberty.

DeShaney is best understood in terms of the policy considerations noted previously. A majority of the Court was persuaded by the combination of policy factors regarding the need to preserve legislative and executive discretion in allocating resources, the inflexibility of constitutional rules, and the danger that an affirmative constitutional duty to protect will unduly interfere with individual liberty. Admittedly, it can be difficult to draw a line between cases that warrant an affirmative duty and those that do not, especially one that can be applied with confidence by social workers, police officers, and other officers who deal with situations in which they are pressed for time and lack information. The dissenting justices were convinced that these dangers could be contained by focusing on the facts of specific cases and thought that the facts alleged in *DeShaney* warranted the conclusion that government officials unconstitutionally abused their power by not doing more to protect Joshua.

Affirmative Consitutional Duties after *DeShaney*

Though the Court in *DeShaney* unequivocally rejected a general duty to protect under the Due Process Clause, it acknowledged that such a duty may exist in "certain limited circumstances." The plaintiff's arguments and the Court's opinion in *DeShaney* invoked the term "special relationship" to describe situations in which affirmative duties might be recognized. This term is borrowed from common law torts and reflects the normative conclusion that a duty to help should be recognized in certain situations for reasons of basic fairness. Common law courts have concluded that a special relationship may exist when state officials by affirmative conduct have done something to render the plaintiff especially vulnerable or when the plaintiff detrimentally relies on the specific assurances by government officials that they will protect the plaintiff.[33] It is considered fair to impose an affirmative duty (a) when a defendant is responsible for the plaintiff's need for help, and (b) when the defendant has made a specific promise to help and the plaintiff counted on the aid. With this common law background in mind, we consider whether there are any constitutional affirmative duties.

Special Relationships: Involuntary Confinement

In Estelle v. Gamble (1976) the Court considered the complaint of a state prisoner who alleged that he received inadequate medical care after injuring his back while engaged in prison work. The inmate claimed that this constituted cruel and unusual punishment in violation of the Eighth Amendment. The Court held that "deliberate indifference to serious medical needs of prisoners constitutes the 'unnecessary and wanton infliction of pain'. . . proscribed by the Eighth Amendment." The constitutional obligation to provide medical care stemmed from the state's use of power to place the plaintiff in a position of dependency. As later explained in *DeShaney*, "when the State by the affirmative exercise of its power so restrains an individual's liberty that it renders him unable to care for himself, and at the same time fails to provide for his basic human needs (e.g., food, clothing, shelter, medical care, and reasonable safety) it transgresses the substantive limits on state action set by the Eighth Amendment and the Due Process Clause." The Court carefully emphasized that "an inadvertent failure to provide adequate medical care" would not rise to the level of an Eighth Amendment violation. "Medical malpractice [i.e, a doctor's negligence in ordinary tort law] does not become a constitutional violation merely because the victim is a prisoner." The claim must allege "deliberate indifference to serious medical need." Under this standard, Gamble's claims against prison medical personnel were rejected. He asserted that his back injury was inadequately treated because prison doctors failed to order an X-ray. "A medical decision not to order an X-ray, or like measures, does not represent cruel and unusual punishment."

The inmate in *Estelle* may have lost his personal battle for compensation, but he won the war for recognition of a constitutional affirmative duty under the Eighth Amendment to provide medical care to prison inmates. In the years following *Estelle*, lower courts developed a body of decisional law that fleshed out the constitutional standard of "deliberate indifference to serious medical need." They have ruled, for example, that prison officials violate the Eighth Amendment when they refuse to provide prescribed treatment or know of the inmate's need for immediate medical care yet take no action. On the other hand, obliging the inmate to wait a couple of days before seeing a doctor for nonemergency care is not an Eighth Amendment violation.[34]

The Supreme Court returned to the duty to provide medical care for inmates in Helling v. McKinney (1993), a case in which a prison inmate claimed that exposure to environmental tobacco smoke (ETS) posed an unreasonable danger to his future health. The defendants argued that the Eighth Amendment only required them to provide medical care when the inmate was already sick or injured. The Court rejected that argument, holding that prison officials had a constitutional duty to protect inmates from future health risks as well as to provide for current medical needs. In order to win, the inmate must first prove the objective fact that "he himself is being exposed to unreasonably high levels of [tobacco smoke]." Second, he must prove that prison officials' subjective state of mind reflected "deliberate indifference" to the health risks posed by ETS. The Court cautioned that "it could be very difficult to demonstrate that prison authorities are ignoring the possible dangers posed by exposure to ETS."

Farmer v. Brennan (1994), made clear that prison officials also have an affirmative duty under the Eighth Amendment to protect inmates from threats posed by other inmates. The plaintiff in *Farmer* was a young transsexual man with feminine characteristics who was placed in the general prison population and thereafter beaten and raped by other inmates. The Court held that the Eighth Amendment "imposes duties on [prison] officials . . . [to] 'take reasonable measures to guarantee the safety of the inmates.'" The Court analyzed Farmer's claim by applying the Eighth Amendment standard laid down in *Estelle v. Gamble*. A prison official may be found to have violated an inmate's Eighth Amendment rights only upon proof that (1) the inmate was exposed to a substantial risk of harm and (2) the prison official's state of mind reflected deliberate indifference to that risk. The crucial question is what the prison official actually knew and not merely what he or she should have known. It is not enough for an inmate to prove that a prison official failed to act in the face of an obvious danger. Rather, the inmate must prove that the official actually knew of and disregarded an excessive risk of serious danger.

The Court explained that a prison official's actual knowledge of risk can be established by circumstantial evidence. Specifically, "a factfinder may conclude that a prison official knew of a substantial risk from the very fact that the risk was obvious." The Court concluded that the facts alleged in the complaint, if proven, could support a finding that the defendants were actually aware of the serious dangers facing Farmer and, therefore, could support a finding of deliberate indifference.

In Ingraham v. Wright (1977) the Court determined that the Eighth Amendment applies only to those who have been convicted of a crime. However, it did not say whether officials have any affirmative constitutional duties to those they have taken into custody but who have not been convicted of a crime. In a pair of decisions from the early 1980s the Court ruled that the Due Process Clause requires state officials to protect and provide medical care for persons they have involuntarily taken into custody. In Youngberg v. Romeo (1982), the Court held that a mentally ill person involuntarily committed to a state facility is entitled to protection under the Due Process Clause. The Court reasoned that, if the Eighth Amendment protects prison inmates from unsafe conditions, "it must be unconstitutional to confine the involuntarily committed 'who may not be punished at all' in unsafe conditions." In City of Revere v. Massachusetts General Hospital (1983), the Court held that "[t]he Due Process Clause . . . does require the responsible government or governmental agency to provide medical care to persons . . . who have been injured while being apprehended by the police. . . . [T]he due process rights of a person [arrested but not yet convicted of a crime] are at least as great as the Eighth Amendment protections available to a convicted criminal." Thus, the law is clear that state officials have constitutional obligations under the Eighth and Fourteenth amendments to protect and care for those involuntarily placed in confinement.

Other Special Relationships

The Court in *DeShaney* hinted that affirmative duties might exist in contexts other than involuntary custody. In a footnote the Court suggested that if the state removes a child from his parents and places him or her in a state-sponsored foster home "we might have a situation sufficiently analogous to incarceration or institutionalization to give rise to an affirmative duty to protect." The Court noted that several lower courts had recognized affirmative constitutional duties to protect foster children from mistreatment at the hands of their foster parents. The Court in *DeShaney*, however, "express[ed] no view on the validity of the analogy. . . ." The task of deciding what relationships, if any, are "sufficiently analogous" to incarceration to "give rise to an affirmative duty to protect" has been left largely to the lower courts.

The two contexts that have received the most attention in this matter are foster care and public schools. A typical complaint in these cases alleges that a child was injured by a third party (e.g., sexual abuse by foster parent or fellow student), and the governmental defendant (e.g., social worker or school official) failed to take appropriate measures to protect the child. The common question raised in such cases is whether foster care or attending public schools under compulsory attendance laws is "sufficiently analogous" to incarceration to give rise to an affirmative constitutional duty to protect.

Many lower federal courts have found that state welfare officials must take steps to protect children placed in state-sponsored foster homes. A representative decision, Nicini v. Morra (2000), explains why courts think foster children are in a position similar to that of prison inmates. The Court recognized that the analogy is "incomplete" in that foster children enjoy a greater degree of freedom than do prison inmates or institutionalized mentally retarded persons. Nonetheless, in each instance the state has made the individual substantially dependent upon the state to meet his or her basic needs. Both the inmate and the foster child are placed in a custodial environment and are unable to seek alternative living arrangements. The Court declared, "when the state places a child in state-regulated foster care, the state has entered into a special relationship with that child which imposes upon it certain affirmative duties."

Proponents of affirmative duties in the public school context emphasize that the state has custody of children while attending school. Often the children are compelled by law to be there. These children, the argument continues, are no less dependant on state officials for protection than are foster children or the involuntarily confined. Some of the Supreme Court's reasoning indicates a certain lack of sympathy with this argument. In Veronia School District v. Acton (1995) the issue was totally different from the affirmative duty doctrine. The school had required athletes to submit to random drug testing; a student challenged the practice, claiming it was an unreasonable search, and the Court ruled for the school. In the course of the opinion, the Court emphasized the school's historical role to stand "in loco parentis" (i.e., in the place of the parent) over children entrusted to them. For our purposes, the key point is that the Court refused to go a step further, stating that it did not mean to say "that public schools as a general matter have such a degree of control over children as to give rise to a constitutional 'duty to protect. . . .'"

As illustrated in Hasenfus v. LaJeunesse (1999), courts of appeals generally have agreed that compulsory school attendance and involuntary confinement are not "sufficiently analogous" within the meaning of *DeShaney* to give rise to an affirmative constitutional duty to protect. These courts point out that children live most of their lives outside of school and have persons other than government officials (e.g., their parents) to act as their protectors. Foster children, by contrast, have no one other than state officials to protect them from their state-approved foster parents. Courts do not think the degree of dependence created by state compulsory attendance laws is sufficiently great to justify the recognition of an affirmative constitutional duty to protect. Consequently, lower courts have generally held that school officials do not have a constitutional obligation to protect students from threats posed by other students. In both foster care and public schools, the state has done something that renders the child dependant on government officials for protection. The key distinguishing factor appears to be the extent of state involvement in creating dependency rather than the simple fact of dependency. In the foster care context courts have concluded that the state is sufficiently responsible for the foster child's need for state protection to justify an affirmative constitutional duty. In the public school context courts have concluded that the state is not so deeply involved as to justify a duty. The distinction is one of degree rather than kind and illustrates that fact-specific nuances may determine which relationships are and which are not sufficiently analogous to support an affirmative duty.

State-Created Danger

DeShaney suggests yet a third circumstance in which an affirmative constitutional duty to protect might be found. In explaining why Joshua's claim was properly dismissed, the Court observed that the state "played no part in [the] creation [of the dangers that Joshua faced], nor did it do anything to render him any more vulnerable to them." This phrasing implies that a duty might arise if the state created the danger from which Joshua sought protection. Before and after *DeShaney*, lower courts have applied this rationale to find affirmative constitutional duties when the state played a significant role in creating the danger. As explained by Judge Richard Posner in Bowers v. DeVito (1982), "[i]f a state puts a man in a position of danger from private persons and then fails to protect him, it will not be heard to say that its role is merely passive; it is as much an active tort-feasor as if it had thrown him into a snake pit." The central question under this theory is how significant was the state's contribution to the creation of the risk.

The starting point for understanding the decisions in this area is Martinez v. California (1980). The state parole board had released on parole a violent sex offender who, five months later, tortured and killed a teenage girl. The girl's parents sued the parole board, charging that it acted recklessly in letting the man out of prison. The Supreme Court held that state parole officials could not be held responsible for the girl's death. One factor in the decision was the five-month gap between the release and the murder. The Court also stressed that the parole officials were not aware of any special danger to this victim "as distinguished from the public at large." Although the *Martinez* opinion is couched in very general language, two points are quite clear. First, state action unquestionably created some risk to the fifteen-year-old victim: If the state had not paroled the inmate, he could not have killed her. Second, the risk created by this state action was deemed legally insufficient to support a constitutional obligation.

Following *Martinez*, lower courts have routinely denied claims brought by those suffering at the hands of inmates who were released by parole or furlough or who even escaped. They have also held that police officers have no constitutional duty to arrest a suspected drunk driver (Saenz v. Heldenfels Bros., Inc., 1989) or to protect jail nurses from violent attacks by prisoners (White v. Lemacks, 1999). In these cases the government officials were aware of a generalized risk but not of a particularized danger to a specific victim.

Some lower courts, however, have recognized affirmative duties when the state makes a more substantial or particularized contribution to the risk. In Nishiyama v. Dickson County (1987) a county sheriff routinely allowed a trusty inmate to have unsupervised use of a fully marked and equipped patrol car. On one occasion, the sheriff took no action for ten hours after receiving reports that the trusty was using the patrol car to stop and harass passing motorists; using the car, the man stopped the plaintiff's daughter and murdered her. Under these facts the court of appeals held that the sheriff could be held responsible for the murder. The ruling distinguished *Martinez* on the grounds that, in this case, "state officers by their acts facilitate[d] the crime by providing the criminal with the necessary means and the specific opportunity to commit his crime." Liability also has been based on the allegations that (a) police arrested the driver of a car, took him away, and left the young children passengers alone on a busy highway (White v. Rochford, 1979); (b) police instructed private citizens not to attempt to rescue a drowning man (Ross v. United States, 1990); and (c) police assured skinheads that they would not interfere with members of their group who were beating up political protestors for burning the American flag (Dwares v. City of New York, 1993).

It is an admittedly fine line that separates state contribution to risk giving rise to an affirmative duty from that which does not; predicting results in individual cases is hazardous, at best. Perhaps the most that can be said is that the more specific the state contribution, the more particularized the risk, and the more specifically identifiable the potential victim, the better the chances that a court will recognize an affirmative duty.

Alternative Approaches to the Affirmative Duty Issue

The Supreme Court has sometimes employed alternative ways of analyzing what might appear to be an affirmative duty claim. In *DeShaney* itself, the Court observed in a footnote that discrimination against certain classes of persons in the provision of protective services might violate the equal protection clause of the Fourteenth Amendment. The recent decision of Willowbrook v. Olech (2000) held that a successful equal protection claim can be based on the arbitrary denial of governmental services to a single person. (See the section entitled "Arbitrary Acts and Equal Protection") Courts of Appeals have occasionally upheld claims under an equal protection analysis that might not be successful under an affirmative duty-to-protect theory. In Shipp v. McMahon (2000), for example, the court of appeals refused to dismiss a complaint alleging that the police discriminated against women in how they responded to reports of domestic violence.

While as a matter of substantive due process the police did not have a constitutional duty to protect the plaintiff, it could not intentionally refuse to do so on the basis of her sex. Similarly, in Dwares v. City of New York (1993) the plaintiffs alleged that police intentionally refused to protect them from violent attacks by skinheads because the plaintiffs burned an American flag at a political protest. The court of appeals held that if these facts were proven at trial, the denial of protective services on the basis of political expression would violate the protesters' Fourteenth Amendment right to equal protection. An equal protection violation may be difficult to establish, however, as the plaintiff must prove that the defendant intended to discriminate on a constitutionally impermissible basis (Washington v. Davis, 1976). Thus, the plaintiff in *Shipp* had to prove that the police intended to discriminate against her because of her sex when they failed to protect her from her abusive husband.

A different body of legal doctrine governs claims alleging that a local government or one of its officials failed to protect the plaintiff from harm threatened by another government official. For example, a plaintiff might allege that a sheriff who inadequately supervised a deputy is legally responsible for the beating inflicted upon the plaintiff by the deputy, or that a city is responsible for the unconstitutional acts of an individual police officer becauseits official policies or customs encouraged such behavior. The law pertaining to governmental and supervisory liability is discussed in the section entitled "Liability of Local Governments." For present purposes, we simply observe that this body of law might provide an avenue of recovery when a general constitutional duty to protect otherwise would not apply.

Finally, there are instances where a statute creates a duty to protect even when the Constitution does not. Recall that the courts of appeals have ruled that public school officials have no constitutional duty to protect students from threatened acts of violence by other students. Such a duty has been recognized, however, under a federal civil rights statute, Title IX of the Education Amendments of 1972. Thus, students who are victims of sexual harassment by teachers (Gebser v. Lago Vista Independent School District, 1998) or fellow students (Davis v. Monroe County Board of Education, 1999) may recover damages from school districts if they can prove that someone with authority to take corrective measures acted with deliberate indifference to known acts of harassment.

LIABILITY OF GOVERNMENTAL ENTITIES

Suits seeking compensation for violations of constitutional rights arise in a variety of contexts. Criminal suspects and inmates may claim that their constitutional rights were violated by the arresting officer, jailer, or other correctional official. School teachers and other government employees may allege that they lost their jobs because they exercised their rights to free speech protected by the First Amendment. In these and other instances, the aggrieved party may seek compensation from the individual official who allegedly violated his or her constitutional rights. One may also pursue a claim against the official's governmental employer. In this section we explore the circumstances under which a government may be held liable for the deprivation of constitutional rights.

The liability of governmental entities for constitutional violations is an extremely complex area of law. This complexity stems from several factors. First, the set of rules pertaining to the liability of states is quite different from those governing the liability of local governments. (The term "local governments" as used in this section covers a wide variety of entities, including cities, counties, and school districts. As explained below, the differences in liability rules are due in large part to differences in the historical origins and constitutional status of states and local governments.) Second, the Supreme Court has rejected the general principle that a city is legally responsible for a constitutional violation simply because it employed the individual wrongdoer. Rather, the plaintiff must prove that some "official policy or custom" of the city was "the moving force" behind the violation. These terms have little common law heritage or historical meaning. Consequently, courts have struggled with the articulation and application of rules without being able to draw upon well-settled common law analogies. Third, some important Supreme Court cases in this area do not command a majority opinion. Thus, the governing rules can be elicited only by piecing together plurality and concurring opinions. We will attempt to explain the law in this area first by addressing the rules governing suits brought against a state, then by addressing suits brought against local governments.

Suits Against a State

State governments enjoy sovereign immunity from suit as a matter of federal constitutional law (Alden v. Maine, 1999; Hans v. Louisiana, 1890). "Sovereign immunity" means that a state cannot be sued for damages even if it is plain that the state has violated someone's rights. Even so, there are ways of obtaining relief for a state's breaches of its legal duties. These blanket statements need to be qualified and explained, however, as the law of sovereign immunity actually is quite nuanced. We first identify the constitutional source of sovereign immunity. We then discuss the scope of soverign immunity and a number of recent cases in which the Supreme Court has considered whether and in what circumstances Congress has the power to abrogate state sovereign immunity.

The Source of State Sovereign Immunity

According to the Supreme Court, the source of state sovereign immunity is the original Constitution, adopted in 1787. We will see that a number of features of the doctrine turn on this seemingly technical issue of where the immunity comes from. For that reason, we need to explain with some care how the Court reached this conclusion. As an initial matter, there is a problem with locating the immunity in the original document, for the 1787 Constitution does not mention sovereign immunity. It does not appear until 1798, with the ratification of the Eleventh Amendment. That amendment provides that "the judicial power of the United States shall not be construed to extend to any suit in law or equity, commenced or prosecuted against one of the United States by citizens of another state, or by citizens or subjects of any foreign state."

Taken at face value, this provision seems to enact a relatively narrow immunity rule under which states would not be subject to suit by outsiders in federal court. As we shall see, the Supreme Court has preferred a broader immunity doctrine. Locating the immunity in the original Constitution has permitted the Court to find immunity in situations that are not covered by the specific language of the Eleventh Amendment. But the question remains: Given the absence of any mention of immunity in the original document, how does the Court justify finding it there?

The answer lies in the historical circumstances of the adoption of the Constitution and the Eleventh Amendment.[35] In the debates over ratification of the Constitution, opponents noted the absence of any mention of sovereign immunity, while proponents offered assurances that states would indeed be immune from suit in federal court. A few years after ratification, the Supreme Court confirmed the critics' fears, deciding in Chisholm v. Georgia (1793) that a citizen of South Carolina could sue the state of Georgia in federal court to recover money owed to him. The Eleventh Amendment was adopted in response to that ruling. By a 5–4 margin, the current Supreme Court takes the view that it was generally understood at the time of ratification that states would be broadly immune from suit. *Chisholm* was an error on the part of the Supreme Court; the Eleventh Amendment is written so narrowly because it was intended merely to correct the Court's mistake, restoring the broad immunity states enjoyed under the original Constitution (Seminole Tribe of Florida v. Florida, 1996). *Seminole Tribe* is not the first case to endorse this thesis, which dates from Hans v. Louisiana (1890). Keep in mind, however, that this and other Eleventh Amendment issues are hotly disputed points. As the composition of the Court changes, the majority may take a different view of the source of state sovereign immunity. This, in turn, could have significant implications for the rest of immunity doctrine. Broadly speaking, arguments in favor of sovereign immunity would have less persuasive force if they were denied a grounding in the original Constitution.

The Scope of Immunity

Ever since *Hans*, the Supreme Court has applied state sovereign immunity in many situations not covered by the language of the Eleventh Amendment.[36] For example, immunity applies to citizens of the state being sued and to foreign governments, but not to suits by other states or to suits by the United States. It also applies to suits "in admiralty" (i.e., involving maritime matters). On the other hand, there is an important limit on its real-world scope, one that relies on the distinction explored previously between prospective and retrospective relief. Retrospective relief against a state, in the form of damages or another backward-looking remedy, is forbidden by the sovereign immunity doctrine. But prospective relief is another matter. Although a state itself cannot be sued for prospective relief, a litigant may sue an officer and seek an injunction directing the officer to comply with federal law (Ex Parte Young, 1908). This type of lawsuit is discussed in detail in the section entitled "Prospective Relief," where we analyze the remedies available for constitutional violations.

Apart from the prospective/retrospective distinction, there are other limits on the scope of state sovereign immunity from suit in state court, especially in suits based on federal constitutional grounds. States may not assert immunity as a ground for refusing to pay for private property they have taken for public use (First Evangelical Lutheran Church of Glendale v. County of Los Angeles, 1987). And they may not invoke it as a ground for refusing to repay unconstitutionally collected taxes unless they have made some other remedy available (Reich v. Collins, 1994). Whether these cases stand for a broader principle that the Constitution presumptively obliges states to accord a remedy for the violation of constitutional rights is an issue the Court has not yet resolved.[37] In Nevada v. Hall (1979) the Court ruled that California courts did not have to recognize the sovereign immunity claim of the state of Nevada, even though the suit involved no constitutional issues but only ordinary matters of state law.

Congressional Power to Abrogate Immunity

The big issue in Eleventh Amendment law in recent years has been whether Congress may abrogate the states' sovereign immunity. In exploring this question, two grants of power to Congress must be distinguished. First, Article 1 accords a number of powers to Congress, including, for example, the power to regulate commerce among the states and with Indian tribes, the power to protect intellectual property rights, and the power to collect taxes and pay debts. We call these "Article 1 powers." Second, § 5 of the Fourteenth Amendment grants Congress the authority to enforce the substantive rights guaranteed by that amendment (including equal protection, due process, and all the rights incorporated into the Fourteenth Amendment from the Bill of Rights)[38] by "appropriate legislation." We call this the "section 5 power." Note, however, that similar provisions appear in other constitutional amendments enacted after the Civil War, specifically, the Thirteenth Amendment (outlawing slavery) and the Fifteenth Amendment (forbidding states from denying former slaves the right to vote.) Though there are no cases concerning the scope of congressional power to enforce these provisions, it is likely that the "section 5" doctrine discussed below would apply to them as well.

In earlier times, Congress did not attempt to subject states to suit by private individuals. This attitude began to change in the 1970s. In a number of statutes enacted over the past thirty years Congress has attempted to authorize private individuals to sue state governments for violations of their federal rights. When challenged in the Supreme Court, its efforts have met with decidedly mixed results.

In describing the Supreme Court's body of doctrine on Congressional abrogation, it is useful to begin by focusing on the source of authority on which Congress draws when it seeks to abrogate immunity. With regard to cases in which Congress relies on its Article 1 powers, the Supreme Court first took one path and then turned around and went in the opposite direction. In Pennsylvania v. Union Gas (1989) the Court ruled by a 5–4 majority that Congress may subject states to suit in federal court. Congress had enacted a statute that obliged states to pay for environmental cleanup efforts and that allowed private persons to sue states in order to enforce the law. The Court allowed the suit to go forward, reasoning that the states surrendered some of their immunity when they ratified the Constitution. Specifically, they gave up immunity to the extent Congress chooses to override it when acting within its Article 1 powers. Seven years later and after the composition of the Court had changed, a different 5–4 majority reached the opposite conclusion. In Seminole Tribe of Florida v. Florida (1996) the Court overruled *Union Gas*, holding that the immunity overrides any exercise of Article 1 powers. Like *Union Gas*, *Seminole Tribe* was a suit in federal court. After *Seminole Tribe*, litigants attempted to avoid the bar erected by that case by suing in state court. But the Supreme Court cut off that avenue as well, holding in Alden v. Maine (1999) that the sovereign immunity bar applied in state court as well as federal court. As of today, then, the rule is that Congress may not override state sovereign immunity when acting under Article 1 powers.

With regard to § 5, the doctrinal situation is more complicated. In Fitzpatrick v. Bitzer (1976) Congress had subjected states to suit for discriminating on the basis of sex in employment. Since the Fourteenth Amendment prohibits sex discrimination, and the statute enforced that prohibition, the Supreme Court upheld this statute as a valid exercise of § 5 power to enforce the substantive provisions of the amendment by appropriate legislation. Using the same reasoning, the Court shortly afterward upheld Congress' statute subjecting states to liability for attorneys' fees to successful plaintiffs in § 1983 cases (Hutto v. Finney, 1978).

After *Hutto*, however, the Court began to whittle away at this doctrine. First, in Quern v. Jordan (1979) it announced a "clear statement rule," under which abrogation would be found only where Congress had explicitly stated its intent to do so. In *Quern*, itself, the issue was how to interpret the provision of § 1983 that authorizes a cause of action against "every person" who violates rights. Citing *Fitzpatrick* and *Hutto*, the plaintiff maintained that the provision allowed federal court suits against state governments despite sovereign immunity. Shortly before, the Court had held that local governments are persons subject to suit, and the plaintiffs argued that the same result should hold for states as well. The Court rejected this reasoning, pointing out that the two situations are not perfectly analogous. Unlike state governments, local governments have no sovereign immunity. There is, therefore, a stronger interest in finding that states remain immune. A clear statement rule serves the goal of assuring that the states' immunity interest has received due consideration from Congress.[39] Applying this principle to the question of whether § 1983 contains such a clear statement of intent to subject states to suit, the Court found that the term "person" was not sufficiently explicit. Later the Court held that plaintiffs could not escape this rule by bringing suit in state court rather than federal court (Will v. Michigan Department of State Police, 1989).

A second limit on "section 5 abrogation" derives from a distinction the Court has made between rights and remedies in delineating the scope of Congress' power under § 5. The leading case is City of Boerne v. Flores (1997), which concerned the validity of the Religious Freedom Restoration Act (RFRA). In order to understand the case, we must make a brief detour into First Amendment law. The First Amendment forbids governments from "prohibiting the free exercise" of religion. This language leaves open many questions as to how far government may go in regulating religion. Suppose, for example, that a genuine religious practice involves smoking peyote, and the state has a law that forbids the possession of peyote. The issue is whether the state may, consistently with the "free exercise" clause, impose sanctions on someone who uses peyote as part of religious practice.

Some years ago the Supreme Court held that the state may do so, reasoning that so long as the state applies its law in a neutral fashion to anyone who smokes peyote, without targeting religion, there is no free exercise violation (Employment Division v. Smith, 1990). After that case Congress enacted RFRA, which forbids governments from substantially burdening religion even by laws of general applicability unless compelling government interests can be achieved in no other way. Congress relied on its section § 5 to enforce the substantive provisions of the Fourteenth Amendment, which include the free exercise right. In *Flores* the Supreme Court ruled that the statute could not be applied to state laws, as Congress had exceeded the scope of its § 5 power. The Court relied on the distinction between rights and remedies and held that the section five power is mainly remedial (though the power also extends to making rules that will deter future violations, if there is a strong enough need for such rules). That is, Congress may not use § 5 as a basis for defining the content of substantive constitutional rights in a way that differs from the Supreme Court's own constitutional decisions. With RFRA, Congress had attempted to do just that.

Flores did not concern a "Congressional abrogation of sovereign immunity" issue, yet it is highly relevant to the scope of Congress's § 5 abrogation power. *Flores* means that any effort by Congress to abrogate state sovereign immunity must get over the hurdle of the right/remedy distinction. In Kimel v. Florida Board of Regents (2000), for example, Congress had attempted to abrogate state immunity in enacting the Age Discrimination in Employment Act (ADEA), which protects workers over forty from being fired because of their age and allows them to sue state governments as well as other employers for damages. Under the Court's substantive equal protection doctrine, age discrimination is unconstitutional only when it is irrational. The statute prohibits age discrimination in a far broader category of cases. Under *Flores*, then, the ADEA could not validly abrogate state sovereign immunity.

Another recent case concerns the Americans with Disabilities Act (ADA), in which Congress had outlawed certain kinds of discrimination against persons with disabilities and had imposed liability for damages on violators, including state governments. As in *Kimel*, the Supreme Court's substantive constitutional standard under the equal protection clause for testing the legality of such discrimination is that it must not be irrational (Cleburne v. Cleburne Living Center, 1985). Yet the ADA prohibited discrimination even if it had a rational basis. Moreover, it is not enough to show isolated instances of unconstitutional discrimination. There must be a sufficient showing of widespread violations in order to justify abrogation. Because Congress had not identified any "history and pattern of unconstitutional job discrimination against the disabled," its abrogating legislation again crossed the line between rights and remedies (Board of Trustees of University of Alabama v. Garrett, 2001). The Court also ruled in *Garrett* that Congress may not base § 5 abrogation on actions of local governments, explaining that those governments do not have immunity in the first place. For that reason, "[i]t would make no sense to consider constitutional violations on their part, as well as by the States themselves, when only the States are the beneficiaries of the Eleventh Amendment."

The Liability of Local Governments

We are accustomed to thinking of local governments as divisions of the state government. Local governments have no status independent of the state in which they are located. Their powers come from the state legislature, whose laws they enforce throughout the state, and state and local governments share tax revenue. And yet, for purposes of immunity from suit, there is a sharp distinction between local governments and the state government: In Lincoln County v. Luning (1890) the Supreme Court ruled that counties do not share the state government's sovereign immunity under the U.S. Constitution. Subsequent cases have extended this ruling to cities and school boards (Workman v. New York, 1900; Mount Healthy City School District v. Doyle, 1977). There is a historical explanation for this distinction. Many local governments were initially established as private associations that took on certain functions of government. In the eighteenth century, at the time the Eleventh Amendment was adopted, the legal status of local governments was closer to that of a private corporation. "By the time that the municipal corporation came to be seen as a distinct legal form exercising governmental powers delegated by the state, the amenability of local governments to suit in federal court had long been established."[40]

Therefore none of the doctrine examined thus far has any application to suits against a local government. The distinction does raise an issue as to whether a given governmental entity is an "arm of the state" or part of a local government. Consider, for example, a local community college. Would it be viewed as an arm of the state (thus sharing the state's sovereign immunity) or as a part of the local government? There is surprisingly little Supreme Court doctrine on this issue. In the lower courts, the answer in any given case depends on such factors as whether a judgment against the entity would be paid from state or from local government funds and whether the entity performs functions of the central state government (e.g., Hale v. Arizona, 1993). In the discussion that follows, we will assume that the entity in question is not an arm of the state and therefore does not share the state government's federal sovereign immunity.

Local Governments as Subject to Suit Under 42 U.S.C. § 1983

Most suits against local governments are brought under 42 U.S.C. § 1983, which authorizes suits against "every person" who subjects another to a deprivation of rights secured by the Constitution. In the context of governmental liability, the threshold question is whether a local government is a "person" within the meaning of § 1983.

The Supreme Court initially answered this question negativly in the seminal case Monroe v. Pape (1961). *Monroe* involved a suit brought against individual police officers and the City of Chicago for the forcible entry and search of the plaintiffs' residence and for detention of the plaintiffs without a warrant. The City of Chicago moved to dismiss the complaint on the grounds that it was not subject to suit under 42 U.S.C. § 1983. The Supreme Court reviewed the legislative history of § 1983 and concluded that Congress did not intend to subject municipalities to suit. Hence, cities could not be considered "persons" within the meaning of the statute. The Court's conclusion rested primarily on Congress' rejection of the so-called "Sherman Amendment" (named after its sponsor, a senator). This proposed amendment to the Civil Rights Act of 1871 would have imposed liability on municipal corporations for damage done to the person or property of its inhabitants by private persons "riotously and tumultuously assembled." The legislative debates reveal that many members of Congress doubted that the federal government could constitutionally impose an obligation on cities to protect their citizens from riots. The *Monroe* Court reasoned that if Congress in 1871 did not believe it had the constitutional power to enact the Sherman Amendment, it must not have intended to create any type of liability upon a municipality as an entity.

The Supreme Court revisited this issue in Monell v. Department of Social Services (1978). A detailed examination of the legislative history of the Civil Rights Act of 1871 convinced the *Monell* Court that the concerns leading Congress to reject the Sherman Amendment did not apply to the more general question of municipal liability for its own wrongdoing. The Sherman Amendment was seen as an attempt to impose a federal obligation to keep the peace. The legislative debates over the Sherman Amendment are replete with expressions of doubt regarding Congress' constitutional power to impose a duty on a local government to control the conduct of private citizens. Section 1983 as enacted, however, merely authorized civil liability for a person's own constitutional wrongdoing. The Court concluded that "nothing said in the debate on the Sherman amendment would have prevented holding a municipality liable . . . for its own violations of the Fourteenth Amendment." Furthermore, it was commonly understood in 1871 that corporations, including municipal corporations, should be treated as natural persons for "virtually all purposes of constitutional and statutory analysis," including tort liability. Thus, "the 'usual meaning' of the word 'person' [in 1871] would extend to municipal corporations . . ." The Court held that the history and language of the Civil Rights Act of 1871 "compels the conclusion that Congress did intend municipalities and other local government units to be included among those persons to whom Section 1983 applies."

Monell's ruling that cities are "persons" subject to suit opened the door to municipal liability for certain constitutional violations. That opening was narrowed by the second holding in *Monell*, which pertained to the circumstances under which a city could be deemed responsible for a constitutional violation. To put this portion of *Monell* in perspective, some common law background is helpful. Under well-settled principles of common law, an employer is legally responsible for the wrongs committed by its employees within the scope of their employment. This principle is known as "respondeat superior" or "vicarious liability." Under the rule of respondeat superior, a trucking company is responsible for injuries caused by the negligent driving of its employees. If this principle were to apply to claims brought under 42 U.S.C. § 1983, cities would be responsible for the constitutional violations committed by police officers and other officials in the course of their duties.

The Court in *Monell*, however, held that "a municipality cannot be held liable under § 1983 on a respondeat superior theory." This holding was based in substantial part on the use of the word "causes" in the statute. According to the Court, for a city to cause a constitutional violation it must do more than simply employ the individual wrongdoer. The statutory language "plainly imposes liability on a government that, under color of some official policy, 'causes' an employee to violate another's constitutional right." Moreover, the Court viewed the Congressional rejection of the Sherman Amendment as a tacit rejection of all forms of vicarious liability. It reasoned that the adoption of a federal rule of respondeat superior "would have raised all the constitutional problems" that led to the rejection of the Sherman Amendment. Thus, the rejection of the Sherman Amendment was also a rejection of respondeat superior. The Court concluded:

> a local government may not be sued under § 1983 for an injury inflicted solely by its employees or agents. Instead, it is when execution of a government's policy or custom, whether

by its lawmakers or those whose edicts or acts may fairly be said to represent official policy, inflicts the injury that the government as an entity is responsible under § 1983.

Monell established two fundamental principles. First, local governments are "persons" subject to suit under § 1983. Second, to establish liability, the plaintiff must prove that some official policy or custom of the local government caused the constitutional violation. What is "official policy or custom" and when does it "cause" someone to violate another's constitutional rights? These are the questions that have produced a sizable and confusing body of law. Before addressing the "policy or custom" cases in detail, we describe immunities that are or are not available to local governments. An understanding of the scope of immunities available to local governments helps explain the strategic importance of determining what constitutes a city's policy or custom and when a policy or custom can be said to cause a violation of constitutional rights.

Immunity of Local Governments

Before *Monell,* suits seeking recovery of damages for violations of constitutional rights were brought exclusively against individual government officials. Part of the law that had developed in this context was a defense of qualified immunity. The evolution and parameters of various immunities are discussed in the sections entitled "Absolute Immunity" and "Qualified Immunity." At the time *Monell* was decided, an individual government official who acted in good faith and with reasonable grounds was immune from liability for compensatory damages even if his or her conduct was later found to have violated the constitutional rights of the plaintiff (Scheuer v. Rhodes, 1974). An important question raised after *Monell* was whether a local government was also protected by qualified immunity.

The Supreme Court addressed the issue of immunity for local governments in Owen v. City of Independence (1980). George Owen was dismissed from his position as chief of police following an investigation of alleged improper administration of the police property room. At a city council meeting, a councilman publicly charged that Owen "had misappropriated Police Department property for his own use, that narcotics and money had 'mysteriously disappeared' from his office, that traffic tickets had been manipulated, that high-ranking police officials had made 'inappropriate' requests affecting the police court, and that 'things have occurred causing the unusual release of felons.'" The city council then passed a resolution directing the city manager to "take all direct and appropriate action" against those persons "involved in illegal, wrongful, or gross inefficient activities brought out in the investigative report." Chief Owen was dismissed the next day without a notice of reasons or an opportunity to refute the allegations made at the city council meeting. Owen then sued, claiming that the city's actions violated his substantive and procedural due process rights under the Fourteenth Amendment.

Two months after Owen's termination the Supreme Court decided two cases, Board of Regents v. Roth (1972) and Perry v. Sindermann (1972), that recognized a constitutional right under the Due Process Clause of the Fourteenth Amendment to a "name-clearing hearing for a government employee stigmatized in the course of his discharge." Since *Roth* and *Perry* were decided after Owen's discharge, city officials could not have been aware of Owen's constitutional right to a name-clearing hearing at the time he was fired. Consequently, the city argued, under the rules of qualified immunity the city should not be subject to liability for compensatory damages.

A bare majority of a sharply divided Supreme Court rejected this argument and held that "municipalities have no immunity from damages liability flowing from their constitutional violations. . . ." The majority relied on traditional historical materials and a surprisingly candid assessment of contemporary tort policy to support this holding. With regard to the historical materials, the Court observed that cities were not afforded a "good faith" immunity at common law at the time Congress enacted the Civil Rights Act of 1871 (the statute that has since been codified as 42 U.S.C. § 1983 and is commonly referred to simply as "§1983"). Nor is there any mention of such an immunity in the debates and legislative history of the Civil Rights Act of 1871. Finally, the Court noted that such common law immunities that were recognized in 1871 would not have applied to the circumstances surrounding the firing of Chief Owen.

The Court's consideration of public policy focused on vindication, deterrence, and fairness. With regard to vindication, the Court observed that a "damages remedy against the offending party is a vital component of any scheme for vindicating cherished constitutional guarantees, and the importance of assuring its efficacy is only accentuated when the wrongdoer is the institution that has been established to protect the very rights it has transgressed." With regard to deterrence, the Court opined that the "knowledge that a municipality will be liable for all of its injurious conduct, whether committed in good faith or not, should create an incentive for officials who may harbor doubts about the lawfulness of their intended actions to err on the side of protecting citizens' constitutional rights." Individual government officials would not be overdeterred in their discharge of public responsibilities because "the damage award comes not from the official's pocket, but from the public treasury." Finally, the rejection of qualified immunity for cities was considered just because "it is fairer to allocate any resulting financial loss to the inevitable costs of government borne by all the taxpayers, than to allow its impact to be felt solely by those whose rights, albeit newly recognized, have been violated."

This last quotation reflects a view of fairness that incorporates principles of cost internalization frequently found in regimes of enterprise liability. Proponents of enterprise liability maintain that it is fair to allocate the injury costs caused by an enterprise's activities to the enterprise. These injury costs would then be internalized and reflected in prices of goods and services provided by the enterprise. Thus, the injury costs associated with an enterprise's activities would ultimately be born by those who benefit from those activities.[41] In the context of remedies for constitutional violations, the enterprise is the local government, the injury costs are damages caused by the violation of constitutional rights, and most of the city's revenue comes from taxes. In the view of the *Owen* majority, the cost of governing should include compensating persons whose constitutional rights are violated by governmental policy or custom even when individual officials act in good faith. These costs would be spread through taxation among the public, who presumably benefit from aggressive policing and other acts of government.

When viewed in conjunction with other legal doctrines that recognized a defense of qualified immunity for individual government officials, along with the *Monell* requirement of an "official policy or custom," the rejection of qualified immunity for local governments was seen by the majority as creating a body of law that appropriately balanced the competing interests of victims, government officials, and governments. The majority explained the application of these rules:

> The innocent individual who is harmed by an abuse of governmental authority is assured that he will be compensated for his injury. The offending official, so long as he conducts himself in good faith, may go about his business secure in the knowledge that a qualified immunity defense will protect him from personal liability for damages. . . . And the public will be forced to bear only the costs of injury inflicted by the "execution of a government's policy or custom, whether made by its lawmakers or by those whose edicts or acts may fairly be said to represent official policy."

The four dissenting justices, in an opinion authored by Justice Powell, disagreed both with the majority's reading of history and with its assessment of public policy. The dissenters noted that municipal immunity in the nineteenth century was far more widespread than the majority opinion would suggest and that forty-four states and the District of Columbia currently recognize a "municipal immunity at least analogous to a 'good faith' defense against liability for constitutional torts." Moreover, the dissenters feared that government officials would be overdeterred by the rejection of a good faith immunity. "If officials must look over their shoulders at strict municipal liability for unknowable constitutional deprivations, the resulting degree of governmental paralysis will be little different from that caused by fear of personal liability." In their view, "basic fairness requires a qualified immunity for municipalities." Many local governments "lack the resources to withstand substantial unanticipated liability under [§] 1983" and thus will be unable to "spread the costs of any judgment across the local population. . . . By simply applying the theorems of welfare economics and ignoring the reality of municipal finance, the Court imposes strict liability on the level of government least able to bear it."

Despite the narrow margin of the majority and the blistering attack by the dissenting justices and some academic commentators,[42] *Owen* remains good law today. Cities and other local governments are not protected by the doctrine of qualified immunity that applies to claims against individual governmental officials. Thus, cities may be held liable for compensatory damages when their official policies or customs bring about a violation of a constitutional right, even if their officers and employees act in good faith.

While local governments are denied a defense available to individual defendants regarding compensatory damages, they receive greater protection from punitive damages. As discussed in detail in the section entitled "Punitive Damages: Newport v. Fact Concerts and Smith v. Wade," punitive damages are designed to punish and deter aggravated wrongdoing. Prior to *Monell* and *Owen*, lower courts had awarded punitive damages against individual government officials who flagrantly violated the constitutional rights of the plaintiff. A year after *Owen* was decided, the Supreme Court ruled in City of Newport v. Fact Concerts, Inc. (1981) that, unlike individual officials, local governments could not be held liable for punitive damages. As in *Owen*, the Court justified this result by looking at nineteenth-century common law, legislative history, and public policy. The Court found that at the time Congress enacted §1983 cities were largely immune from liability for punitive damages under common law. Moreover, there was nothing in the legislative history of § 1983 indicating that Congress intended to depart from this well-established common law background. Finally, as a matter of policy, the Court found that potential liability for compensatory damages provided local governments with sufficient incentives to avoid policies that could lead to the deprivation of constitutional rights. Punitive damage awards against individual officials provided additional deterrence. The Court also expressed its concern that a different result would create serious risks to the financial stability of local governments by exposing them to unpredictable punitive damage awards at the hands of juries.

The different scope of immunities and defenses afforded individual defendants and local governments produces certain strategic or tactical incentives. Suits against individual officials are subject to a defense of qualified immunity but can produce an award of punitive damages if the underlying conduct is sufficiently egregious. Cities are insulated from liability for punitive damages but do not have the benefit of qualified immunity with regard to compensatory damages. This latter point is especially important. Because the city does not have a defense that is available to individual officials, there is a powerful incentive for plaintiffs to attempt to establish municipal liability for compensatory damages. If the plaintiff can establish that some official policy or custom of the city caused the alleged deprivation of constitutional rights, he or she can recover compensatory damages from the city without regard to immunity. This tactical incentive helps explain the importance of determining the standards by which official policy and custom are measured. We now turn to this issue.

Official Policy or Custom

Monell clearly held that a local government cannot be held liable unless the constitutional violation was brought about by an official policy or custom. In the aftermath of *Monell*, courts have struggled with the issue of what constitutes a policy or custom of a government. We organize our discussion of this issue by the following recurring fact patterns: formal policy, acts of "policymakers," inadequate training, inadequate hiring, and custom.

The clearest form of official policy is found in ordinances, regulations, and other types of deliberative formal declarations of governing bodies. The dispute in *Monell* provides a good example of formal official policy. In this case the Board of Education and the Department of Social Services of the City of New York promulgated rules requiring pregnant employees to take unpaid leaves of absence before such leaves were required for medical reasons. The defendants in *Monell* did not dispute that this was the formal policy of those two municipal departments. Mandatory maternity leave was a policy of general application affecting all female employees. Formal official policy also may be found in actions affecting only a single person. In *Owen*, for example, the termination of the police chief and refusal to conduct a name-clearing hearing affected only one person—Chief Owen. Since these actions were taken by the city manager following a formal motion passed by the city council, the majority had no difficulty in finding them to be the official policy of the City of Independence.

Monell also made clear that an official policy can provide the basis for municipal liability only if it causes a violation of the constitutional rights of the plaintiff; it must be "the moving force" behind the constitutional violation. This causal connection is readily apparent in cases such as *Monell* involving ordinances, regulations and other types of formal, deliberative declarations of policy. Once the mandatory maternity leave policy is declared unconstitutional, the causal relationship between that policy violation of the plaintiff's constitutional rights is both direct and obvious. Similarly, there was no disputing the causal connection between the city council's resolution and the city manager's termination of the chief of police in *Owen*.

Municipal ordinances, administrative regulations, and other formal declarations by governing bodies are the least controversial examples of official policy. They are also the least frequently litigated. Far more frequent and controversial are claims discussed in the ensuing paragraphs alleging that municipal policy is reflected in the decisions of individual city officials or employees.

Pembaur v. City of Cincinnati (1986) was one of the first post-*Monell* Supreme Court decisions that spoke to the question of whether a single act of a city official can constitute municipal policy. The *Pembaur* litigation began when two deputy sheriffs in Hamilton County, Ohio, used force to break down a locked door in a medical clinic. The deputies were at the clinic to serve arrest warrants on two clinic employees in order to oblige them to testify at a grand jury proceeding. When the two county deputy sheriffs arrived at the clinic to serve the warrants, Dr. Pembaur locked the door and refused to let them enter. Upon advice of their supervisors, the deputy sheriffs called an assistant prosecuting attorney for the county who, after consulting with his superiors, instructed the deputies to "go in and get" the witnesses. The deputy sheriffs then used an ax to chop down the door. Although two people were detained, the individuals named in the warrants were not found on the premises. Dr. Pembaur later filed an action against several defendants, including Hamilton County, claiming that the forcible entry violated his rights under the Fourth Amendment to be free from unreasonable searches and seizures.

Four years after the incident, the Supreme Court held that, absent exigent circumstances, the police cannot enter a person's home or business without a search warrant to execute an arrest warrant for a third person (Steagald v. United States, 1981). In other words, the police must have both an arrest warrant authorizing the seizure of the third person and a search warrant to enter the premises of another to look for the person named in the arrest warrant. Since the deputy sheriffs did not have a search warrant, the forced entry into Dr. Pembaur's clinic was unconstitutional under *Steagald. Monell* would authorize holding the county liable for the violation of Dr. Pembaur's Fourth Amendment rights if the forcible entry was made pursuant to official county policy. Under *Owen*, the county would not be protected by qualified immunity even though this constitutional right had not been clearly established at the time of the forced entry. Thus, the central question in *Pembaur* became whether the instructions of the assistant prosecuting attorney to the deputy sheriffs to "go in and get" the witnesses was official county policy within the meaning of *Monell*.

Pembaur produced five separate opinions, none of which received the support of a majority of the Court in its entirety. Nonetheless, several key principles emerge from the various opinions. One point upon which a majority of the justices did agree was that "municipal liability may be imposed for a single decision by municipal policymakers under appropriate circumstances." Thus, *Pembaur* held that single acts can constitute official policy under *Monell*. In an opinion authored by Justice Brennan, four justices (a plurality of the nine justices on the Court) endorsed other guidelines. According to the plurality, municipal liability may result when the action in question was the result of a decision of an official who possesses "final authority to establish municipal policy with respect to the action taken." Moreover, "whether an official had final policymaking authority is a question of state law." Since the lower courts had found and the parties did not dispute that the assistant prosecuting attorney had authority under Ohio law to establish county policy regarding the execution of warrants, the unconstitutional entry of Dr. Pembaur's clinic was deemed to have been made pursuant to county policy.

Three justices concurred in this result but did not join in the reasoning of the plurality opinion. Justice White agreed with the plurality's conclusion that the forcible entry was made pursuant to county policy. However, his reasoning was less sweeping than that of Justice Brennan. The key point, according to Justice White, was the lack of a constitutional or statutory prohibition on warrantless forcible entries at the time of the deputies' action in this case. He expressed doubt that actions taken in violation of "controlling law" could ever be considered official policy. "Had the Sheriff or Prosecutor in this case failed to follow an existing warrant requirement, it would be absurd to say that he was nevertheless executing county policy in authorizing the forceful entry. . . ." Justice O'Connor agreed with Justice White on this point and cautioned that some of the standards suggested in the Brennan plurality opinion "may be misread to expose municipalities to liability beyond that envisioned by the Court in *Monell*." Justice Stevens, writing separately, reiterated his view that the "broad remedial purpose of [§ 1983] and the fact that it embodied contemporaneous common-law doctrine, including *respondeat superior*, require a conclusion that Congress intended that a governmental entity be liable for the constitutional deprivations committed by its agents in the course of their duties." In other words, Justice Stevens just disagrees with the "official policy" ruling in *Monell*.

Justice Powell, in an opinion joined by Chief Justice Burger and Justice Rehnquist, dissented and offered a more narrow and formal view of the official policy requirement of *Monell*. In Justice Powell's view, official policy could not be found in "a brief response to a single question over the telephone." Rather, a court must look to "the nature of the decision reached" and "the process by which the decision was reached or the action was taken." Under this approach, "most policies embody a rule of general applicability" rather than ad hoc decisions. Moreover, an important "factor indicating that policy has been formed is the process by which the decision at issue was reached. Formal procedures that involve, for example, voting by elected officials, prepared reports, extended deliberation, or official records indicate that the resulting decisions taken 'may fairly be said to represent official policy.'" Under these standards, the telephoned instruction to "go in and get" the witnesses could not be said to be official county policy.

The many opinions in *Pembaur* suggest that the Court had not yet gotten very far in reaching even a partial consensus as to the content of "official policy." The Court's next effort to explicate what is official policy came in City of St. Louis v. Praprotnik (1988). Praprotnik sued the City of St. Louis, claiming that he was transferred to a less desirable position and ultimately was laid off in retaliation for exercising his First Amendment right to appeal a previous workplace suspension. Many of the adverse employment actions were initiated by Praprotnik's supervisor. Praprotnik had then appealed to the city's Civil Service Commission. In two separate opinions, neither of which commanded the support of a majority of the Court, seven justices agreed with the general conclusion that the city could not be held liable, even assuming that Praprotnik's First Amendment rights were violated.

Justice O'Connor, writing for four conservative justices, analyzed the issue of municipal liability through the formal lens of state law. Relying on what she described as the "guiding principles" from the *Pembaur* plurality opinion, Justice

O'Connor focused on the question of which officials had "final policymaking authority." Her opinion began "by reiterating that the identification of policy making officials is a question of state law." This "is not a question of federal law, and it is not a question of fact in the usual sense." That is, identifying who is a final policymaker is a task for the trial judge looking at state law. Under state law (including municipal ordinances), the only entities authorized to make employment policy for the City of St. Louis were the mayor, the aldermen, and the civil service commission. "The Mayor and Aldermen enacted no ordinance designed to retaliate against [Praprotnik] or against similarly situated employees . . . and the Civil Service Commission never so much as hinted that retaliatory transfers or layoffs were permissible." Consequently, the dissenting Justices would have ruled that the adverse actions taken against Praprotnik could not be said to reflect the official city policy.

Justice Brennan, in an opinion joined by two other liberal justices, concurred in the judgment but labeled Justice O'Connor's reasoning as "both unduly narrow and unrealistic." According to Justice Brennan, state law is only "an appropriate starting point" in determining who is a final policymaker for a city. To look exclusively at the city charter and municipal ordinances would "turn a blind eye to reality." The focus should be on "the realities of municipal decision making, and any assessment of a municipality's actual power structure is necessarily a factual and practical one." Consequently, the "identification of municipal policymakers is an essentially factual determination 'in the usual sense' and is therefore rightly entrusted to a properly instructed jury." These justices were clearly concerned that under the plurality's approach, a city could insulate itself from liability by constructing a formal facade of administrative review of employment decisions when de facto policymaking power rested with lower level supervisors. They concurred in the judgment, however, because the record did not show that Praprotnik's supervisor "possessed any policymaking authority with respect to lateral transfers."

Justice Stevens was the only justice who would allow Praprotnik to recover from the city and his opinion focused on the rank of the city officials in question. If the officials who took retaliatory actions against Praprotnik were sufficiently high ranking, then their actions can be said to constitute city policy. In his view, the evidence supported a finding that "top officials in the city administration" took retaliatory actions against Praprotnik because he testified truthfully in official proceedings. Justice Stevens concluded that a city should be accountable "when many of its high officials . . . cooperate to retaliate against a whistleblower for the exercise of his First Amendment rights."

By piecing together the votes of the various justices in *Pembaur* and *Praprotnik*, a majority of the Court had come to agree that municipal liability could be based on the single acts of "final policymakers" and that the Court should look to state law to determine who had final decision-making authority on a given subject. What was not clear was just how rigid or flexible this state law inquiry was to be.

More light was shed on this issue in Jett v. Dallas Independent School District (1989). *Jett* dealt primarily with the issue of whether the official policy requirement first articulated in *Monell* would also apply to claims brought against a local government under a different civil rights statute. In the course of ruling that the official policy requirement did apply to municipal liability under other civil rights statutes, a majority of the Court articulated the general principles of municipal liability:

"whether a particular official has 'final policymaking authority' is a question of state law". . . . As with other questions of state law relevant to the application of federal law, the identification of those officials whose decisions represent the official policy of the local governmental unit is itself a legal question to be resolved by the trial judge before the case is submitted to the jury. . . . Once those officials who have the power to make official policy on a particular issue have been identified [by the judge], it is for the jury to determine whether their decisions have caused the deprivation of rights at issue by policies which affirmatively command that it occur . . . or by acquiescence in a long standing practice which constitutes the "standard operating procedure" of the local governmental entity.

What is significant about *Jett* is that a majority of the Court has made it clear that state law governs the "who is a final policymaker" issue. At the same time, the references to "longstanding practice," "custom," and "standard operating procedure" indicate that trial courts should look to more than formal municipal ordinances, codes, and organizational charts in determining where final policymaking authority resides.[43]

As is the case with formal declarations of municipal policy, the issue of causation is often undisputed in final policymaker cases. In cases such as *Pembaur*, the primary contested issue is whether the person who made the decision or issued the order was the final policymaker for the local government. If the decision itself is unconstitutional and the person who made the decision is a final policymaker, the causal connection between the decision and the constitutional violation is clear. In *Pembaur*, for example, once the Court concluded that (a) the forcible entry without a search warrant violated the Fourth Amendment, (b) the assistant prosecuting attorney was a final policymaker for the county under state law, and (c) the assistant prosecuting attorney instructed the deputy sheriffs to enter the premises without a search warrant, the causal connection between the county's policy and the violation of the plaintiff's constitutional rights is apparent. There may be instances in which the parties agree that someone is a policymaker, but they disagree as to the level of government for which that person acts. Such was the case in McMillian v. Monroe County (1997). Walter McMillian had been convicted of murder and sentenced to death; after serving six years in prison, McMillian's conviction was reversed on the grounds that various law enforcement officials, including Sheriff Tate of Monroe County, Alabama, suppressed exculpatory evidence in violation of his rights under the Sixth Amendment. McMillian sued Monroe County under the theory that Sheriff Tate was the final policymaker for the county on issues of law enforcement and his conduct represented county policy. The parties agreed that the sheriff was a policymaker for purposes of § 1983 but disagreed about whether he was a policymaker for the county or the state. (If the latter, the issue of governmental liability would be resolved by the doctrine on state sovereign immunity discussed in the section entitled "Suits Against a State.") A sharply divided Supreme Court held that under Alabama law Sheriff Tate was a policymaker for the state and, consequently, the county was not liable for his actions.

The majority opinion relied on a provision of the Alabama Constitution that listed sheriffs as members of the state's executive department. The inclusion of sheriffs within the state's executive department was brought about by a post–Civil War amendment to the Alabama Constitution. It was ratified at a time when local sheriffs were perceived as not protecting African-American citizens from terrorist activity and greater accountability to the state for law enforcement activity was needed. The majority also cited an opinion of the Alabama Supreme Court holding that sheriffs were state officials for purposes of tort liability, as well as various statutory provisions regarding the relationship between the sheriff and other state and local officials.

The four dissenting justices emphasized that under Alabama law the sheriff is paid by the county, receives equipment and supplies from the county, is elected locally by voters in the county, and has law enforcement authority limited to the geographic borders of the county. They also cited numerous provisions of the Alabama code that list the sheriff as a "county officer" or "county employee" for various purposes. The dissent concluded that "[a] sheriff locally elected, paid, and equipped, who autonomously sets and implements law enforcement policies operative within the geographic confines of a county, is ordinarily just what he seems to be: a county official."

The immediate impact of the Court's ruling was to determine who could and could not be held liable for the deprivation of McMillian's constitutional rights. Since Sheriff Tate was not a county official for these purposes, the county could not be held liable. Nor could McMillian secure compensation from the state, because states are not subject to suit under § 1983. His sole recourse would lie, if at all, against Sheriff Tate individually, subject to the defense of qualified immunity.

On a broader level, *McMillian* illustrates the vagueness of the doctrine on official policy. It is apparent that litigants and courts must deal with substantial uncertainty and lack of predictability in determining who is a policymaker under state law. As in *McMillian*, it may often happen that state constitutions, code provisions, case law, and local practices do not point clearly in a single direction. Moreover, much may depend on the specific purpose for which the policymaking determination was made. The same official may be a local policymaker for one purpose but not for another. As noted by the dissent in *McMillian*, sheriffs in Alabama had been considered county policymakers for purposes of hiring a jailer (Parker v. Williams, 1989), but were found to be state policymakers for purposes of law enforcement. This is an issue that demands more attention from the Supreme Court.

A different set of issues is presented when municipal liability is based on an alleged policy or custom of inadequate training. This type of case frequently arises in the context of law enforcement and incarceration. The plaintiff has been injured in a scuffle with the police, or while locked up in jail awaiting a criminal trial or serving time for a minor offense. (If he is convicted of a major crime and put in a state prison, the relevant governmental entity is, of course, the state, and the doctrines discussed in the preceeding section entitled "Suits Against the State" will apply. Notably, a § 1983 suit will not be available against the state, because the ruling in Quern v. Jordan (1979) established that the state is not a "person" subject to suit.) He may allege that the city failed to train its police officers in the proper use of force, or failed to train correctional personnel in providing medical care to inmates. In each of these instances, the plaintiff is attempting to hold a city responsible for the unconstitutional acts of employees who admittedly are not final policymakers under state law. Thus, the purported basis for municipal liability cannot stand on cases like *Pembaur* and *Praprotnik*. Rather, municipal liability is based on an alleged policy of inadequate training practices.

The Supreme Court recognized that a city could be held liable for a "failure to train" in City of Canton v. Harris (1989). In this case the plaintiff, Mrs. Harris, was arrested and taken to jail. Although she was incoherent and twice fell to the floor during her incarceration, Mrs. Harris did not receive any medical attention. Upon her release, Mrs. Harris' family arranged for her to be taken to a nearby hospital where she was diagnosed as suffering from several emotional ailments. The evidence established that pursuant to a municipal regulation, "shift commanders [at the jail] were authorized to determine, in their sole discretion, whether a detainee required medical care." Moreover, shift commanders "were not provided with any special training (beyond first-aid training)" to make such a determination. Mrs. Harris brought suit against the City of Canton, alleging that the municipal policy of inadequate training of shift commanders caused a violation of her constitutional right to medical care.

All nine justices agreed that "there are limited circumstances in which an allegation of a 'failure to train' can be the basis for liability under § 1983." The plaintiff's burden in such cases is to prove that "the failure to train amounts to deliberate indifference to the rights of persons with whom the police come into contact." This standard would be met when, "in light of the duties assigned to specific officers or employees the need for more or different training is so obvious, and the inadequacy so likely to result in the violation of constitutional rights, that the policymakers of the city can reasonably be said to have been deliberately indifferent to the need . . . [T]he focus must be on adequacy of the training program in relation to the tasks the particular officer must perform."

The phrase "deliberate indifference" has been used by the Court on several occasions to describe the level of culpability needed to support recovery for a constitutional violation. That phrase is potentially confusing because the Court has given it different meanings in various contexts. For example, in Farmer v. Brennan (1994) the issue was whether failure to protect a prisoner from sexual assault by other prisoners was a form of cruel or unusual punishment forbidden by the Eighth Amendment. The Court held that a plaintiff must prove a prison official disregarded "actual knowledge" of an excessive risk to inmate safety or health to establish "deliberate indifference" in that context. The *Farmer* Court acknowledged that a different analysis was required under *City of Canton*. To establish municipal liability for a failure to train, the plaintiff can establish deliberate indifference with evidence that city leaders disregarded obvious needs (whether or not the officers knew of those needs). One way to separate the two uses of deliberate indifference is by distinguishing between "objective" and "subjective" legal standards. An objective test is one that holds the actor to a standard that is external to his own perceptions and thoughts, whereas a subjective one focuses on what this actor really knew. Thus, deliberate indifference is an objective standard of culpability with regard to municipal liability under *City of Canton*, but is a subjective standard of culpability with regard to individual liability for certain violations of the Eighth Amendment under *Farmer*.

The Court in *City of Canton* stated in a footnote that the "deliberate indifference" standard needed to support a claim based on alleged inadequate training was independent from the state-of-mind requirement needed to establish the underlying constitutional violation. Thus, failure to train claims require proof of two distinct types of culpability: one involving the state of mind of the individual official and the other involving the municipality. First, the plaintiff must prove that the individual official acted with a sufficiently culpable state of mind to establish a violation of a constitutional right. As discussed in detail in the section entitled "State of Mind," the state of mind necessary to establish a constitutional violation varies with the particular constitutional right in question. Second, the plaintiff must prove that the city's training policies were so deficient as to evidence deliberate indifference to the likelihood that the employee would violate those rights. For example, suppose a jailor uses force in dealing with a prisoner at a city jail. The victim sues the city that employs the officer, claiming that he was inadequately trained. First, the plaintiff must show that the officer acted recklessly (i.e., with subjective fault) in order to make out an Eighth Amendment violation under Whitley v. Albers. (See the section entitled "Abuse of Power and the 'Shocks the Conscience' Test.") Second, in order to meet the "official policy" test, he must show that city officials were, in their training practices and under the objective standard of *City of Canton*, deliberately indifferent to the risk that such incidents may occur. Or suppose a city police officer uses force in arresting a suspect. The first prong of the case then requires the plaintiff to prove that the officer acted unreasonably under the objective test of Graham v. Connor (1989). (See the section entitled "Unreasonable Searches and Seizures and the Fouth Amendment.") The second prong is, of course, the same as in the previous example.

City of Canton is an important decision. From the plaintiff's perspective, the decision provides a blueprint for potential municipal liability for the unconstitutional acts of lower-level employees that does not involve the factually and legally complex search for personal responsibility of a final policymaker. For the same reason, local governments fear that a loosely applied "failure to train" claim could produce de facto *respondeat superior* liability in violation of the spirit, if not the letter, of *Monell.*

The Court in *City of Canton* also stressed that there must be a close causal connection between the inadequate training and the underlying violation of the plaintiff's constitutional rights. "[T]he identified deficiency in the city's training program must be closely related to the ultimate injury." Specifically, Mrs. Harris must prove "that the deficiency in training actually caused the police officers' indifference to her medical needs." The Court framed the causal inquiry in terms of a variation of the common law "but-for" test discussed in the section entitled "Cause in Fact." It is not enough to for the plaintiff to prove that a constitutional injury might have been avoided had the city employed a better training program. Rather, the plaintiff must prove that "the injury would have been avoided had the employee been trained under a program that was not deficient in the identified respect." In other words, the plaintiff must prove that her constitutional rights would not have been violated if the city had an adequate training program. If this officer would have committed the violation in any event, no matter how well trained, the plaintiff cannot win. The Court recognized that predicting "how a hypothetically well-trained officer would have acted under the circumstances may not be an easy task," but expressed confidence that the "judge and jury, doing their respective jobs, will be up to the task."

One other aspect of the causation issue merits brief mention. In City of Los Angeles v. Heller (1985), the Court held that a city cannot be held liable for compensatory damages for allegedly deficient policies unless they lead to a violation of constitutional rights. *Heller* involved a claim brought against the city and two police officers for an allegedly illegal arrest and use of excessive force. The claims against one of the police officers was dismissed prior to trial, while the claims against the second officer were submitted to a jury. The jury was instructed that the plaintiff was entitled to recovery if he was arrested without probable cause or with unreasonable force. The jury decided in favor of the police officer. Notwithstanding this verdict, the plaintiff sought to recover damages from the city on the grounds that its policies authorized the use of excessive force. The Court held that the claim against the city must also be dismissed because, given the jury's verdict in favor of the police officer, the plaintiff suffered "no constitutional injury." At any rate, none had been established. If the plaintiff "has suffered no constitutional injury at the hands of the individual police officer, the fact that the departmental regulations might have authorized the use of constitutionally excessive force is quite beyond the point." *Heller* makes clear that local government liability must be premised on a constitutional violation by someone. It is not enough to prove that a city's training policy is so flawed as to meet *City of Canton's* standard of deliberate indifference. The plaintiff wins only if the flawed policy caused the official to violate the plaintiff's constitutional rights.

The Court addressed potential municipal liability for allegedly inadequate hiring policies in Board of County Commissioners of Bryan County v. Brown (1997). In *Bryan County* a jury found that Brown suffered serious injuries when a sheriff's deputy, Burns, used excessive force while arresting her without probable cause; Brown sought to hold Bryan County responsible for her injuries under theories of inadequate hiring and training policies. The county stipulated that Sheriff Moore was the policymaker for Bryan County regarding the Sheriff's Department. Deputy Burns was the 21-year-old son of Sheriff Moore's nephew. Burns had a history driving infractions and had pled guilty to various misdemeanors, including assault and battery, resisting arrest, and public drunkenness within sixteen months of having been hired as a deputy sheriff. A jury found that the hiring and training policies of Bryan County "as instituted by its policymaker, B.J. Moore, were so inadequate as to amount to deliberate indifference to the constitutional needs of the Plaintiff."

In a decision that addressed only the allegation of inadequate hiring practices, a bare majority of a sharply divided Supreme Court held that the evidence was insufficient to hold the county responsible for the unconstitutional acts of the deputy. Identifying the precise rationale for this outcome is a true challenge. As one commentator put it, "[t]o say that *Brown* is not a model of clarity would be a model of understatement."[44] The majority, in an opinion written by Justice O'Connor, "assumed" that Sheriff Moore's assessment of Burns' background was "inadequate." It also "assum[ed] without deciding that proof of a single instance of inadequate screening could ever trigger municipal liability. . . ." Nonetheless, it concluded that "the evidence in this case was insufficient to support a finding that, in hiring Burns, Sheriff Moore disregarded a known or obvious risk of injury."

The majority emphasized that "rigorous standards of culpability and causation must be applied to ensure that the municipality is not held liable solely for the actions of its employees." Those "rigorous standards" were not met in this case, according to the majority, because there was "no pattern of injuries linked to Sheriff Moore's hiring practices." The sole instance of inadequate screening pertained to the hiring of Deputy Burns. "The only evidence on this point at trial suggested that Sheriff Moore had adequately screened the backgrounds of all prior deputies hired." Moreover, Burns' criminal record did not disqualify him from serving as a deputy sheriff under Oklahoma law. Nor was there any evidence that the county (acting through its commissioners or the Sheriff) directed or authorized the use of excessive force. Moreover, the majority found that Burns' criminal record would not "necessarily" make "Burns' use of excessive force . . . a plain and obvious risk of the hiring decision."

The majority distinguished *City of Canton* by arguing that it is more predictable that improper training will lead to subsequent deprivations of constitutional rights than it is that inadequate screening of potential employees will do so. As stated by the majority,

> [P]rediciting the consequence of a single hiring decision . . . is far more difficult than predicting what might flow from the failure to train a single law enforcement officer as to a specific skill necessary to discharge his duties. . . . Unlike the risk from a particular glaring omission in a training regimen, the risk from a single instance of inadequate screening of an applicant's background is not "obvious" in the abstract; rather it depends upon the background of the applicant.

In other words, there is a "high degree of predictability" that an improperly trained city employee will violate the constitutional rights of others while deficient screening creates only a "generalized . . . risk."

Causation

The Court in *Bryan County* also emphasized the importance of causation. Brown's claimed failed, in part, because a majority of the Court found insufficient evidence to link the hiring decision to the constitutional injury. It was not enough to argue that if Deputy Burns had not been hired he would not have been in a position to use excessive force in arresting Brown. Such a generalized formulation "pose[s] the greatest risk that a municipality will be held liable for an injury that it did not cause." The causal inquiry is more particularized. As framed by the Court, the question of causation was whether a proper screening of Burns' application "reveals that Sheriff Moore should have concluded that Burns' use of excessive force would be a plainly obvious consequence of the hiring decision." Without adherence to "rigorous requirements of culpability and causation, municipal liability collapses into *respondeat superior* liability."

Four justices dissented in two separate opinions. Justices Souter, Stevens, and Breyer believed the findings of the jury supported liability under *Monell* and *City of Canton*. "Under this prior law, Sheriff Moore's failure to screen out his 21-year-old great-nephew Burns on the basis of his criminal record, and the decision instead to authorize Burns to act as a deputy sheriff, constitutes a policy choice attributable to Bryan County . . . ." This dissenting opinion characterizes the majority opinion as creating a new "high threshold" standard of "plainly obvious consequence of a particular injury" that goes "a step further" than required by prior cases.

Justice Breyer, writing for himself and Justices Stevens and Ginsberg, stated that *Bryan County* illustrates the increasing difficulty of trying "to apply *Monell*'s basic distinction between liability that rests upon policy and liability that is vicarious." Efforts to articulate standards for formal policy, final policymakers, and distinctions between training and hiring have "generated a body of interpretive law so complex that the law has become difficult to apply." According to these justices, it is time to "reexamine the legal soundness" of the "basic distinction" in *Monell* between constitutional violations caused by municipal policy and principles of *respondeat superior*.

Taken together, *City of Canton* and *Bryan County* reflect the continuing disagreement among the justices about the appropriate scope of the liability of local governments for constitutional violations committed by lower-level officials. *City of Canton* marked a potential expansion of municipal liability by recognizing that inadequate training could be considered a municipal policy. Many constitutional violations might be traced in some manner to the training the offending employee received. *Bryan County*, on the other hand, sends a signal that lower courts should not routinely submit "failure to" claims to juries; the jury, trial judge, and court of appeals in the case had ruled for the plaintiff. By vacating the judgment for the plaintiff, the Supreme Court warns lower courts that they must carefully consider whether a single bad decision of a policymaker genuinely reflects governmental policy. At the very least, *Bryan County* suggests that a single improper hiring decision can rarely be found to cause a subsequent constitutional violation. Unless and until a majority of the Court accept Justice Breyer's invitation to "reexamine" *Monell*'s rejection of *respondeat superior*, distinguishing unconstitutional acts that reflect governmental policy from those that do not will likely remain difficult.

Custom

The wording of § 1983 does not limit recovery to people whose constitutional rights are violated by governmental policy. The statute specifically provides a remedy for those whose rights are violated "under color of any . . . custom, or usage" of any state. Despite the express inclusion of the phrase "custom or usage" within the body of the statute, there are surprisingly few cases that address what constitutes a custom that might give rise to governmental liability.

In Adickes v. S.H. Kress (1970), a white civil rights protester sued a Mississippi restaurant for its refusal to serve her lunch while in the company of African-Americans. The restaurant argued it could not be held liable under federal civil rights laws because, as a private entity, it did not act under color of state law. Adickes' legal theory was that her suit could be brought under federal civil rights laws because the store was acting pursuant to a "custom or usage" having force of law. In support of this theory, the plaintiff pointed out that local police officers were present at the time the restaurant refused to serve her. The Supreme Court held that Adickes could prevail if she could prove that she was denied service due to a state-enforced custom of racial segregation in public eating places. In the course of its ruling, the Court explained the importance of custom as follows:

> Congress included customs and usages within its definition of law in § 1983 because of the persistent and widespread discriminatory practices of state officials in some areas of the post-bellum South. . . . Although not authorized by written law, such practices of state officials could well be so permanent and well settled to constitute a "custom or usage" with

the force of law. . . . This interpretation of custom recognizes that settled-practices of state officials may, by imposing sanctions or withholding benefits, transform private predilections into compulsory rules of behavior no less than legislative pronouncements.

Adickes was decided before *Monell* held that local governments were subject to suit under Section 1983. Consequently, *Adickes* did not speak to the question of whether a city could be held liable due to a custom as distinguished from an official policy. *Monell* itself, however, stated that "local governments . . . may be sued for constitutional deprivations visited pursuant to governmental custom even though such a custom has not received formal approval through the body's official decision making channels." Thus, *Monell* recognized that governmental custom may be an independent basis for municipal liability. The *Monell* Court was not pressed to elaborate further, because the mandatory maternity leave challenged in that case was an official city policy.

Remarkably, the Supreme Court has yet to decide a case in which governmental liability was premised on an alleged customary practice. However, lower federal courts have occasionally awarded damages based on a governmental custom. The few cases that exist indicate that to sustain a claim on a theory of governmental custom, the plaintiff must prove that the challenged conduct is widely practiced and tolerated by high-level officials. In Garza v. City of Omaha (1987), for example, the court of appeals ruled that the "evidence was sufficient for the jury to conclude that the discrimination [against Hispanics in employment] was so permanent and well settled as to constitute a custom with the force of law." In Webster v. City of Houston (1982) the court of appeals affirmed a jury verdict in favor of the family of a person shot and killed by a police officer. Liability was premised on a custom of the police to plant a "throw down" weapon near an unarmed suspect who had been shot by police officers so as to justify the shooting. The evidence presented at trial supported findings that, even though this practice had not been affirmatively endorsed by any final policymaker, it was universally used in the police department, widely known to high-ranking police officials, and no actions had ever been taken to discourage it.

Some academic critics suggest that courts should make greater use of "custom" as a way of expanding municipal liability without the complexity and rigidity of current doctrine regarding official policy. Focusing on governmental custom, it is argued, would encourage courts to look more at what governments actually do rather than at what they say they do. This, in turn, would be consistent with the original understanding of § 1983.[45] Although such a shift in legal doctrine is theoretically possible, it remains to be seen whether it will take place.

Supervisory Liability

Civil rights plaintiffs often bring claims against three types of defendants: the individual official who actively violated the plaintiff's constitutional rights, the supervisor of the offending official, and the local government that employed them both. For example, a person who was injured through the use of excessive force by a deputy sheriff may sue the deputy (who inflicted the unconstitutional force), the county (claiming that some official policy or custom of the county was the moving force behind the unconstitutional use of force) and the sheriff individually (claiming the sheriff did not adequately supervise the deputy). The preceding discussion has focused on claims against governments. We now briefly address claims that might be brought against supervisors.

Under the right set of facts, supervisors have been held individually responsible for their subordinate's unconstitutional treatment of the plaintiff. Since this type of claim imposes individual liability, the supervisor may assert any defenses available to individual defendants, including qualified immunity discussed in the section entitled "Qualified Immunity." It is also important to recognize that this type of claim is not based on principles of vicarious liability. The supervisor is held liable because he or she did something wrong—not simply for being in charge of someone else who did something wrong.

The Supreme Court has not fully addressed the issue of when a supervisor may be held liable for constitutional violations inflicted by a subordinate. In Rizzo v. Goode (1976), the Court declined to permit an injunction to be issued against the mayor and other high-ranking officials of the City of Philadelphia to stop alleged police brutality. Among the reasons given why an injunction should not be issued were the broad scope of the relief, the extensive federal court supervision that would be required to enforce such an injunction, the degree of federal intrusion into matters traditionally left to states to regulate, and the absence of any showing of any "personal involvement" by supervisory personnel in the unconstitutional conduct of various police officers. *Monell* later seized upon this last reason and cited *Rizzo* for the proposition that supervisors are not responsible for the unconstitutional acts of their subordinates absent some personal involvement by the supervisor.

The negative implication of this proposition is that supervisors may be responsible for the unconstitutional acts of their subordinates when there is personal involvement on the part of the supervisor and lower federal courts have so held. The standard for imposing liability on a supervisor is often phrased in terms reminiscent of "deliberate indifference." As recently stated the by Court of Appeals for the Seventh Circuit, the supervisor "must know about the [unconstitutional] conduct and facilitate it, approve it, condone it, or turn a blind eye. . . ." (Zentmyer v. Kendall County, 2000) . The First Circuit Court of Appeals articulated the standard as follows: "[T]o impose supervisory liability . . . [the plaintiff] must establish that [the supervisor's] conduct or inaction amounts to 'reckless or callous indifference' of [the plaintiff's] constitutional rights and that an 'affirmative link' existed between the constitutional violation and [the supervisor's] acts or omissions" (Miller v. Kennebec County, 2000).

Conclusion

This section has attempted to explain a complex web of legal doctrine. Claims for money damages may not be asserted against a state but can be made against individual state officials. Local governments are subject to liability if their official policies or customs cause a constitutional violation. Official policy is often found in the acts of policymakers, the identification of whom turns on the intricacies of state law. Claims based on an alleged municipal policy of inadequate training are treated differently from those grounded in an alleged policy of inadequate screening of potential employees. Supervisors may be individually responsible for the unconstitutional acts of their subordinates, but only if the supervisor was personally involved in the offending conduct.

The complexity of these various sets of rules has drawn criticism from academics and members of the Court. Important distinctions depend on fine factual nuances that may be difficult to appreciate in the immediate heat of litigation. What the practicing lawyer and informed citizen must remember is that there are different rules governing claims against individual government officials and claims against governments as entities, different rules governing claims against states and claims against local governments, and different rules governing claims against "street-level" government officials who actively violate the constitutional rights of others (e.g., police officers) and claims against those who supervise the street-level official (e.g., police chiefs).

CAUSATION

To sustain a claim against a defendant, a plaintiff must do more than prove that his or her constitutional rights were violated and that he or she suffered some injury. The plaintiff must also prove a causal link between the defendant's wrongful conduct and the injury. Despite its central place in the law of constitutional torts, the element of causation has received little analytical attention. Courts and commentators have focused more on the substantive aspects of a constitutional tort claim, such as whether a particular arrest was legal or whether certain speech was protected by the First Amendment.

When the issue of causation is directly addressed, the analysis seldom goes beyond a superficial recital of principles that were first developed in the context of common law torts. Thus, the starting point for understanding causation in the constitutional tort context is a brief review of traditional common law principles. We then address the issues that arise in "mixed motive" cases, where one of the reasons for an official's act is constitutionally permissible and another is not. We then discuss the special causation issues that arise when the defendant is a government or a supervisor. Finally, we exam "proximate cause" issues, which involve the scope of liability rather than the existence of a causal connection.

Basic Common Law Principles

Cause in Fact

Causation has a long and rich history in the context of common law torts. Hundreds of law review articles and books explore the nuances of causation in tort. The orthodox approach divides causation into two separate inquires: cause in fact and proximate cause. "Cause in fact" refers to a threshold factual connection between a defendant's conduct and the plaintiff's injury. Common law courts will find a causal connection between conduct and injury if the conduct was a necessary condition for the injury to occur.[46] In other words, conduct is the cause in fact of an injury if the injury would not have occurred without the conduct. The converse, of course, is that conduct is not the factual cause of an injury that would have occurred even in the absence of the conduct. For example, speeding can be considered a cause in fact of an automobile accident if the accident would not have occurred had the defendant been driving within the speed limit. Conversely, the defendant's speeding will not be considered a cause in fact of an accident that would have occurred even if the defendant had been driving within the speed limit. This test of causality if often referred to as the "but-for" test.[47]

An alternative common law approach to cause in fact is referred to as the "substantial factor" test.[48] Under this approach, conduct can be considered a cause in fact of an injury if it was a substantial factor in bringing about the harm. Something can be considered a substantial factor even if it does not meet the but-for test of causation. The substantial factor test was adopted by common law courts to rectify limitations of the but-for test in cases involving multiple, independently sufficient causal forces. The but-for test proves to be problematic in cases in which there is more than one causal force in operation, each of which would have been sufficient by itself to produce the injury. The classic common law example involves merging fires. Assume that two fires merge and the combined fire destroys the plaintiff's property. Also assume that either fire alone would have been sufficient to cause the harm. Finally, assume that one fire was started by the negligence of the defendant and the other started by a bolt of lightning. A strict application of the but-for test under these circumstances would lead to the conclusion that the defendant's negligence was not a cause of the plaintiff's harm, since the property would have burned even in its absence.[49] Courts and commentators thought it was unjust to allow the negligent defendant to avoid liability in such instances. Under the substantial factor test, however, the negligent defendant could not escape liability. Because each fire was independently sufficient to destroy the plaintiff's property, each could be considered a substantial factor in producing the harm, so that the defendant's negligence could be considered the cause in fact of the plaintiff's injury. As explained by one commentator,

> The real policy behind imposing liability in such cases . . . is that wrongdoers should not be permitted to escape the consequences of their wrongful acts. Even a showing that the

result would have occurred just the same through other causes is not enough to overcome this. The policy of the law refuses to recognize the distinction where the other cause was innocent and those where it was wrongful.[50]

The substantial factor test has gained general acceptance throughout the states, especially when two or more defendants contribute to a single harm.[51]

Proximate Cause

Proximate cause issues concern limitations placed on the extent of liability for injuries for which the defendant's negligence was a cause in fact.[52] For example, many common law courts limit the extent of a defendant's liability to the "foreseeable consequences" of a negligent act. If the injury for which the plaintiff seeks compensation is not a foreseeable consequence, the defendant can avoid liability—even if the negligent act was a substantial factor or a but-for cause of the injury. Properly understood, the phrase "proximate cause" is a label used to describe various policy-based limitations on liability that have little to do with causality. Proximate cause is essentially a question of whether, as a matter of policy, legal responsibility for wrongful conduct will extend to the particular consequences that have in fact occurred. The policies that underlie judicial assessments of responsibility are often disguised behind the language of causation.[53]

The remainder of Part I will discuss how these general principles have been invoked and applied in the context of constitutional torts.

Causation and Mixed-Motive Decisions

There are many situations in which the constitutionality of government action depends on the motivation of the official. For example, suppose a government employee is fired from his or her job. If he or she is fired because of inefficiency or insubordination, the termination is perfectly legal. On the other hand, if the employee is fired for engaging in constitutionally protected speech, the termination violates his or her First Amendment rights. The constitutionality of the termination thus depends on the motivation of the supervisor. The case is easy to resolve if only one of the reasons was the actual basis for the termination. But what if both reasons influenced the decision? Under these circumstances can it be said that the employee's constitutional rights have been violated or that his or her engaging in protected speech caused the termination?

Mt. Healthy City School District Board of Education v. Doyle

This precise issue arose in Mt. Healthy City School District Board of Education v. Doyle (1977). Doyle was a nontenured public school teacher whose contract was not renewed by the school district. The school board notified Doyle that he was not being rehired because of "a notable lack of tact in handling professional matters," citing two specific incidents. The first cited incident involved Doyle contacting a local radio station to criticize a proposed dress code for teachers. In the second incident Doyle made an "obscene gesture to two girls in connection with their failure to obey commands made in his capacity as cafeteria supervisor." The lower courts found that Doyle's communication with the radio station "was protected by the First and Fourteenth Amendments" and played a "substantial part" in the board's decision not to renew Doyle's contract. On the strength of these findings, both the District Court and the Court of Appeals concluded that the school board violated Doyle's rights under the First Amendment and that he was entitled to reinstatement and back pay.

The Supreme Court reversed the decision of the lower courts. It accepted the finding that Doyle's communication with the radio station was speech protected by the First Amendment. However, the Court held that Doyle would not be entitled to relief if the school board could prove that he would have been fired anyway, for the constitutionally permissible reasons. The Court adopted a two-part test for causation in mixed-motive cases. First, the plaintiff must show that a constitutionally impermissible motive was a "substantial factor" or a "motivating factor" in the board's decision. Once the plaintiff meets this substantial factor test, the burden of proof shifts to the defendants to show "by a preponderance of evidence that it would have reached the same decision . . . even in the absence of the protected conduct." The Supreme Court remanded the case for a determination of whether Doyle's contract would not have been removed even if he had not contacted the radio station regarding the proposed dress code.

Mt. Healthy adopts a variant of the common law but-for test of causation, differing only in the allocation of the burden of proof. Under *Mt. Healthy*, a defendant will prevail on the grounds of lack of causation if the plaintiff fails to prove that a constitutionally impermissible reason was a substantial factor in the decision to terminate his employment, or if the defendant establishes that the same decision would have been made even if the constitutionally impermissible factor had not been considered. The plaintiff prevails only when there is a finding that absent the constitutionally impermissible motive, the plaintiff would not have been injured.

The Court explained that unless some form of a but-for test were applied, the employee "could [be] in a better position as a result of the exercise of constitutionally protected conduct than he would have occupied had he done nothing at all." In the Court's view, the substantial factor test applied by the lower courts could produce a windfall to Doyle by allowing him to recover for an injury (e.g., job loss) that would have occurred even if the school board had not considered Doyle's exercise of his First Amendment freedoms. The but-for test as articulated by the Court allows government employers to implement independently justified employment decisions.

Criticism of the *Mt. Healthy* Rule

Mt. Healthy has been roundly criticized by academic commentators. One set of criticisms focus on traditional tort policy. Both constitutional and common law torts have as their stated goals the vindication of rights and the deterrence of wrongdoing. Some commentators argue that the but-for test adopted in *Mt. Healthy* achieves less vindication and deterrence than alternative approaches to causation that have been applied in analogous common law tort settings.[54] Recall our earlier discussion that common law courts generally apply the substantial factor test in cases in which multiple causal forces are in operation. Common law courts have concluded that the substantial factor test is superior to the but-for test in vindicating rights and deterring wrongful conduct in situations in which there is more than one sufficient cause of an injury. These critics argue that vindication and deterrence considerations also support the application of the substantial factor test in constitutional tort cases. In the words of one critic,

> The conduct sought to be deterred in *Mt. Healthy* is retaliation by government officials against employees who exercise their First Amendment rights. . . . Surely a school administrator would be less likely to base a termination decision substantially on unconstitutional considerations if that administrator could not avoid liability by pointing to an alternative justification for the decision.[55]

It has also been suggested that the common law of defamation provides an appropriate analogy to mixed-motive decisions.[56] At common law, a defendant is sometimes privileged to make what would otherwise be a defamatory statement so long as the speaker had a legitimate personal or professional interest in making the statement. The privilege does not apply, however, if the speaker is actually motivated by a desire to injure the plaintiff. When the motive of the speaker is disputed, courts instruct the jury to determine which was the "dominant purpose."[57] It has been suggested that the dominant purpose test represents a compromise between the substantial factor test applied by the court of appeals in *Mt. Healthy* and the but-for test adopted by the Supreme Court.[58] If the dominant purpose test were applied to the facts of *Mt. Healthy*, Doyle could not recover simply by establishing that his constitutionally protected speech was a substantial factor in the decision not to rehire him, and the school board could not escape liability by showing that it would have made the same decision even if Doyle had not spoken to the media. The outcome of the case would depend on whether the dominant purpose of the decision was to retaliate against Doyle's exercise of free speech or simply to remove a quarrelsome and unprofessional teacher from the school district.

Other criticisms focus on special features of constitutional tort law and the fragile nature of the First Amendment in particular. These considerations may justify the adoption of causation rules that offer greater protection of constitutional rights than does the but-for test of *Mt. Healthy*. As stated by Professor Wells, "In constitutional tort law, the rights at stake are fundamental liberties. Perhaps the but-for test provides adequate protection for the plaintiff's interests in compensation for personal injury and property damage. It does not follow that the same judgment should be made when constitutional rights are at issue."[59]

Wells argues that a more protective causation standard is especially warranted in public employee free speech cases, such as in *Mt. Healthy.* The Supreme Court has recognized in other contexts that free speech is a "delicate and vulnerable" right that needs special protection to flourish.[60] Under *Mt. Healthy*, the employee who speaks on an issue of public concern always has to worry that the employer may have some other reason sufficient to fire him or her or can convince a jury that there is such a reason. The constitutional values and interests underlying the First Amendment would be better protected by rules of causation other than the but-for test, such as the substantial factor and dominant purpose rules discussed previously.

Finally, other critics have noted the tension between the but-for test of *Mt. Healthy* and other strains of constitutional tort doctrine. Sheldon Nahmod has argued that the *Mt. Healthy* test is inconsistent with the rules pertaining to compensatory damages set forth in Carey v. Piphus (1978). Piphus was a public high school student who was suspected of smoking marijuana and suspended without a hearing. The suspension violated Piphus' right to procedural due process under the Fourteenth Amendment, but the principal argued that Piphus would have been suspended even if a hearing had been held. The Supreme Court addressed the question of what damages Piphus could recover if his due process rights had been violated, but the suspension was ultimately justified. The Court held that although there could be no recovery of "presumed damages," a plaintiff could recover for proven emotional distress caused by the violation of constitutional rights. The Court went further and stated that "we believe that the denial of procedural due process should be actionable for nominal damages without proof of injury." Professor Nahmod maintains that

> [w]hat the Court said about procedural due process violations should apply with at least as much force to First Amendment violations in the employment setting . . . [A]n adverse governmental employment decision . . . tainted by an impermissible First Amendment motivation . . . should constitute a First Amendment violation that caused harm, even apart from the job loss, possibly consisting of emotional distress stemming from the insult to the plaintiff . . . [T]he constitutional violations and resulting harm have occurred in both situations, justifying at least an award of nominal damages and the chance to prove general damages.[61]

Beyond Mixed Motives: Texas v. Lesage

Despite academic criticism, the Court has steadfastly adhered to the *Mt. Healthy* rule. In fact, the Court has extended its application to racial discrimination claims brought under the equal protection clause of the Fourteenth Amendment. In Texas v. Lesage (1999) "an African immigrant of Caucasian descent" who was denied admission into a PhD program at the University of Texas filed suit, challenging the constitutionality of the university's race-conscious admission policy. The university defended on the grounds that even if the school's admissions process had been completely color-blind, Lesage would not have been admitted. Thus, the university made the *Mt Healthy*-like argument that even if the constitutionally impermissible factor had not been considered, the plaintiff would have suffered the same fate. Lesage framed his claims in terms reminiscent of Carey v. Piphus (1978). Lesage contended that his constitutional rights were violated simply by being subjected to different admissions standards. The constitutional injury, according to Lesage, was "the inability to compete on an equal footing." If the principles articulated in *Carey* were applied in this context, Lesage could recover at least nominal damages and perhaps compensatory damages for emotional distress.

The Supreme Court resolved this case by distinguishing between claims for damages and those seeking injunctive relief. With regard to the claim for damages, the Court reaffirmed the "well-established framework" of *Mt. Healthy* and held that "[t]he government can avoid liability by proving that it would have made the same decision without the impermissible motive." The Court suggested that plaintiffs such as Lesage could be entitled to injunctive relief even if they could not recover damages. "Of course, a plaintiff who challenges an ongoing race conscious program and seeks forward-looking relief need not affirmatively establish that he would receive the benefit in question if race were not considered. The relevant injury in such cases is the 'inability to compete on an equal footing.'" The Court did not reach the question of whether such forward-looking relief was justified in this particular case because it appeared that Lesage had abandoned his claim for an injunction.

Lesage thus unequivocally confirms the Court's continued commitment to *Mt. Healthy* as the basic test of causation in constitutional tort claims seeking compensatory damages. Whether plaintiffs allege a violation of free speech or equal protection rights, defendants will prevail if they can establish that the same injury would have resulted even if the constitutionally impermissible factor had not been considered. *Lesage* may also signal, as one commentator has suggested, "that the Court is backing away from the affirmative promise of *Carey* in all section 1983 cases. . . . Read broadly, it suggests that the Court is no longer comfortable with the possibility that civil rights plaintiffs can seek nominal or emotional distress damages when their material situation would be unaffected by a change in government behavior."[62]

Causation and the Liability of Governmental Entities and Supervisors

Recall from our previous discussion that governments are sometimes held liable for the constitutional violations inflicted by their officials, and supervisors may be found individually responsible for the unconstitutional acts of their subordinates.

For example, cities are sometimes held liable for the use of excessive force by their police officers, and sheriffs are sometimes individually liable when their deputies unconstitutionally deny medical care to inmates. But recall also that such claims cannot be based on principles of vicarious liability. The plaintiff must prove that some official policy or custom of the local government was the cause of the constitutional violation or that the supervisor had some personal involvement with the unconstitutional misconduct of his subordinate. The question addressed here is how to determine whether a governmental policy or a lack of proper supervision caused a violation of constitutional rights.

The Easy Cases: Formal, Deliberate Governmental Policy As a Cause of a Violation of Constitutional Rights

In Monell v. Department of Social Services (1978), the Court held that municipalities are subject to suit under § 1983, but they cannot be held liable under principles of *respondeat superior*. That is, a city cannot be held liable simply because it employed the individual police officer or other official who violated the plaintiff's constitutional rights. Causation under *Monell* requires the plaintiff must prove that some official policy or custom of the city was "responsible for" or the "moving force" behind the deprivation of constitutional rights.

Monell's rejection of vicarious liability and its requirement that plaintiffs prove that policy was the moving force behind the violation of constitutional rights injects a potentially difficult causation issue into constitutional tort litigation. The causation issue is difficult for two reasons. First, state courts have long applied principles of vicarious liability to determine municipal liability for common law torts committed by their employees. By rejecting this longstanding framework, *Monell* forces lower courts to develop new principles of causation without the benefit of common law analogies. Second, whether governmental policy caused an individual official to deprive the plaintiff of his or her constitutional rights is a question fraught with uncertainty. The causal connection between policy and conduct requires the fact finder, usually a jury, to determine whether an individual official's conduct would have been different if governmental policy had been different. How sure can we ever be, for example, that better training or supervision would have prevented the use of excessive force by an officer making an arrest? The hypothetical nature of the question produces inherently uncertain answers.[63] The Supreme Court recognized as much in City of Canton v. Harris (1989). There the Court acknowledged that "predicting how a hypothetically well-trained officer would have acted under the circumstances may not be an easy task for the factfinder," but expressed confidence that the "judge and jury, doing their respective jobs, will be adequate to the task."

Despite these difficulties, some general guidelines have emerged. A causal relationship is most readily found in formal, deliberative declarations of policy that are themselves unconstitutional. Examples of formal, deliberative declarations of policy would include municipal ordinances, administrative regulations, or other formal decisions of governmental bodies. For example, the plaintiff in *Monell* challenged the constitutionality of policies promulgated by the board of education and the department of social services compelling pregnant employees to take unpaid leaves of absences before such leaves were required for medical reasons. Once the policy of compulsory unpaid maternity leave is found to be unconstitutional, the causal connection between that policy and the violation of the plaintiff's constitutional rights is apparent.[64] As noted by Professor Kritchevsky, "[w]hen an unconstitutional policy is proved, courts generally assume that the policy alone caused the injury. The courts *assume* that the violation of the plaintiff's constitutional rights occurred because the state actor was following a municipal policy, and not because of any improper personal motive."[65]

Professor Kritchevsky's observation holds even when the "policy" consists of a single, random decision of a final policymaker. Recall from that in Pembaur v. City of Cincinnati (1986), the Court held that a single ad hoc decision of an assistant prosecuting attorney could be considered an official policy of the county. The attorney in question had authorized the forcible entry into the plaintiff's premises without a search warrant, a practice the Court had previously found to be unconstitutional. The causal connection between the policy and the violation of the plaintiff's constitutional rights was deemed established once the Court concluded that the warrantless entry was unconstitutional and had been authorized by a final policymaker for the county.

The More Difficult Cases: Failure to Train and Improper Hiring as Causes of Violations of Constitutional Rights

The Court has demanded more exacting proof of causation in cases based on a government's alleged inadequate training, supervision, or hiring. The Court in *City of Canton* emphasized that there must be a close causal connection between a city's inadequate training and the specific injury suffered by the plaintiff. In that case, the plaintiff did not receive any medical care during her incarceration in a city jail despite being incoherent and having fallen twice. The police were aware of her condition and decided to leave the incoherent Harris lying on the floor of the jail so she would not fall again. Upon her release, Harris was taken to a hospital where she was diagnosed as suffering from several emotional ailments; she later claimed that she was deprived of her constitutional right to receive adequate medical care while confined in jail. Harris sought to hold the city liable under a theory that its failure to properly train the jail's shift commander regarding the medical care of inmates caused the deprivation of her constitutional rights.

The Supreme Court framed the causation question in terms of the common law but-for test previously discussed. The Court stated that it would not be sufficient for the plaintiff to prove that her injury "could have been avoided if an officer had had better" training. Rather, the [plaintiff] must . . . prove that the deficiency in training actually caused the police officers' indifference to her medical needs. Would the injury have been avoided had the employee been trained under a program that was not deficient in the identified respect?" Thus, the plaintiff must identify the specific manner in which the training was inadequate and determine if the outcome would have been different if that particular deficiency had been remedied. In other words, if the shift commander would have failed to summon treatment for Harris even if he had received adequate training, the city's policy could not be said to have caused her injury.[66]

The Court employed what it termed a "rigorous" standard of causation in Bryan County v. Brown, (1997). The plaintiff, Brown, was the victim of the use of excessive force by Deputy Burns, who had been hired by his great uncle, Sheriff Moore. At the time he was hired, Burns had a history of driving infractions and had been convicted of several misdemeanors, including assault and battery, resisting arrest, and public drunkenness. The county stipulated that Sheriff Moore was the policymaker for Bryan County's sheriff's department; a jury found that the hiring and training practices of the county as instituted by Moore were so inadequate as to amount to deliberate indifference to the constitutional needs of the plaintiff.

A majority of the Court held that this evidence did not supply a sufficient link between the decision to hire Burns and the deprivation of Brown's constitutional rights. It was not enough to show that Deputy Burns would not have been in a position to inflict excessive force on Mrs. Brown if he had not been hired. Rather, Mrs. Brown needed to prove that if Sheriff Moore had performed a proper screening of Burns' application, he would have realized that hiring Burns created a "plainly obvious" risk that Burns would use excessive force. Three dissenting justices would have upheld the lower courts and affirmed the judgment for the plaintiff; they criticized the majority for establishing a new "high threshold" standard of causation. In their view, the "plainly obvious consequence of a particular injury" went a "step further" than required by *City of Canton* and other prior decisions.

Causation and the Liability of Supervisors

The Supreme Court has not directly addressed the circumstances under which a supervisor (e.g., a prison warden) may be held individually liable for the deprivations of constitutional rights inflicted by those whom he supervises (e.g., prison guards). The Court considered supervisory liability in the context of injunctive relief in Rizzo v. Goode (1976). In *Rizzo*, the Supreme Court reversed a lower court injunction issued against several individuals for their alleged failure to adequately supervise and discipline police officers who engaged in unconstitutional conduct. Among the reasons given by the Court as to why an injunction should not have been issued was the absence of evidence that the named defendants were "directly responsible" for the offending officers' conduct.[67] The Court expressly refused to embrace a theory that "without a showing of direct responsibility for the actions of a small percentage of the police force, [defendants'] *failure* to act in the face of a statistical pattern" could support a request for injunctive relief under § 1983. The negative implication of this statement is that a supervisor may be held liable if he or she had "direct responsibility" for the actions of the offending subordinates.

The Courts of Appeals have unanimously accepted the principle that supervisors can be held liable for the violations of constitutional rights committed by those whom they supervise.

The various cases are summarized by one commentator as follows:

> supervisory liability is imposed in the supervisor's individual capacity for his own culpable action or inaction in supervising, training, or controlling subordinates; for acquiescing, condoning of fostering constitutional violations; . . . for tolerating dangerous reckless conduct by subordinates in a way that tends to prove the supervisor's pre-existing disposition and policy; . . . for failing to reprimand or discharge; . . . [or for promulgating] a departmental policy that permitted or encouraged an unconstitutional [act].[68]

Although lower courts agree in principle that supervisors may be individually liable for the unconstitutional acts of their subordinates, they disagree as to the level of culpability needed to support such claims. Some courts articulate the standard in terms of "gross negligence," while others phrase the standard in terms of "recklessness" or "deliberate indifference." Still others demand proof that the supervisor had actual knowledge of and acquiescence in the subordinate's constitutional violation.[69] What is really at stake in these various formulations of culpability is what the plaintiff must prove regarding the supervisor's knowledge of the risk of a constitutional violation. The "gross negligence" standard implies that liability may lie when the supervisor had constructive knowledge (i.e., should have known) that his subordinate would violate the plaintiff's constitutional rights. The more demanding standards require proof of actual knowledge of and acquiescence in the unconstitutional conduct of the subordinate.

Regardless of which particular verbal formula is used to express the level of culpability needed to support a claim against a supervisor, the issue of causation must be addressed. When can it be said that the deliberate indifference of a supervisor caused his subordinate to violate the constitutional rights of the plaintiff? Again, this issue has not received sufficient analytical attention by commentators and judicial opinions on this point are not a model of clarity. However, lower court opinions appear to be influenced by standards developed by the Supreme Court in cases involving municipal liability, such as City of Canton v. Harris (1989) and Bryan County v. Brown (1997).[70]

Consider the case of LaMarca v. Turner (1993), in which a prison inmate (LaMarca) sued the superintendent (Turner) of the facility in which he was confined.

The suit alleged that Turner violated LaMarca's rights under the Eighth Amendment to be free of cruel and unusual punishment by tolerating conditions at the facility that exposed inmates like LaMarca to widespread acts of violence and sexual assaults. Among the specific conditions about which LaMarca complained were "a lack of adequate patrols, . . . the lack of adequate reporting procedures for rapes and assaults, . . . and . . . a lack of supervision of [prison guards] leading to corruption and incompetence." A federal magistrate ruled in favor of LaMarca and this ruling was appealed to the Eleventh Circuit Court of Appeals. The Court of Appeals agreed that there was sufficient evidence to support the magistrate's findings that Turner had actual knowledge of an unreasonable risk of violence at the facility and failed to take certain measures within budget constraints to improve security. Nonetheless, it reversed the lower court and remanded the case due to the magistrate's failure to make certain "essential findings of fact" regarding causation. The Court of Appeals stated:

> "more is required than [a] naked assertion that the assault would not have occurred but-for the offensive conditions" . . . [To establish causation,] merely showing that an official had the means to correct a constitutional infirmity will not suffice. For the plaintiffs to demonstrate the requisite causal nexus, Turner must not only have had the means to correct the alleged constitutional infirmities, but also must have at least recklessly disregarded the inadequacy of the approach he took, the availability of other approaches, and their capacity to provide a cure.

The lower court was instructed to "reconsider the issue of causation and determine whether Turner knowingly or recklessly disregarded any corrective measures. If he did, the court must then determine whether, taken as a whole, these measures would have eliminated the infirm conditions for which he was responsible."

LaMarca illustrates an approach to causation similar to that subsequently applied by the Supreme Court in *Bryan County*. In both cases the plaintiffs presented evidence of misconduct. In *Bryan County* the misconduct was the sheriff's failure to adequately screen his nephew's employment application. In *LaMarca* it was the superintendent's failure to take protective measures in the face of actual knowledge of an unreasonable risk of prison violence. In both cases the lower courts found that the misconduct was a cause of the deprivation of the plaintiffs' constitutional rights. And in both cases the reviewing courts concluded that a simple but-for connection between the general misconduct and the injury was not sufficient to establish causation. Rather, LaMarca had to connect his injuries to specific and particularized decisions of the superintendent, while Brown had to prove that the inadequate screening of Burns posed an obvious risk of the use of excessive force. Thus, in both cases the courts employed a rigorous test of causation that requires a close connection between the specific governmental policy or supervisory misconduct at issue and the particular constitutional injury for which the plaintiff seeks compensation.

Proximate Cause Issues in Constitutional Torts

As discussed earlier, "proximate cause" is a shorthand expression for a variety of issues that essentially reduce to whether the law, as a matter of policy, will extend responsibility for the conduct to the particular consequences that have in fact occurred. As stated by one leading commentator, "[t]he proximate cause issue, in spite of its terminology, is not about causation at all but about the appropriate scope of responsibility."[71] Several principles of proximate cause that were developed in the context of common law torts have been invoked by courts in constitutional tort cases. The following are three common law proximate cause maxims that appear in constitutional tort cases: a defendant is responsible for the foreseeable consequences of his wrongful act; a defendant's conduct is not the proximate cause of an injury that is deemed to be "too remote" in time or space; and a defendant sometimes may avoid liability if an intervening act or force comes into play after the defendant's wrongful conduct.

While these principles were developed in state courts as a matter of state law, it should be recognized that proximate cause rules applied in constitutional tort cases are a matter of federal law. This is so because proximate cause defines the extent of responsibility for the violation of legal rights, and, in constitutional tort litigation, the source of the plaintiff's legal right is the United States Constitution. The extent of responsibility for the violation of federal constitutional rights should be considered a matter of federal law. Thus, while "courts may be guided by [state] common law principles in establishing federal rules of proximate cause governing section 1983 claims, [they] are not bound by decisions of state courts."[72]

Remote Consequences of a Violation of Constitutional Rights

Martinez v. California (1980), involved a suit brought against state officials who released an inmate (Thomas) on parole who tortured and murdered a fifteen-year-old girl five months after his release. The plaintiffs' characterized the decision to parole Thomas as reckless, alleging that, at the time the defendant parole officials released Thomas, they knew he had been convicted of attempted rape, had first been committed to a state mental hospital as a "Mentally Disordered Sex Offender not amenable to treatment," was later sentenced to a term of imprisonment of one to twenty years with a recommendation that he not be paroled, and had been informed of "the likelihood that he would commit another violent crime." The plaintiffs claimed that the reckless decision to place Thomas on parole deprived their daughter of her life without due process in violation of her rights under the Fourteenth Amendment.

The Supreme Court held that "taking these particular allegations as true, [the parole officials] did not 'deprive' [the plaintiffs' daughter] of life within the meaning of the Fourteenth Amendment." The Court emphasized two facts in support of its holding: First, "[h]er life was taken by [Thomas] five months after his release";

and second, "the parole board was not aware that [the plaintiffs' daughter], as distinguished from the public at large, faced any special danger." In light of these two facts, the Court concluded that the torture and murder of the plaintiffs' daughter was "too remote a consequence of the parole officers' action to hold them responsible under the federal civil rights law."

Martinez invokes proximate cause terminology when it speaks of remote consequences. The Court accepted the plaintiffs' characterization of the decision to parole Thomas as reckless. Moreover, it is clear that this "reckless" decision was a cause in fact of the death of the plaintiffs' daughter; if Thomas had not been released, the girl would not have been murdered. Thus, the Court's decision fits within the traditional guise of proximate cause as a policy-based limitation on the extent of liability for a wrongful act that was a cause in fact of the harm suffered by the plaintiff.

By couching its reasoning in the vague language of proximate cause, the Court resolves the particular case without having to address in detail the difficult policy issues that lurk within the plaintiffs' underlying constitutional claim.[73] When, if ever, can government officials be held responsible under the Fourteenth Amendment for the criminal acts of dangerous persons it releases into society? Would the murder have been "too remote" if it had occurred within hours of Thomas' release?[74] Would it have made any difference if Thomas had made threats against this particular victim?[75] By resolving *Martinez* with a conclusory reference to the proximate cause principle of "remoteness" and by limiting the decision to the particular facts of the case, the Court postpones these issues for another day.

Intervening Causes and Shifted Responsibility

In common law torts, the extent of a defendant's liability is sometimes limited either because some intervening force comes into play or because responsibility for a risk has shifted to some other party.[76] Whether an intervening force severs the causal connection between the defendant's wrongful conduct and the plaintiff's injury is often said to depend on whether the intervening force was foreseeable at the time of the wrongful conduct. That is, as a general proposition, common law defendants remain legally responsible for an injury when the intervening force was foreseeable, but their liability is limited when the intervening force was not foreseeable.[77]

These principles have been invoked in constitutional tort cases as well. Consider the extent of potential liability for an unconstitutional search of a criminal suspect. Assume, for example, that a police officer violates the plaintiff's constitutional rights by conducting a search of his car without a warrant or probable cause. The officer finds cocaine in the glove compartment, the driver is charged with possession of illegal drugs, and the drugs are improperly admitted into evidence at trial. The driver is convicted and sent to prison, where he is assaulted by another inmate. An appellate court later rules that the search of the glove compartment was illegal, the drugs should not have been admitted into evidence at trial, and without the drugs the driver would not have been convicted of a crime. Should the arresting officer who conducted the unconstitutional search be held responsible for the criminal conviction and prison assault? Or should the liability of the arresting officer be limited because of the intervening act of the trial judge in admitting the drugs into evidence, or because responsibility for the plaintiff's safety shifted to prison officials?

Variations of this hypothetical appear in reported constitutional tort decisions. Several lower courts have invoked "intervening cause" principles to limit the extent of a law enforcement officer's liability. In Duncan v. Nelson (1972), the Seventh Circuit Court of Appeals held that police officers who coerced a confession from a suspect were not liable for the plaintiff's nine-year incarceration because it was "untenable" to believe that the officers could foresee that a trial judge would improperly admit the confession into evidence. Other decisions have held that the independent decisions of prosecutors, grand juries, and judges break the chain of causation between an illegal arrest and subsequent injury.[78]

To the extent such cases are correctly decided, the justification must rest in judgments regarding ultimate responsibility rather than foresight. It was surely foreseeable to the police officers in *Duncan* that the coerced confession would be admitted into evidence at trial and lead to the conviction and incarceration of the plaintiff. Indeed, conviction and incarceration were probably the very purposes of the interrogation that was later found to exceed constitutional bounds. Perhaps a more plausible explanation for why the officers are not held liable for the conviction and incarceration is the notion of shifted responsibility. That is, once the trial begins, the responsibility for protecting the plaintiff's constitutional rights shifts from the police officers to the trial judge. This notion of shifted responsibility might also explain why some courts have concluded that a police officer who framed a criminal suspect is not liable for a sexual assault that occurs in prison.[79] Prison officials, not the arresting officers, are responsible for providing security to prison inmates.

The Supreme Court has only spoken once to these issues. In Malley v. Briggs (1986) the plaintiffs sued a state trooper who obtained an arrest warrant based on information obtained from a court-authorized wiretap. The plaintiffs alleged that the trooper violated their rights under the Fourth Amendment by presenting the state judge who issued the arrest warrant with a complaint and supporting affidavit that failed to establish probable cause. The trial judge in the constitutional tort case directed a verdict in favor of the defendant trooper on two grounds: first, that the state judge's issuance of an arrest warrant "broke the causal chain" between the trooper's filing of the allegedly deficient complaint and the plaintiffs' arrests; and second, an officer who believes the facts stated in his or her affidavit are true and who submits them to a neutral magistrate is entitled to qualified immunity.

The Court of Appeals reversed the trial court, holding that qualified immunity does not apply unless the trooper has an objectively reasonable basis for believing the facts alleged in his or her affidavit are sufficient to establish probable cause.

The Supreme Court affirmed the Court of Appeals ruling regarding qualified immunity. As to the trial court's causation rationale, the Court maintained that

> It should be clear . . . that the District Court's "no causation" rationale in this case is inconsistent with our interpretation of § 1983. As we stated in Monroe v. Pape [1961], § 1983 "should be read against the background of tort liability that makes a man responsible for the natural consequences of his actions." Since the common law recognized the causal link between the submission of a complaint and an ensuing arrest, we read § 1983 as recognizing the same causal link.

Thus, the Supreme Court rejected the trooper's argument that "the judge's decision to issue the warrant [broke] the causal chain between the application of the warrant and the improvident arrest."

Conclusion

This section ends as it began, with the puzzling observation that causation is both an indispensable and underdeveloped element of every constitutional tort action. The plaintiff must prove that the defendant's conduct caused him or her to be deprived of a constitutional right, yet the standards for establishing causation have not been fleshed out to the same extent as have other elements of the claim. The most elaborate treatment of causation issues is found in the context of *Mt. Healthy* and similar cases. Despite academic criticisms, the Supreme Court has steadfastly adhered to a variant of the common law but-for test to deny recovery to plaintiffs who would have suffered the same injury if the defendants had not infringed on their constitutionally protected interests. Thus, a public employee who is punished for engaging in protected speech cannot recover damages if he or she would have received the same punishment for other reasons. Nor is a damage remedy available for an applicant who, pursuant to a racially discriminatory admissions policy, is denied admission to a graduate program at a state university if he or she would have been denied admission under a constitutionally valid policy.

Causation issues in other constitutional tort contexts receive only infrequent and fragmentary treatment. The Supreme Court recognizes the importance of causation in the context of governmental and supervisory liability but has yet to articulate a coherent set of guiding principles. Discussions of proximate cause issues have not progressed beyond an occasional perfunctory recitation of common law maxims. Causation is one area of constitutional tort doctrine ripe for further analytical growth.

ABSOLUTE IMMUNITY

The statute that authorizes suits to recover damages for violations of constitutional rights (42 U.S.C. § 1983) is written in very broad terms. It provides that "every person who under color of . . . [state law or custom] subjects or causes to be subjected . . . any citizen. . . or other person . . . to the deprivation of any rights . . . secured by the Constitution . . . shall be liable to the party injured. . . . " On its face, the statute does not provide for any "defenses." That is, once the plaintiff shows that someone has violated his constitutional rights, it appears that there are no excuses that would save the defendant from responsibility for the violation and its consequences. Despite the absence of any statutory language establishing a defense, the Supreme Court has consistently held that certain defendants may avoid liability on account of a doctrine called "official immunity." The Court's decisions in this area emphasize two points: (1) such immunities were widely recognized at common law in 1871 (the date § 1983 was enacted), and (2) there was no affirmative indication that Congress intended to depart from the well-established tradition of immunities.

Types of Immunities: Absolute and Qualified

An immunity is a powerful defense. It protects defendants from having to compensate those whose constitutional rights they violated. It also often protects defendants from having to defend the case at all. In certain (rare) cases it even frees the defendant from any obligation to change his illegal behavior in the future. The cases recognize two types of immunities: "absolute" and "qualified." Absolute immunities are the subject of this section. An immunity is absolute when it applies regardless of the motive, intent, or state of mind of the official. It protects a government official whose conduct violates the clearly established constitutional rights of the plaintiff. It even defeats the claim of a plaintiff who can prove that the defendant acted with the specific intent to harm the plaintiff. For example, a criminal defendant cannot recover money damages even if he or she can prove that a judge knowingly violated her constitutional rights during the course of a trial. The Supreme Court has defined the scope of absolute immunity in terms of what it describes as a "functional approach." This means that absolute immunity only applies to certain types of acts or functions. For example, absolute immunity protects a judge who violates constitutional rights when acting in a judicial function (e.g., presiding over a trial), but not when acting in an administrative function (e.g., hiring or firing personnel).

When absolute immunity does not apply, a defendant may still be protected by qualified immunity. As its name suggests, a qualified immunity is of a more limited nature. It only applies when a government official would not have reason to know that his or her conduct would violate the clearly established constitutional rights of the plaintiff. While narrower in scope than absolute immunity, qualified immunity potentially applies to more defendants. Its application does not depend so heavily on the type of act or function being performed by the official and is potentially available to nearly all § 1983 defendants. An important point to keep in mind in reading this section is that qualified immunity may protect a defendant even if absolute immunity does not apply. As we shall see, qualified immunity is itself a powerful defense, though less complete than absolute immunity.

Rationale for Immunity: Avoiding Overdeterrence

We are concerned here only with the personal liability of individual government officials. These are the only defendants for whom official immunity is an issue. Recall that states are not subject to suit and that under Owen v. City of Independence (1980) local governments are not protected by any immunity. The basic argument in favor of granting an immunity to a government official is the fear of overdeterrence. Specifically, the concern is that the cost and inconvenience of defending a lawsuit and the potential personal liability for compensatory damages would inhibit government officials from vigorously discharging their public responsibilities. That is, the prospect of defending lawsuits and paying damages may lead officials to be too cautious in doing their jobs.

In private tort law, ordinary citizens have no immunity of the kind enjoyed by government officers in § 1983 suits. Officers receive special treatment because the deterrent impact of potential liability is thought to be different for government officials (public actors) and individuals or businesses in the private sector (private actors). Private actors, such as businesses, engage in conduct that creates risk of injury to others (e.g., selling a product) in expectation of financial gain. The private actor expects to capture the full benefit of this risk-creating activity. Potential liability is needed to give the private actor an incentive to take precautions to reduce risk to some acceptable level. Government officials, on the other hand, act in the public interest. Police officers who make an arrests or a public school teachers who discipline unruly students may not stand personally to benefit from their actions. Yet an individual might bear the costs of his or her actions were they later found to violate the constitutional rights of the criminal suspect or student. Faced with the prospect of personal liability, the police officers and teachers in certain circumstances may decide not to act at all. In this way, potential liability may skew the incentives of government officials, as compared to private actors, toward inaction or defensive behavior (Harlow v. Fitzgerald, 1982).

No doubt government officers are more likely to err on the side of caution than people who can reap the benefits of their risky actions. Still, the force of the overdeterrence argument is not so clear. A critic of the Court's immunity doctrines might argue that the case for immunity is weaker than it seems, because it overlooks the widespread practice of state and local governments supplying officials with defense counsel paying judgments when officials' conduct is found to have violated plaintiffs' constitutional rights. This practice is commonly referred to as indemnification. Indemnification results in governments, not individual officials, paying the costs of defending lawsuits and paying judgments. Since individual officials do not ultimately incur the out-of-pocket expenses in defending suits, one may question whether they will be overly deterred from discharging their public responsibilities.

Professor John Jeffries defends the doctrine of immunity for public officials.[80] He argues that even though indemnification reduces the individual officer's incentives for inaction, the incentives are still skewed in that direction. Jeffries identifies three factors that create incentives for government employees to remain passive despite indemnification. First, he maintains that because of the "tradition of civil service" in public employment, it is more difficult to terminate a government employee for relative inefficiency or lack of productivity than his or her counterpart in the private sector. Government workers enjoy relatively strong job security in the absence of provable acts of misconduct. In other words, a public employee who does nothing is less likely to lose his or her job than one who takes action that later turns out to be unconstitutional. Second, Jeffries asserts that "psychological self-selection" results in risk-averse persons gravitating to governmental employment while risk-taking individuals tend to seek jobs in the private sector, where risk-taking is more likely to be rewarded. Third, and most important for Jeffries, is a "political culture that punishes" costs that come out of an entity's budget (such as the actual costs of defending lawsuits and paying judgments) more than the less precisely measurable costs of governmental inaction (such as the failure to arrest a criminal suspect or to discipline an unruly student). These factors convince Jeffries that notwithstanding the widespread practice of indemnification, some form of immunity is necessary to encourage public officials to vigorously discharge their public responsibilities.

The arguments for and against immunities are based largely on assumptions regarding human behavior that are not readily subject to empirical verification. Regardless of one's view of these arguments, the Court appears to be steadfastly committed to the defense of absolute immunity in some contexts. We now turn to the specific settings in which the defense of absolute immunity may apply.

Legislative Immunity

The General Rule: Absolute Immunity for Legislative Functions

The first group of cases we discuss involve suits brought against legislators. In Tenney v. Brandhove (1951), Brandhove sued members of the California Senate Fact-Finding Committee on Un-American Activities, claiming that they held hearings designed "to intimidate and silence the plaintiff" in violation of his constitutional rights. *Tenney* held that even assuming these allegations were true, the individual legislators were immune from suit.

The Court began its opinion with a summary of the historical development of legislative immunity. The Court traced the "taproots" of this doctrine to the English Civil War and the "Parliamentary Struggles of the Sixteenth and Seventeenth Centuries." At the time of our nation's founding, some form of immunity for legislators was recognized in the Articles of Confederation, the Speech and Debate clause of the United States Constitution (article I, section 6), and in virtually every state constitution. The Court then concluded that Congress did not intend "to overturn the tradition of legislative freedom" through the "general language" of § 1983.

The policy justifications for legislative immunity are grounded in democratic theory and the principle of separation of powers. As stated by the *Tenney* Court,

> Legislators are immune from deterrents to the uninhibited discharge of their legislative duty, not for their private indulgence but-for the public good. One must not expect uncommon courage even in legislators. The privilege would be of little value if they could be subjected to the cost and inconvenience and distraction of a trial upon a conclusion of the pleader, or the hazard of a judgment against them based upon a jury's speculation as to motives.

Courts are not the appropriate forum to rectify excesses in legislative action prompted by "political passion, dishonest or vindictive motives. . . ." Rather, "[s]elf-discipline and the voters must be the ultimate reliance for discouraging or correcting such abuses."

The Court in *Tenney* did not purport to define the precise scope of legislative immunity. It left open the possibility that "there may . . . be things done . . . of an extraordinary character, for which the members who take part in the act may be held legally responsible." It concluded simply that in this case the "individual defendants and the legislative committee were acting in a field where legislators traditionally have power to act."

Subsequent decisions extended the protection of absolute legislative immunity beyond state legislators. In Lake Country Estates, Inc. v. Tahoe Regional Planning Agency (1979), a majority of the Court held that individual officers of an interstate compact planning agency (a cooperative effort involving officials from more than one state) should be considered regional legislators. As such, they were absolutely immune from suit. Justices Brennan, Marshall, and Blackmun dissented, arguing that these officials should not be characterized as regional legislators. "Their duties are not solely legislative: they possess some executive powers . . . the concept of separation of powers has no relevance to them. They are not subject to the responsibility and the brake of the electoral process."

In Bogan v. Scott-Harris (1998), the plaintiff was a local official in Fall River, Massachusetts. She had upset some members of the city council, who then passed a budget that eliminated the plaintiff's department (and her position). She sued and a jury found that the elimination of the plaintiff's job was done in order to punish her for having exercised her right of free speech. Yet she was unable to recover any damages, because the city council members were legislators and the enacting of a budget was a legislative act. The Supreme Court held that local legislators enjoy the same immunity as do federal, state, and regional legislators. The Court reasoned that the "common law accorded local legislators the same absolute immunity it accorded legislators at other levels of government, and . . . the rationales for such immunity are fully applicable to local legislators."

The Scope of Absolute Legislative Immunity: What Are Legislative Acts or Functions?

Not every act of a legislator is protected by absolute immunity. As stated in *Bogan*, the immunity applies only to "actions taken 'in the sphere of legitimate legislative activities.'" The plaintiff in Bogan argued that even if the immunity protects local legislators, it did not apply in this case because the conduct in question did not lie within "the sphere of legitimate legislative activities." Specifically, Ms. Scott-Harris maintained that the budgetary action taken against her and her department was not a legitimate legislative activity because it was substantially motivated by a desire to punish her for engaging in constitutionally protected speech.

The Supreme Court rejected this argument. It stated that "[w]hether an act is legislative turns on the nature of the act, rather than on the motive or intent of the official performing it." The Court had "little trouble" concluding that the conduct at issue was legislative in nature. The acts of introducing a budget and voting for an ordinance "were, in form, quintessentially legislative." They were also legislative in substance as the budget ordinance "reflected a discretionary, policymaking decision implicating the budgetary priorities of the city and the services the city provides to its constituents." The elimination of a department through the budgetary process was, in the Court's view, "undoubtedly legislative."

An example of conduct that does not involve a legislative function can be found in Davis v. Passman (1979). In this case, a congressman was sued by a former staff member who alleged that her termination was the result of unconstitutional sex discrimination. The termination letter informed the plaintiff that although she had been an "able, energetic, and a very hard worker . . . it was essential that the understudy to my Administrative Assistant be a man." The Court ruled that the Congressman could be held liable for sex discrimination as the hiring and firing of staff was not a legislative activity.

Together, *Bogan* and *Passman* illustrate what the Supreme Court has referred to as the "functional" approach to absolute immunity. Whether absolute immunity applies to a given action depends on the function the officer is performing at the time, not simply the office held by the defendant. Legislators enjoy an absolute immunity insofar as they act in a legislative function, such as voting on bills, conducting hearings, participating in legislative debates, and so on. When acting outside the legislative sphere, as in *Passman*, the legislator is subject to suit to the same extent, as are other government officials. Conversely, an actor may engage mainly in executive functions yet be able to take advantage of absolute legislative immunity on those occasions when he or she takes part in a legislative function. Suppose the mayor of a city is, under the city charter, allowed to vote on all business that comes before the city council. He or she would ordinarily be deemed an executive officer but would probably receive legislative immunity for voting on the budget at a city council meeting.

The Practical Impact of Absolute Legislative Immunity

Absolute legislative immunity will not prevent redress of constitutional violations in a great number of cases. In most instances, the unconstitutional acts or policies of a legislature must be implemented or enforced by executive officials who are subject to suit under § 1983. Consider, for example, a hypothetical case in which a legislator votes to impose compulsory prayer in public schools in violation of the First Amendment. A claim against a sponsoring legislator would be barred by the doctrine of absolute immunity. However, an aggrieved party could sue school officials who attempt to enforce the unconstitutional policy. Thus, in most instances, the practical impact of absolute legislative immunity is to redirect litigation away from the legislator to other government officials. *Bogan* is one of the relatively few instances in which executive officers were not needed to implement the allegedly unconstitutional actions of legislators. In that instance, absolute immunity foreclosed the opportunity for the plaintiff to recover compensatory damages from officers for the violation of her constitutional rights.

Even in a case like *Bogan*, all is not necessarily lost for the plaintiff. It may be possible to obtain damages from the city under the principles previously discussed (see "Liability of Governmental Entities"). After all, the decisions of the city council are surely city policy, and the city does not enjoy immunity. In *Bogan* itself, the plaintiff tried this theory. She lost only because the vote to eliminate her job was 6–2, and the evidence suggested that only two of the six were badly motivated. Given these figures, a lower court found that "municipal liability could not rest 'on so frail a foundation.'"

Absolute Judicial Immunity

The General Rule: Absolute Immunity for Judicial Functions

The very year that Congress enacted the civil rights law that eventually became codified as § 1983, the Supreme Court decided Bradley v. Fisher (1871). The defendant in Bradley was a criminal court judge of the District of Columbia who was sued for damages by a lawyer whom he removed from practice before his court without giving the lawyer notice and an opportunity to defend. The Court held that "judges of courts of superior or general jurisdictions are not liable to civil actions for their judicial acts, even when such acts are in excess of their jurisdiction, and are alleged to have been done maliciously or corruptly." Thus, the Court embraced the general principle of absolute judicial immunity.

In the course of its opinion, the Court distinguished between judicial acts "in excess of jurisdiction" and acts taken in "the clear absence of all jurisdiction over the subject matter." Absolute immunity protects the former but not the latter. The Court offered one example of a situation in which absolute immunity would apply and another in which it would not. A criminal court judge who sentenced a prisoner to a greater punishment than authorized by statute would have acted "in excess of jurisdiction" but would be absolutely immune from civil liability. On the other hand, a probate court judge who unlawfully tried criminal cases would not be absolutely immune from suit because the subject matter jurisdiction of a probate court is limited to claims involving wills and estates.

In applying these principles to the facts before it, the Supreme Court in *Bradley* observed that the judge had the legal authority to remove lawyers from the bar, although ordinarily this should not be done without giving the attorney notice and an opportunity to defend. The judge erred in not giving the plaintiff such notice. The wrongful action of the judge, however, was at most an excess of jurisdiction. The failure to give notice "did not make the act any less a judicial act" because the criminal court had "jurisdiction . . . over its attorneys." Consequently, the Court concluded, the defendant judge was absolutely immune from liability for damages for the disbarment.

Nearly a century later, in Pierson v. Ray (1967), the Supreme Court applied absolute judicial immunity in a § 1983 case. Its reasoning combined the jurisdictional language from *Bradley* and the policy analysis from *Tenney*. In *Pierson*, civil rights protestors sued a municipal police court justice who sentenced them to jail for violating an unconstitutional state statute. The Court invoked *Bradley* when it said that judges are absolutely immune from liability for damages for "acts committed within their judicial jurisdiction . . . even when the judge is accused of acting maliciously and corruptly." The Court in *Pierson* gave a policy rationale in support of absolute judicial immunity similar to the one it had invoked in *Tenney* to justify legislative immunity. Judges need the immunity to allow them to discharge their responsibilities:

> It is a judge's duty to decide all cases within his judicial jurisdiction that are brought before him, including controversial cases that arouse the most intense feelings in the litigants. His errors may be corrected on appeal, but he should not have to fear that unsatisfied litigants may hound him with litigation charging malice or corruption. Imposing such a burden on judges would contribute not to principled and fearless decision making but to intimidation.

Pierson also borrowed from *Tenney* in interpreting § 1983 by reference to common law principies. The Court noted that "the immunity of judges for acts within the judicial role is equally well established [as absolute legislative immunity], and we presume that Congress would have specifically so provided had it wished to abolish the doctrine."

Dissenting in *Pierson*, Justice Douglas maintained that Congress did intend for judges to be subject to liability under § 1983. He said that "it was recognized [in 1871] that certain members of the judiciary were instruments of oppression and were partially responsible for the wrongs to be remedied [by section 1983]." Some commentators have also argued that the common law tradition of judicial immunity was not as well established in 1871 as was absolute legislative immunity.[81]

Despite these historical misgivings, the general rule of absolute judicial immunity remains firmly in place. The primary area of contention today concerns the scope of the immunity.

The Scope of Absolute Judicial Immunity: What Are Judicial Acts or Functions?

In Stump v. Sparkman (1978) the mother of a fifteen-year-old mentally retarded girl asked a judge in Indiana to authorize the sterilization of her child. The judge granted this request without observing many of the formalities that customarily accompany a judicial proceeding. Specifically, "the petition was not given a docket number, was not placed on file with the clerk's office, and was approved in an ex parte proceeding without notice to the minor, without a hearing, and without the appointment of a guardian ad litem." The child was told that the medical procedure was an appendectomy and did not learn that she had been sterilized until after she was married and could not become pregnant. She and her husband brought suit against several defendants, including the judge who had approved the petition.

The Supreme Court held that Judge Stump was absolutely immune from suit, emphasizing that "there was no Indiana statute and no case law . . . prohibiting a circuit court, a court of general jurisdiction, from considering a petition of the type presented to Judge Stump." The plaintiffs argued that the approval of the petition should not be considered a "judicial act" because it was not accompanied by the traditional formalities of judicial proceedings. The Court rejected this argument. The two relevant factors in determining whether the challenged conduct is a protected judicial act, according to the Court, are "whether it is a function normally performed by a judge, and . . . the expectations of parties, i.e., whether they dealt with the judge in his judicial capacity." Both of these factors indicated that Judge Stump's approval of the petition was a "judicial act" for which he was "immune from damages liability even if his approval of the petition was in error."

Justices Stewart, Marshall, and Powell dissented. Focusing on the absence of judicial formalities in Judge Stump's handling of this matter, the dissenting justices concluded that the approval of the petition should not be considered a judicial act. They would define a judicial act in terms of "the factors [summarized in

Pierson] that support immunity from liability . . ." and "[n]ot one" of which they found here. As stated by Justice Stewart, "[t]here was no 'case', controversial or otherwise. There were no litigants. There was and could be no appeal. And there was not even the pretext of principled decision making. The total absence of any of these normal attributes of a judicial proceeding convinces me that the conduct complained of was not a judicial act."

Judicial acts encompass more than just decisions the judge makes about the litigants. In Mireles v. Waco (1991), a lawyer claimed that a judge ordered police to use excessive force to arrest him for failing to appear in court. The judge raised judicial immunity as a shield against liability, and the Supreme Court ruled in his favor. Although directing police to use excessive force is "not a function normally performed by a judge," ordering police to bring an attorney in a pending case before the court is a traditional act of a judge. Since the conduct in question involved "a general function normally performed by a judge," the judge was absolutely immune from civil liability.

Though *Stump* and *Mireles* give a broad scope to judicial immunity, not all acts of judges are judicial acts. The judge in Forrester v. White (1988) had the authority to hire and fire probation officers. The plaintiff claimed that he fired her on account of her sex, in violation of her Fourteenth Amendment right to equal protection. Rejecting the judge's claim of absolute immunity, the Supreme Court explicitly embraced what it referred to as a "functional approach" in defining the scope of absolute judicial immunity. Hiring and firing were administrative, not judicial, functions.

The Court's decisions establish that approving a petition to sterilize a teenage girl is a judicial function protected by absolute immunity, while the hiring and firing of a probation officer is not. Thus, the cases distinguish between the judge as a decider of cases and the judge as workplace supervisor. Should absolute immunity protect a judge who coerces sex from women who have cases pending before the court? On the one hand, sexual exploitation is not, in the words of the Court in *Stump*, a "function normally performed by a judge." On the other hand, the offending conduct occurred while the judge presided over ongoing litigation, which undoubtedly is a function normally performed by a judge. In Archie v. Lanier (1996), the Sixth Circuit Court of Appeals considered a case involving a judge who coerced sex and rejected Judge Lanier's claim of absolute immunity. The Court of Appeals reasoned that "stalking and sexually assaulting a person, no matter what the circumstances, do not constitute 'judicial acts.' The fact that, regrettably, Lanier happened to be a judge when he committed these reprehensible acts is not relevant to the question of whether he is entitled to immunity. Clearly he is not." In a related criminal case, the Supreme Court affirmed Judge Lanier's conviction for violating his victims' civil rights over his complaint that he was not given fair notice that what he did was a crime (United States v. Lanier, 1997).

Absolute Prosecutorial Immunity

The General Rule: Absolute Immunity for Prosecutorial Functions

Imbler v. Pachtman (1976) established the general principle that prosecutors, like legislators and judges, are absolutely immune from liability for damages. The plaintiff (Imbler) had been a criminal defendant. He sued the prosecutor (Pachtman), alleging that Pachtman intentionally allowed a witness to give false testimony, suppressed exculpatory evidence, and had a police sketch of the suspect altered to resemble Imbler more closely after the investigation had focused on him. The Supreme Court held that even if these allegations were true, Pachtman was immune from liability for damages because his actions "were intimately associated with the judicial phase of the criminal process."

The Court in *Imbler* relied on the same type of analysis used in the legislative and judicial immunity cases. It found that the "common-law rule of immunity [for prosecutors] is . . . well settled." The need for such an immunity stems from the concern that "harassment by unfounded litigation would cause a deflection of the prosecutor's energies from his public duties, and the possibility that he would shade his decisions instead of exercising the independence of judgment required by his public trust." The need to defend lawsuits "could impose unique and intolerable burdens upon a prosecutor responsible annually for hundreds of indictments and trials."

The Court also observed that the criminal justice system provides checks against prosecutorial abuse. The "ultimate fairness" of the criminal process is protected by the "[v]arious post-trial procedures" available to the criminal defendant, including "the remedial powers of the trial judge, appellate review, and state and federal post-conviction collateral remedies." Those remedies, of course, provide relief only to people who are wrongfully convicted of a crime. They are of no benefit to the criminal defendant whose constitutional rights were violated but who was found to be not guilty of the charge. Nor do appeals or other post-conviction remedies provide monetary compensation for the violation of constitutional rights. The Court responded to these limitations with the comment that "it is . . . better in the end to leave unredressed the wrongs done by dishonest officers than subject those who try to do their duty to the constant dread of retaliation."

The Court further noted that the ultimate power of the public to deter prosecutorial misconduct rests in criminal law and disciplinary action by the state bar. Absolute immunity may protect the abusive prosecutor from civil liability, but it does not place him "beyond the reach of the criminal law." Moreover, a prosecutor who deprives others of constitutional rights is subject to "professional discipline by an association of his peers."

The Scope of Absolute Prosecutorial Immunity: What Are "Activities Intimately Associated with the Judicial Phase of the Criminal Process"?

Imbler granted prosecutors immunity for "activities intimately associated with the judicial phase of the criminal process." The *Imbler* Court expressly refused to decide whether an absolute immunity would protect the prosecutor whose allegedly unconstitutional conduct occurred in the context of his or her role of administrator or investigative officer. Subsequent decisions more precisely shaped the contours and limits of absolute prosecutorial immunity.

The difficulty of defining the various functions of a prosecutor was illustrated in Burns v. Reed (1991). In this case the police hypnotized a criminal suspect and induced her to confess to a crime. The prosecuting attorney allegedly advised the police on how to procure this evidence and falsely represented the confession as truth at the probable cause hearing at which a search warrant was obtained. (In order to get permission to search someone's property, the police must show that there is good reason—"probable cause"— to think they will find evidence of crime. The proceeding at which this request is made to a judge is called a probable cause hearing.) The trial judge later dismissed all charges when he learned that the confession was obtained by hypnosis. The plaintiff then sued the prosecutor for advising the police on the use of hypnosis and participating in the probable cause hearing. In the Supreme Court, the issue was whether the prosecutor was entitled to absolute immunity.

The Court distinguished between the two things the prosecutor had done. It held that the prosecutor was absolutely immune from civil liability because of his participation in the probable cause hearing, but that he was subject to suit for the dubious legal advice. Appearing before a judge and presenting evidence in support of a motion for a search warrant clearly involves "the prosecutor's 'role as advocate for the State,' rather than his role as 'administrator or investigative officer.'" Pretrial court appearances are "intimately associated with the judicial phase of the criminal process" and, under *Imbler*, are protected by absolute immunity. The "judicial process is available as a check on prosecutorial actions at a probable cause hearing." However, the prosecutor was not absolutely immune from civil liability stemming from legal advice. Central to the Court's reasoning was the absence of "any historical or common-law support for extending absolute immunity to such actions by prosecutors." In addition, the policy needs for absolute immunity were seen as less compelling in the context of providing legal advice. Most criminal suspects are "not likely to be as aware of a prosecutor's role in giving advice as a prosecutor's role in initiating and conducting a prosecution." As a result, a prosecutor's risk of "becoming entangled in litigation based on his or her role as legal advisor" is not as great.

The boundaries of absolute prosecutorial immunity were further tested in Buckley v. Fitzsimmons (1993). The prosecutors in this case (Fitzsimmons and others) allegedly manufactured evidence of a boot print placing Buckley at the scene of a highly publicized murder, used it to procure an indictment, and held a pretrial press conference implicating him. After all the criminal charges were dismissed, Buckley became a civil rights plaintiff and sued Fitzsimmons for fabricating evidence and for his statements at the press conference.

The Court unanimously held that Fitzsimmons was not shielded by absolute immunity for statements made at a press conference. Holding a press conference was not considered a prosecutorial function. Informing the public about a pending prosecution may be effective public relations, but it is too far removed from the judicial phase of a criminal proceeding to warrant this level of protection. A harder question was whether absolute immunity should protect the prosecutor from claims stemming from the alleged fabrication of evidence leading to the arrest of the plaintiff. A bare majority of the Court held that absolute immunity did not apply in this context, the key point being that the allegedly unconstitutional conduct occurred before the existence of probable cause (i.e., before there were good reasons to believe that Buckley committed the crime and should be prosecuted for it). Therefore, it could not be considered part of the prosecutor's role as advocate for the state. The Court noted that police who manufacture false evidence are not protected by absolute immunity. Prosecutors who engage in the same unconstitutional conduct should not benefit from any greater protection.

In Kalina v. Fletcher (1997), the Court considered the case of a prosecuting attorney who made a false statement in an affidavit supporting an application to a judge for an arrest warrant. Again the issue was whether the prosecutor was protected by absolute immunity. On the one hand, a false statement made to a judge by a prosecutor might be considered "intimately associated with the judicial phase of the criminal process" under *Imbler*. On the other hand, the Supreme Court in Malley v. Briggs (1986) had previously ruled that police officers are not absolutely immune for false statements made to secure arrest warrants. In *Kalina* the Court held that absolute immunity does not apply, reasoning that a prosecutor who makes a false affidavit is acting as a witness, not as a legal advocate for the state. This was considered too far removed from the core prosecutorial function of advocacy in the judicial phase of the criminal procedure to merit the protection of absolute immunity.

We now see that prosecutors perform many functions, only some of which are protected by absolute immunity. Absolute immunity from civil liability protects the prosecutor who knowingly presents false evidence at trial (*Imbler*) and who advocates on behalf of the state in probable cause hearings (*Burns*), but only qualified immunity applies when the prosecutor allegedly fabricates evidence to establish probable cause (*Fitzsimmons*), issues false statements at a press conference (*Fitzsimmons*), gives faulty legal advice to police (*Burns*), or makes false statements in an affidavit to secure an arrest warrant (*Kalina*). The practical lesson for the prosecutor is that absolute immunity is most likely to apply when the alleged unconstitutional misconduct occurs in the context of in-court advocacy. The further removed the alleged misconduct is from this core prosecutorial function, the less likely it will be protected by absolute immunity.

Other Participants in the Judicial Process: Witnesses

Suppose a police officer tells a lie while under oath at a criminal trial, doing so for the purpose of getting the jury to convict an innocent person. Later he or she is sued under § 1983 by the victim. The suit will fail because the Supreme Court has held that police officers are absolutely immune from § 1983 liability for damages based on their testimony as witnesses (Briscoe v. LaHue, 1983). Justice Stevens, writing for the Court, noted that at common law witnesses could not be sued for damages "even if the witness knew the statements were false and made them with malice." Absolute immunity was needed to prevent witness "self-censorship." "A witness who knows that he might be forced to defend a subsequent lawsuit, and perhaps to pay damages, might be inclined to shade his testimony in favor of the potential plaintiff, to magnify uncertainties, and thus to deprive the finder of fact of candid, objective, and undistorted evidence."

The plaintiff in *Briscoe* argued that police witnesses were less likely to engage in self-censorship or be intimidated by the threat of lawsuits. Unlike other witnesses, police officers have a legal duty to testify and a "professional interest in obtaining convictions which would counterbalance any tendency to shade testimony in favor of potentially vindictive defendants." Moreover, the plaintiff argued, "perjured testimony by police officers is likely to be more damaging to constitutional rights than such testimony by ordinary citizens." Finally, the plaintiff asserted that policemen were less likely to be prosecuted for perjury because of their close working relationships with prosecuting attorneys.

Although the Court recognized that these "contentions have some force," it refused to establish different immunity rules for ordinary witnesses and police officers. The Court emphasized first that its immunity doctrine "rests on functional categories, not on the status of the defendant." A police officer on the witness stand performs the same functions as any other witness. Second, the number of potential suits convinced the Court that absolute immunity was appropriate. Like prosecutors, police officers could be subject to an overwhelming number of suits because they "testify in scores of cases every year, and defendants often will transform resentment at being convicted into allegations of perjury by the state's official witnesses."

Functional Categories by Analogy: Prison Discipline and Court Reporters

Some defendants who are not part of the judiciary have argued that they perform functions that are analogous to those performed by judges, and, therefore, they too should be protected by absolute immunity. The defendants in Cleavinger v. Saxner (1985) were members of a prison disciplinary committee. An inmate sued them, charging that they treated him unfairly, denying his right to due process, in the course of a prison disciplinary action. The defendants argued that they should be protected by absolute immunity because resolving prison disciplinary matters is analogous to adjudication. The Court rejected the functional comparison between judges and prison disciplinary officials. The prison officials, unlike judges, were not truly independent and often faced pressure to resolve disputes in favor of the institution. The Court concluded that the more limited defense of qualified immunity was appropriate in this context.

This absolute immunity by analogy argument was again made and rejected in Antoine v. Byers & Anderson, Inc. (1993), a case involving a suit against a court reporter. The plaintiff alleged that the court reporter (Byers & Anderson) deprived him of his constitutional rights by failing to prepare a trial transcript in a timely manner. The defendant argued that a court reporter's transcription of a trial is functionally analogous to the older practice of judicial note-taking. Byers & Anderson maintained that it should be protected by absolute immunity since a judge would be absolutely immune from civil liability for any alleged wrongdoing in taking notes. The Court rejected this position. The Court first noted that there was no common law history of immunity for court reporters, because they did not exist when the common law of judicial immunity developed. Moreover, note-taking, verbatim or otherwise, was considered to be an administrative and not a judicial function.

The Special Case of the President of the United States

For most purposes, the immunities afforded state and federal officials are identical. That is, a federal judge, legislator, or prosecutor who is alleged to have violated the constitutional rights of the plaintiff is protected by absolute immunity to the same extent as is his or her state counterpart. The one exception lies in the executive branch of government. Governors and other state executive officials are protected by qualified, not absolute, immunity. However, claims against the president for alleged unconstitutional conduct while in office are barred by absolute immunity.

Absolute immunity for the president for official misconduct was established in Nixon v. Fitzgerald (1982). The Court's opinion is filled with references to the "unique position" the President occupies in our constitutional scheme and the "singular importance" of his or her duties in explaining why a president needs broader immunity than that given a governor. Moreover, the Court emphasized the "unique risks" that would be posed by subjecting a president to lawsuits. Litigation "could distract a president from his public duties, to the detriment not only of the President and his office but also the nation that the presidency was designed to serve."

Absolute immunity for the president does not extend, however, to pre-presidential misconduct. In Clinton v. Jones (1997) a unanimous Supreme Court held that a sexual harassment claim against President Clinton could proceed with discovery and, if necessary, trial when the alleged acts of misconduct occurred while Clinton was the governor of Arkansas. Rather than recognize an immunity for pre-presidential misconduct or postponing the litigation until after Clinton left office, the Court relied on the sound discretion of the trial judge to manage the litigation to protect sitting presidents from harassment, frivolous claims, and excessive distraction.

Absolute Immunity and Prospective Relief

Thus far, we have discussed absolute immunity in the context of a lawsuit in which the plaintiff seeks damages. The final issue addressed in this section is whether absolute immunity also applies to bar claims seeking declaratory or injunctive relief. As discussed in "Types of Constitutional Remedies," compensatory damages are a retrospective remedy. That is, they compensate an injured party for a wrong that has already occurred. An award of compensatory damages restores the plaintiff to the same position he or she was in prior to the wrongful act of the defendant. Other remedies are prospective in nature. That is, they are intended to directly affect the future conduct of the defendant by ordering him or her to do or not to do something, or by stating that a given act is or is not legal. Two types of prospective remedies are declaratory judgments and injunctions. As the term implies, a declaratory judgment is a judicial declaration of the rights of the parties; it does not by itself order any specific changes in conduct. An injunction is a court order for one party to perform a specific act or to refrain from certain conduct. In the context of remedies for constitutional violations, plaintiffs sometimes seek a declaratory judgment that certain conduct is unconstitutional and an injunction prohibiting the unconstitutional practice in the future.

Whether absolute immunity precludes declaratory and injunctive relief is an important issue for two reasons. The first and most obvious reason is that an injunction may halt ongoing unconstitutional practices. In this respect, a prospective remedy can have a direct affect on the defendant's future conduct. Second, under another federal statute (42 U.S.C. § 1988), attorney's fees may be awarded to a plaintiff who prevails in a civil rights case. A plaintiff who obtains declaratory or injunctive relief can be entitled to an award of attorney's fees, even if compensatory damages are barred by immunity. In many of the cases that follow, the defendant's liability for attorney's fees was an important practical issue that depended on whether prospective remedies were subject to absolute immunity.

The Supreme Court gave detailed consideration to this issue in Supreme Court of Virginia v. Consumers Union (1980). Under Virginia law the Supreme Court of Virginia regulated advertising by lawyers. This case involved a challenge by a consumer advocacy group to rules issued by the Supreme Court of Virginia that prohibited attorneys from advertising the fees they charged for certain routine legal services. Consumers Union contended that these rules were a suppression of free speech in violation of the First Amendment. The plaintiff sought declaratory and injunctive relief from the various defendants, including the members of the Virginia Supreme Court. Under a ruling in an earlier case (Bates v. State Bar of Arizona, 1977), the defendants conceded that the Virginia bar rule was unconstitutional. Nonetheless, the defendants sought to dismiss the action against them on the grounds of absolute immunity.

Applying its customary "functional approach," the United States Supreme Court first held that the Virginia Supreme Court acted in a legislative capacity in promulgating the bar disciplinary rules in question. The Court agreed with the analysis of a lower court judge who concluded that "in enacting the disciplinary rules, the Supreme Court of Virginia is constituted as a legislature." It then held that in its prior decisions establishing absolute legislative immunity, "we did not distinguish between actions for damages and those for prospective relief." Consistent with those prior decisions, Consumers Union held that absolute legislative immunity forbids both damages and prospective relief against legislators. Thus, the Virginia Supreme Court could not be ordered to repeal the unconstitutional bar disciplinary rule.

The decision did not end there, for the plaintiffs also sought an injunction preventing the enforcement of the unconstitutional rule. The Virginia Supreme Court played two roles with regard to enforcement: It "hears appeals from lower court decisions in disciplinary cases . . . ; and in addition, it has independent enforcement authority of its own." Hearing appeals was clearly a judicial function, whereas enforcement was a prosecutorial function. The issue thus became whether the Justices of the Virginia Supreme Court could be enjoined in their judicial or prosecutorial capacities, or whether such claims were barred by absolute judicial or prosecutorial immunity.

The Supreme Court did not reach the issue of whether judicial immunity precludes prospective relief. Instead, it focused on absolute prosecutorial immunity. The Court noted that absolute immunity has never prevented a lower court from issuing an injunction prohibiting the enforcement of an unconstitutional law. Without the availability of prospective relief, "putative plaintiffs would have to await the institution of state-court proceedings against them in order to assert their federal constitutional claims. This is not the way the law has developed. . . ." Consequently, the justices of the Virginia Supreme Court could be enjoined from enforcing the unconstitutional bar disciplinary rule, and they could be liable for attorney's fees in the litigation leading to the injunction.

Consumers Union established that absolute immunity foreclosed prospective relief against legislators, but not prosecutors. It left open the question of whether declaratory and injunctive relief may be obtained against judges. This question was answered a few years later in Pulliam v. Allen (1984). This case concerned a Virginia magistrate who routinely required persons arrested for minor criminal offenses to "post bail" as a condition for release even though incarceration was not a possible punishment for the offenses in question. He then would lock up defendants if they could not meet bail. The plaintiff in *Pulliam* sued the magistrate in federal court under § 1983, seeking an order directing the magistrate to stop this practice. The lower court held that the practice was unconstitutional and enjoined its enforcement. The magistrate appealed to the Supreme Court, contending that prospective relief was barred by absolute judicial immunity.

A bare majority of a sharply divided Supreme Court upheld the injunction. The Court admitted that there was not a common law tradition of issuing injunctions against judges. Long ago in England, however, there had been a close parallel in the relief available through the use of "the King's prerogative writs," especially the writs of prohibition and mandamus. The Court was also influenced by the fact that the prevailing practice in the lower federal courts was to allow prospective relief against judges in appropriate circumstances. This practice was not seen to have had any "chilling effect" on judges in their discharge of their official duties.

The Court did caution that courts ought to enjoin judges only as a last resort, when other methods of getting compliance with federal constitutional guarantees were unavailing. A key practical consideration is that, absent the power to order the judge to stop an illegal practice, there is sometimes no other way to accomplish that goal. In many circumstances an injunction against the prosecutor will be sufficient, for much of what judges do is instigated by prosecutors. But the particular practice at issue in Pulliam concerned only the judge and not the prosecutor. Together, *Consumers Union* and *Pulliam* establish that absolute immunity from prospective relief applies to legislators but not to prosecutors or judges.

QUALIFIED IMMUNITY

The Supreme Court has recognized two types of immunity: absolute and qualified. Absolute immunity, discussed in the previous section, only protects certain government officials (e.g., legislators, judges, prosecutors) who perform specific functions (e.g., legislative, judicial, or prosecutorial functions). Absolute immunity protects these officials from suit even if the plaintiff can prove that the defendant knew his or her actions were unconstitutional. Qualified immunity is available only when the law is unclear. Unlike absolute immunity, qualified immunity is not a defense when a reasonable official would know that his or her conduct violates the clearly established constitutional rights of the plaintiff. At the same time, qualified immunity applies to more defendants; it is available to all government officials who exercise "discretionary" functions. (This includes virtually all actions that could give rise to constitutional tort liability.) The Court has distinguished these from "ministerial" functions, which do not involve the exercise of judgment. Though the Court has not squarely ruled one way or the other on this issue in a § 1983 case, there may be no immunity whatever for ministerial actions (Westfall v. Erwin, 1988). Because it has little practical relevance, we will set aside the topic of ministerial functions and direct our attention to the doctrine of qualified immunity for discretionary functions.

As explained in more detail in "Absolute Immunity," the rationale underlying both immunity defenses is avoidance of overdeterrence. Subjecting government officials to personal liability for violations of constitutional rights is thought to deter those officials from acting unconstitutionally. Of course, deterring unconstitutional conduct is one of the primary purposes of § 1983 and constitutional tort litigation in general. Proponents of immunities maintain, however, that the risk of being sued and incurring personal liability will do more than deter unconstitutional behavior. Rather, government officials will become "overdeterred," or excessively cautious in performing their official duties. In this way, overdeterrence impedes the efficient operation of government, and some form of immunity is needed to prevent it. The challenge of formulating rules of liability and immunity is how to advance the goal of deterring unconstitutional conduct and yet avoid the dangers of overdeterrence.

Viewed in terms of policy, the difference between absolute and qualified immunity concerns how to strike the balance between the competing goals of achieving deterrence and avoiding overdeterrence. Absolute immunity gives greater weight to risks of overdeterrence by protecting a limited number of government officials even when they knowingly violate the constitutional rights of others. Qualified immunity treats other government officials differently, protecting them only when—based on the state of the law when they acted— they may have "reasonably" believed they were acting properly. We shall see that though less sweeping than absolute immunity, the doctrine of qualified immunity has evolved over time to become a very powerful defense.

Evolution of Qualified Immunity and the Shrinking Role of "State-of-Mind" Inquiries

The Original Formulation: Objective Reasonableness and Subjective Good Faith

The Supreme Court's first consideration of qualified immunity under § 1983 came in Pierson v. Ray (1967). Mississippi police officers were sued by civil rights protesters arrested for breach of the peace when attempting to integrate an interstate bus terminal. The Court held that "the defense of good faith and probable cause . . . is . . . available to [the police officers] in the action under § 1983." Even though a defense of "good faith and probable cause" is not mentioned in the text of § 1983, it was well recognized at common law at the time § 1983 was enacted and "the legislative record gives no clear indication that Congress meant to abolish wholesale all common-law immunities."

The Court further held that, notwithstanding the recognition of this defense, the claims against the police officers should not be dismissed. The plaintiffs argued that the police arrested them "solely for attempting to use the "White Only" waiting room. . . ." The defendant officers claimed that they arrested the plaintiffs "solely for the purpose of preventing violence" because "a crowd gathered and imminent violence was likely." The plaintiffs testified that "no crowd was present, and that no one threatened violence or seemed about to cause a disturbance." Given these disputed factual issues, a new trial was necessary to determine whether the "officers reasonably believed in good faith that the arrest was constitutional."

Pierson was an important case for three reasons. First, drawing on defenses available at common law, the Court recognized that government officials other than judges or legislators would have some defense against claims brought under § 1983. Second, the defense recognized by the Court was more limited in nature than the absolute immunity afforded judges and legislators. The defense includes both an objective (probable cause) and a subjective (good faith) component. The "good faith" element of the defense focuses on the state of mind of the arresting officers: Did they mean well, or were they actually malicious or indifferent to the plaintiffs' rights? "Probable cause" is an objective test: Quite apart from the subjective motivations of the officers, would a "reasonable" person confronted with the situation conclude that an arrest may be justified? In contrast to absolute immunity, the officers would have no defense if either of these inquiries were resolved against them. Third, the Court recognized that given the disputed versions of the facts, a trial was necessary to determine whether these officers acted in reasonable good faith.

After *Pierson*, the Court made clear that the two-part qualified immunity test applied to all those federal, state, and local government officials not covered by absolute immunity. Thus, qualified immunity applied to claims brought against the governor of Ohio who called out the national guard to quell an anti-war protest at Kent State University (Scheuer v. Rhodes, 1974); a state mental health official who confined a patient against his wishes (O'Connor v. Donaldson, 1975); local school board officials who suspended students from high school without giving them a hearing (Wood v. Strickland, 1975); a prison guard who allegedly violated the free speech rights of an inmate by interfering with his mail (Procunier v. Navarette, 1978); and even the Secretary of Agriculture, who was charged with retaliating against a commodities broker for criticism of federal officials (Butz v. Economou, 1978).

Wood v. Strickland (1975) was especially significant because it explicated the two-part test in considerable detail. The following quote from *Wood* is necessary for understanding subsequent Supreme Court decisions bearing on qualified immunity.

> The official himself must be acting sincerely and with a belief that he is doing right, but an act violating a student's constitutional rights can no more be justified by ignorance or disregard of settled, indisputable law. . . . To be entitled to [qualified immunity] . . . a school board member . . . must be held to a standard of conduct based not only on permissible intentions, but also on knowledge of the basic, unquestioned constitutional rights of his charges. . . . [A] school board member is not immune from liability for damages under § 1983 if he knew or reasonably should have known that the action he took . . . would violate the constitutional rights of the student affected, or if he took the action with the malicious intention to cause a deprivation of constitutional rights or other injury to the student.

The objective prong of the qualified immunity test (identified by the "should have known" language in the quotation) prevented officials from escaping liability by claiming ignorance of the law. Thus, the objective standard elevated the standard of conduct. Subjective good faith was an essential, but not an independently sufficient, basis for the immunity. (One who knows he or she is violating constitutional rights or who "maliciously intends" to cause injury does not act with subjective good faith.)

The Transformation of Qualified Immunity: The Demise of Subjective Good Faith

Beginning with Harlow v. Fitzgerald (1982), the two-part test of *Wood* underwent considerable transformation. *Harlow* was a suit brought against aides to former president Richard Nixon, claiming that they fired Fitzgerald in retaliation for his testifying to Congress about cost overruns in the Air Force. (As described in "Absolute Immunity," the case against Nixon himself was dismissed on absolute immunity grounds.) The Court used this case to catalog deficiencies with the existing law and to reformulate the test for qualified immunity. The *Wood* approach was unsatisfactory because the subjective prong of the qualified immunity test forced too many cases to trial. "[A]n official's subjective good faith has been considered to be a question of fact that some courts have regarded as inherently requiring resolution by a jury." The routine submission of cases to trial was considered a problem because "claims frequently run against the innocent as well as the guilty—at a cost not only to the defendant officials, but to society as a whole." The "social costs" of litigating claims—even those in which the defendant ultimately prevailed—included "the expenses of litigation, the diversion of official energy from pressing public issues and the deterrence of able citizens from acceptance of public office." Moreover, the Court continued, the fear of being sued "will 'dampen the ardor of all but the most resolute, or the most irresponsible [public officials] in the unflinching discharge of their duties.'" The subjective good faith element of qualified immunity was also seen as posing "special costs" because "inquiry into subjective motivation . . . may entail broad-ranging discovery and the deposing of numerous persons, including an official's professional colleagues. Inquiries of this kind can be particularly disruptive of effective government."

Given these problems, the Court concluded that "an adjustment of the 'good faith' standard" was needed to facilitate "the dismissal of insubstantial lawsuits without trial." It held that "bare allegations of malice should not suffice to subject government officials to the costs of trial or the burdens of broad-reaching discovery." Furthermore, "government officials performing discretionary functions generally are shielded from liability for civil damages insofar as their conduct does not violate clearly established statutory or constitutional rights of which a reasonable person would have known."

The qualified immunity test as restructured by *Harlow* focuses on "the objective reasonableness of an official's conduct, as measured by reference to clearly established law. . . ." The *Harlow* Court envisioned a process in which the presiding trial judge would determine "whether the law was clearly established at the time an action occurred." This determination would be made shortly after the suit was filed and without extensive discovery. If the alleged conduct of the defendant did not violate "clearly established law," the defendant would be entitled to summary judgment (i.e., the matter would be dismissed without a trial).If the alleged conduct did violate clearly settled law, the "immunity defense ordinarily should fail, since a reasonably competent public official should know the law governing his conduct."

The next step in reformulating the doctrine of qualified immunity came in Anderson v. Creighton (1987). This case involved a claim brought against an FBI agent who entered the plaintiffs' home without a warrant to search for a suspected bank robber. The Court of Appeals had ruled that agent Anderson was not protected by qualified immunity because it was "clearly established" at the time of his actions that a law enforcement officer could not enter the home of a person to search for a criminal suspect without a warrant except in an emergency (in legal terms, the exception is for "probable cause and exigent circumstances"). For example, suppose the officer saw the suspect enter the house with cocaine. This would establish probable cause. Suppose the suspect knew the officer saw him and, given a few minutes, could flush the cocaine down the toilet, thus disposing of the evidence against him. This danger would constitute exigent circumstances, excusing the officer's failure first to obtain a warrant from a judge.

In *Anderson* the issue was whether an officer had qualified immunity when the general legal standard was clearly established, but it is unclear whether the particular situation faced by an officer did or did not constitute probable cause and exigent circumstances. In other words, the question was the level of generality at which the "clearly established law" inquiry should be resolved. The plaintiffs and the Court of Appeals couched the inquiry at a high level of generality: Was it clearly settled that an FBI agent could not enter a house without a warrant absent probable cause and exigent circumstances? (The answer to this question is clearly no.) The defendant, on the other hand, stated the issue at a more fact-specific level: Was it clearly settled that the facts presented to agent Anderson did not constitute probable cause and exigent circumstances? The Court held that whether a right was "clearly established" for purposes of qualified immunity should be analyzed on the fact-specific level. That is,

> the right the official is alleged to have violated must have been "clearly established" in a more particularized, and hence more relevant sense. . . . The relevant question in this case, for example, is the objective (albeit fact-specific) question of whether a reasonable officer could have believed Anderson's warrantless search to be lawful, in light of clearly established law and the information the searching officer possessed.

This reasoning indicates that a determination of whether law was clearly settled is to be made on a fact-specific level. For example, a plaintiff could not defeat a claim of qualified immunity by showing that it was clearly settled that a police officer could not lawfully arrest a suspect absent probable cause. Rather, the plaintiff would have to establish that a reasonable officer could not have believed there was probable cause to make an arrest under the specific facts of the case.

Another aspect of *Anderson* also deserves mention. If *Harlow* left any doubt, it now became clear that the two-part test of qualified immunity originating in *Pierson* was dead, to be replaced in *Harlow* and *Anderson* with a single standard of objective legal reasonableness. The subjective "good faith" of the defendant officer had become, in the words of the *Anderson* Court, "irrelevant." The sole question was whether a reasonable official could reasonably believe his or her conduct was lawful under then existing law. If so, the defendant official would be immune from liability even though his own motive was to violate the plaintiff's constitutional rights.

When Is Law "Clearly Established" for Purposes of Qualified Immunity?

After *Harlow*, a defendant's assertion of qualified immunity will often depend on whether the law was clearly established or clearly settled at the time of the incident. *Anderson* instructs lower courts to frame this question in a fact-specific manner. But other than this general guideline, what standards should govern the "clearly settled" law inquiry? How many similar cases need to have been decided? From which courts? Surprisingly, the Supreme Court has rarely spoken to these pivotal issues. There are three cases, however, that merit attention.

"Clearly Established Law" in the Supreme Court

The Supreme Court's most elaborate discussion of when law is clearly established is found in Wilson v. Layne, 1999. This case addressed the constitutionality of reporters accompanying law enforcement officers when they entered a home to execute an arrest warrant. Several warrants had been issued for the arrest of Dominic Wilson, but they made no mention of media presence or assistance. Even so, federal and local law enforcement officials invited a reporter and photographer to accompany them as they arrested their suspect. The address listed for Dominic Wilson in the warrants was actually the residence of his parents, Charles and Geraldine Wilson. The officers and the media representatives entered the parents' home at 6:45 A.M., and after a verbal confrontation the officers arrested Charles Wilson, mistakenly believing him to be Dominic. Charles sued them for a constitutional tort, claiming that they violated his Fourth Amendment right against unreasonable searches and seizures.

A unanimous Supreme Court agreed with the elder Wilson that the police had committed a constitutional violation, holding that "it is a violation of the Fourth Amendment for police to bring members of the media or other third parties into a home during the execution of a warrant when the presence of the third parties in the home was not in aid of the execution of the warrant." However, the Court also held that the officers were protected by qualified immunity, so the Wilsons were not entitled to compensation for their constitutional injury. Qualified immunity applied, the Court said, because it was not clearly established at the time of the incident that the Fourth Amendment prohibited media entry into a home during the execution of a warrant. (The mistaken address was not a factor in the case.)

The Court gave three reasons why it concluded that the inclusion of the media in the execution of the warrant did not violate "settled" constitutional law. First, the Court observed that "the constitutional issue presented by this case is by no means open and shut . . . and it is not obvious from general principles of the Fourth Amendment. . . ." Second, there were no judicial opinions that had squarely held that the officers conduct violated the Constitution. The Court emphasized that

> [the Wilsons] have not brought to our attention any cases of controlling authority in their jurisdiction at the time of the incident which clearly established the rule on which they seek to rely, nor have they identified a consensus of cases of persuasive authority such that a reasonable officer could not have believed that his actions were lawful.

The strongest authority the plaintiffs could find was a Court of Appeals ruling in an earlier case that the police may violate the Fourth Amendment by bringing a private security guard along on a search. The Supreme Court reasoned that this single opinion did not clearly establish that media entry into the premises violated the Wilsons' Fourth Amendment rights because it was decided by a court from a different jurisdiction "a mere five weeks before the events of this case. . . ." Third, the ride-along policies of federal and local agencies either explicitly contemplated media entry into the premises or did not expressly prohibit it. Given the "undeveloped" state of the law, "it was not unreasonable for law enforcement officials to look and rely on their formal ride-along policies."

Wilson thus offers several guidelines for lower courts in determining whether a defendant is entitled to qualified immunity. A defendant will be protected by qualified immunity unless (1) the conduct in question is so obviously unconstitutional that it can be labeled an "open and shut" case, (2) there is factually similar case law decided by courts of "controlling authority" (e.g., United States Supreme Court or Court of Appeals for the circuit in which the incident occurred or the state supreme court in the state in which it occurred) holding the contested conduct to be unconstitutional; or (3) unless there is a "consensus" of factually similar opinions from other jurisdictions reaching that conclusion.

United States v. Lanier (1997), provides an example of what the *Wilson* Court may have had in mind as an "open and shut" case. Lanier, a state judge, was prosecuted under federal criminal law for violating the federal civil rights of several women. The indictment alleged, among other things, that Judge Lanier used his official power to extort sexual favors from a woman whose divorce and child custody matters were subject to the court's jurisdiction. The defendant argued that he could not be prosecuted under these facts because no prior cases had clearly established that soliciting sexual favors from litigants violated any federal constitutional rights. The Supreme Court unanimously rejected his argument, holding that despite the absence of a specific prior court opinion, the defendant had fair warning that his conduct violated his victim's constitutional rights. The absence of explicit case law was explained by quoting a lower court judge: "The easiest cases don't even arise. There has never been . . . a Section 1983 case accusing welfare officials of selling foster children into slavery; it does not follow that if such a case arose, the officials would be immune from damages [or criminal] liability."

In Elder v. Holloway (1994), the problem was not the lack of precedent on the point at issue but the obscurity of the prior cases. The plaintiff's lawyer was unable to locate the earlier decisions that established a clear violation of law by the defendant, and the first judge who heard the case could not find them either. The issue was whether the law was "clearly established" for immunity purposes, and the Supreme Court held that it was. The relevant universe of cases was "all relevant precedent, not simply those cited to or discovered by the district court." This was better than limiting the inquiry to cases found by the lawyers or the judge because the latter approach would be entirely unpredictable. Thus, it would not give officials any real protection from lawsuits. Nor, of course, would it "further the interests on the other side of the balance: deterring public officials' unlawful actions and compensating victims of such conduct."

"Clearly Established Law" in the Lower Courts

While the Supreme Court has spoken infrequently and in general terms regarding the standards for determining when law is clearly settled, the lower courts confront this issue on a daily and fact-specific basis. Lower courts have developed a body of case law that has made qualified immunity a formidable defense in many of them. A graphic example of this is found in the case of Lassiter v. Alabama A & M University (1994). In this case the Court of Appeals for the eleventh Circuit described the role of qualified immunity in the following forceful terms:

qualified immunity . . . is the usual rule; only in exceptional cases will government actors have no shield against claims made against them. . . . [Defendants] are entitled to immunity except in the extraordinary case where [the case law] would lead to the inevitable conclusion [that the act was unlawful]. . . . For qualified immunity to be surrendered, pre-existing law must dictate, that is, truly compel (not just suggest or allow or raise a question about), the conclusion for every like-situated, reasonable government agent that what defendant is doing violates federal law *in the circumstances.* (28 F.3d at 1149–50, emphasis in the original)

As noted by one commentator, *Lassiter*'s "emphasis on factual specificity and the use of verbs like 'dictate' and 'compel' and adjectives like 'exceptional,' 'extraordinary,' and 'inevitable,' all combine to leave the impression that only an egregious violation can override immunity."[82] *Lassiter* continues to be cited favorably in the Eleventh Circuit and in other circuits as well.[83] To put *Lassiter* in perspective, it should be noted that a good many courts reject immunity claims without ensuring that the demanding standard of that case has been met.[84] Until the Supreme Court gives clearer directions on this issue, lower courts will be left to their own devices and will probably continue to reach results that are hard to reconcile with one another.[84a]

Thus far we have addressed the substantive elements of qualified immunity. We have seen that this defense, as it has evolved in the Supreme Court and as applied by lower courts, poses a significant obstacle to victims who seek compensation for violations of their constitutional rights. The next section describes various procedural aspects of the defense that also tend, on the whole, to work in favor of the defendant.

Procedural Aspects of Qualified Immunity

Procedural rules often have more or as much influence on the outcome of litigation as does the substantive law—a generalization that holds true for constitutional torts as well. The procedures used to raise and adjudicate claims of qualified immunity can have an important bearing on the outcome of constitutional litigation. This section will discuss three procedural aspects of the qualified immunity defense: the order in which a court considers the issues of immunity and the substantive constitutional claim; the standards applied by a court in deciding whether an issue can be summarily resolved without a trial; and the rules regarding when a party may appeal an adverse ruling by a trial judge.

Which Should Be Decided First, the Issue of Qualified Immunity or the Substantive Constitutional Issue?

In Siegert v. Gilley (1991) the plaintiff alleged that a federal official deprived him of liberty without due process by writing a highly unfavorable reference letter, a letter he claimed was written in bad faith. In order to win the lawsuit, the plaintiff had to prevail on two issues: He had to show (1) that the sending of the letter violated his constitutional rights, and (2) that this right was clearly established at the time the defendant sent the letter. The former is a substantive issue of constitutional law, whereas the latter, of course, is the immunity issue discussed previously. One way to approach the case—and a method that proved quite popular with lower courts—is to avoid facing the substantive issue directly and instead assume for the sake of argument that the plaintiff can win on the merits. Then a court could merely ask whether the right was clearly established. Given the murkiness of much constitutional law, it may be easy to conclude that it was not. In this way, a court can dispose of the case without directly facing the often difficult constitutional issue it presents.

But in *Siegert* the Supreme Court disapproved of this practice. It ruled that courts should first decide the substantive constitutional issue and only proceed to the immunity issue if they have found for the plaintiff on the substantive merits. In *Siegert* itself the Court held that the facts alleged by the plaintiff did not amount to a constitutional violation. It stated that the defendant's conduct did not deprive the plaintiff of liberty, but at most constituted common law defamation. The plaintiff's constitutional tort claim was lost at what the Court referred to as the "analytically earlier stage" of deciding whether a constitutional right had been violated, rather than at the later stage of determining whether the defendant violated clearly settled law.

Siegert thus approved a decisional methodology whereby courts would decide the substantive constitutional issue before addressing the defense of qualified immunity. That is, the court should first consider whether the complaint alleges a violation of a constitutional right before deciding whether the law was clearly settled at the time of the incident. This means that the judge should first assume the factual allegations contained in the complaint to be true and then determine whether the alleged conduct violated a constitutional right. If, as in *Gilley*, the facts alleged do not state a constitutional violation, the case can be dismissed on that basis. If the facts alleged do state a violation of constitutional rights, the court would then consider whether the defendant is entitled to qualified immunity (i.e., whether the alleged conduct violated clearly established law). If the plaintiff wins on both these issues, and there are disputed facts, it is then appropriate to proceed to trial.

This methodology was also employed in *Wilson*. Recall that in that case the Court in *Wilson* first decided that media entry into a home during the execution of an arrest warrant violated the Fourth Amendment rights of the plaintiffs. It then held that the law in this area had not been clearly established at the time of the incident, so the defendants were entitled to qualified immunity.

Note that the decisional methodology laid down in *Gilley* and applied in *Wilson* requires the Court to reach the merits of substantive constitutional issues even though the resolution of the merits may not be necessary to decide the case. (A finding of immunity would suffice for that.) But the Court has concluded that the advantages of first facing the substantive issue outweigh any objections. In *Wil-*

son it cited *Siegert* and said that "[t]his order of procedure is designed to spare a defendant not only unwarranted liability, but unwarranted demands customarily imposed upon those defending a long drawn-out lawsuit." In addition, "[d]eciding the constitutional question before addressing the qualified immunity question also promotes clarity in the legal standards for official conduct, to the benefit of both the officers and the general public." For example, if the Court in *Wilson* had simply held that the defendants were entitled to qualified immunity because the law was unsettled, law enforcement officials would still not know whether media entry into a home during the execution of an arrest warrant violates the Fourth Amendment's rule against unreasonable searches and seizures. If the clearly established law issue were addressed first, courts could continually avoid reaching the merits of the substantive constitutional issue and the law would remain unsettled.

Professor Jeffries defends the Court's decisional methodology in *Siegert* and *Wilson* by calling attention to the costs of constitutional innovation. This approach allows the Court to clarify the law for future cases without triggering damages liability for past conduct. In this sense, the decisional methodology places greater importance on prevention of future constitutional violations than on reparations for past injury.[85]

Summary Judgment and the Role of Judge and Jury

The clear thrust of *Harlow* and its progeny is to encourage courts to decide the qualified immunity issue as quickly as possible so as to spare government officials not only the costs of liability but the costs and inconvenience of defending lawsuits as well. The procedural mechanism most frequently employed for the prompt resolution of the qualified immunity defense is known as summary judgment. Summary judgment is authorized by Federal Rules of Civil Procedure, Rule 56. It empowers a judge to decide (without the need for a jury trial) a case, or an issue within a case, if the material facts are not disputed. ("Material" facts are facts that matter to the outcome of the litigation, for example, in a case concerning a car accident, whether the driver was drunk would be a material fact, but whether the car was blue or red probably would not be one.) The party seeking summary judgment alleges that under the undisputed facts it is entitled to a judgment as a matter of law. Summary judgment will be granted unless the party opposing it demonstrates that material facts are in dispute. In the constitutional tort context, the government official typically will ask for summary judgment on qualified immunity by claiming that, under the undisputed facts, no reasonable officer in the defendant's position could have known that his or her conduct violated clearly settled law. The burden then becomes the plaintiff's to demonstrate either that the material facts are disputed or that under the undisputed facts the defendant's conduct violated clearly settled law.

In Hunter v. Bryant (1991) two Secret Service agents arrested Bryant because they believed he had threatened the life of President Reagan. The charges were later dropped and Bryant sued the agents, alleging that the arrest was made without a warrant and without probable cause, in violation of his Fourth Amendment rights. The agents moved for summary judgment on the grounds of qualified immunity. Lower courts denied the motion, explaining that whether reasonable officers could have believed they had probable cause to arrest Bryant was a disputed issue of material fact and therefore a full trial was necessary. The Supreme Court reversed this decision:

> The decision of the [Court of Appeals] . . . is wrong for two reasons. First, it routinely places the question of immunity in the hands of the jury. Immunity ordinarily should be decided by the court long before trial. Second, the court should ask whether the agents acted reasonably under settled law in the circumstances, not whether another reasonable, or more reasonable, interpretation of the events can be constructed five years after the fact.

The Court then examined the facts known to the agents at the time of the arrest and concluded that they were entitled to qualified immunity.

The primary lesson of *Hunter* is that both the questions of (1) whether law was clearly settled and (2) whether a reasonable government official would know that his or her conduct violated clearly settled law are themselves questions of law to be decided by the court, rather than questions of fact to be decided by a jury. This characterization encourages the summary resolution of the issue of qualified immunity, thereby eliminating the need for jury trials in a great number of cases.

Appeals of Decisions Denying Defendants' Motions for Summary Judgment on Qualified Immunity

In constitutional torts, as in all types of civil litigation, a trial court is likely to rule on a host of motions before the case is actually brought to trial. Ordinarily, a party cannot appeal an adverse ruling on a pretrial motion until the court has entered a "final decision" that disposes of the entire litigation. The requirement of a final decision usually means that adverse rulings on pretrial motions cannot be appealed until after the conclusion of the trial. An exception to this general practice is found under what is known as the "collateral order doctrine." Under this doctrine, certain pretrial rulings are subject to "interlocutory appeal"; that is, they may be appealed before the entry of a final order that disposes of the entire case. The collateral order doctrine as explained in Cohen v. Beneficial Industrial Loan Corp. (1949) applies to a "small class [of decisions] which finally determine claims of rights separable from, and collateral to, rights asserted in the action, too important to be denied review and too independent of the cause itself to require that appellate consideration be deferred until the whole case is adjudicated."

In Mitchell v. Forsyth (1985) the Supreme Court considered whether the collateral order doctrine applies to District Court rulings denying summary judgment to government officials claiming qualified immunity. Forsyth brought suit against Attorney General John Mitchell for Mitchell's authorization of a wiretap without first securing a warrant. Mitchell asserted that he was entitled to qualified immunity, as it was not clearly established at the time of the incident that warrantless wiretaps were unconstitutional. The District Court denied Mitchell's motion for summary judgment and Mitchell immediately appealed.

The Supreme Court held that a ruling denying a motion for summary judgment on qualified immunity was subject to an interlocutory appeal under the collateral order doctrine. The Court reasoned that qualified immunity is "an entitlement not to stand trial or face the other burdens of litigation." This right would be "effectively lost if a case is erroneously permitted to go to trial." Thus, the denial of a defendant's motion for summary judgment on qualified immunity "finally and conclusively determines the defendant's claim of right not to stand trial." Moreover, the Court said that "the question of immunity is separate from the merits of the underlying action" because it does not depend "on the correctness of the plaintiff's version of the facts. . ." Rather, the Court need only consider "a question of law: whether the legal norms allegedly violated by the defendant were clearly established at the time of the challenged actions. . . ."

Mitchell adopts what may appear to be an arcane procedural rule. However, this rule has a tremendous practical impact on constitutional tort litigation. After *Mitchell*, a defendant who seeks summary judgment on the grounds of qualified immunity can routinely appeal an adverse ruling before the trial. Once this interlocutory appeal is filed, the District Court cannot proceed with the claim against the defendant who filed the appeal and often will not proceed with claims against other defendants. Thus, the case will not go to trial until after the Court of Appeals has ruled on the interlocutory appeal. This means a plaintiff in a constitutional tort case must be prepared to litigate the qualified immunity issue at least once in the Court of Appeals before going to trial on the merits of the claim. This adds considerable delay and cost to the litigation of constitutional tort claims.

Such cost and delay are exacerbated when the defendant is allowed to file more than one interlocutory appeal before trial. In Behrens v. Pelletier (1996) the defendant first raised the defense of qualified immunity in a motion to dismiss. (A motion to dismiss, which addresses the adequacy of the pleadings, is filed immediately after the complaint and is decided before either side has engaged in the fact-developing process known as "discovery." That is, one takes at face value the propositions asserted by the plaintiff in his or her request for relief and asks whether, even if they are true, the plaintiff has stated a sound claim under the governing law.) The trial judge ruled against the defendant, who immediately but unsuccessfully appealed. The case was then returned to the trial court, and the parties proceeded with discovery.

The defendant then moved for summary judgment on the grounds of qualified immunity based on the facts developed during discovery, and again the motion was denied by the trial court and the defendant appealed. The plaintiff argued that the defendant should be allowed only one interlocutory appeal and that the second should be dismissed. The Supreme Court ruled for the defendant. It held that a defendant can immediately appeal the denial of summary judgment on the grounds of qualified immunity even if he or shehad previously lodged an unsuccessful appeal of a motion to dismiss. Each motion, the Court reasoned, is subject to different standards and is itself an appealable order under *Mitchell.* Thus, in some instances, a plaintiff may have to prevail in two appeals before proceeding to trial.

The Court limited the application of collateral order doctrine in the context of qualified immunity in the case of Johnson v. Jones (1995). Jones was arrested for being drunk on public streets, though he actually suffered an insulin seizure. He was taken to the police station but later found himself in a hospital with several broken ribs. Jones sued five police, officers alleging that they inflicted excessive force during the course of his arrest and incarceration. Three of the officers moved for summary judgment on the grounds that there was no evidence they had beaten Jones or were present while others did so. The District Court denied their motion, ruling that circumstantial evidence supported Jones' theory of the case. The officers filed an interlocutory appeal that was dismissed by the Court of Appeals.

The Supreme Court held that the officers' appeal did not fall within the collateral order doctrine as applied in *Mitchell.* The primary distinction between the two cases related to the grounds asserted for summary judgment by the respective defendants. The interlocutory appeal in *Mitchell* "concerned, not which facts the parties might be able to prove, but, rather, whether or not certain given facts showed a violation of 'clearly established' law." *Jones*, on the other hand, was exclusively concerned with factual disputes and the sufficiency of the evidence. In such instances, the motion for summary judgment does not raise a legal question collateral to and independent of the merits of the underlying claim. "The upshot is that, compared to *Mitchell*, considerations of delay, comparative expertise of trial and appellate courts, and wise use of appellate resources argue in favor of limiting interlocutory appeals of 'qualified immunity' matters to cases presenting more abstract issues of law."

One other limitation on *Mitchell* merits brief mention. Most constitutional tort claims are filed in federal courts and are subject to the federal rules of civil procedure. Such suits, howerver, can be filed in state courts, as well. (See "Liability of Governmental Entities"). In Johnson v. Fankell (1997), the Supreme Court held that defendants in constitutional tort actions brought in state courts do not have a federal right to an interlocutory appeal from a denial of qualified immunity. The Court reasoned that the collateral order doctrine is an interpretation of a federal statute (28 U.S.C. § 1291) that does not purport to govern judicial proceedings in state court. Thus, the availability of an interlocutory appeal will depend on state law and not the collateral order doctrine as applied in *Mitchell* and *Jones*.

The Relationship Between Qualified Immunity and the Substantive Constitutional Right

When the Constitutional Violation Depends on the Defendant's State of Mind

We have seen that *Harlow* makes the defendant's subjective state of mind irrelevant to the issue of qualified immunity. The defendant's state of mind may be of critical importance, however, in determining whether there is a violation of substantive constitutional rights. There are many situations in which the plaintiff must prove an improper motive to establish a violation of a constitutional right (see "Due Process and other Constitutional Rights"). For example, plaintiffs must prove that the defendant intended to discriminate on a constitutionally impermissible basis to establish a violation of the equal protection clause of the Fourteenth Amendment for race or gender discrimination. Similarly, improper motive is an element of claims alleging cruel and unusual punishment (Eight Amendment), termination of government employment based on political affiliation (First Amendment), and retaliation by government officials against those who exercise their right to free speech (first Amendment). Because intent is an essential element of the substantive constitutional claim in many cases, the defendant's subjective state of mind becomes a key issue in the litigation.

A tension is thus created when the defendant's state of mind is an essential element of substantive constitutional claim but is deemed irrelevant for purposes of qualified immunity. What are lower courts to do when *Harlow* instructs them not to allow intrusive inquiries into a government official's motive, but the plaintiff must prove improper motive in order to establish a constitutional violation? The critical practical issue faced by lower courts is how a plaintiff can be given a chance to prove improper motive without incurring the "special costs" of state-of-mind inquiries decried in *Harlow*?

In Crawford-El v. Britton (1998) the Court considered the relationship between the irrelevance of good faith in the context of qualified immunity and the requirement of improper motive in establishing a First Amendment retaliation claim. Crawford-El, described by the Court as a "litigious and outspoken prisoner," was transferred to a number of different prisons. During one of these transfers, boxes of Crawford-El's personal belongings, including legal materials, were given to his brother-in-law instead of being shipped directly to the prison facility. Shipping the boxes outside official prison channels resulted in a delay of several months in his receiving the materials. The plaintiff alleged that the defendant intentionally misdirected the boxes to punish him for exercising his First Amendment rights.

The District Court dismissed Crawford-El's complaint because he did not allege any "direct evidence" of unconstitutional motive. The Court of Appeals held that the plaintiff may rely on circumstantial as well as direct evidence of improper motive to support his claim. However, the plaintiff must establish that motive by "clear and convincing" evidence—a standard of proof more demanding than the "preponderance of evidence" standard that governs most civil cases. According to the Court of Appeals, a "heightened burden of proof" was required by the reasoning of *Harlow* in order to protect government officials from the costs of litigation in unconstitutional-motive cases.

A closely divided Supreme Court reversed this decision. Justice Stevens began the majority opinion by explaining that *Harlow* spoke only to the defense of qualified immunity and not to the substantive constitutional right. Thus, according to the majority, *Harlow* could not be fairly read to change the nature of the plaintiff's burden of proving a constitutional violation. Justice Stevens acknowledged that some of the concerns that led the *Harlow* Court to eliminate the state-of-mind component of the qualified immunity defense might also apply when the state-of-mind inquiry is raised in the context of establishing a substantive constitutional violation. But, he wrote, "there are countervailing concerns that must be considered."

The majority reasoned that the "special costs" of state-of-mind inquiries were less disruptive of government when raised in the context of an alleged violation of a specific substantive constitutional right than when framed in terms of "the bare allegations of malice" that were used to rebut a qualified immunity defense before *Harlow*. That is, an inquiry into an alleged retaliatory motive is "more specific" (and hence, less intrusive) than an "open-ended inquiry into subjective motivation." Furthermore, defendants in improper-motive cases might be able to avoid unnecessary trials if the plaintiff cannot establish other elements of the claim, such as causation. Trial judges can employ "existing procedures" to control pleadings and discovery so as to "facilitate prompt and efficient resolution of the lawsuit." The bottom-line assessment of the majority was that "broad discretion in the management of the factfinding process may be more useful and equitable to all the parties than the categorical rule imposed by the Court of Appeals."

The dissenting justices believed that the majority did not give appropriate weight to *Harlow*'s policies counseling against inquiries into the subjective state of mind of government officials. Justices Rehnquist and O'Connor would embrace a rule "that a government official who is a defendant in a motive-based tort suit is entitled to immunity from suit so long as he can offer a legitimate reason for the action that is being challenged, and the plaintiff is unable to establish, by reliance on objective evidence, that the offered reason is actually a pretext." Justices Scalia and Thomas would go further and grant immunity to a government official who can articulate a legitimate justification for the challenged action. They would refuse to permit any rebuttal by the plaintiff even if he or she can offer objective evidence of pretext. Justice Kennedy agreed with the dissenting justices that there were "serious concerns" that motive-based claims could give rise to "frivolous and farcical" lawsuits but concurred in the majority opinion because "the authority to propose those far-reaching solutions lies with the legislative branch, not with us."

The essential policy question posed by both *Harlow* and *Crawford-El* is how to balance the plaintiff's and public's interest in securing redress when badly motivated government officials injure a person against the defendant's and public's interest in avoiding litigation that will unduly interfere with the efficient operation of government. *Harlow* strikes this balance in favor of defendants when the state-of-mind inquiry arises in the context of a qualified immunity defense. The majority in *Crawford-El* strikes the balance in favor of plaintiffs when improper motivation is an essential element of the substantive constitutional claim. The practical effect of the majority opinion in *Crawford-El* is that more motive-based constitutional tort claims will proceed to trial.

When Objective Legal Reasonableness Is an Element of the Constitutional Right

Harlow and *Anderson* eliminated the subjective element of qualified immunity and transformed the defense into one based on objective reasonableness. That is, the defendant's own good faith, malice, or other state of mind does not matter. A government official is immune from liability unless it would be clear to a reasonable official that his conduct was unlawful in the situation he confronted. A similar standard has evolved for evaluating claims based on the alleged use of excessive force during an arrest. In Graham v. Connor (1989) the Supreme Court held that claims of excessive force in the context of arrests should be analyzed under the Fourth Amendment's "objective reasonableness" standard. This means that the use of force during an arrest will not be considered unconstitutionally excessive unless it would be clear to a reasonable officer that under the circumstances the force employed was unlawful. Again, the test does not depend on the defendant's state of mind. Thus, both the general standard of qualified immunity and the Fourth Amendment standard for excessive force are grounded in objective reasonableness.

The common emphasis on objective reasonableness has raised the question of whether the standards for recognizing qualified immunity and the substantive standards of the Fourth Amendment are identical. The practical importance of this issue arises in the context of summary judgment. As discussed previously, trial courts will deny defense motions for summary judgment if there are disputed issues of material fact. Often there are disputed factual issues in an excessive force case, such as need for the use of force and the amount of force actually used. If disputed issues of this nature would preclude summary judgment on the substantive question of whether the force used was unconstitutionally excessive, and if the standard for determining whether force is excessive is identical to that used to determine qualified immunity, defense motions for summary judgment on qualified immunity would also be denied.

The Supreme Court addressed the relationship between qualified immunity and the substantive Fourth Amendment standards for excessive force in Saucier v. Katz (2001). Officer Saucier arrested Katz, an animal rights protester who was trying to display a banner at a speech given by Vice President Gore at the Presidio Army Base. Katz alleged that Saucier used excessive force in removing him from the crowd and violently shoving him into a van. Saucier filed a motion for summary judgment claiming that the forced used was not unconstitutionally excessive and that he was entitled to qualified immunity. The lower courts ruled that Saucier's motion for summary judgment should be denied and that the case should proceed to trial. They reasoned that there were disputed issues of material fact concerning whether the force used was excessive. Thus, summary judgment could not be entered on the merits of the constitutional claim. Nor could Saucier be granted summary judgment on qualified immunity, because, in the view of the lower courts, the standard for qualified immunity was identical to that used to determine whether force was excessive.

The Supreme Court reversed the ruling of the the lower courts, holding that Saucier was entitled to summary judgment on qualified immunity. A majority of the Court "assumed" that a jury could find that Katz was the victim of excessive force. Nonetheless, the lower courts erred in concluding Saucier was not entitled to summary judgment on qualified immunity. The Court held that the standard for evaluating the merits of the excessive force claim was not identical to that used to determine qualified immunity. In the view of a majority of the justices, Saucier was entitled to qualified immunity because "[i]t cannot be said there was a clearly established rule that would prohibit using the force [Saucier] did to place [Katz] into the van to accomplish [the] objectives" of protecting the vice president and restoring order to the scene.

Three justices disagreed with the majority on whether the standards used to evaluate the merits of an excessive force claim differed from those used to decide qualified immunity. These Justices concluded that "the determination of police misconduct in excessive force cases and the availability of qualified immunity hinge on the same question: Taking into account the particular circumstances confronting the defendant officer, could a reasonable officer, identically situated, have believed the force employed was lawful?" The concurring justices agreed with the majority, however, that Saucier should prevail. In their view, Katz presented no evidence to support his claim that Saucier used unconstitutionally excessive force. Thus, Saucier was entitled to summary judgment—not because of qualified immunity—but because Katz could not prove that his Fourth Amendment rights had been violated.

Under the majority opinion, qualified immunity and the merits of an excessive force claim are separate and distinct issues. It is theoretically possible for a lower court to conclude that a jury could find that the amount of force used to make an arrest was not objectively reasonable (and, hence, a violation of the Fourth Amendment under *Graham*), but it would not be clear to a reasonable officer that his or her conduct was unlawful under the circumstances (and, hence, he or she would be protected by qualified immunity under *Harlow*). Whether such a distinction proves to be linguistically or conceptually sound remains to be seen. What is clear for the moment, however, is that an officer may be entitled to qualified immunity even if a court concludes a jury could find that the use of force was not objectively reasonable.

Persons Not Protected by Qualified Immunity

Most defendants in constitutional tort actions are government officials. There are situations, however, when private persons may be named as defendants. One such situation involves a private person who acts under color of state law to deprive the plaintiff of constitutional rights. These cases, which were discussed in "Self-Help Remedies," frequently involve private citizens who invoke state law to seize or recover property without a trial. Another situation involves government contracting with a private person or company to provide governmental services, such as when a state privatizes the operation of a jail or prison. The question arises in such cases whether these nominally private defendants are entitled to the same qualified immunity that protects government officials.

In Wyatt v. Cole (1992) one partner in a business (Cole) used state procedures to seize cattle and other property of another partner (Wyatt) without the benefit of any judicial hearing. When Cole refused to return the property, Wyatt brought suit under § 1983. He charged that Cole acted under color of state law to deprive Wyatt of property without due process of law in violation of the Due Process Clause of the Fourteenth Amendment. The Supreme Court held that Cole had no immunity in this situation, explaining that private persons were not afforded an immunity at common law at the time § 1983 was enacted, and that the policy considerations giving rise to the defense did not apply when the defendant was not a government official. But the Court's opinion was a narrow one. The Court did "not foreclose the possibility that private defendants faced with § 1983 liability . . . could be entitled to an affirmative defense based on good faith. . ." In this way, the Court set the stage for a subtle distinction between an "immunity," which the private actor could not assert, and a "good faith defense," which may be available to him or her.

The case was remanded to the Court of Appeals, which subsequently recognized a defense of good faith.[86] Although an affirmative defense of good faith may appear to be the same thing as a defense of qualified immunity, there are important differences. The good faith defense turns on the subjective state of mind of the defendant, something deemed irrelevant to qualified immunity under *Harlow*. Thus, the private defendant is not protected from what the *Harlow* Court described as intrusive inquiries into motivation. Moreover, qualified immunity is a protection against having to defend the lawsuit, so that under *Mitchell*, denials of defendants' motions for summary judgment are often subject to interlocutory appeal. By contrast, a denial of a motion for summary judgment on the affirmative defense of good faith would not be immediately appealable.

A later case extends this reasoning to another context in which private actors may be sued under § 1983. In Richardson v. McKnight (1997) the issue was whether guards at a privately operated prison were entitled to the same qualified immunity as guards at a state-run facility. A sharply divided Court by a 5–4 margin held that they were not. Although conceding that the private prison guard's claim of immunity was stronger than that of the private businessman in *Wyatt*, Justice Breyer's majority opinion held that it ultimately fell short. The majority reasoned that there was no "firmly rooted" tradition of immunity applicable to private prison guards at common law. More importantly, it concluded that the policy considerations that support conferring qualified immunity on state prison guards did not apply with equal force in the context of a privatized facility. The opinion emphasized the presence of market forces in the privatized prison that are not present in the state-run facility. A private prison is operated by

> a private company subject to competitive market pressures . . . that mean not only that a firm whose guards are too aggressive will face damages that raise costs, thereby threatening its replacement, but also that a firm whose guards are too timid will face threats of replacement by other firms with records that demonstrate their ability to do both a safer and more effective job.

Moreover, a private firm is not constrained by civil service laws applicable to public employment. This "permits the private firm, unlike a government department, to offset any increased employee liability risk with higher pay or extra benefits."

The dissenting justices, speaking through Justice Scalia, were not convinced that market forces obviated the need for an immunity. In the first place, it is "fanciful to speak of the consequences of 'market' pressures where public officials are the only purchaser and other people's money the medium of payment." Second, even if market forces did apply, "*price* (not discipline) will be the predominating factor in such a regime's selection of a contractor." Third, there was no reason to believe that private prison guards were more likely to violate inmates' constitutional rights than were state prison guards.

Together, *Wyatt* and *Richardson* signal that private persons who act under color of state law to deprive a person of rights secured by the Constitution will receive less protection than government officials. The Court does not appear to be convinced that immunity is needed to prevent overdeterrence of private parties. The key to this reasoning is that private persons stand to gain by their actions. They are in a position to assess whether the potential personal gain outweighs the liability risks of their actions, and the prospect of personal gain will prevent them from acting too cautiously. By contrast, government officials personally do not gain from their official actions. Consequently greater special insulation from liability is thought to be needed to keep them from becoming too timid.

Conclusion

Qualified immunity as described in this chapter reflects a judicial balancing of competing goals and objectives. On the one hand, the plaintiff and the public have an interest in compensating victims of constitutional wrongs and deterring future misconduct. On the other hand, the defendant and the public have an interest in avoiding overdeterrence. The balance struck by the Court's current case law tilts in favor of the latter set of interests. Both the substantive doctrine and procedural rules elevate qualified immunity to a formidable defense. *Harlow*'s elimination of the good faith element means that even the badly motivated government official is insulated from liability so long as the conduct was objectively reasonable. *Anderson*'s emphasis on factual specificity makes more difficult the plaintiff's burden of showing clearly established law. The standards for summary judgment and the interlocutory appeals authorized by *Mitchell* guarantee there will be additional cost and delay before a plaintiff can present his or her claim to a jury. The net effect of these substantive and procedural rules has been described by one prominent commentator as "instruct[ing] the decision-maker, the judge (and *not* the jury), to empathize with the defendant. . . , thus forcing § 1983 plaintiffs to bear their own losses even when their constitutional rights are violated."[87]

REMEDIES: DAMAGES, INJUNCTIONS, DECLARATORY RELIEF, AND ATTORNEY'S FEES

Throughout this book we explore the issues that arise when someone goes on the offense, so to speak, against government action that may be unconstitutional. In these suits the citizen is the plaintiff in litigation that challenges the validity of action by a government official. Of course, the point of bringing such a suit is to obtain a remedy of some kind. This section takes it as a given that the plaintiff has established a constitutional violation and has overcome other potential obstacles such as the immunity doctrines discussed in "Qualified Immunity" and "Absolute Immunity." This section deals with the remedies available to a successful plaintiff in a § 1983 suit, including the recovery of attorney's fees.

At the outset, a basic distinction should be noted between prospective and retrospective remedies, for different principles apply to these two categories of relief. A "prospective" remedy is one that looks to the future. It gives directions to the government as to how it must or must not behave going forward. These remedies may include the "injunction" (an order forbidding or compelling the government to act in a certain way) and the "declaratory judgment" (which simply states the rights and duties of the two sides without issuing any immediately enforceable orders). These remedies are discussed later in this section. The main "retrospective" remedy is damages: a payment of money that is, in principle, equal to the injury done to the plaintiff by the defendant's wrong. By contrast to prospective remedies, the focus of attention is on a constitutional wrong that has already taken place. The award of money to the injured party is supposed to make up for that wrong.

In order to avoid confusion, a curious feature of the remedial law ought to be noted before going any further with the substantive analysis. One may sue local and state officials and local governments on constitutional grounds for damages, but such suits for retrospective relief cannot be maintained against state governments. One may obtain prospective relief against not only local officials and governments but also against state government officials. The practical effect of these rules is that one may obtain prospective relief against a state government but not backward-looking relieflike damages. This distinction raises two questions: (a) Why do courts distinguish so sharply between prospective and retrospective relief? and (b) What relief may be obtained under the rule that, in effect, allows prospective remedies against state governments?

By distinguishing between prospective and retrospective remedies, we do not mean to give the impression that the plaintiff is required to make a choice between pursuing one or the other kind of remedy. In some cases, both damages and injunctive relief may be appropriate. In others, it will be apparent from the circumstances that only one or the other can be an effective remedy. The test for which remedy should be sought is the timing of the constitutional violation. A number of fact patterns need to be distinguished: (a) If the violation is altogether finished by the time of the trial, and there is little chance it will be repeated, then damages for the past injury is the only relief that may be obtained. An example would be a suit brought by the victim of a beating by the police at the local jail, who cannot show that the beating of suspects is an ongoing practice at the jail. (b) On the other hand, if the violation has not yet taken place but is threatened in the future, then there is no point in seeking damages as there is not yet any harm to be remedied. An injunction or a declaratory judgment is the proper remedy against the future threat of a constitutional violation. Suppose, for example, a state enacts a law that forbids protected speech, but the law has not yet been applied to anyone. (c) In some cases, the violation began in the past and continues up to the moment of the judge's ruling. In that event, both damages (for the harm that has already occurred) and prospective relief (to stop the continuing violation) should be available. Suppose, for example, that the plaintiff is a government employee who was dismissed for engaging in speech protected by the First Amendment. Damages should be awarded for the harm already suffered, and an injunction may be issued as well, ordering the agency to reinstate the plaintiff in the position from which he or she was, and remains, illegally removed. (d) Occasionally there will be a past violation, the threat of a future violation, yet no present violation. For an illustration, return to fact pattern (a) above. Suppose the jailor has beaten suspects in the past, and has ceased beating suspects for the time being. Yet it can be shown that he is likely to do it in the future (once the litigation with its increased scrutiny of his practices is over and the press is diverted to other matters). In such a case, of course, it may be appropriate to award both damages and an injunction.

Damages

The plaintiff in a constitutional tort case may obtain compensatory and punitive damages on account of injuries suffered in the past. These two kinds of damages serve somewhat different purposes. Compensatory damages are awarded in order to make up for the harm suffered by the plaintiff, and their amount depends on the extent of that harm. The focus of an award of punitive damages is not the plaintiff's injury but the egregiousness of the defendant's conduct; it is aimed at expressing society's disapproval of that conduct and at deterring similar behavior in the future. There is overlap as to the functions served by compensatory and punitive damages. We shall see that deterrence is an aim of compensatory damages as well. But there are important differences between compensatory and punitive damages, and, to avoid confusion, it is wise to keep them separate. We first deal with the issues raised by compensatory damages and then turn to punitive damages later in this section.

We shall see that principles drawn from the common law of torts are highly relevant to the resolution of damages issues in constitutional tort cases. Setting forth some of those principles now will provide the necessary context for understanding the Supreme Court's approach to damages in constitutional torts. In the common law, a central aim of damages is to "make the plaintiff whole" by obliging the wrongdoer to pay him an amount of money equivalent to what the plaintiff lost in the accident. If the plaintiff is physically injured, the defendant must pay the medical expenses, both for services already rendered and for those likely to be needed in the future. The same is true for the services of a psychologist in the event the plaintiff suffered emotional distress because of the defendant's wrong. If the plaintiff has missed work or will likely miss work in the future, the defendant is obliged to pay the lost salary, past and future. These are called "pecuniary" losses because they can be measured in dollars. The injured plaintiff is also entitled to "nonpecuniary" compensatory damages. These damages do not make up for money the plaintiff has paid or has been unable to earn on account of the accident. They are aimed at compensating the plaintiff for a category of harms called "pain and suffering" by common law courts. But the name may be a bit misleading. This group of harms includes not only the pain of the accident but such experiences as anxiety, depression, humiliation, embarrassment, and loss of enjoyment of life, even if the plaintiff cannot show that the injury cost him any money.[88]

One general aspect of damages law that is relevant to all the issues discussed herein is the division of decision making between the judge and the jury. In deciding damages issues, the role of the jury is to determine their amount, and the role of the judge is to inform (or "instruct") the jurors as to the legal rules they should apply in determining the damages. Hence, we shall see that one important question is the content of those instructions. Judges have another role as well. After the jury returns from its deliberations with an award, the trial judge and the appellate court must determine whether the amount is justified by the evidence. One approach to answering this question, though not necessarily the best, is to compare the award made in this case with the amounts awarded in similar cases in the past.[89]

Carey v. Piphus: The Supreme Court's First Section 1983 Damages Case

The Supreme Court first addressed damages issues in constitutional tort suits in Carey v. Piphus (1978), setting forth guidelines that still govern damage awards today. Piphus was a junior high school student who got into trouble when the principal observed him smoking an irregular-looking cigarette. Without holding any kind of hearing to determine whether this was a marijuana cigarette, the principal concluded that it was and summarily ordered that Piphus be suspended from school. The Supreme Court subsequently ruled, in Goss v. Lopez (1975), that a student is entitled to a hearing, as a matter of procedural due process, before being suspended. Piphus sued, seeking damages for denial of his right to procedural due process, and the Circuit Court of Appeals held that he was entitled to obtain substantial damages for the violation of procedural due process even if the suspension itself was justified. The Supreme Court reversed this decision, ruling that "the basic purpose of a § 1983 damages award should be to compensate persons for injuries caused by the deprivation of constitutional rights." Piphus could recover substantial non-punitive damages only if he could prove the constitutional violation caused an actual injury. He could not recover for injuries that could not be traced to the violation of his constitutional rights.[90]

Notice the implications of this ruling for various possible scenarios: (1) If the suspension were not justified, and a hearing would have prevented the suspension from occurring, then Piphus would be entitled to damages due to the suspension. (2) If the suspension were in fact justified, he could obtain damages only for harm caused by the denial of due process. For example, in theory one may be able to show that denial of due process causes emotional distress, or even physical symptoms resulting from emotional distress, however improbable this may be in practice. But there would be no recovery for emotional distress caused by a justified dismissal. (3) In the event the suspension were justified, and Pipus could not prove any emotional distress or other damages resulting from the denial of due process, then he would only obtain "nominal" damages (typically, one dollar) as a symbolic recognition that a constitutional violation occurred. He would receive nominal damages even though no substantial damage occurred. The practical importance of such an award is twofold: First, the lawsuit will have determined that the conduct of which the plaintiff complains was in fact unconstitutional, and this determination (rather than an award of money) may be the main point of the litigation. Second, nominal damages may be a sufficient ground for an award of attorney's fees. See "When May a Party Recover Attorney's Fees: Who Is a Prevailing Party." Whether the plaintiff may obtain punitive damages is, of course, a separate question, (Attorney's fees and punitive damages will be discussed later in this section.)

In reaching this result, the Supreme Court could not rely on the text of § 1983, for the statute says absolutely nothing about the principles that are to determine damages awards in constitutional tort cases. The Supreme Court's reasoning relies heavily on principles of damages that have been developed through the years in the common law of torts. But the Court did not simply borrow the common law because it is a convenient source of rules for constitutional tort. Explaining its reference to the common law, the Court stated, "The Members of the Congress that enacted § 1983 did not directly address the question of damages, but the principle that damages are designed to compensate persons for injuries caused by the deprivation of rights hardly could have been foreign to the many lawyers in Congress in 1871." This reasoning suggests that the Court's justification for using the common law is that this is what the framers of the statute intended. The 1871 Congress that enacted § 1983 acted against the background of common law rules, and meant to have damages issues resolved by reference to those rules. Thus, in support of its adoption of the compensation principle, the Court quoted a torts treatise for the proposition that "the cardinal principle of damages in Anglo-American law is that of compensation for the injury caused to plaintiff by defendant's breach of duty."[91]

Memphis Independent School District v. Stachura: Damages for Substantive Rights

An important question remained open after *Carey*. From the perspective of damages, the violation of procedural due process rights (as in *Carey*) differs from most constitutional rights because a procedural violation does not necessarily produce any substantive harm. Therefore, a procedural violation does not always justify a recovery for the substantive harm suffered by the plaintiff. The substantive penalty may be entirely justified and noncompensable. For example, if the school principal could show that Piphus was in fact smoking marijuana, and that his suspension from school was in fact justified, then Piphus could not in any event recover for the harm due to the suspension, only for whatever harm may have occurred solely on account of the due process violation. This means that in many cases there will be no significant harm due to the simple violation of procedural due process. Given this feature of procedural due process, it is easy to see why the Court would be reluctant to allow a substantial recovery of money without some proof that, in the circumstances of a given case, the procedural violation really did produce some harm.

Substantive constitutional rights may receive more sympathetic treatment. In *Carey* itself the Court's reasoning suggested that a different approach to damages may be needed for such cases. The Court in *Carey* did not rule that the common law "compensation principle" should necessarily be applied in the same way to every constitutional tort case. It said that, sometimes, "the interests protected by a particular branch of the common law of torts . . . parallel closely the interests protected by a particular constitutional right. In such cases, it may be appropriate to apply the tort rules of damages directly to the § 1983 action." But "[i]n other cases, the interests protected by a particular constitutional right may not also be protected by an analogous branch of the common law of torts." In that event, "the task will be the more difficult one of adapting common-law rules of damages to provide fair compensation for injuries caused by the deprivation of a constitutional right." Because of the differences between constitutional and common law rights, "the rules governing compensation for injuries caused by the deprivation of constitutional rights should be tailored to the interests protected by the particular right in question."

Eight years after *Carey*, in Memphis Community School District v. Stachura (1986), the Court considered the issue of damages for substantive constitutional violations. The plaintiff was a public school teacher who had been suspended, with pay, when a controversy arose regarding his methods of teaching about human reproduction. Assuming that the suspension violated his right of free speech, the Supreme Court examined the judge's instruction to the jury concerning damages for violations of the substantive right of freedom of speech. The judge was obviously concerned with the difficulty of placing a monetary value on free speech rights. He had told the jury that "[d]amages for this type of injury are more difficult to measure than damages for physical injury or injury to one's property" because "[t]here are no medical bills or other expenses by which you can judge how much compensation is appropriate." But "just because these rights are not capable of precise evaluation does not mean that an appropriate monetary amount should not be awarded." Thus, he told the jury that they could award damages for the "value" of freedom of speech and that they "may wish to consider the importance of the right in our system of government, the role which this right has played in the history of our republic, [and] the significance of the right in the context of the activities which the plaintiff was engaged in at the time of the violation of that right." The jury awarded $275,000 in compensatory damages (an amount the judge reduced to $266,750).

The Supreme Court ruled that the judge committed an error when he gave this instruction on damages. The Court seemed to give little weight to its comments in *Carey* that some constitutional rights may receive different treatment from the strict limits on damages for violations of procedural due process. Instead, it reiterated its premise that "the level of damages [in § 1983 cases] is ordinarily determined according to principles derived from the common law of torts" and reaffirmed the central ruling of *Carey*, that "damages in tort cases are designed to provide compensation for the injury caused to plaintiff by defendant's breach of duty." The problem with the judge's instruction was that it focused "not on compensation for provable injury, but on the jury's subjective perception of the importance of constitutional rights as an abstract matter. *Carey* establishes that such an approach is impermissible." The Court rejected the notion that substantive rights should receive different treatment: *Carey* did "not establish a two-tiered system of constitutional rights, with substantive rights afforded greater protection than 'mere' procedural safeguards." Since the compensation principle governs both substantive and procedural rights, there is "no room for noncompensatory damages measured by the jury's perception of the abstract 'importance' of a constitutional right."

Compensation for Harm and Vindication of Constitutional Rights

So far in this section we have described the Supreme Court's adoption for constitutional torts of the common law tort principle that the aim of damages is to compensate the plaintiff for the loss he or she has suffered. *Stachura* established that the Court would apply this principle to violations of substantive constitutional rights as well as to those of procedural due process. In order to fully understand this rule, we need to examine in greater detail the purposes served by compensation in tort law. In addition, we must consider whether certain special features of constitutional tort may bear on the role of compensation in the § 1983 context. Identifying and explaining the functions served by compensatory damages for constitutional torts is the aim of this and the next section.

Compensating the victim of an accident (or of a constitutional violation) serves two distinct goals. One is "corrective justice" (discussed in this section) and the other is "deterrence" (discussed in the next section). The point of corrective justice is to vindicate the plaintiff's rights, whether one's rights are defined by the law of torts and its rules governing the care actors must take to avoid injuring others, or by the Bill of Rights and the Fourteenth Amendment.[92] In either kind of case, the damages issue is reached only after the plaintiff has established a violation of those rights. By awarding damages for the injury caused by the violation, the courts recognize and reaffirm the rights themselves. By contrast, allowing the injury to go uncompensated would send a signal that the rights themselves are worthless and can be trampled upon with impunity. Common law courts have held that the amount of damages necessary to vindicate the plaintiff's rights is measured by the amount of harm the plaintiff has suffered as a result of the violation. *Carey* and *Stachura* adopt this principle for the constitutional context as well. The reason why this basis for awarding damages is sometimes called "corrective justice" is that the defendant has committed a wrong, the plaintiff has suffered as a result, and the role of damages is to undo, or correct, the wrong by obliging the defendant to make the plaintiff whole.

One lesson of *Carey*, and especially of *Stachura*, is that the logic of corrective justice not only justifies damages but places limits on their recovery. For it implies that the simple fact of a constitutional violation, without doing any harm, does not require any vindication or correction. At any rate, this is clearly the Court's view. One may argue, to the contrary, that constitutional rights are different from other rights; by their nature, these are fundamental rights. Because they are the most important rights we hold, there may be good reason to vindicate them by an award of damages even where no harm results from their violation. This seems to have been the reasoning underlying the trial judge's instruction to the jury in *Stachura* on the nonmonetary value of constitutional rights. Though the Supreme Court rejected this view, it may resurface in the future.

On the other hand, the Court's view of the importance of vindication may be vulnerable to attack from the opposite direction as well. Even where the plaintiff has suffered harm as a result of a constitutional violation, there is an argument that justice, properly understood, does not justify recovery. The argument is that justice has at least two dimensions. Conceding that corrective justice favors recovery, considerations of "distributive" justice must also be taken into account. While corrective justice addresses the appropriate response to violations of rights, distributive justice is concerned with the overall allocation of resources in society. The relevance of this notion to our subject is that an advocate of a more equal distribution of wealth may favor using government's resources to achieve greater equality rather than using them to correct injustices. The point is not that distributive justice must necessarily take precedence over corrective justice, but merely that arguments based on "justice" may be made both for and against constitutional tort liability.[93]

Deterring Constitutional Violations

In both *Carey* and *Stachura* the Supreme Court declares that the aim of damages is to compensate the plaintiff for losses due to constitutional violations. Besides vindicating the plaintiff's rights, in both cases the Court affirms that compensation also serves the goal of deterring constitutional violations. Yet the measure of deterrence is defined by the amount of compensatory damages. In meeting arguments by the plaintiffs that deterrence may require damage awards larger than the amounts of damages plaintiffs can prove, the Court's response in *Stachura* was that deterrence "operates through the mechanism of damages that are compensatory—damages grounded in determinations of plaintiffs' actual losses." And in *Carey* the Court asserted that there was "no evidence that [Congress] meant to establish a deterrent more formidable than that inherent in the award of compensatory damages."

Though the Court never specifies exactly how deterrence should operate, the reasoning is clear to anyone familiar with the way economists explain human behavior. The reasoning begins with a hypothetical world in which there are no penalties for committing wrongs. Given a choice between acting as one pleases and doing what is required by some legal norm, many people will do as they please, including committing constitutional violations. In order to counter this tendency to pursue our own preferences rather than to obey the law, it is necessary to attach sanctions to the breach of legal norms, including violations of constitutional rights. If actors know that doing as they please without regard for others will have bad consequences for their own welfare, through litigation that will extract money from their bank accounts, then they will be dissuaded from illegal conduct. A premise of this reasoning is that people are generally rational; they will prefer a state of affairs in which they are better off to one in which they are worse off. Thus, they will prefer to obey the law and keep their money rather than violate the law and hand it over to the victim of the wrong. Assessing damages equal to the amount of harm suffered by the victim will, it is argued, provide the right incentive to avoid harm to others.

For the sake of focusing on the constitutional tort context, let us assume that this reasoning is sound with regard to private actors and ordinary torts. (Note, however, that some critics find fault with it even in that context.)[94] In the constitutional tort context, an argument can be made for a stronger deterrent than is provided by compensatory damages. Much of the value of constitutional rights is, as the trial judge in *Stachura* recognized, nonmonetary, and much of that value is shared in common with everyone. One cannot easily prove a nonmonetary loss, and it is not possible under common law tort principles to recover for a loss that was suffered by others. If these things are true, a rule that the plaintiff may recover only for losses he or she has suffered (and can prove) will systematically undervalue constitutional rights and too feebly deter their violation.[95]

Conversely, one may maintain that in the constitutional context, or indeed whenever a government or official is the defendant, it may be futile to expect that damages will deter violations. The point is that the payment of damages assessed against the government comes out of tax revenues. When officials are held liable, they are very often indemnified by the government for which they work. This being so, officials will not respond to the prospect of tort liability by weighing the pluses of engaging in the forbidden activity against the minuses of having to pay damages. Any deterrence will come not from the requirement that damages be paid (a disincentive they will not feel) but rather from the prospect of losing the next election (or, in the case of an unelected the prospect of being fired by elected officers). In some circumstances, officials will change their behavior if there is any chance they may be held liable. But in other situations, officials may be personally better off, in terms of staying in power, by violating the Constitution and using tax dollars to pay damages. One cannot say with confidence, as a general proposition, that the threat of damages will go very far toward deterring violations. How they will behave depends on a range of circumstances not taken into account under the current legal regime.[96]

So far, neither the arguments against deterrence nor the arguments for allowing damages over and above what is needed to compensate the plaintiff have had any impact on the Supreme Court's doctrine. But the state of the law is sufficiently fluid to permit the Court to take either set of arguments into account when and if it revisits this topic. Since *Stachura*, decided in 1986, the Supreme Court has not returned to the problem of constitutional tort damages. This means that there are only two precedents in the area and plenty of room for drawing distinctions and exploring new directions, if the Court chooses to do so.

Presumed Damages

One means by which the Court may choose to reconsider damages doctrine is to address the question of whether presumed damages may be awarded for constitutional violations. "Presumed damages" is a common law doctrine that allows the jury to award substantial compensatory damages to the plaintiff even though he or she cannot prove harm. The rationale for these damages is that there are situations in which it is likely that the plaintiff has suffered an injury, yet the harm is difficult to prove.[97]

Courts decide whether presumed damages are proper by asking whether the rationale applies to a given type of case. For example, presumed damages are frequently allowed in defamation law. The theory of recovery in defamation is that a plaintiff's reputation deserves legal protection from false statements that are communicated to third persons. "Libel" is the name of the tort when a defendant puts the statements in writing or in some other permanent form. "Slander" is the term used to denote spoken words. The general rule is that a defendant may be liable when his or her written or spoken statements falsely accuse the plaintiff of lying, or of criminal conduct, or of some other behavior that threatens the plaintiff's standing with others. With regard to damages, the victim of libel or slander faces a problem that does not come up in physical injury cases. The harm is that others may, upon hearing or reading the defamatory statement, choose not to have relations with the plaintiff. But the plaintiff may have no idea who these people are and no way of finding out who they are. Courts try to cope with the difficulty of proof by allowing the jury to "presume" damages, without proof, in certain circumstances in which the likelihood of harm seems great. Presumed damages are permitted, for example, where slander undermines the plaintiff's standing in his profession.

The argument for applying the presumed damages doctrine to constitutional tort rests on the premise that the victim of a constitutional violation suffers an injury, even if the violation has no economic, physical, or emotional impact. If this is so, then constitutional tort is similar to defamation in that there may be real harm even though that harm is difficult to prove because it is not only nonmonetary but also nonphysical.[98] Admittedly, the analogy is not perfect, for there is an important difference between constitutional tort and defamation. The reason for the difficulty of proof in defamation is that the harm involves the behavior of unknown third parties, while the reason for the difficulty of proof in constitutional tort is the intangible nature of the injury. But this is not a critical difference, for the underlying rationale for presumed damages is the same: The difficulty of proof is the key, and the difference between the two areas has to do merely with why there is a difficulty of proof. Note also that presumed damages are sometimes awarded in the common law for "dignitary" torts, for example, where the defendant spits in the plaintiff's face, causing no monetary or even emotional harm that could serve as the basis for a traditional award of damages. Perhaps this is a closer analogy to constitutional tort, if one is needed.[99]

Adopting presumed damages for constitutional tort would not violate the central proposition established in *Carey* and *Stachura*, that the aim of constitutional tort damages is to compensate the plaintiff for the harm done by the constitutional violation. The point of presumed damages is not to award extra-compensatory damages, but to recognize that real harm can be impossible to establish, so that an exception may need to be made to the general rule that the plaintiff may recover only the amount of harm he or she can prove. Moreover, presumed damages should not be permitted across the entire range of constitutional torts. As in the common law, they should be allowed only where the circumstances fit the rationale for presumed damages. The victim of excessive police force or the employee fired from his or her job for protected speech will have no difficulty proving substantial damages.

Significant presumed damages would probably not be appropriate in such cases (though one could plausibly argue that the full harm due to the constitutional violation is not reflected in the medical bills and other provable injuries). On the other hand, someone who, in violation of freedom of speech, is denied a permit for a demonstration is in a different situation. The would-be demonstrator certainly suffers a real injury but cannot show any monetary harm as a result. There is a strong case for punitive damages in a situation of that kind. Other rights that fall within this category include the right to vote and the right of religious freedom.

The Court's reasoning in *Stachura* does pose one potential obstacle to the recognition of presumed damages for constitutional torts, though a careful analysis of the opinion shows that the Court actually did not take a position one way or the other. The plaintiff in this case tried unsuccessfully to defend the trial judge's instruction by characterizing it as authorizing a form of presumed damages. Though the Court rejected this argument, it also affirmed that "[w]hen a plaintiff seeks compensation for an injury that is likely to have occurred but difficult to establish, some form of presumed damages may possibly be appropriate." In such a case, "presumed damages may roughly approximate the harm that the plaintiff suffered and thereby compensate for harms that may be impossible to measure." The problem with the plaintiff's theory was that the instruction given by the judge on the societal value of First Amendment rights "did not serve this purpose, but instead called on the jury to measure damages based on a subjective evaluation of the importance of particular constitutional values." Thus, the Court found that the instruction was not really aimed at authorizing presumed damages. It did not decide that a properly worded presumed damages instruction would be unacceptable, nor did it declare that a presumed damages instruction would be upheld; it simply did not reach the issue of whether presumed damages could be awarded in constitutional tort cases.

Punitive Damages: Newport v. Fact Concerts and Smith v. Wade

In *Carey* and *Stachura*, the Supreme Court adopts as its central premise the principle that the purpose of damages in constitutional torts is to compensate the plaintiff for harm caused by the violation. Relying on that principle, the Court has rebuffed attempts to obtain damages without showing harm. In one area of damages doctrine, however, proof of harm is not required, either in common law torts or in constitutional torts. In addition to the compensatory damages discussed in the previous sections, the victim of a common law tort may, on a proper showing, obtain punitive damages. According to the punitive and deterrent goals such damages would serve, a jury has wide discretion both whether to award them and how much to award in the circumstances of a given case.

Like compensatory damages, punitives were among the common law principles familiar to the framers of § 1983, and they remain an important part of common law tort doctrine today. Applying the framework it had established in *Carey* for compensatory damages, the Supreme Court addressed punitive damages issues in City of Newport v. Fact Concerts (1981) and Smith v. Wade (1983). The Court held, first of all, that punitive damages may be awarded in § 1983 cases. This seems to be a sound rule from the perspective of constitutional tort policy. If punishment and deterrence are worthy goals in ordinary accident law involving a private defendant who endangers the plaintiff's physical safety, then the imposition of similarly heavy sanctions for violations of constitutional rights, in order to express society's disapproval of them and to deter officers from committing such acts, is at least an equally worthy goal, if not a more compelling one.

One issue the Supreme Court has faced in connection with punitive damages for constitutional torts is identifying the appropriate instruction to the jury as to what kinds of circumstances call for a punitive award. Smith and the other defendants in the case were prison guards. The plaintiff, Wade, was an inmate who, before the incident that gave rise to the lawsuit, had been attacked by other prisoners. He charged that the guards knew or should have known that certain other inmates were likely to hurt him if given a chance. Despite this awareness, the guards put two dangerous prisoners in a cell with Wade. As the plaintiff feared, he was attacked again. The substantive constitutional right at stake in the case was the Eighth Amendment right not to be subjected to cruel and unusual punishment. If Wade could show that Smith and the other guards failed to protect him despite knowledge of the danger, he would succeed in establishing an Eighth Amendment violation. As for punitive damages, the district judge instructed the jury that

> [I]f the conduct of one or more of the defendants is shown to be a reckless or callous disregard of, or indifference to, the rights or safety of others, then you may assess punitive or exemplary damages in addition to any award of actual damages. . . . The amount of punitive or exemplary damages assessed against any defendant may be such sum as you believe will serve to punish that defendant and to deter him and others from like conduct.

The jury found Smith liable, and awarded $25,000 in compensatory damages and $5,000 in punitive damages. The issue addressed by the Supreme Court was the propriety of the instruction on punitive damages.

Smith objected to the instruction on the ground that reckless disregard or indifference to the plaintiff's rights would not warrant punitive damages. He argued that "the proper test is one of actual malicious intent—'ill will, spite, or intent to injure.'" He argued that recklessness or callous indifference "is too uncertain a standard to achieve deterrence rationally and fairly" because one cannot always know when one is being reckless or indifferent.

But the Court disagreed, by ruling that the instruction was correct and affirming the judgment. Much of the majority opinion, and of Justice Rehnquist's dissent, is devoted to analyses of the nineteenth-century tort law bearing on the question of the appropriate standard for awarding punitive damages. After satisfying itself that both nineteenth- and twentieth-century courts awarded punitives without a showing of malicious intent, the Court turned to the question of tort policy presented by the case. Rejecting the view that "a recklessness standard is too vague to be fair or useful," the Court pointed out that the main deterrent to violations would be substantive constitutional law. This being so, it was not necessary to adopt fixed and rigid rules as the test for punitive damages. Accordingly, "in the absence of any persuasive argument to the contrary based on the policies of § 1983," the Court was "content to adopt the policy judgment of the common law—that reckless or callous disregard for the plaintiff's rights, as well as intentional violations of federal law, should be sufficient to trigger a jury's consideration of the appropriateness of punitive damages."

Besides *Smith*, the Supreme Court has decided one other § 1983 punitive damages case. In City of Newport v. Fact Concerts (1981) it held that municipal governments may not be held liable for punitive damages. The Court examined nineteenth-century tort law and concluded that "[b]y the time Congress enacted what is now § 1983, the immunity of a municipal corporation from punitive damages at common law was not open to serious question." With regard to policy considerations, the Court pointed out that punitive damages "are not intended to compensate the injured party, but rather to punish the tortfeasor whose wrongful action was intentional or malicious, and to deter him and others from similar extreme conduct." This means the target of punitive damages should be the officials who act and not the municipality in whose name they act. For "[i]t is far from clear that municipal officials . . . would be deterred from wrongdoing by the knowledge that large punitive awards could be assessed based on the wealth of their municipality." In addition, "a more effective means of deterrence" is to allow "juries and courts to assess punitive damages in appropriate circumstances against the offending official." The noncompensatory windfall to the plaintiff cannot be defended on the ground that he deserves it, and may well be accompanied by unfortunate consequences, including increased taxes on citizens who had nothing to do with the egregious conduct, as well as threats to the "fiscal integrity" of the affected governments.

In a footnote, the Court in *City of Newport* left room for an exception to its ban on punitives, conceding that "[i]t is perhaps possible to imagine an extreme situation where the taxpayers are directly responsible for perpetrating an outrageous abuse of constitutional rights." But "such an occurrence is sufficiently unlikely" that the Court saw no need to decide whether punitives may ever be appropriate against municipalities. Perhaps the Court's hypothetical case would be presented if the voters enacted laws mandating racial discrimination, though even here the Court's emphasis on the unfairness of punitives to the taxpayers suggests that it may not be willing to impose punitives on taxpayers for something the voters have done. Granting that the current Court has shown no indication that it will depart from *City of Newport*, one could argue on policy grounds that punitive damages would in fact be a strong deterrent against some kinds of municipal wrongdoing and, hence, that the Court ought to reconsider the holding of that case.[100]

One general issue in the law of punitive damages may have particular importance in the constitutional tort context and therefore requires our attention here. The Supreme Court has held that awards of punitive damages are themselves subject to constitutional scrutiny under the Due Process Clause. Among other things, the Court has held that a punitive award may violate the defendant's right to due process of law in the event there is a big disparity between the harm suffered (as measured by the compensatory damages) and the punitive award. For example, in one case the Court noted that the punitive award was "500 times the amount of [plaintiff's] actual harm as determined by the jury," and said that this "breathtaking" ratio "must surely raise a suspicious judicial eyebrow" (BMW v. Gore, 1996).

The relevance of this feature of the Court's doctrine to punitive damages to § 1983 litigation becomes clear when one recalls that substantial compensatory damages can be hard to come by in constitutional tort cases. The intangible nature of many constitutional rights, coupled with the Supreme Court's "compensation principle" can easily produce a ruling for the plaintiff on the merits, together with an award of nominal damages. This may happen even if the defendant's conduct is egregious. In such a case, the only way for a jury to show its strong disapproval of the defendant's conduct, and to try to deter such conduct in the future, is to grant an award of punitive damages. But any punitive award with teeth will involve a ratio of punitives to the nominal compensatory damages that is far higher than the 500-to-1 ratio the Court found suspect in *BMW*. In setting forth its concern about that ratio, the Court obviously did not have the constitutional tort context in mind, and it was careful to reject any "simple mathematical formula" for evaluating the ratio between punitive and compensatory damages. If and when the issue of the appropriate ratio arises in the constitutional tort context, the Court ought to make clear that the special features of this kind of litigation would justify a far higher ratio of punitives to compensatory damages than may be appropriate in the common law of torts.[101]

Survival and Wrongful Death

Under the rulings in *Carey* and *Stachura*, courts are supposed to use the common law of torts—which judges have made over the years in order to deal with ordinary tort suits arising between private individuals— as their benchmark in devising damages principles for constitutional tort cases. But this approach does not always work, because some aspects of ordinary tort law are not covered by judge-made common law. They are governed by statutes enacted separately in each state, and the Court has had to face the question of whether courts in constitutional tort cases should follow these statutes.

The reason why there are gaps in the common law is that long ago courts foreclosed the development of common law rules on some matters. Nineteenth-century courts held that when the victim of the tort dies before a court has handed down a judgment, the tort case dies with him. In addition, nineteenth-century courts held that even when the tort itself results in the death of the victim, his family may not sue for the harm done. Because these holdings seemed unjust, legislatures in every state enacted two kinds of statutes to fill in the gaps they created in the remedies available for ordinary torts. These statutes are not mutually exclusive. On the contrary, each complements the other, and both may be applicable to the same tort. Though these statutes differ among themselves in matters of detail, most of them share certain features in common.[102]

One kind of statute is called a "survival" statute. Its aim is to permit the tort suit to continue even after the death of the victim, whether or not the death resulted from the tort. In place of the tort victim, the plaintiff in the lawsuit is the "estate" of the victim. (This term refers to the legal entity that represents the deceased's continuing rights and obligations, including his property, his debts, and his to right bring a lawsuit.) In most states, the measure of damages in the lawsuit is the harm suffered by the deceased before his death. For example, the estate may recover for medical expenses, lost income, and pain and suffering incurred between the tort and the death. The other kind of statute is called a "wrongful death" act. Unlike the survival statute, this statute applies only when the death results from the tort. It authorizes certain family members to bring suit to recover the benefits they could have expected to receive from the deceased in the future, had he lived. In most states, the measure of recovery is not the whole value of the deceased's life but only the amounts that he would have spent for the benefit of these plaintiffs. Note, however, that generalizations about these statutes are perilous. They vary from one state to another.

In Robertson v. Wegmann (1978) the Supreme Court addressed the "survival" problem in a constitutional tort case. The plaintiff in a constitutional tort case died of causes unrelated to the constitutional tort before the suit was resolved. The case arose in Louisiana, and the issue was whether the federal court should borrow the Louisiana survival statute or make a common law rule to govern the case. The Supreme Court ruled that federal courts in § 1983 cases should usually borrow the state's survival statute in such a case. In reaching this result, it relied on another federal statute, 42 U.S.C. § 1988. That statute, as it is interpreted by the Supreme Court, directs federal courts in § 1983 cases to borrow state statutes for issues that are not covered by federal law. Because survival is normally covered by statute, and because there is no federal statute on survival, federal courts should use the state statute. And because survival statutes may vary from state to state, the outcome of a given case may depend on the state in which it is brought.

Section 1988 does contain a limitation on the use of state statutes, specifying that they should not be used when they are "inconsistent with the Constitution and laws of the United States." The problem in *Robertson* was that the Louisiana survival statute, in effect, foreclosed any survival unless certain close relatives survived the deceased, a condition that was not met in this case. Consequently, the lucky defendant escaped liability. The estate contended that this feature of the statute made it inconsistent with the remedial purpose of § 1983 and therefore should not be used. But the Court rejected this argument on the ground that the peculiar facts of the case were hardly typical. Ordinarily, the Louisiana statute would provide an adequate remedy, for "surely few persons are not survived by one of these close relatives, and in any event no contention is made here that Louisiana's decision to restrict certain survivorship rights in this manner is an unreasonable one." According to the Court, the absence of a remedy in this case would not interfere with the compensatory goal of § 1983 because, in the absence of close relatives, there appeared to be no one who needed to be compensated for the death. The deterrent goal would not be affected, because an official "contemplating illegal activity" would almost certainly not be able to predict that the victim would die without survivors. Thus, the disincentive provided by the prospect of liability for damages would remain intact.

Though the Court applied the Louisiana survival statute in *Robertson*, it stressed that its holding was "a narrow one, limited to situations in which no claim is made that state law generally is inhospitable to survival of § 1983 actions and in which the particular application of state survivorship law, while it may cause abatement of the action, has no independent adverse effect on the policies underlying § 1983." It warned that a state law prohibiting or severely restricting survival may receive different treatment. In addition, the Court reserved the issue of whether a state law prohibiting survival would be borrowed in the event the constitutional violation caused the death. Later, in Carlson v. Green (1980), the Court refused to follow state law in such a case, explaining that the deterrence goal of constitutional tort would be frustrated by disallowing recovery. Notice, however, that *Carlson* was not a § 1983 case but an action brought against a federal official under the *Bivens* doctrine discussed in "Suing Federal Officers," Though *Carlson* is not directly controlling in the § 1983 context, it seems likely the Court will apply it there as well, since the deterrence policy is equally relevant to § 1983 cases.

Prospective Relief

Now we turn to cases in which the constitutional violation is ongoing or absent judicial intervention, is likely to occur in the future. These cases present an entirely different set of issues from those we have identified in connection with retrospective relief. In some ways, the remedial issues are simple in these cases. Because the judge merely commands the official to do or not do something, the Constitution is implemented directly, without any need to worry about putting a dollar figure on intangible harm or determining how to influence official behavior through monetary awards. Nor is there usually any "official immunity" barrier to obtaining prospective relief, unless the defendant is a legislator or a judge.[103] Sovereign immunity is an obstacle to obtaining an award of money from the state, but it does not preclude prospective relief against a state officer.

There are two main vehicles for seeking prospective relief: the suit for an injunction and the suit for a declaratory judgment. The differences between these two remedies are discussed first. Historically, the plaintiff was obliged to make a special showing in order to obtain injunctive relief; otherwise, he was required to sue for damages. We then explain the reasoning behind this rule and why it is rarely a problem for plaintiffs in constitutional litigation. But problems do arise in constitutional litigation involving prospective relief. One of these, discussed separately, is determining what kinds of relief are encompassed by the rule allowing prospective relief against a state officer. We then address issues that relate to the uncertainty and diffuseness of potential future injuries. A characteristic of certain constitutional rights is that everyone holds them even though no one may suffer any particular injury when government crosses the line into illegality. The question is who, if anyone, should be allowed to obtain prospective relief in such a case. When the unconstitutional action is merely a possibility and not a reality, courts must ask whether any judicial intervention is appropriate. Another set of problems results from the brutal simplicity of prospective relief. In one sense an award of damages is far less intrusive than prospective relief, for it does not actually compel the government to do anything. But some kinds of injunctive relief can be quite intrusive, turning the judge into a manager of state institutions. In these cases a conflict may exist between, on the one hand, effective judicial intervention, and on the other, avoiding too much intrusion into the day-to-day operations of government. Finally, we describe the law bearing on requests for interim relief. The issue here is whether the defendant government should be allowed to do as it pleases while the litigation is in progress and before a final resolution of the merits.

Injunctions and Declaratory Judgments

Two forms of prospective relief need to be distinguished: "injunction" is an order handed down by the judge telling an official what he or she must or must not do. Having originated in England over five hundred years ago, the injunction has been a feature of both private and public law throughout our history. Second, a "declaratory judgment" merely states the judge's conclusions as to the rights and obligations of the parties. Declaratory judgments are authorized in the federal courts by 28 U.S.C. § 2201, a federal statute enacted in the 1930s. The aim of this statute was to enable litigants to obtain a judicial ruling as to their rights and liabilities in circumstances in which a good argument could be made for allowing access to the courts, even though the traditional requirements for obtaining injunctive relief would be hard to meet.

Historically, the test for obtaining injunctive relief could be demanding, and the declaratory judgment acts were a needed reform. There is, in fact, little practical difference today between the two remedies, except that an injunction can be immediately enforced while a declaratory judgment cannot be. A leading authority on the law of remedies has written, "In practice, declaratory judgments that statutes are unconstitutional appear to have been as effective as injunctions against enforcement."[104] If a judge issues an injunction and the official violates its terms, the judge may hold the official in contempt, which can include a fine or imprisonment until he or she complies. If the official fails to comply with a declaratory judgment, an immediate contempt citation would not be available. However, the plaintiff would be entitled to go back to the judge and obtain an injunction to enforce the declaratory judgment. From this time forward, any further violations by the official could put him in contempt. Because this is the main difference between the two remedies, we will in general not distinguish between them in discussing prospective relief. Unless we indicate otherwise, references in this section to the law governing injunctions should be taken as referring to declaratory judgments as well.

The "Irreparable Injury" Requirement

Historically, courts regarded injunctive relief as an extraordinary (or "equitable") remedy, available only in the event "legal" remedies (e.g., damages, raising one's rights as a defense) were inadequate. As an equitable remedy, an injunction would be granted only if "irreparable injury" would occur in its absence. For example, courts held that damages would be an inadequate remedy for the harm done by the defendant's cutting trees on the plaintiff's property because the recovery of damages could not reconvert lumber into live trees. Accordingly, an injunction forbidding the cutting was the appropriate remedy. Ordinarily, however, damages were considered adequate to make up for most harms. The historical explanation for this limit on access to injunctive remedies is that equitable remedies arose after legal remedies. In order to justify their use, it was necessary to show that there was some problem with the legal remedy.[105] Besides history, there may be functional justifications for the preference for awarding damages rather than injunctions. Thus, "[i]t is sometimes said that injunctions impose a greater burden on the court, because they have to be enforced over time, . . . [and] that the injunction is a greater intrusion on the defendant's liberty."[106] On the other hand, one expert has argued that the irreparable injury rule actually has little force today because "any litigant with a plausible need for specific relief can satisfy the irreparable injury rule."[107]

Whatever may be the case generally, it is clear that the irreparable injury rule carries little weight in the context of constitutional remedies. Courts give scant credence to the notion that legal remedies may be adequate and thus foreclose an injunction against continuing or threatened violations of constitutional rights. With regard to these "intangible rights that are never bought or sold in any market . . . injunctions are the standard remedy."[108] In one situation, however, the "irreparable injury/adequate remedy at law" notion does have weight. This is when the plaintiff seeking an injunction is also a defendant in a state court case (usually a criminal case) who asks a federal court to stop the state proceeding because it would be unconstitutional to convict him or her of a crime. The Supreme Court's rule in such cases is that the constitutional issue should be litigated in the state court, one reason being that the challenger has an adequate remedy at law available in that court.[109] It may be the case that, even in this context, the "irreparable injury/adequate remedy at law" principle is not the major justification for refusing an injunction. What is certain is that, in the absence of some state proceeding in which the challenger could raise his or her federal rights, that principle rarely proves decisive in constitutional litigation.

Sovereign Immunity and the Prospective–Retrospective Distinction

Damages are available only from officials and local governments. With regard to state governments the law is complex, but the bottom line is that because of sovereign immunity they cannot be sued for damages. In "Liability of Government Entities" we explained that Congress has the power to take away the state's sovereign immunity from suit on Fourteenth Amendment claims, and these are, of course, just the kinds of claims that arise in suits seeking constitutional remedies. Strictly speaking, then, there is no insuperable theoretical objection to any remedy whatsoever, prospective or retrospective. But in practice there are barriers nonetheless. The Supreme Court has ruled that, in enacting § 1983, Congress did not in fact expose the states to suits for damages (Quern v. Jordan, 1979). Even so, one can obtain injunctive relief from state government officials for actions that violate the Fourteenth Amendment or other constitutional provisions (Ex parte Young, 1908). But a great many things may be included within injunctive relief, and a question arises as to which of these are permissible given the restraints imposed by sovereign immunity.

In *Ex Parte Young* the Supreme Court ruled that injunctive relief was available against the officer in spite of sovereign immunity because the officer who violates federal constitutional law is "stripped of his official or representative character and is subjected in his person to the consequences of his individual conduct." The logic of this ruling has been questioned because the plaintiff's substantive theory of recovery must be that state action has taken place (see "State Action"). Otherwise, no Fourteenth Amendment violation would have occurred. It seems that the officer acts for the state for purposes of the Fourteenth Amendment but not for purposes of sovereign immunity. Later, in Pennhurst State School and Hospital v. Halderman (1984), the Court explained that the *Young* principle was a "fiction" that was justified by the need for an "offensive" prospective remedy for Fourteenth Amendment violations. Thus, in *Pennhurst* the Court ruled that a plaintiff could not obtain prospective relief in federal court against a state officer on state law grounds.

As to what kinds of relief may be awarded under the heading of "injunctive" relief, the leading case is Edelman v. Jordan (1974). The plaintiffs in *Edelman* were Social Security recipients in Illinois. Edelman, the state official in charge of the program, had illegally delayed the starting date for their benefits, costing them money they were entitled to receive. They brought a suit to challenge this practice, seeking not only an injunction ordering Edelman to obey the law in the future (the standard *Ex Parte Young* relief, which of course raised no objection) but also an order that he give to them money they should have and would have received if not for the illegal conduct. The Supreme Court rejected this latter kind of relief, holding that although Edelman was named as defendant, this relief would have to come from the state itself. "These funds obviously will not be paid out of the pocket of . . . Edelman." Because allowing the plaintiffs to recover money from the state would in effect take away sovereign immunity altogether, the Court drew a line between prospective and retrospective relief, by stating that one could only obtain a prospective remedy under the principle of *Young*. The line between these two types of relief is not always clear. In one later case the Court upheld an injunction requiring that funds be spent for a remedial education program for children who had been denied their right to a desegregated public education (Milliken v. Bradley, 1977). Although it is true that this relief applies to the future, and thus may be viewed as prospective, the function of the remedial reading program was to make up for a past wrong, and in this regard the relief approved in *Milliken* seems to be essentially retrospective in nature.

Standing, Ripeness, and Mootness

Suits seeking damages are generally brought in well-defined disputes in which the focus of the litigation is an event that took place in the past (though its impact may continue into the present). When someone seeks prospective relief, however, the restraints that are more or less automatically imposed on the scope of the litigation by the requirement that the plaintiff show damages are now lifted. The harm may be diffuse, in the future or in the past, or borne by someone other than the plaintiff. The consequences of granting prospective relief may be far greater than the simple obligation to pay damages, as government may have to change its operations in important ways. The Supreme Court has devised three doctrines—standing, ripeness, and mootness—in order to assure that suits for prospective relief really need to be decided, and are fit to be decided, by a Court at this time.

The law of "standing" is concerned with determining who should be allowed to bring suit. The Constitution requires that the plaintiff show a present or threatened "injury in fact." This is not a problem in suits for damages. Under *Carey* and *Stachura* (discussed previously in this section), a plaintiff cannot win a substantial award without proving that he has suffered a significant injury of some kind. In litigation for injunctive relief, the unconstitutional act may not yet have occurred. Even if the illegal activity is already underway, the focus of the plaintiff's lawsuit will often be the defendant's conduct, and the need to stop it, not the harm suffered by any particular person. For example, the plaintiff in an injunction suit may challenge the state's use of religious symbols, its proposed legislative districts, or its system for assigning children to schools. One need not meet the requirements of *Carey* and *Stachura* in order to obtain an injunction in such cases. Even so, the Supreme Court requires an "injury in fact" for the plaintiff to have "standing to sue," and the question we must address is what "injury in fact" means.

The policies behind the standing requirement are (1) that courts should not intervene unless there is a need to do so, and if no one suffers any particular harm, there is no need to do so; (2) assuming there is an injury to someone, that person and not someone else should be the plaintiff because the injured person can be counted on to vigorously pursue his or her rights and will more likely be able to present the court with a typical fact situation. While these policies make sense, the meaning of "injury" in the law of standing has proven to be elusive. We can begin by identifying the two ends of a spectrum of harm and then note some of the difficult cases in the middle. At one end of the spectrum is the plaintiff who has suffered the kind of harm *Carey* and *Stachura* demand for recovery of damages. This plaintiff would also be able to show an injury-in-fact for purposes of standing to obtain injunctive relief, so long as he or she could establish a real threat of recurrence in the future. But harm to an intangible interest, which may not suffice for damages under *Carey* and *Stachura*, can still give one standing to seek prospective relief. A voter whose vote is diluted or otherwise diminished in value by the state's practice of drawing legislative districts has standing to challenge the law whether or not he can prove any damages.[110] At the other end of the spectrum, someone who simply disagrees with a law but is not directly affected by it would not have standing. For example, a plaintiff who has no children in the public schools would not have standing to challenge racial discrimination in those schools (Allen v. Wright, 1984).

In between these poles, it is hard to draw the line between what is and what is not a sufficient "injury" to give someone the necessary standing. Consider, for example, a line of cases in which federal taxpayers sought to challenge various uses of tax dollars, asserting that they were injured by being taxed for illegal ends. This kind of governmental activity is especially likely to give rise to litigation over standing because no one can show that he or she is hurt by it. The amount of the spending traceable to any given taxpayer is likely to be minuscule, and a taxpayer would have great difficulty showing that his or her bill would be lower if this particular expenditure were forbidden. Thus, a question arises as to whether anyone has suffered an injury no matter how illegal the expenditure may be. In one case the Supreme Court ruled that a federal taxpayer does not have standing to challenge congressional legislation merely because his or her tax dollars would be illegally expended (Frothingham v. Mellon, 1923). But a federal taxpayer does have standing to challenge congressional legislation giving money to religious schools on the ground that it would violate the First Amendment's prohibition on maintaining an establishment of religion (Flast v. Cohen, 1968). On the other hand, a federal taxpayer does not have standing to challenge a government agency's decision to hand over government property to a religious institution even if one claims that this violates the Establishment Clause (Valley Forge Christian College v. Americans United for Separation of Church and State, 1982).

Besides having an "injury," there is another constitutional requirement for standing to sue. The plaintiff must show that the injury was caused by the constitutional violation. The problem here is that the plaintiff's situation may be the result of several factors working at the same time, and it is not clear that the constitutional violation was primarily responsible for it. In such cases, the Supreme Court sometimes rules that this "causation" aspect of standing is not met. In one case, for example, the plaintiffs claimed that zoning regulations contributing to high prices for housing prevented low-income people from moving into a town. But there were other reasons for the high prices as well, and the Court took the view that the link between the zoning regulations and the inability to reside in the town was too speculative to warrant a finding that the plaintiffs had standing. In the Supreme Court's jargon, one must show that the injury was "traceable" to the constitutional wrong and would be "redressable" by correcting that wrong. In this case, it appeared that the low-income residents would have been unable to afford housing in the town in any event (Warth v. Seldin, 1975).

In addition to these constitutional requirements for standing, a further "subconstitutional" rule should be mentioned. In some cases the Supreme Court has denied standing to persons who can show an injury and who can show that the injury was caused by the unconstitutional conduct. The problem is that these litigants have no rights at stake in the litigation; they seek instead to raise the rights of others ("jus tertii"). Suppose Person A stashes marijuana in Person B's house. The police conduct a search that fails to meet the requirements of the Fourth Amendment, in violation of Person B's rights. They find the marijuana and seek to use it as evidence in a criminal prosecution of Person A. Though Person A is injured by the constitutional violation, there was no violation of his or her Fourth Amendment rights. Person A may not rely on the violation of Person B's rights in this instance.[111] Over the past twenty-five years, however, the Court has frequently made exceptions to this principle in cases in which the litigation involved a request for prospective relief. For example, the Court has permitted doctors to assert the rights of their patients and bartenders to assert the rights of their patrons (Singleton v. Wulff, 1976; Craig v. Boren, 1976). While it would be incautious to say that the old doctrine has been overturned, it does not appear to have as much force as it once did, at least in the context of constitutional litigation. Also, one should distinguish this problem from the situation in which an organization seeks to assert the rights of its members. So long as some of its members can show injury and causation, there is no difficulty with standing in that kind of lawsuit.[112] For example, the NAACP would have standing to challenge racial discrimination suffered by some of its members.

While suits for damages are necessarily brought after an injury has occurred (or while it is ongoing), a plaintiff may sue for prospective relief before the government's alleged unconstitutional action has taken place. Suppose, for example, that the legislature enacts a statute forbidding the distribution of pornography and imposes criminal penalties for violation of the prohibition. A distributor of books who thinks that the statute violates freedom of speech would obviously prefer to get a court ruling on its validity sooner rather than later, and he or she would prefer to test the validity of the statute without actually violating it, taking the risk of losing his challenge and being convicted of a crime. From the plaintiff's perspective, the main advantage of trying to nip the unconstitutional statute in the bud is that one never has to put up with it at all. So far as standing is concerned, the plaintiff merely needs to show a real threat that the statute will be enforced against him or her. That threat would be a sufficient "injury" to meet the standing requirement.

But policies similar to those underlying standing doctrine have led the Supreme Court to impose a "ripeness" requirement as well (e.g., United Public Workers v. Mitchell, 1947). It may be that the antipornography statute will be interpreted by state law enforcement agencies in such a way that it does not interfere with any legitimate business, so there arises no need for judicial intervention. In addition, a court may benefit from being able to evaluate the statute's impact in a real-world fact situation rather than considering it in the abstract. For these reasons, the court may conclude that the suit is not ripe until the state prosecutors actually try to enforce the statute. Though the vocabulary of "ripeness" is used both in suits for injunctive relief and for declaratory judgments, it may play a bigger role in the latter kind of litigation than in the former. Courts are perhaps more likely to focus on the "irreparable injury" requirement in injunction suits. The two inquiries are functionally quite similar. Any time there is an irreparable injury, the case is ripe. Conversely, if a request for declaratory relief is ripe, the likely reason is that the plaintiff would suffer an irreparable injury if forced to wait.

Under the Supreme Court's ripeness doctrine, courts make judgments on a case-by-case basis, balancing the desirability of waiting for a traditional injury to take place against the benefits of immediate intervention. If our hypothetical statute is written in such a way as to make it quite likely to apply to the plaintiff's business, and if the prosecutor has publicly stated his or her intention to bring a suit against the plaintiff, then the argument for immediate intervention will be stronger. But if the statute's wording makes it uncertain that the plaintiff is one of its targets, and the prosecutor has disavowed any intent to pursue him or her, then the Court is more likely to find a lack of ripeness. Another factor that bears on ripeness is whether the court can competently rule without more facts. In situations in which the legal rule is clear and depends on a few facts that are already available, a case is more likely to be ripe. But if the governing legal standard directs courts to consider a large number of circumstances on a case-by-case basis, the Court is more likely to rule that the dispute is not ripe until the parties interact enough to produce a concrete set of facts that can be examined and evaluated.[113]

Just as a challenge to government action may be premature and thereby raise a ripeness problem, the passage of time may change the circumstances so much that a dispute about legal rights, once alive, no longer makes much difference. Consider the antipornography statute used to illustrate ripeness. Perhaps the bookseller had a ripe dispute with the prosecutor, but now he has decided to enter the grocery business instead of selling books, or perhaps the statute has been repealed. In either case, the dispute may no longer need to be resolved, because a judicial decision would have little or no impact on the rights and duties of the parties. Deciding such cases may not be a wise use of scarce judicial resources, and there is a danger that the quality of any decision reached will be compromised by the parties' lack of vigor in debating an issue that is largely irrelevant to either of them. As with standing and ripeness, mootness plays no role in suits seeking only damages. A plaintiff who has suffered compensable past injury always has a live dispute as long as the defendant has not paid the damages that are due. Mootness is a problem when the litigant seeks only prospective relief, or when his claim for damages has failed on account of official immunity or for some other reason unrelated to the merits of the claim.

One problem courts face in deciding whether a case is moot is that the continuing vitality of a given dispute is not an all-or-nothing question. It is sometimes necessary to decide not just whether there is a need to intervene, but how likely it is that the dispute will require resolution. In DeFunis v. Odegaard (1974), for example, the plaintiff was (at the outset of the litigation) a law school applicant who challenged the University of Washington's admissions policy on the ground that it discriminated on the basis of race in violation of the equal protection clause of the Fourteenth Amendment. He was admitted to the school on a provisional basis during the litigation, and by the time the case was decided by the Supreme Court he was just two months from graduation. The university had promised that even if it won, it would not expel him from school at that late date. The Court ruled that the case was moot because no matter how it ruled DeFunis would be allowed to finish school. Of course, DeFunis may have failed a course or fallen sick and found himself unable to complete the year. For such circumstances, the university had reserved the right to keep him from continuing. In the Court's view, however, the possibility of these events was too small to keep the case alive. But this was a matter of judgment that may have gone either way.

Another issue in mootness cases is determining whether an apparently moot case is, in fact, still vital in one way or another. Suppose the antipornography statute were repealed solely to put an end to the lawsuit, with the aim of reinstating it once the threat of litigation had passed. Applying the "voluntary cessation" doctrine, the Court would probably rule that the dispute is still ongoing because the constitutional issue will likely arise under any new statute as well (Vitek v. Jones, 1980). Or a case may be "capable of repetition, yet evading review." Suppose, for example, a newspaper seeks to challenge an order excluding reporters from a trial. Once the trial is over, the dispute may appear to be moot. But the same issue will likely arise again, as the newspaper will doubtless want to cover other trials. And there will always be difficulty getting it resolved before it becomes moot on account of the short duration of most trials. Thus, it is both "capable of repetition" and "evading review" and can be decided in spite of the mootness problem (Globe Newspaper Co. v. Superior Court, 1982). An important rule to keep in mind with regard to this doctrine is that it applies only if the same issue is "capable of repetition yet evading review" with regard to the plaintiff in this case. Thus, Defunis could not satisfy the requirements of this doctrine by showing that other law school applicants may face the same problem in the future.

Though standing, ripeness, and mootness are not barriers to obtaining damages, these doctrines do stand in the way of prospective relief. Suppose, however, a plaintiff has suffered a past injury and therefore has a good suit for damages. And suppose the government practice that produced the past injury is still in force, thus threatening to do more harm in the future. It may be possible to obtain both damages and prospective relief in such a case. The point of this section, however, is that the effort to obtain prospective relief must be kept separate from the request for damages. The Supreme Court has ruled that the fact that the plaintiff has a good suit for damages does not necessarily enable him to meet the standing, ripeness, and mootness requirements (City of Los Angeles v. Lyons).

In *Lyons* the plaintiff, Adolph Lyons, had been stopped by the police for a traffic offense. According to Lyons, though he offered no resistance or threat, the police caused him harm by applying a chokehold to his neck. Claiming that the police routinely used such chokeholds on nonthreatening arrestees, he sought damages for excessive force as well as an injunction against the use of chokeholds in cases in which the arrestee poses no danger. Invoking principles of standing and ripeness, the Supreme Court ruled that his request for injunctive relief could not go forward. He had suffered an injury and could obtain damages for it. But for injunctive relief he would need to show that "he was likely to suffer future injury from the use of the chokeholds by police officers." Even if he had been illegally choked in the past, this "does nothing to establish a real and immediate threat that he would again be stopped for a traffic violation" and choked again. Though the city had not disavowed the use of chokeholds in the future, he had not shown that he was particularly likely to be a victim.

Critics of this ruling point out that the policies behind standing and ripeness doctrine are weak in this situation. Lyons was not simply pursuing an abstract disagreement with the city. He had suffered a concrete injury, which ought to be enough for standing. Moreover, there probably is a need to address the substantive issue in order to adjudicate Lyons' suit for damages. The facts may show that an injunction is inappropriate because chokeholds are typically used properly, but the Court's ruling is that an injunction may not be granted no matter how egregious the city's use of chokeholds may be.[114] Later cases have refused to extend the scope of the *Lyons* rule. Thus, a person who has been stopped by the police not once but fifteen times does have standing to seek an injunction. The number of times he or she has been stopped means it is sufficiently likely that this would continue to happen (Kolender v. Lawson, 1983; City of Houston v. Hill, 1987).

Public Law Litigation

If the plaintiff surmounts the obstacles described in the preceding sections, he or she will ordinarily be able to obtain an injunction that orders government officials to change their behavior in some way. Used as a means of enforcing constitutional rights, the injunction has over the past fifty years become a powerful tool for reforming the institutions of government. As government at all levels has grown in scope and extended its impact on people's lives, litigants have increasingly sought injunctive remedies to vindicate their constitutional rights (as well as other rights). In an influential law review article, Professor Abram Chayes described this new kind of lawsuit (which he called "public law litigation") and contrasted it with traditional "private law litigation."[115] Examples of public law litigation include suits brought in connection with public school desegregation, reform of state prisons and hospitals, legislative reapportionment, and employment discrimination.

Chayes explained that in traditional litigation, the lawsuit is "bipolar," typically pitting the plaintiff claiming wrongful injury against the person who committed the injury. The point of the litigation is to make up for a past wrong, and the impact of the judgment is limited to the parties. The plaintiff begins and controls his or her side of the litigation, and the defendant controls the other side. If they decide to settle the case, the role of the judge is merely to ratify what they have chosen to do. By contrast, in public law litigation there may be many parties, and parties may come and go throughout the litigation. "The traditional adversary relationship is suffused and intermixed with negotiating and mediating processes at every point." Moreover, "[t]he judge is the dominant figure in organizing and guiding the case." The judge does not merely decide legal issues and put an end to the litigation. Rather, "the trial judge has increasingly become the creator and manager of complex forms of ongoing relief, which have widespread effects on persons not before the court and require the judge's continuing involvement in administration and implementation."

Two features of public law litigation deserve special attention as they are particularly important in suits brought to enforce constitutional rights. One of these is the "class action." This is a type of lawsuit in which one or a few named plaintiffs are permitted to represent the interests of, and obtain relief for, a large number of other people who share the same legal claim against the defendant. The other noteworthy feature of public law litigation is the "structural injunction," by which the judge does not merely tell officials what they must not do. In this kind of litigation, the judge undertakes to reform institutions by directing officials as to what actions they must take to eradicate unconstitutional conditions, and the judge typically engages in ongoing supervision of officials' compliance efforts.

Some constitutional violations, of course, affect only one or a few people. An example is the use of excessive force by a police officer in making an arrest. But suppose the officer uses excessive force because it is the general policy of the local police department to do so. In that case, the violation has a more systematic impact on a large group of people. Other examples of constitutional violations that affect a large number of people include (a) drawing legislative districts so that the votes of some citizens count for less than those of others, (b) operating a prison in which the conditions are so bad as to amount to cruel and unusual punishment of the inmates, and (c) using racial classifications to segregate public schools. In situations like these, a particular plaintiff may choose to sue solely on his or her own behalf, but it is more likely he will bring a class action. Under Rule 23 of the Federal Rules of Civil Procedure, such a lawsuit may be maintained to obtain prospective relief against unconstitutional actions if (a) the group of affected persons is so large that it would be impracticable to name them all as plaintiffs, (b) the issues are common to all members of group, and (c) the court is convinced that the person or persons seeking to represent the interests of others will do so adequately. Assuming the named plaintiffs can show that they are responsible people and have adequate resources to finance the litigation, all the hypothetical cases mentioned in this paragraph would probably qualify as class actions.

It should be evident that a class action is a powerful tool for reforming the way government operates. Rather than each affected person incurring the expense and effort of bringing suit and obtaining relief limited only to his or her situation, one can divide the expenses among a large number of people and obtain a sweeping court order that directs officials to change their behavior generally, not merely to stop misbehaving toward one particular plaintiff. In addition, two of the obstacles to obtaining prospective relief that were discussed previously can be avoided if the case can be framed as a class action.

Recall that a case may become moot if conditions change so that there is no longer a live dispute between the defendant and the plaintiff. The "capable of repetition, yet evading review" rule helps to ameliorate this problem in some cases, but that doctrine applies only when the dispute is "capable of repetition" with regard to this plaintiff. For example, a state may have a "durational residency" requirement for voting or obtaining some state benefit, and this may be challenged as a violation of the equal protection of the laws. No particular plaintiff can credibly claim that he or she will be subjected to it more than once, so the "capable of repetition" condition will not be met in the event he or she brings a traditional lawsuit. The Supreme Court has held that when the case is a class action, the claim need only be capable of repetition with regard to some, but not all, members of the class (Sosna v. Iowa, 1975). In our durational residency example, the class can be defined as including all new residents of the state, and this definition can embrace not only new residents at the time the suit was filed but also people who come to the state during the litigation. There will always be someone in the class for whom the case is not moot.

Bringing a case as a class action may also avoid the ripeness and standing problems that presented difficulty for the plaintiff in *Lyons*. In this case Lyons could not credibly claim that he would likely be subjected to a chokehold in the future, so, under the Court's reasoning, he lacked standing to obtain forward-looking relief. If he had brought the suit as a class action on behalf of all persons stopped for traffic offenses and posing no threat to the police, then there seems to be a compelling argument that some members of the class will be treated this way (so long as the city does not abandon the practice). Hence, there would be a threat to some plaintiffs and a need to resolve the dispute as to whether chokeholds may generally be used in these circumstances. (The problem with the "class action" approach is that each instance of chokehold use may be so different from others that there is no truly common issue.)

Whether a suit for prospective relief is brought as a class action, the traditional and most common function of an injunction in constitutional litigation is to stop the defendant from doing something (in the present or in the future) that is unconstitutional. Besides this preventive role, an injunction may be used to make up for the affects of past illegality and to reform government institutions.[116] The former are sometimes labeled "reparative" injunctions in the scholarly literature. A reparative injunction is not just another name for damages, which look solely to the past. By contrast, "a reparative injunction is appropriate only when plaintiff will suffer additional harm in the future [as a result of the past violation] . . . and when it is possible to prevent that additional harm from happening."[117] Examples include (a) the remedial education program that the Supreme Court approved in Milliken v. Bradley (1997), (b) setting aside a tainted election and ordering a new one, and (c) requiring that affirmative steps be taken to hire members of minority groups who have suffered discrimination in the past. Recall that some reparative injunctions are forbidden by sovereign immunity when they would require that the state government pay money to make up for a past wrong (Edelman v. Jordan, 1974).

The third use of an injunction in constitutional litigation is to reform government institutions, such as prisons, schools, and workplaces. The distinctive characteristic of these "structural" injunctions, as they are often called, is that the judge does not simply order relief and punish noncompliance with the order. He or she engages in ongoing supervision of the prison, the school system, or other institution and may issue orders that deal with the details of their operation, such as methods of assigning students to schools (Swann v. Charlotte-Mecklenburg Board of Education, 1971) or the number of prisoners that may be put in a cell and the quality of food that must be served in the prison cafeteria (Hutto v. Finney, 1978). The judge may also pursue innovative remedial theories. In *Swann* the Supreme Court upheld an order that students be bused across town to better integrate the schools in spite of segregated housing patterns. In another school desegregation case the Court upheld an order that the school district establish a remedial education program (Milliken v. Bradley, 1977).

There are limits, however. The Court was more skeptical of a decree ordering higher teacher salaries and other improvements in the public schools. The district judge's rationale was that by making the schools more attractive, they would attract more white students. The Supreme Court thought that, without greater justification than had been given, the salary order was "simply too far removed from an acceptable implementation of a permissible means to remedy previous illegally mandated segregation" (Missouri v. Jenkins, 1995). And once the school system has been desegregated, judicial supervision should cease (Board of Education v. Dowell, 1991). Similar issues arise regarding the relation of constitutional rights to remedies in prison reform litigation.[118]

Often, the judge's remedial order in a structural injunction case will be the outcome of negotiation between the parties, in which the judge may participate as well. The result will be a "consent decree," so named because it is, at least nominally, an arrangement that both the defendants and the plaintiffs have accepted, though neither may be entirely satisfied with it. If the first efforts to achieve the desired result do not produce the preferred outcome, or if conditions change so much that the initial remedy no longer works, the judge may modify the remedies at a later point in time even if they are the product of a consent decree. The Supreme Court has ruled that in "institutional reform litigation" (the kind of litigation that gives rise to structural injunctions), "a party seeking modification of a consent decree must establish that a significant change in facts or law warrants revision of the decree and that the proposed modification is suitably tailored to the changed circumstance" (Rufo v. Inmates of the Suffolk County Jail, 1992).

Preliminary Relief

Some rights are ephemeral and may be partially or entirely lost unless they are protected immediately. Suppose, for example, the plaintiff wants to ship perishable foods without obtaining a state permit and charges that the state law requiring the permit is unconstitutional. He or she may bring a lawsuit to challenge the law, but the suit could drag on for years. If the plaintiff is obliged to wait until the litigation is finished before vindicating his or her rights, those rights may be lost for no good reason. Even if the plaintiff ultimately wins, his or her rights will have been lost during the time when the litigation was ongoing.

The solution to this problem is a "preliminary injunction." This is an order, issued by the judge hearing the case, that tells the defendant to cease the allegedly illegal activity while the case is under consideration. It is not a ruling on the merits, and does not mean that the plaintiff will eventually prevail. It merely gives the plaintiff temporary relief. Every plaintiff would like to obtain such an order, of course, but preliminary injunctions are not granted automatically. Courts apply a balancing test in deciding whether to grant them. One factor is whether and how much harm the plaintiff will suffer unless he or she receives interim relief. If the rights are not time-sensitive (like the right to ship perishable food) then it will be hard for him or her to establish a need for preliminary relief. A second factor is the defendant's hardship in case the preliminary relief is granted. If the balance of hardships favors the plaintiff, he or she is more likely to secure preliminary relief. Third, the judge must make a tentative estimation of the ultimate resolution of the case; finding that it is more likely than not the plaintiff will eventually prevail counts in favor of preliminary relief. Fourth, courts look beyond the parties and consider whether the public interest would be served by preliminary relief. Some courts depart from this "balancing" framework. They treat these four tests as rules, and require the plaintiff to prevail on all four in order to win a preliminary injunction.[119] However the test is characterized, the overriding point is that the district judge has broad discretion to consider an array of factors in deciding whether to award preliminary relief.

It is important not to confuse preliminary injunctions with another type of order that may be issued at the outset of the litigation, called a "temporary restraining order." A judge should not issue a preliminary injunction without first hearing arguments from both sides and carefully applying the criteria described in the preceding paragraph. Once issued, a preliminary injunction may remain in force throughout the litigation, which may continue for years (though changed circumstances may require modifying or lifting it). A temporary restraining order ("TRO," in the jargon) is different. This is an order that may be sought in circumstances in which immediate action is necessary for one reason or another. "Temporary restraining orders are designed to prevent irreparable harm that will occur even before a preliminary injunction hearing can be held. In a sufficiently urgent case, a judge will issue a TRO from home, in the middle of the night."[120] For example, some group may plan to hold a demonstration at a given time and place; government officials, learning of this hours before the event and fearing violence, may go to court to obtain a temporary restraining order forbidding the demonstration until its legality can be litigated at leisure. If the protest proceeds as planned, the participants may be convicted of contempt of the restraining order even if, strictly in terms of free speech principles, their activities would be constitutionally protected (Walker v. City of Birmingham, 1967).

The key inquiry in deciding whether to grant a TRO is whether immediate action is needed. Little emphasis is placed on the "ultimate success on the merits" issue. In exceptional circumstances, such an order may be issued "ex parte" (i.e., without an adversary hearing at which the side opposing the order may present its arguments), but only if (a) there is a compelling need, (b) it is impracticable to give the other side notice and an opportunity to be heard, and (c) an adversary hearing will be held soon afterward.[121] An ex parte restraining order is especially vulnerable to attack in cases such as our hypothetical. When a restraining order threatens free speech rights, such an ex parte order is invalid unless a "showing is made that it is impossible to serve or to notify the opposing parties and to give them an opportunity to participate" (Carroll v. President of Princess Anne, 1968). Of course, a person asserting constitutional rights may also, in a proper case, seek a temporary restraining order against government action that threatens those rights. Thus, someone about to be deported from the United States on orders from the Immigration and Naturalization Service may obtain a temporary restraining order until the merits of the government's action can be litigated.

Attorney's Fees

Potential awards of compensatory damages or injunctive relief are of little practical benefit unless victims can effectively pursue their claims in court. Representation by competent counsel is generally necessary for the victim of a constitutional violation to have a meaningful chance of redress. Lawyers are more likely to engage in this type of practice if they can expect reasonable compensation for their services. This section addresses the issue of when an award of attorney's fees can be made part of the remedy in a constitutional tort case. We will first describe the historical background and policy considerations that bear on this issue. We then describe the circumstances in which a party is or is not entitled to an award of attorney's fees. Finally, we will explain how reasonable attorney's fees are calculated.

Historical Background and Policy Considerations

It has long been the general rule in the United States that attorney's fees are not awarded to the prevailing party in civil litigation in the absence of a specific authorizing statute. Under what is commonly known as the "American Rule," the winning and losing parties are expected to pay their own attorneys. Courts used to make an exception to this rule in some civil rights cases, reasoning that the public interest would be served by allowing these plaintiffs to obtain fees. These are cases in which important public values are at stake even though, for reasons discussed previously, the monetary value of the plaintiffs' claims may be small. In Alyeska Pipeline Service Co. v. Wilderness Society (1975) the Supreme Court put a temporary stop to this practice. The Court reaffirmed the American Rule and disapproved lower court awards of attorney's fees to successful civil rights plaintiffs. The *Alyeska* decision made it clear that attorney's fees would be awarded to prevailing civil rights plaintiffs only if Congress expressly authorized this remedy. Within a year of the *Alyeska* decision, Congress enacted the Civil Rights Attorney's Fees Award Act of 1976,[122] which provides that "In any action or proceeding to enforce [certain civil rights laws, including 42 U.S.C. § 1983], the court, in its discretion, may allow the prevailing party, other than the United States, a reasonable attorney's fee as part of the costs."

The legislative history of this statute emphasizes two points: First, Congress believed that an award of attorney's fees to prevailing plaintiffs was necessary to enable civil rights plaintiffs to secure the services of competent counsel; and, second, private enforcement of civil rights laws serves a public purpose. As stated in the Senate report accompanying the legislation,

> [C]ivil rights law[s] depend heavily upon private enforcement, and fee awards have proved an essential remedy if private citizens are to have a meaningful opportunity to vindicate the important Congressional policies which these laws contain. In many cases arising under our civil rights laws, the citizen who must sue to enforce the law has little or no money with which to hire a lawyer. If private citizens are to be able to assert their civil rights, and

if those who violate the Nation's fundamental laws are not to proceed with impunity, then citizens must have the opportunity to recover what it costs them to vindicate these rights in court. If the cost of private enforcement actions becomes too great, there will be no private enforcement. If our civil rights laws are not to become hollow pronouncements which the average citizen cannot enforce, we must maintain the traditionally effective remedy of fee shifting in these cases.[123]

The public benefit of private enforcement was emphasized throughout the Senate report. The citizen who filed suit to enforce civil rights laws was referred to as a "private attorney general." Such suits were said to "vindicat[e] a policy that Congress considered of the highest priority." The attorney's fees statute was seen by Congress as "enabling vigorous enforcement of modern civil rights legislation, while at the same time limiting the growth of the enforcement bureaucracy." In order to achieve these public goals, the amount of fees awarded under this statute should be "adequate to attract competent counsel, but . . . not produce windfalls to attorneys."[124]

When May a Party Recover Attorney's Fees: Who Is a "Prevailing Party"?

Under the Civil Rights Attorney's Fees Awards Act of 1976, attorney's fees may be awarded to a "prevailing party." When a party seeks to recover millions of dollars but obtains a judgment for $1, can he or she be said to have "prevailed?" The Supreme Court addressed this question in Farrar v. Hobby (1992). Joseph Farrar sued the then–lieutenant governor of Texas, William Hobby, alleging that Hobby and others conspired to deprive Farrar of liberty and property without due process through malicious prosecution aimed at closing a school Farrar owned and operated. Farrar sought $17 million in compensatory damages. The jury found that Hobby had indeed conspired to deprive Farrar of his constitutional rights, but this conspiracy was not the proximate cause of any injury. The District Court ultimately entered a judgment in favor of Farrar for nominal compensatory damages ($1) and for $280,000 in attorney's fees. The Court of Appeals held that given the limited compensatory damage award, Farrar could not be considered a prevailing party and was not entitled to attorney's fees.

The Supreme Court agreed with the Court of Appeals that Farrar was not entitled to attorney's fees, but did so for different reasons. All nine justices concluded that Farrar was a "prevailing party" within the meaning of the attorney's fees statute because he secured an "enforceable judgment" for nominal damages. "In short, a plaintiff 'prevails' when actual relief on the merits of his claim materially alters the legal relationship between the parties by modifying the defendant's behavior in a way that directly benefits the plaintiff." A majority of the Court, however, characterized Farrar's victory as merely "technical" and "pyrrhic" in nature. Given the huge discrepancy between the compensatory damages sought ($17 million) and those awarded ($1), the majority concluded that "the only reasonable fee is . . . no fee at all."

Justice O'Connor cast the decisive fifth vote to make up the majority. In her view, not "all nominal damages awards are de minimis." Lower courts should consider three factors in deciding whether attorney's fees should be awarded when a plaintiff secures a judgment for nominal damages. The first consideration is whether there is "a substantial difference between the judgment recovered and the recovery sought . . ." The second factor is "the significance of the legal issue on which the plaintiff claims to have prevailed." Finally, the lower court should consider whether the litigation "accomplished some public goal other than occupying the time and energy of counsel, court, and client . . ." Justice O'Connor joined the majority because, in her view, these three factors "all point to a single conclusion: Joseph Farrar achieved only a de minimis victory." The four dissenting justices agreed with the majority that securing an enforceable judgment for nominal damages made Farrar a "prevailing party," but would have remanded the case to the lower courts to determine whether a $280,000 fee award was excessive in light of the limited success of the litigation.

The fundamental issue presented in *Farrar* is whether a plaintiff who achieves only limited success can recover attorney's fees. Commentators have characterized *Farrar* as attempting to answer this question in a "somewhat odd" manner and through "seemingly contradictory conclusions."[125] On the one hand, *Farrar* unequivocally holds that an award of nominal damages confers prevailing party status on the plaintiff. This holding offers the promise of attorney's fees to the civil rights plaintiff who cannot prove substantial actual damages. But this promise seemingly evaporates by the second holding in *Farrar* that when the plaintiff recovers only nominal damages, "the only reasonable fee is usually no fee at all." However, this second prong of *Farrar* must be read in light of Justice O'Connor's concurring opinion because the ruling could not stand without her vote. Justice O'Connor leaves open the possibility that an award of attorney's fees may be appropriate even when the plaintiff only recovers nominal damages. Under her reasoning, for example, it appears that a substantial attorney's fee can be awarded when the main motive for the litigation is to establish the illegality of the defendant's conduct, rather than to show that this illegality caused substantial harm. The plaintiff who does not claim any substantial harm may be in a better position to receive attorney's fees than the plaintiff who does claim to have been harmed but fails to prove it. Given the division of the Court in *Farrar*, perhaps it is not surprising that lower courts continue to express different views on whether to award attorney's fees when the plaintiff secures only a limited recovery.[126]

Farrar's pronouncement that attorney's fees usually should not be awarded when the plaintiff obtains only nominal damages may prove especially troublesome in light of the Court's rulings that one must prove harm in order to recover substantial damages. Recall the Supreme Court's ruling in Carey v. Piphus (1978) that absent proof of actual injury, a plaintiff would be entitled only to a judgment for nominal damages for a violation of procedural due process. In Memphis Community School District v. Stachura (1986), the Court disapproved of an instruction that would allow a jury to award damages based on the value or importance of the constitutional right violated. The limitations on damages recoverable under *Carey* and *Stachura*, coupled with *Farrar*'s disallowance of attorney's fees when the only damages are nominal may create an economic disincentive for lawyers to represent civil rights plaintiffs seeking redress for constitutional violations. The problem is especially severe in procedural due process cases. As stated by one pair of commentators, "[a]fter *Farrar*, it is difficult to understand how, when there is little or no actual economic or emotional injury, the Court contemplates that [procedural due process] rights will be enforced if attorney's fees are only theoretically and not practically available to plaintiffs who successfully prosecuted suits for their violations."[127]

A pair of cases illustrate how immunity rules (discussed previously in "Absolute Immunity" and "Qualified Immunity") and limitations on the granting of injunctive relief (discussed previously in this section) may also foreclose an award of attorney's fees even when a constitutional violation is proven. In Hewitt v. Helms (1987) an inmate sued prison officials seeking damages and injunctive relief to redress his unconstitutional confinement. Although the Supreme Court agreed that the plaintiff's due process rights had been violated, his claim for damages was defeated by the doctrine of qualified immunity. State correctional officials subsequently revised their disciplinary procedures. But by that time the inmate had abandoned his claim for injunctive relief because he had been released from prison before the end of the litigation. Under these facts, the Court held that the inmate could not be considered a prevailing party. In Rhodes v. Stewart (1988) a judge found that prison officials violated the free speech rights of two inmates by denying them access to certain magazines. Before the judge ruled, however, one of the plaintiffs had died and the other had been released from custody. The Supreme Court held that the inmates could not be considered "prevailing parties" to whom attorney's fees could be awarded, because the declaratory judgment did not affect the behavior of the prison officials towards the plaintiffs. Together, *Hewitt* and *Rhodes* send a cautionary signal to the attorney who is deciding whether to represent a civil rights plaintiff. If, as Congress assumed, most civil rights plaintiffs do not have the resources to hire a lawyer, the attorney will ordinarily look to statutory attorney's fees for compensation. In assessing the prospects of prevailing, the attorney must consider not only the merits of the constitutional claim but also the intricacies of absolute immunity, qualified immunity, and the limitations on the granting of injunctive and declaratory relief.

Suppose that a plaintiff filed suit challenging the constitutionality of a governmental policy and seeks only prospective relief, such as an injunction ordering a modification of the policy. (Prospective remedies are discussed in "Remedies.") Also suppose that after the suit was filed, the defendant changed the challenged policy in the manner sought by the plaintiff so that injunctive relief was no longer needed. Under these circumstances could the plaintiff be considered a prevailing party entitled to an award of attorney's fees on the theory that the lawsuit was the catalyst for the change in policy? Prior to 1994, every Court of Appeals to consider the issue concluded that a fee award could be made under these facts.[128] This practice ended with the Supreme Court's decision in Buckhannon Board and Care Home, Inc. v. West Virginia Department of Human Resources (2001).

In *Buckhannon*, an assisted living facility filed suit seeking an injunction to prohibit the enforcement of certain state regulations that the plaintiff claimed violated federal civil rights laws. While the suit was pending, the state legislature eliminated the challenged regulations and the suit was dismissed as moot. The plaintiff then requested attorney's fees under the "catalyst theory," claiming that it was a prevailing party because the lawsuit was the catalyst for changing the contested policy in a manner sought by the plaintiff. A bare majority of a sharply divided Supreme Court held that "the 'catalyst theory' is not a permissible basis for the award of attorney's fees."

The majority rested its opinion on the "plain language" of the attorney's fee statute and the "holdings" of prior cases. Citing Black's Law Dictionary, the majority argued that the phrase "prevailing party" is a "legal term of art" that describes a person "who has been awarded some relief by the court." Moreover, prior decisions had recognized "prevailing party" status only "where the plaintiff has received a judgment on the merits . . . or obtained a court-ordered consent decree." The dissenting justices chided the majority for upsetting "long-prevailing Circuit precedent applicable to scores of federal fee-shifting statutes." The dissenting opinion cited examples of the application of the catalyst theory that predated the enactment of federal fee-shifting statutes and references in both the House and Senate reports on the Civil Rights Attorney's Fee Award Act of 1976, which indicated that Congress was aware and approved of such practices.

Although it is far too early to assess the impact of *Buckhannon*'s rejection of the catalyst theory on civil rights litigation, it appears to be the most recent in a line of cases that narrowly define the term "prevailing party" for purposes of fee awards.

The attorney's fee statute, 42 U.S.C. § 1988 (b), states that the prevailing party may obtain fees in a proper case. On its face, the statute does not distinguish between prevailing plaintiffs and prevailing defendants. The legislative history, however, clearly reflects a Congressional intent that the standards for awarding attorney's fees to a prevailing defendant are quite different from those used when the plaintiff prevails. For example, the Senate Report states that prevailing civil rights plaintiffs "should ordinarily recover an attorney's fee unless special circumstances would render such an award unjust." The same report states, however, that plaintiffs "should not be deterred from bringing good faith actions to vindicate the fundamental rights here involved by the prospect of having to pay their opponents counsel fees should they lose . . . This bill thus deters frivolous suits by authorizing an award of attorney's fees against a party shown to have litigated in 'bad faith.'"[129]

The Supreme Court has applied the attorney's fee statute in a manner consistent with this expression of congressional intent. In Hensley v. Eckerhart (1983) the Court held an award of attorney's fees under 42 U.S.C. § 1988 should be made to a prevailing defendant "only where the suit was vexatious, frivolous, or brought to harass or embarrass the defendant." This standard was drawn from cases decided under other civil rights statutes.[130] Since the "vexatious or frivolous" standard is difficult to meet, awards of attorney's fees to prevailing defendants are quite rare. The more exacting standard applied to prevailing defendants reflects a policy judgment that plaintiffs should be encouraged to bring colorable civil rights claims, even if those claims are ultimately unsuccessful.

What Is a Reasonable Fee?

Once a plaintiff has achieved "prevailing party" status under *Farrar*, the court must then determine what constitutes a reasonable fee. The mechanics of this calculation are of greater interest to practicing attorneys than to the general public, so the following discussion will simply highlight the general principles.

The principal Supreme Court decision that outlines how to calculate attorney's fees is Hensley v. Eckerhart (1983). The plaintiffs in *Hensley* challenged a variety of practices at a state facility for the involuntarily confined. Over the course of eight years of litigation, some of the claims were abandoned by the plaintiffs and others were dismissed as moot after the defendants changed their policies. Ultimately, however, the plaintiffs prevailed on their claim that persons involuntarily confined in state facilities were being denied their constitutional right to minimally adequate care. The District Court's award of $133,332.25 in attorney's fees was affirmed by the Court of Appeals.

The Supreme Court used *Hensley* to describe how to calculate an award of attorney's fees: "The most useful starting point for determining the amount of a reasonable fee is the number of hours reasonably expended on the litigation multiplied by a reasonable hourly rate." The formula of "number of hours × hourly rate" is commonly referred to as the "lodestar." The first factor in computing the lodestar is the number of hours. The Court in *Hensley* directed lower courts to exercise "billing judgment" and exclude from the lodestar time that was not reasonably expended, such as "hours that are excessive, redundant or otherwise unnecessary." Courts may exclude from the lodestar hours that are not properly documented or that are spent on activities not closely related to the prosecution of the case.

The second component of the lodestar is the reasonable hourly rate. In Blum v. Stenson (1984), the Supreme Court held that a reasonable hourly rate is ordinarily determined by looking at the "prevailing market rates in the relevant community." The premise of looking to prevailing market rates is to compensate the attorney for "the opportunity cost of that time, the income foregone by [the lawyer in] representing the plaintiff."

An award of attorney's fees may include more than payments for the time expended by a lawyer. In Missouri v. Jenkins (1989) the Supreme Court ruled that an attorney's fee award may include compensation for paralegals, law clerks, and other support personnel. Inclusion of these expenses was needed so that "an attorney's fee awarded under § 1988 . . . yield[s] the same level of compensation that would be available from the market . . ." But in West Virginia University Hospitals, Inc. v. Casey (1991) the Court ruled that the costs of securing the services of expert witnesses are not to be included in an award of attorney's fees. This limitation was seen by many civil rights advocates as a major barrier to effective representation. Shortly after *Casey* was decided, Congress enacted the Civil Rights Act of 1991, which authorizes the inclusion of expert witness fees in an attorney's fee award in some, but not all, civil rights cases. Significantly, this legislation does not authorize an award for expert witness costs for actions brought under 42 U.S.C. § 1983. Consequently, an attorney's fee award will not include payment for expert witnesses in the bulk of constitutional tort claims, which are the subject of this book.

Once a court has fixed the number of hours and the hourly rate, it should consider whether any adjustments to the lodestar are appropriate. The *Hensley* Court made it clear that "the most crucial factor" to consider in making any adjustments to the lodestar is the "degree of success obtained." This is an especially important factor in cases, such as *Hensley*, in which the plaintiff succeeded on some but not all of the claims. In such cases, the court should consider whether the successful and unsuccessful claims are distinct or interconnected. That is, the court must evaluate the extent to which the successful and unsuccessful claims rest on a "common core or facts" and "related legal theories." The stronger the factual and legal connection between the successful and unsuccessful claims, the less the justification for a downward adjustment of the fee. The court should also consider the overall "level of success." The *Hensley* Court stated that "[w]hen the plaintiff has obtained excellent results, his attorney should recover a fully compensatory fee. . . and indeed, in some cases of exceptional success an enhanced award may be justified." On the other hand, if the plaintiff has achieved only limited or partial success, a downward adjustment of the lodestar may be appropriate.

Another important issue is whether the lodestar should be enhanced to compensate plaintiffs' attorneys for the risk of receiving no fee should they not prevail. This is commonly referred to as a contingency multiplier. The economic theory underlying a contingency multiplier was explained by one commentator as follows:

> A lawyer who bears both the risk of not being paid and provides legal services is not receiving the fair market value of his work if he is paid only for the second of these functions. If he is paid no more, competent counsel will be reluctant to accept fee award cases.[131]

Prior to 1992, lower courts had adopted varying approaches in allowing contingency multipliers and the Supreme Court had not spoken clearly on the issue.[132] This matter was put to rest when the Supreme Court in City of Burlington v. Dague (1992) held that an enhancement of the lodestar for contingent recovery was not permitted under federal fee-shifting statutes. The majority reasoned that a contingency enhancement was not needed to attract competent counsel and posed a danger of encouraging the filing of nonmeritorious claims.

The possibility that attorney's fees may be awarded to a prevailing plaintiff can influence litigation strategies and settlement negotiations. Nowhere was this made clearer than in Evans v. Jeff D. (1986), in which the plaintiff sought changes in state policies regarding the education and medical care provided children with emotional and mental disabilities. The plaintiff was represented by a lawyer affiliated with the Legal Aid Society. Because the Legal Aid Society was prohibited from representing persons capable of paying attorney's fees, the only potential source of compensation was a statutory award of attorney's fees. The defendants offered to settle the case by providing "virtually all of the injunctive relief . . . sought in the complaint" in exchange for the plaintiff waiving any claim he might have to attorney's fees. The plaintiff's counsel argued that the fee waiver agreement should not be enforced because it "exploited his ethical duty to his clients—that he was 'forced,' by an offer giving his clients 'the best result [they] could have gotten in this court or any other court,' to waive his attorney's fees." The District Court rejected this argument and approved the settlement, including the fee waiver. The Court of Appeals upheld the portion of the settlement that would improve medical services but invalidated the fee waiver agreement as contrary to public policy.

The Supreme Court reversed the Court of Appeals and held that the fee waiver agreement did not violate public policy and should be enforced. The majority disagreed with the assertion that a fee waiver agreement created an ethical dilemma for the plaintiff's attorney. The plaintiff's attorney "has no ethical obligation to seek a statutory fee award. His ethical duty was to serve his clients loyally and competently." Attorney's fees are a part of the plaintiff's "arsenal of remedies," not a right of the plaintiff's lawyer. Moreover, there was nothing in the statute to suggest that attorney's fees were "nonwaivable or nonnegotiable." Finally, the Court reasoned that not enforcing fee waiver agreements would impede settlements because "[m]ost defendants are unlikely to settle" if they remained responsible for attorney's fees that are of "potentially large and typically uncertain magnitude."

Another strategic device to limit liability for attorney's fees is known as an offer of judgment. An offer of judgment is authorized by Federal Rules of Civil Procedure, Rule 68. Under this rule of procedure, a defendant may offer to allow judgment to be taken against him. If the offer is refused and the plaintiff prevails, but fails to obtain a result more favorable than the offer, the plaintiff is responsible for "costs" incurred after the date the offer was made. In practical terms, this means that a constitutional tort plaintiff who fails to improve on the offer of judgment will not recover attorney's fees for the portion of the litigation occurring after the date of the offer.

The practical effect of a Rule 68 offer of judgment on constitutional tort litigation was well illustrated in the Supreme Court decision of Marek v. Chesny (1985). In *Marek*, three police officers shot and killed a man when responding to a domestic disturbance. The plaintiff claimed the officers used unconstitutionally excessive force. Prior to trial, the officers offered to have a judgment entered against them in the amount of $100.000, an offer that did not separate damages from attorney's fees. At the time the offer was made, the plaintiff had incurred costs, including attorney's fees of $32,000. The plaintiff refused the offer and proceeded to trial, at which the jury awarded $60,000 in compensatory and punitive damages. Because the outcome at trial was less than the offer of judgment under Rule 68,[133] the plaintiff was not entitled to the $140,000 in attorney's fees incurred after the date of the offer. In upholding the application of Rule 68 under these facts, the Court said

> We are convinced that applying Rule 68 in the context of a § 1983 action is consistent with the policies and objectives of § 1988 [the Attorney's Fees Award statute]. Section 1988 encourages plaintiffs to bring meritorious civil rights suits; Rule 68 simply encourages settlements. There is nothing incompatible in these two objectives.

Theory and Practice

An attorney deciding whether to represent a constitutional tort plaintiff must consider a number of factors in addition to the merits of the constitutional claim. He or she needs to be aware that substantial damages may be difficult to prove (e.g., Carey v. Piphus, 1978) and that any fee award may be severely reduced and perhaps denied if the overall success is limited (e.g., Farrar v. Hobby, 1992). Official immunity and limitations on the granting of injunctive relief may prevent his client from prevailing even if the plaintiff's constitutional rights were violated (e.g., Hewitt v. Helms, 1987; Rhodes v. Stewart, 1988). The court will not enhance a fee award to account for the risk that the attorney will receive no fee in some cases. (e.g., City of Burlington v. Dague, 1992). Defendants can avoid or limit the award of fees through negotiated fee waiver agreements (e.g., Evans v. Jeff D., 1986) or through a well-crafted offer of judgment (e.g., Marek v. Chesny, 1985). In light of these considerations, is the potential statutory fee award sufficient to attract the services of competent counsel?

Some academic critics argue that many of the Supreme Court decisions discussed in this section undermine the congressional goal of encouraging attorneys to represent civil rights plaintiffs.[134] There is some indication, however, that these decisions may not have had the adverse impact that critics have predicted. Professor Julie Davies interviewed attorneys who represent plaintiffs in civil rights matters and found some interesting results.[135] Plaintiffs' lawyers generally agreed that elimination of the contingency multiplier in *Dague* reduced the plaintiff's leverage in settlement negotiations but had little actual effect on overall compensation. These attorneys reported that under the lodestar formula they are paid at relatively high hourly rates and that lower courts have adjusted for the lack of a multiplier by awarding them a greater percentage of the hours billed. These lawyers also said that defendants rarely condition a settlement offer on a waiver of attorney's fees and that when made, such requests are generally refused. More common are lump-sum settlement offers that leave it to the plaintiff and his or her lawyer to decide how much goes to compensating the plaintiff for injuries and how much goes to compensating the lawyer for services. The plaintiffs' lawyers felt that lump-sum settlement offers generally produce smaller fees for their services than would result if payment to the plaintiff and attorney's fees were negotiated separately. Finally, Professor Davies found that plaintiffs' lawyers rarely encounter Rule 68 offers of judgments. She suggests two reasons why Rule 68 offers are not made more often: First, defense counsel may not be able to accurately estimate the value of a case, including attorney's fees, to derive an offer that is serious enough to get the plaintiff's attorney's attention; and second, defendants may be reluctant to authorize a realistic settlement offer at an early date.

Scholars may debate whether the leading Supreme Court decisions on attorney's fees are consistent with congressional intent or whether they serve to attract or discourage lawyers from engaging in a civil rights practice. It is undeniable, however, that attorney's fees play a significant role in constitutional tort litigation. Attorneys who engage in constitutional litigation plainly need to understand the law in this area as part of the practical economics of law practice. But the statute and the Court's construction of it is of interest not only to lawyers but to anyone seeking to understand how rules related to the availability of attorney's fees can help or hinder efforts to enforce the Constitution.

FEDERALISM AND CONSTITUTIONAL TORTS

Law consists not only of substantive and remedial rules of the kind described in earlier sections of this book but also of courts and procedures for adjudicating disputes about the scope of those rights and remedies. In a simple legal system the substantive law would be enforced in a single system of courts through a single body of procedural rules. We live in a more complex "federal" legal system, in which authority for making and enforcing legal norms is divided between the national government and the state governments. This section addresses a number of legal issues that arise from the adjudication of constitutional tort suits in a federal system.

These issues can be divided into two broad categories. One set of problems relates to the source or "pedigree," of the rule governing a particular issue in the litigation. Some legal rules are creatures of federal law, whereas others are matters of state law. National (or what is more commonly called "federal") law rarely covers every issue in a given field. More often, it is "interstitial," governing some but not all of the issues in a case.[136] In the event of a conflict, of course, federal law will override state law. Though this principle is well settled, questions do arise as to whether or not a particular difference between the requirements of federal and state law amounts to a "conflict." In constitutional torts there is no question about the source of the substantive rights and remedies discussed in previous sections. They are mainly matters of federal constitutional and (under 42 U.S.C. § 1983) statutory law. But federal statutory and constitutional law do not cover all the issues that may arise in a constitutional tort case. Courts must decide whether state law rules will be allowed to govern other aspects of the litigation, such as the period of time within which a suit must be brought or the enforceability of an agreement by the constitutional tort plaintiff to release the defendant from liability.

Second, the dual judicial system presents a distinct group of legal issues. In every state there are two systems of courts with overlapping jurisdiction. As a result, many constitutional issues may be litigated in either the federal court system or the state court system. The focus here is not on the source of the substantive law that controls a given issue but on identifying the court that will adjudicate the dispute. The parties may agree that federal law governs a given issue yet disagree about whether a federal court or a state court should decide that issue. Many litigants think the choice of a forum can be critical to the outcome of a constitutional tort case because they perceive the federal courts to be more sympathetic than state courts are to their claims, or more competent at resolving them. Rightly or wrongly, they believe that state courts are less familiar than federal courts with the substantive law bearing on constitutional challenges to state action and less willing than federal courts to rule that state officers have violated the federal Constitution.[137]

Choosing Between Federal and State Law

Constitutional tort law is only partly a matter of federal constitutional law. It is a complex hybrid of federal law and state law, and its federal component is itself only partly constitutional law. We have seen in earlier sections that the United States Constitution is the source of the rights that one may assert in a constitutional tort case, but it does not contain many remedial provisions. These are supplied by section 1983 and by federal judge-made rules (such as those described in "Remedies"). Moreover, on some issues the courts look to state law to resolve particular issues that arise in constitutional tort suits. Three prominent examples of this practice are (a) time limits on bringing suit, (b) whether suit may be maintained after the death of the victim, and (c) whether the court should honor a prior agreement by the plaintiff not to bring suit when the plaintiff now wishes to sue despite the agreement.

Time Limits on Bringing Suit

As a general rule, a person who has suffered an injury must sue within a specified period of time or else forfeit his or her rights against the offender. This rule applies to virtually every kind of lawsuit and is enforced by statutes in every state. These are called "statutes of limitations." The time period typically varies depending on the type of lawsuit and the state in which it is brought, so that a given claim may be "time-barred" in one state but not in another. The main policy behind these time limits is that the value of repose deserves respect (Wilson v. Garcia, 1985). Even a wrongdoer should not have to worry constantly about the possibility of being sued. There is also a concern that, over time, the evidence of what happened will become less reliable as memories fade and as physical evidence decays. Often, of course, the merits of a lawsuit will not be clear ahead of time, so it would be misleading to say that the beneficiaries of these rules are necessarily wrongdoers. Some will be the innocent targets of belated litigation. Thus, we give persons who think they have been wronged a strong incentive to bring suit within a specified number of years of the alleged wrong by forbidding them to sue after that time. Though the statutes do vary greatly, for the most part the time limits are somewhere between one and four years.

As the term "statute of limitations" indicates, these time limits are not judge-made rules but are contained in statutes enacted by Congress and the state legislatures. There are federal statutes of limitations for a variety of federal lawsuits, but there is no federal statute bearing on the time limit for filing a constitutional tort suit. The Supreme Court might have borrowed some other federal statute of limitations for this purpose, or it might have made its own rule, or it might even have decided that, in the absence of action by Congress imposing a limitations period on constitutional tort suits, there would be no limit. But it chose none of these alternatives. Instead, it ruled in *Wilson* that the federal courts should borrow state statutes of limitations. This decision can be justified on a number of grounds. There is a general principle that federal law should not displace state law unless there is a good reason for doing so. The mere fact that a federal alternative is available is typically not a sufficiently good reason. Also, setting fixed times within which suits may be brought is typically a subject for statutory action, so the Court probably felt uncomfortable with the notion of making its own rule. It may have preferred state rules over simply using a federal statute enacted for some other purpose because the appropriate time period may vary according to the nature of the rights being asserted. (In the extreme case of murder, for example, there is typically no statute of limitations because the crime is so heinous that the need for justice overwhelms the interest in repose.) No federal statute speaks to the appropriate time period for constitutional tort claims. There are, however, state statutes dealing with analogous problems. Those statutes may reflect considered judgments as to what is an appropriate limitations period for constitutional tort cases as well.

Having decided generally to borrow state statutes of limitations, the Court in *Wilson* then faced a further question. In any given state there will be a number of statutes of limitations, each directed at particular types of lawsuits. *Wilson*, for example, was a case from New Mexico. The constitutional tort claim was that police officers had violated the plaintiff's Fourth, Fifth, and Fourteenth Amendment rights by using excessive force in the course of an arrest. The officers argued that the appropriate statute of limitations was New Mexico's two-year limit on suing the state for damages for torts committed by its officers. Had the Court adopted this view, the claim would have been barred, as suit was brought more than two years after the incident took place. But there were other New Mexico statutes of limitations, including a three-year limit on bringing suits to recover for "injury to the person." Under this statute, the plaintiff's claim would not be barred, as the case was brought within three years of the incident. This statute applied to ordinary tort cases and the Supreme Court ruled that it ought to apply to constitutional tort as well.

The Court explained that the best way to choose among the alternatives was to identify the state statute of limitations for causes of action that most closely resemble constitutional tort cases. The "injury to the person" statute for ordinary tort ought to apply because constitutional tort is simply another type of tort suit. Thus, "[t]he atrocities that concerned Congress in 1871 [when § 1983 was enacted] plainly sounded in tort." Also, as we have seen in other sections of this book, the Court has "found tort analogies compelling in establishing the elements of a cause of action under § 1983, and in identifying the immunities available to defendants." It followed that "[a]mong the potential analogies, Congress would unquestionably have considered the remedies established in [§ 1983] to be more analogous to tort claims for personal injury than, for example, to claims for damages to property or breach of contract."

Wilson established that courts should try to borrow just one state statute of limitations for all constitutional tort claims within that state, and that the appropriate statute for constitutional tort suits is the one covering personal injury claims. In many states, however, this rule does not settle the issue, for in these states there are two or more statutes covering various kinds of personal injury claims. Typically, some of the statutes will cover certain specified tort suits, and then a general statute will cover all other tort claims not mentioned in the narrower statutes. In Owens v. Okure (1989) the Court ruled that the general or residual limitations period for personal injury actions should govern § 1983 claims. In *Owens*, a case from New York, the plaintiff's claim that the police used constitutionally excessive force would be controlled by New York's three-year general personal injury statute of limitations rather than by its one-year limitations period for intentional torts, even though the § 1983 excessive force claim closely resembles a common law intentional tort claim. The general principle set forth in *Owens* is that the residual limitations period is appropriate when "state law provides multiple statutes of limitations for personal injury actions and the residual one embraces, either explicitly or by judicial construction, unspecified personal injury actions."

Besides the length of time within which a constitutional tort suit must be brought, the Court has addressed two other issues related to limitations on suing. One is the identification of the day from which the time is measured, an issue called "accrual" in the jargon. The other is whether a litigant may have a good excuse for not bringing his or her case within the ordinary limitations period, which is called "tolling." The Court faced the tolling issue in Board of Regents v. Tomanio (1980). Having been denied a license to practice as a chiropractor in New York, the plaintiff first pursued state remedies. Time passed, the effort proved futile, and then the plaintiff brought a federal suit. The narrow issue in this case was whether the time spent in trying to obtain a state remedy ought to count in calculating the limitations period. But underlying this issue was the question of whether the Court should borrow state law or make a federal rule instead. A lower court had opted for a federal rule that the pursuit of the state remedy would "toll" (i.e., stop the running of) the statute. Under New York law it would not, and the plaintiff would be time-barred in federal court. The Supreme Court held that state law governed tolling; thus, the New York rule applied and the plaintiff lost. Note that the case may come out differently in another state with a different tolling rule.

The "accrual" issue is illustrated by Delaware State College v. Ricks (1980), which concerned a complaint by a college professor at a state school in Delaware that he had been denied tenure because of his national origin. The issue was whether the time period began on the day of the adverse tenure decision (an earlier point in time) or on the day his contract expired (a later point in time). The Supreme Court ruled that the claim accrued on the day of the adverse decision. Rather than making a special rule for constitutional tort, the Court applied the general federal rule, applicable to a broad range of litigation, that a claim begins to accrue on the day the plaintiff reasonably should know the facts supporting a cause of action (United States v. Kubrick, 1979). In this case the Court did not have to face the issue of whether federal or state law governed the accrual issue, because the Delaware rule on accrual was the same as the general federal rule. Whether the Court would apply the general federal rule in a constitutional tort case in which the state law diverged from it seems to be an open question.

Though the Court's general practice is to borrow state law for most issues relating to time limits, this practice is subject to an important qualification: The Court will not borrow state law if the particular state rule is incompatible with the purposes of constitutional torts. For example, in Felder v. Casey (1988) a state statute required that anyone contemplating a suit in state court against a state or local governmental officer must notify the prospective defendant within 120 days of the alleged injury. Under the statute, the officer or agency then has 120 days to decide whether to grant or deny the requested relief. If it is denied, the plaintiff must then bring suit within six months or else forfeit the claim. This statute in effect sets up two stringent limitations periods for the plaintiff, one of 120 days, followed by an interim period of 120 days, and then a six-month time limit on bringing suit. The Court held that the statute could not be applied in § 1983 cases, because the burden it put on the plaintiff interfered too much with the remedial purpose of § 1983. The Court made it clear that its ruling applied to suits filed in federal court as well as those brought to state court. The general principle *Felder* stands for is that a state statute of limitations (or any other state rule that otherwise may be borrowed) will be ignored in constitutional tort suits if the Court deems it insufficiently accommodating to the federal interest in providing an effective remedy for constitutional violations. Applying this principle, one lower court refused to apply a Utah statute that was enacted specifically for constitutional tort cases, explaining that the two-year limitations period the statute established was inconsistent with federal law and policy given that Utah's residual limitations period for torts was four years (Arnold v. Duchesne County, 1994).

Survival and Wrongful Death

Previously, in "Remedies," we described in some detail the doctrine bearing on the "survival" of constitutional tort actions after the death of the victim, and on suits by the dead victim's close relatives for damages they may have suffered as a result of his or her "wrongful death" caused by the constitutional tort. Here we briefly return to this topic to point out that this, too, is an area in which the Supreme Court often borrows state law as the federal rule. In Robertson v. Wegmann (1978) the Court decided that it would, in general, adopt state law on whether a constitutional tort cause of action survived the death of the victim. This case was from Louisiana, where the relevant statute provided that a tort case would not survive the victim's death unless a close relative of the victim was available to pursue it. The problem in this case was that the plaintiff died without any close relatives. Because this does not happen very often, the Court did not think that using the Louisiana statute would interfere much with the § 1983 aims of deterring constitutional violations and vindicating constitutional rights. But the Court was careful to leave the door open to refusing to borrow a survival statute that had a broader impact. While adopting Louisiana law on survival, the Court cautioned that its ruling was

> a narrow one, limited to situations in which no claim is made that state law generally is inhospitable to survival of § 1983 actions and in which the particular application of state survivorship law, while it may cause abatement of the action, has no independent adverse effect on the policies underlying § 1983.

The outcome may be different if the state law allowed for very limited survival or otherwise interfered with the deterrent and compensatory policies of § 1983. For example, the Court has refused to apply a state law that would deny the cause of action in a case in which the death was caused by the constitutional tort. (Carlson v. Green 1980).

Releases of Liability

A common practice in tort litigation is for the parties to settle the case themselves before a court resolves it for them. The defendant may pay the plaintiff a sum of money or agree to change his or her behavior, but without admitting any wrongdoing. In exchange, the plaintiff agrees to drop the lawsuit and "release" the defendant from any further threat of liability arising out of the incident that gave rise to the litigation. Both parties can benefit from such a settlement in that each avoids the risk of an adverse ruling on the merits. The plaintiff gets at least some of what he or she sought in the litigation and the defendant escapes the worst potential consequences of losing the case.

In constitutional tort law, one particular type of settlement raises special issues. These are cases in which the constitutional tort plaintiff is a defendant in a criminal case. In fact, the alleged constitutional tort often arises out of the criminal prosecution in some way. For example, the constitutional tort plaintiff may complain that the police used excessive force in the course of arresting him or her. The settlement in such a case may include a provision that the state will dismiss the criminal charges in exchange for a release of the police officers from liability. These "release-dismissal" agreements differ from ordinary settlements in that some of the costs and benefits of the settlement fall on different actors. The defendant officers benefit from the release, but the "cost" of this is paid by the state criminal justice system, which is denied the opportunity to prosecute a putative crime. Also, there is a danger that officials will bring insubstantial criminal charges against the victim of the constitutional tort so as to have a bargaining chip to use in the settlement negotiations.[138]

Despite these concerns, settlements of this kind are typically allowed under ordinary principles of state contract law. In Town of Newton v. Rumery (1987) the Supreme Court was asked to outlaw them in the constitutional tort field. The facts are typical of the kind of case that gives rise to the release-dismissal issue. Rumery was arrested for allegedly intimidating a witness (the victim of an earlier attack by a friend of Rumery), but the charges were dropped in exchange for an agreement by Rumery not to sue the town or its officials for an illegal arrest. Rumery was represented by a lawyer, who drafted the agreement and explained it to him before he signed it. Despite the agreement, Rumery later brought a § 1983 suit seeking damages for illegal arrest and incarceration. The town and its officials defended on the ground that the release-dismissal agreement was a valid contract under state law. In response Rumery proposed a blanket rule of federal law that such agreements may not be enforced to bar constitutional tort suits. Viewed from the perspective of federalism, the issue for the Court was whether the federal interest in enforcing constitutional rights through § 1983 suits justified a federal rule overriding state contract law.

In a 5–4 decision the Court rejected Rumery's request for a per se rule against the enforcement of release-dismissal agreements, or at least against the enforcement of the one that he signed. Justice Stevens, joined by justices Brennan, Marshall, and Blackmun, wrote the dissent. The four dissenters maintained that a blanket rule was needed because the state prosecutors who negotiate such agreements represent several interests that are potentially in conflict with one another. These include

(a) the state's interest in "the evenhanded and effective enforcement of its criminal laws," (b) "the interests of the town . . . and its Police Department in connection with their possible civil liability;" and (c) the interest of the witness whom Rumery had allegedly threatened. The dissenters were concerned that there is "an obvious potential conflict between the prosecutor's duty to enforce the law and his objective of protecting members of the Police Department who are accused of unlawful conduct." Moreover, there is a danger that the prosecutor will bring prosecutions he or she knows are not justified on the merits simply to put pressure on the constitutional tort plaintiff to drop his or her lawsuit. Finally, the prosecutor should not be overly influenced by the interests of the witness, who may prefer not to testify. For these reasons, Justice Stevens argued, the agreement entered into in this case should not be enforced, and more generally, there should be a "strong presumption against the enforcability of such agreements."

Justice Powell, joined by Chief Justice Rehnquist, Justice White, and Justice Scalia, took a different view. First, Justice Powell rejected the notion that such agreements are inherently coercive, noting that the constitutional tort plaintiff may have very good reasons for preferring the "certain benefits of escaping criminal prosecution" to the "speculative benefits of prevailing in a civil action." While a badly motivated prosecutor may fabricate criminal charges to use as a bargaining chip, it would be wrong to presume that this practice is widespread. There are often legitimate reasons for a prosecutor to make such a deal, notably the public interest in "protecting public officials from the burdens of defending . . . unjust claims." Prosecutors always must weigh a number of factors in deciding whether to prosecute, including "the strength and importance of a case," "government enforcement priorities," and "how best to allocate the scarce resources of a criminal justice system that simply cannot accommodate the litigation of every serious criminal charge." Justice Powell pointed out that courts normally defer to prosecutorial discretion in such matters and maintained that they should do so here as well. At any rate, a per se rule against enforcing such agreements would be unwise.

Justice O'Connor cast the deciding vote against the per se rule. She agreed with much of Justice Powell's reasoning but feared that he gave too little credit to the objections to these release-dismissal agreements. In her view, courts should not presume that such agreements are valid. Rather, on a case-by-case basis the official seeking to enforce the agreement bears the burden of proving that it "was voluntarily made, not the product of prosecutorial overreaching, and in the public interest." In her view, the agreement in this case met these standards.

Though Justice O'Connor wrote only for herself, the four dissenters would surely share her view that the constitutional tort defendant bears the burden of proving the validity of a release-dismissal agreement. Paradoxically, her position has become the rule in such cases. Applying that rule in the years since *Rumery* was decided, lower courts have generally found that significant factors bearing on enforceability include (a) whether the criminal defendant/tort plaintiff was represented by counsel at the time of the agreement, (b) whether he or she was incarcerated at that time, (c) the sophistication of the signer, and (d) whether the prosecutor has legitimate motives for making the agreement.[139] It is important to note that, quite apart from whether federal law allows release-dismissal agreements to be enforced, a given state may have its own rule forbidding such agreements. For example, in Colorado the Bar has enacted a rule forbidding prosecutors from exacting a release as a condition of dropping a criminal prosecution.[140]

Coordinating Federal Court and State Court Jurisdiction

When representatives of the thirteen independent states met in Philadelphia in 1787 to reform the Articles of Confederation, they differed on a number of points. But there was common ground on many matters as well. No one seems to have contemplated doing away with the state judicial systems then in place. Indeed, it was generally agreed that state courts would adjudicate claims arising under federal law as well as claims under state law. Only if and when Congress deemed it necessary were lower federal courts to be created. In 1789 the first Congress did enact legislation to set up a federal judicial system, and the result is the coexistence of two systems of courts in every state.[141] Some matters may only be litigated in federal courts, and some may be taken only to state courts. There is, however, much overlap in the jurisdiction of the two systems. In particular, federal constitutional issues may be litigated in either of them and constitutional remedies may be sought in either of them.

Thus, the Supreme Court held in Monroe v. Pape (1961) that constitutional remedies could be pursued in federal court even if a state remedy is available. In Howlett v. Rose (1990) it ruled that state courts may not refuse to hear constitutional tort claims merely because the state's "public policy" opposes suits against the state. Even though state court is available, most constitutional tort plaintiffs prefer to sue in federal court. There are a variety of reasons for this preference. Because federal judges are chosen from a smaller pool, they may be more competent than state judges, at least at the resolution of the federal issues that regularly arise in constitutional litigation but that state judges may rarely encounter. State judges may be accountable to a state electorate or state legislators and in any event may feel loyalty toward the state government that pays their salaries. Federal judges have life tenure during good behavior, and are altogether independent of any allegiance to the state government. They may be more willing than state judges to find that state officers have violated the federal Constitution and therefore must change their behavior and pay damages. Besides this perception of disparity, plaintiffs may simply prefer the procedural rules used in federal court or the fact that juries are chosen from a broader range of potential jurors.[142]

Of course, some constitutional tort plaintiffs prefer to litigate in state courts. One reason is that such judicial disparity may not be present in a given state. Another is that state judges in a particular area may be more sympathetic than federal judges to federal issues. In a given case the plaintiff's lawyer may prefer a jury chosen from the local area where the alleged tort occurred, or a given state procedural rule may favor the plaintiff.[143] For example, as discussed in "Appeals of Decisions Denying Defendants' Motions for Summary Judgment on Qualified Immunity", in federal court the defendant officer has the right to an interlocutory appeal from a denial of immunity. That is, he or she may insist that the litigation be suspended while the immunity ruling in higher courts is appealed, a process that adds delay and expense to the litigation. The Supreme Court ruled in Johnson v. Fankell (1997) that state courts are not obliged to grant the constitutional tort defendant such an interlocutory appeal. This difference may prompt the plaintiff to take his or her-case to state court rather than to federal court. Yet it is important to note that the case still may end up in federal court if the defendant wants it there. The reason is that the federal "removal" statute allows the defendant to transfer to federal court a case the plaintiff could originally have taken to federal court.[144] The very factor that incited the plaintiff to go to state court may lead the defendant to remove the case to federal court.

There is another reason why the plaintiff may prefer state court: He or she may wish to bring both federal constitutional claims and state tort claims in the same litigation. This may be easier to do in state than in federal court. One reason is that certain state claims may not be brought in federal court. The Supreme Court held in Pennhurst State School and Hospital v. Halderman (1984) that suits against state officers for relief on state law grounds ordinarily may not be heard in federal court because of the principle of state sovereign immunity embodied in the Eleventh Amendment. (This rule does not apply to suits against local governments and local government officers, because they are not protected by Eleventh Amendment immunity.)[145] If the case is against the state and its officers, the only way to litigate federal claims and state claims at the same time is to take them all to state court. Even if *Pennhurst* is not a problem, the Supreme Court has ruled that federal jurisdiction extends to state claims only if they arise out of the "same nucleus of operative fact" as the federal claims (called"pendent jurisdiction.") (United Mine Workers of America v. Gibbs, 1966).[146] In any given case, the facts supporting the state claims may differ too much from those underlying the federal claims for this condition to be met. Neither of these obstacles is an impediment to taking all the claims to state court. Keep in mind, however, that in any given state there may be rules that bar suits against the state in state court or that forbid joining dissimilar state and federal claims. In that event, there may be no alternative but to try the claims separately.

For whatever reason, most constitutional tort plaintiffs prefer federal court over state court. Yet state courts will often also have jurisdiction over the federal constitutional issues raised in the federal litigation. The individual may prefer federal court while the state wants to try the case in state court, for any of the reasons we have discussed in the foregoing paragraphs. This situation gives rise to the potential for conflict between federal and state courts, duplication of effort, and confusion as to which court should rule on a given issue. The Supreme Court has developed several doctrines to address these problems.

Exhaustion of State Remedies

Remedies for constitutional violations may be available in the state courts or other state tribunals. One way of avoiding interference by the federal courts in the affairs of the states would be to require plaintiffs to exhaust these state remedies first before taking their cases to federal court. In this way the state courts would have the initial opportunity to correct constitutional errors by state officers and to interpret state laws so that they do not raise constitutional questions. These are worthy goals, and the case for requiring exhaustion is not an insubstantial one. In one important area of federal–state relations—federal review of state criminal convictions by habeas corpus—it has proven strong enough to support a general exhaustion requirement. Nonetheless, the argument has not prevailed as a general rule in the constitutional tort context. Monroe v. Pape (1961), the seminal constitutional tort decision, is the leading case for the proposition that exhaustion is not required. Though the Court in *Monroe* did not state its decision as a "no exhaustion" rule, this is the necessary implication of its holding that the federal remedy is supplementary to any state remedy.[147] The main reason for this rejection of exhaustion is probably a judgment by the Court that constitutional tort plaintiffs ought to have access to the forum of their choice, and many would prefer a federal forum for the reasons discussed previously.

Through forty years of constitutional tort litigation since *Monroe*, the Court has never wavered from its general rule that exhaustion of state remedies is not a prerequisite to filing a § 1983 suit in federal court. Moreover, in the years since *Monroe* the Court has reaffirmed and expanded the ruling of that case in one important way, by rejecting any general requirement that administrative remedies be exhausted. The states often handle disputes between citizens and government officers through nonjudicial or administrative bodies, such as the internal review mechanisms of a university system. In Patsy v. Board of Regents (1982) the plaintiff took issue with an action by officers of Florida's university system. He brought a § 1983 suit, though the decision could have been challenged through an administrative remedy available within the system. The issue was whether the plaintiff was obliged to pursue the administrative remedy before suing under § 1983. The Supreme Court took the case not only to consider the question of whether administrative exhaustion should be distinguished from exhaustion of judicial remedies but also to reevaluate the "no exhaustion" rule as a whole. Some of the justices would have demanded that litigants exhaust administrative remedies. They maintained that exhaustion should be required in order to conserve federal judicial resources, to show respect for state processes, and to give the agency an opportunity to bring its expertise to bear on the issues. But these arguments were to no avail. The majority reaffirmed the "no exhaustion" rule and its application to administrative as well as judicial remedies, emphasizing that Congress in enacting § 1983 had shown distrust of state processes and had assigned to the federal courts "a paramount role in protecting constitutional rights." There are some exceptions to the general "no exhaustion" rule, however, and these are taken up in the ensuing sections.

Despite *Monroe* and *Patsy*, people are obliged to exhaust state remedies in certain situations. One of these concerns litigation by persons who have been convicted of crimes in state court. In dealing with exhaustion in this context, we need first to describe the relation between suits brought under § 1983, in which exhaustion is not required, and habeas corpus litigation, in which exhaustion is necessary. When a state prisoner brings a § 1983 suit claiming a violation of his or her constitutional rights, the federal court does not merely accept jurisdiction because of the "section 1983" label the prisoner puts on it. Instead, the court must examine the complaint to determine the nature of the claims advanced.[148] If the prisoner challenges the conditions of his confinement, such as brutality by guards or lack of medical attention, then his suit is properly within § 1983. But if his challenge goes to the fact of his confinement, then it must be brought within the habeas corpus rules, and state remedies must be exhausted before the federal suit is filed (Preiser v. Rodriguez, 1973).

Suppose the plaintiff does not seek release, but his or her suit nonetheless rests on the premise that the conviction was illegal. (We need not be concerned with the reasons why he does not seek release from confinement. Two possibilities are that (a) he may have never been sentenced to prison, or (b) his sentence may be over by the time he brings a § 1983 suit.) Does this fall on the "exhaustion" or the "no exhaustion required" side of the line? The Court addressed this question in Heck v. Humphrey (1994) and decided that exhaustion was required. After his conviction for manslaughter, Heck brought a § 1983 suit against two prosecutors and an investigator. He claimed that they knowingly destroyed exculpatory evidence and otherwise deliberately used illegal evidence to have him convicted. A key feature of the case is that Heck sought only damages, not release from custody. The Court held that "in order to recover damages for allegedly unconstitutional conviction or imprisonment, or for other harm caused by actions whose unlawfulness would render a conviction or sentence invalid, a § 1983 plaintiff must prove that the conviction or sentence has been reversed on direct appeal, [or otherwise nullified]." *Heck* obliges lower courts in § 1983 cases to ask whether granting relief for the plaintiff would "necessarily imply the invalidity of his conviction or sentence." If it would, they must dismiss. In effect, *Heck* imposes an exhaustion requirement in this particular category of § 1983 cases despite the general rule of *Monroe*.

Besides these problems resulting from the habeas corpus/constitutional tort distinction, there is one other special exhaustion rule relating to prisoners. Many constitutional tort suits are brought by prisoners complaining about the conditions of their confinement. Prisoners do live in disagreeable circumstances, and they have plenty of time to devote to litigation. In order to lessen the perceived burdens these suits place on the federal courts, Congress several years ago enacted the Prison Litigation Reform Act, which provides that "[n]o action shall be brought with respect to prison conditions under section 1983 . . . or any other federal law, by a prisoner . . . until such administrative remedies as are available are exhausted."[149] Two points should be noted in connection with this requirement. First, it may be satisfied without formally pursuing every administrative remedy that may be available so long as the allegations "have been fully examined *on the merits* by the ultimate administrative authority" (Camp v. Brennan, 2000). Second, the statute also provides that the court can dismiss the case immediately in the event it finds that the claim is "frivolous, malicious, fails to state a claim upon which relief can be granted, or seeks monetary relief from a defendant who is immune from such relief."[150] In such a case exhaustion would be pointless.

In certain circumstances, the plaintiff cannot establish a constitutional violation without first showing that the state judicial process does not furnish an adequate remedy for the harm he or she has suffered. In case the plaintiff does not seek state remedies, the formal rationale for rejecting the federal claim is not "failure to exhaust." It is that no constitutional violation has occurred. Nonetheless, the practical effect of these constitutional doctrines is to require the exhaustion of state remedies.

One such constitutional doctrine relates to the "takings" clause of the Constitution. When the government takes private property for public use, that clause requires that it pay "just compensation." Typically, a government will institute a "condemnation" proceeding in which a court will determine what the property is worth. But sometimes the government "takes" property indirectly, for example, by regulating its use so severely that it becomes worthless. The substantive issue is whether the plaintiff has been denied all beneficial or productive use of the property. In such a case, the only way for the property owner to obtain compensation is to bring a lawsuit of his or her own. One alternative, of course, is to file a § 1983 suit. In Williamson County Regional Planning Commission v. Hamilton Bank (1985) the issue was whether a zoning regulation brought about a taking. The Supreme Court ruled that a court cannot determine whether the owner has been denied all reasonable beneficial use of the property until he or she applies for a variance and receives a final ruling. The practical impact of this rule is to require the exhaustion of state remedies before bringing this type of claim in a § 1983 suit. In a later case the Court applied a similar rule to a claim that the state had deprived the holder of a patent of his property rights when it used the plaintiff's invention without paying for it (Florida Prepaid Postsecondary Education Expense Board v. College Savings Bank, 1999).[151]

One must also resort to state remedies if the claim falls within the doctrine of Parratt v. Taylor (1981). In that case the plaintiff was a prisoner who claimed that guards had lost or destroyed property belonging to him. He brought suit under § 1983, asserting that he had been deprived of property "without due process of law" in violation of the Fourteenth Amendment. The Court noted that the alleged acts of the prison guards were "random and unauthorized" under state law. Thus, the constitutional violation was not established simply by showing that a deprivation had occurred. The plaintiff must also show that the deprivation was "without due process of law." If effective state remedies were available, they would provide the process that was due. The Court explained that allowing such cases into federal court would risk turning the Constitution into a "font of tort law," displacing the state tort system. Respect for the traditional role of state law demanded that the plaintiff take advantage of state remedies.

The effect of the *Parratt* ruling was similar to an exhaustion requirement in that the Court obliged the prisoner to seek state remedies before suing under § 1983. A later case, Zinermon v. Burch (1990), limited the scope of this holding in an important way. *Zinermon* held that the *Parratt* rule only applies to claims that state officers have violated one's right to procedural due process, not to claims that they have violated substantive due process. The distinction between the two is that procedural due process focuses on the procedures used to decide whether a given deprivation is appropriate, whereas substantive due process relates to objections to certain kinds of government invasions of personal interests no matter what procedure is employed in bringing them about. (This distinction is discussed at greater length in "Due Process and Other Constitutional Rights"). The central point here is that, under *Zinermon*, the existence of state remedies is irrelevant to the issue of whether the plaintiff's substantive due process rights have been violated.

Federal Court Abstention

This section describes a group of doctrines that require federal courts to "abstain" from ruling on federal constitutional challenges to state action in favor of directing plaintiffs to the state courts instead. As a functional matter, abstention is often the equivalent of exhaustion. Some of the abstention doctrines are statutory, whereas others are products of judicial law making. Though Congress and the Supreme Court have chosen not to make a general exhaustion rule for § 1983 cases, they have imposed requirements that federal courts abstain from hearing some kinds of § 1983 cases. The general effect of the abstention doctrines has been to strengthen the role of the state courts in the adjudication of certain kinds of constitutional attacks on state practices, and the doctrines are often defended on the ground that they promote "federal–state comity" (e.g., Younger v. Harris, 1971). The reasoning here is that abstention doctrines contribute in a constructive way to federal–state relations by giving state courts more authority than they would otherwise have. These doctrines were initially developed in the context of suits for prospective relief; thus, their central aim is to forbid federal courts from issuing injunctions or declaratory judgments (see "Remedies") rather than to interfere with suits for damages.

Over time the principles first developed in the context of prospective relief have increasingly been applied in suits seeking damages as well.

Beginning in the late nineteenth century and continuing on into the 1930s, the Supreme Court applied a doctrine called "economic due process."[152] Using the Due Process Clause of the Fourteenth Amendment as its doctrinal peg, the Court during this period struck down many efforts by state legislatures to regulate business enterprises. It ruled that much regulation interfered with economic liberty or property rights enough to amount to "deprivation of . . . liberty or property without due process of law." In the 1930s Congress decided that some aspects of this type of constitutional litigation should be conducted in the state courts rather than in the federal courts, no doubt because the state courts would likely be more sympathetic to the state interests that were at stake in these cases. Accordingly, Congress enacted two statutes that channel some constitutional litigation to the state courts. One is the Tax Injunction Act, which bars federal jurisdiction of any case in which a litigant seeks an injunction against "the assessment, levy, or collection of any tax under State law where a plain, speedy and efficient remedy may be had in the courts of such State."[153] In practice, this means that the federal court must abstain whenever a remedy is available in state court even though the state remedy may not be particularly effective.[154] The other statute is the Johnson Act, which limits federal jurisdiction over certain constitutional challenges to state utility rate orders in the same way. So long as a state remedy is available, the federal court may not interfere.[155]

Most of the abstention doctrines are the product of judicial law making. Some of the doctrines draw on the statutory policy underlying the Tax Injunction Act. The act only forbids federal courts from granting injunctions, which are orders directed to state officials to stop enforcing state law. Litigants saw in this language an opportunity to evade the bar to federal court erected by the Tax Injunction Act. They framed their cases as "declaratory judgments" (thus seeking, as an initial matter, merely a statement by the court that the tax was unconstitutional).[156] In Great Lakes Dredge & Dock Co. v. Huffman (1943), the Supreme Court rebuffed this effort, ruling that whether the statute itself forbids declaratory judgments, the availability of adequate state remedies justifies the federal courts in abstaining. Much later the Court ruled that the statute itself implicitly forbids declaratory judgments (California v. Grace Brethren Church, 1982). Another potential remedy is damages after the illegal taxes have been collected. But the Supreme Court has ruled, in Fair Assessment in Real Estate Association, Inc. v. McNary (1981), that the statutory policy of channeling these tax cases to the state courts is strong enough to justify a judge-made rule requiring federal courts to dismiss suits that seek only damages. Writing for the Court, Justice Rehnquist said that "the principle of comity bars federal courts from granting damages relief." He noted that the effect of a judgment for damages would be similar to that of a declaratory judgment, in that the federal court would necessarily have to find the state tax statute unconstitutional in order to give the plaintiff the relief he or she seeks. In a later case the Court ruled that if a state law remedy is available, a § 1983 suit may not be brought even in state court (National Private Truck Council, Inc. v. Oklahoma Tax Commission, 1995).

Other judge-made abstention doctrines do not have their roots in any statute. Their general aim is to promote federal–state comity, by enhancing the role of the state courts in constitutional litigation against state governments and their officers. They also help to minimize friction between the federal and state courts, lessen the amount of interference of federal courts in the affairs of state government, and avoid duplication of effort by the federal and state courts (e.g., Steffel v. Thompson, 1974). A more subtle benefit of abstention doctrines is that, by dividing the work of constitutional litigation between the federal and state courts, they ensure that a broad array of intellectual resources will be brought to bear on their resolution.[157] These doctrines are commonly identified by the names of cases that figured prominently in their development.

The *Pullman* abstention doctrine, named after Railroad Commission of Texas v. Pullman Co. (1941), applies in situations in which someone challenges state action on federal constitutional grounds and in which a state law issue is present as well. In such cases the resolution of the state law issue may obviate the need to decide the federal issue.[158] Suppose, for example, someone brings a § 1983 suit to dispute the validity of a state statute that forbids private individuals from financing political advertisements. The reasoning behind the lawsuit is that the law violates the free speech clause of the First Amendment. But there is also a state constitutional provision that may invalidate the statute. If the state law issue is decided in favor of the plaintiff, there would be no need to resolve the federal issue. The Supreme Court has ruled that federal courts should often abstain from deciding such a case in favor of directing the parties to state court for a resolution of the state law issue.

The Court's reasoning is that several worthy goals are served by abstention. First, it may be possible to avoid resolution of a difficult constitutional issue. Since constitutional adjudication is in some tension with the principle of majority rule, it is best to avoid constitutional decisions whenever possible. Second, it is better that the state law issue be adjudicated in state court because state courts have the final word on state law (Erie Railroad Co. v. Tompkins, 1938; Murdock v. City of Memphis, 1875). Therefore, any ruling made by a federal court would lack the authority a state ruling would have and could be replaced at any time by a contrary ruling from the state court in some later case. Notice that these policies are not equally strong in every case. If the federal constitutional question is an easy one that is clearly governed by precedent, deciding it will produce little increased friction between constitutional adjudication and majority rule. If the state law is clear, there is little chance that the federal court will issue an incorrect ruling on a matter of state law. Thus, the case for *Pullman* abstention is strong only where the federal issue is highly controversial and the prior state cases do not give a straightforward answer to the state law issue.

An important feature of *Pullman* abstention is that the plaintiff is not banished to the state courts forever. Once sent there, he or she must identify his or her federal claims so that the state court can adjudicate the state law issues in their full context. (That court may interpret state law one way rather than another if one alternative may run afoul of the federal Constitution while the other clearly does not.) For that matter, the litigant who is sent to state court under *Pullman* may choose to litigate his or her federal claims there as well. But either side may also reserve the right to return to federal court for resolution of the federal issues in the case (England v. Louisiana State Board of Medical Examiners, 1964).

Our next doctrine arises from the following type of situation: A defendant in a state criminal trial claims that he or she cannot validly be convicted because the statute at issue in the case is itself unconstitutional. He or she seeks to bring a § 1983 suit in order to have the statute struck down and to forbid the prosecutor from continuing with the state prosecution. In Younger v. Harris (1971) the Supreme Court ruled that federal courts should abstain when the federal issue at stake in the case is also a defense in a pending state court prosecution against the federal plaintiff. For example, suppose a state criminal statute makes it a crime to distribute sexually explicit material. A prosecutor brings criminal charges under this statute against a book dealer who then files a § 1983 suit in federal court against the prosecutor, seeking an injunction against the state court prosecution on the ground that the statute violates his or her First Amendment rights. The *Younger* abstention doctrine requires the federal court to dismiss the federal § 1983 case so that the constitutional issue can be litigated in the state criminal case. Unlike *Pullman* abstention, there is no provision for a return to the federal court.

In *Younger* the Court justified the doctrine as an expression of "comity," and defined comity as "a proper respect for state functions, a recognition that the entire country is made up of a Union of separate state governments, and a continuation of the belief that the National Government will fare best if the States and their institutions are left free to perform their separate functions in their separate ways." Later cases have given other reasons as well, such as avoiding the problems caused by disruption of the state case, duplication of effort by the state and federal courts, and disrespect for the state courts.

In the decade following *Younger*, the Court extended its rule beyond the fact pattern presented by *Younger* itself. Thus, federal courts must defer not only to criminal proceedings but to a number of civil proceedings as well (Juidice v. Vail, 1977; Trainor v. Hernandez, 1977). The abstention rule has been applied not only when the federal issue is a defense to the state proceeding but also when it can be raised in some other way. (Moore v. Sims, 1979). It applies not only when the state case is brought before the federal case, but also when it is filed after the federal case but before "proceedings of substance on the merits" in the federal case (Hicks

v. Miranda, 1975). Deference is required not only in favor of state judicial proceedings but also in favor of state administrative proceedings of a judicial nature, such as a state bar disciplinary proceeding (Middlesex County Ethics Commission v. Garden State Bar Association, 1982). The Court has not yet decided whether abstention is required not only where the requested relief is prospective in nature, as in *Younger*, but also when the plaintiff seeks only retrospective relief in the form of damages. It has, however, affirmed a lower court ruling that the federal case must be postponed while the state case goes forward (Deakins v. Monaghan, 1988).

Compared to *Younger*, the *Burford* abstention doctrine has received far less attention from the Supreme Court. The doctrine derives from Burford v. Sun Oil Co. (1943), in which a federal court was asked to rule on the validity of a state administrative order regarding the allocation of rights to drill within an oil field. The Supreme Court said that this type of litigation was best left to the state courts, but it did not make clear exactly why. In the years since the case was decided the Supreme Court has rarely returned to the problem, and "attempts to apply [*Burford*] in the lower courts have frequently spawned confusion."[159] For present purposes the central point is that the case is rarely cited outside the area of business regulation, where there are few constitutional restrictions on government in any event. Unlike *Younger* it is not a serious obstacle to litigating the great majority of viable constitutional challenges to state action. Even within the business regulation area, the doctrine is not likely to be applied if the case raises a substantial constitutional issue.[160]

Issue and Claim Preclusion

For reasons discussed previously, much constitutional litigation takes place in the state courts. The abstention doctrines often require it, and there are situations in which one must exhaust state remedies before bringing suit in federal court. More broadly, state courts have general jurisdiction to consider issues that come before them in the course of their business, and these may include federal issues as well as state issues. In particular, the administration of state criminal law in state courts routinely requires state judges to resolve federal constitutional issues. This section begins from the premise that a state court has already decided a case that may have presented a federal constitutional issue and in which one of the parties later seeks access to federal court to litigate that federal issue in a § 1983 case. The question we address is whether (and in what circumstances) the federal court is precluded from adjudicating the federal claim on account of the prior state proceeding.

At the outset, it will be useful to distinguish between "issue" preclusion and "claim" preclusion. The former doctrine deals with situations in which the state court has decided a federal issue and the federal court is forbidden from revisiting it. Claim preclusion concerns situations in which a federal claim could have been advanced in an earlier state case but was not. Though no court has ruled on the federal issue, the litigant now seeking to pursue it may be foreclosed by the doctrine of claim preclusion. The most important case on this topic is Allen v. McCurry (1980), which involved two pieces of litigation. The first was a criminal prosecution brought by the state of Missouri against McCurry. At the criminal trial McCurry objected to the introduction of some evidence, claiming it had been obtained in violation of his Fourth Amendment right against unreasonable searches and seizures. The state courts rejected this claim and the jury convicted McCurry. He then filed a § 1983 suit in federal court, seeking damages for the allegedly illegal search. Applying the well-established doctrine of "collateral estoppel," the Supreme Court ruled that McCurry could not relitigate the Fourth Amendment issue in federal court; he was bound by the prior adjudication of that issue in state court. The Court explained that "[u]nder collateral estoppel, once a court has decided an issue of fact or law necessary to the judgment, that decision may preclude relitigation of the issue in a suit on a different cause of action involving a party to the first case." This rule "relieve[s] parties of the cost and vexation of multiple lawsuits, conserve[s] judicial resources, and, by preventing inconsistent decisions, encourage[s] reliance on adjudication." When the first case is from state court and the second is in federal court, applying this rule "promote[s] the comity between state and federal courts that has been recognized as a bulwark of the federal system." As for the specific issue of whether the doctrine should apply in constitutional cases, the Court found that neither the language nor the legislative history of § 1983 impeded the application of the collateral estoppel principle. Neither suggested that Congress meant to make an exception to the general rule of collateral estoppel for such cases. Thus, the rule is that federal courts in § 1983 cases must accord to a ruling on a matter of fact or law by state courts the same preclusive effect that the state courts themselves would give the ruling in question. The key to collateral estoppel is that it applies only to a ruling that is necessary to the judgment of the state court. In *Allen* the ruling on the Fourth Amendment issue was necessary to the criminal conviction because the evidence would have been suppressed had McCurry won on the Fourth Amendment issue, and he may then have avoided conviction.

In a later case the Court faced the issue of whether federal courts must give preclusive effect to the determinations of state administrative bodies as well as state courts. It held that the collateral estoppel doctrine applies to the findings of fact of such bodies, provided that they are acting in a judicial capacity, that the parties have had a fair opportunity to litigate the issue, and that the state courts themselves give preclusive effect to administrative determinations of fact in certain circumstances (University of Tennessee v. Elliot, 1986). In *Elliot*, for example, officers of the University of Tennessee fired Elliot. He sought review of this decision in an administrative proceeding, claiming that the dismissal was motivated by racial prejudice against him. The administrative hearing officer found as a matter of fact that it was not. Elliot then brought a § 1983 case, claiming that he was fired because of racial prejudice. The Supreme Court ruled that if the agency acted "in a judicial capacity," the parties had a full opportunity to litigate the relevant issue of fact; if Tennessee courts would give preclusive effect to the administrative finding, then the federal courts must do the same.

On the other hand, when the state courts themselves do not give preclusive effect to a prior ruling, the federal court should not do so either. For example, in Haring v. Prosise (1983) a criminal defendant had pleaded guilty in state court to the crime of manufacturing drugs. (That is, there was no trial; he simply conceded his guilt.) Later he brought a § 1983 suit against the police officers who searched his apartment, charging that they violated his Fourth Amendment rights. The Supreme Court found that the state court would not give preclusive effect to the conviction in this case. In contrast to *Allen*, the Fourth Amendment issue was not litigated in the criminal case. The only issue resolved by the guilty plea was whether Prosise had manufactured drugs, and "[t]his question is simply irrelevant to the legality of the search under the Fourth Amendment or to Prosise's right to compensation from state officials under § 1983."

In Migra v. Warren City School District City Board of Education (1984), the Supreme Court addressed the problem of claim preclusion in constitutional tort litigation. The general rule of claim preclusion is that if a litigant could have brought a particular cause of action in an earlier lawsuit but failed to do so, he or she will be barred from suing on that claim in a later case. As with issue preclusion, the rationale for the doctrine is that it is better to avoid the inefficiency of two lawsuits when one will suffice. In *Migra* a public employee was fired and brought a suit in state court, asserting that the government had broken its contractual obligation to her. She won this case. Migra then brought a § 1983 suit, claiming that she had been fired as punishment for activities that were protected by the First Amendment right of free speech. Thus, her theory was that she should recover damages because the firing was not only a breach of contract but a violation of her constitutional rights. The Supreme Court ruled that the doctrine of claim preclusion applied to her case. Since the free speech claim could have been raised in her earlier breach of contract action, she was precluded from litigating it now. In reaching this result, the Court relied heavily on *Allen*. The Court reasoned that the case for preclusion is, if anything, stronger with regard to claim preclusion than with issue preclusion because Migra voluntarily took her case to state court, unlike McCurry, who was an involuntary criminal defendant in state court. To put this doctrine in perspective, keep in mind two further points: (1) If for some reason the federal claim could not have been litigated in the breach of contract case in state court, the claim preclusion doctrine does not apply; and (2) Migra could have brought the § 1983 suit first and may have been able to litigate the state contract claim along with the federal claim in that suit. Thus, the outcome of the case may be the product of an unfortunate error on the part of Migra's lawyer.

Interaction Among Federalism Doctrines

Having discussed a number of doctrines aimed at coordinating federal and state court jurisdiction in § 1983 cases, we are better able to see how the various rules work together. Several general points should be noted: First, a litigant with a constitutional tort claim is generally not required to exhaust state remedies. If he or she nonetheless takes the case to state court (e.g., because the claims fall under state law as well as federal law), he or she should be sure to litigate the federal claims in the state proceeding, or else the *Migra* rule may preclude litigating them later. Second, if the litigant wants to take the federal claim to state court, the state court must address it unless there is some very good reason, such as a lack of connection between the case and the forum, for refusing to do so. Merely disagreeing with the notion that state officers can be sued for constitutional violations is not a valid excuse for refusing to hear the case. Third, a litigant who must exhaust state remedies, or who is (per the *Younger* doctrine) the target of a pending state case, will be denied access to federal court. If he or she raises federal claims in the state proceeding, the collateral estoppel doctrine will often preclude relitigating them in a later federal case. On the other hand, if the litigant is sent to state court merely because the case meets the requirements of *Pullman* abstention, he or she may reserve the right to a later federal adjudication of federal rights. The *Allen* rule will not apply to such a case.

NOTES

1. Charles Black, "The Supreme Court 1966 Term—Foreword: 'State Action,' Equal Protection, and California's Proposition 14," 81 *Harv. L. Rev.* (1967) 69, 95; Ronna O. Schneider, "State Action—Making Sense Out of Chaos—A Historical Approach," 37 *U. Fla. Rev.* (1985) 737.
2. Paul Brest, "State Action and Liberal Theory: A Casenote on Flagg Brothers v. Brooks," 130 *U. Pa. L. Rev.* (1982) 1296.
3. Kathleen M. Sullivan & Gerald Gunther, *Constitutional Law* (Westbury, N.Y.: Foundation Press, 13th ed. 1997) 433.
4. Brest, "State Action and Liberal Theory."
5. Sheldon H. Nahmod, Michael L. Wells, & Thomas A. Eaton, *Constitutional Torts* (:Anderson Pub. Co., 1995) 66–67.
6. Nahmod et al., *Constitutional Torts* 33–34.
7. Sullivan & Gunther, *Constitutional Law* 432.
8. Stephen Schutte, note, "Doctrinal Foundations of Section 1983 and the Resurgent Dormant Commerce Clause," 77 *Iowa L. Rev.* (1992) 1249.
9. John Hart Ely, *Democracy and Distrust* (1980) 18.
10. Burt Neuborne, "The Myth of Parity," 90 *Harv. L. Rev.* (1977) 1105.
11. Sullivan & Gunther, *Constitutional Law* 45.
12. Larry Alexander, "Constitutional Torts, the Supreme Court, and the Law of Noncontradiction: An Essay on *Zinermon v. Burch*," 87 *Nw. U. L. Rev.* (1993) 576, 589–90.

13. Michael L. Wells & Thomas A. Eaton, "Substantive Due Process and the Scope of Constitutional Torts," 18 *Ga. L. Rev.* (1984) 201.

14. Michael L. Wells, "'Available State Remedies' and the Fourteenth Amendment: Comments on Florida Prepaid v. College Savings Bank," 33 *Loyola L. A. L. Rev.* (2000) 1665.

15. Michael L. Wells, "Constitutional Torts, Common Law Torts, and Due Process of Law," 72 *Chi.-Kent L. Rev.* (1997) 617.

16. Randolph Haines, note, "Reputation, Stigma, and Section 1983: The Lessons of Paul v. Davis," 30 *Stan. L. Rev.* (1977) 191, 204 n.88.

17. See, for example, Richard A. Epstein, "A Theory of Strict Liability," 2 *J. Legal Stud.* (1973) 151.

18. See, for example, George P. Fletcher, "Fairness and Utility in Tort Theory," 85 *Harv. L. Rev.* (1972) 537.

19. Wells, "Available State Remedies, and the Fourteenth Amendment."

20. Richard Fallon, "Some Confusions About Due Process, Judicial Review, and Constitutional Remedies," 93 *Colum. L. Rev.* (1993) 309, 365 n. 307.

21. Sullivan & Gunther, "Constitutional Law" 602 (quotation marks omitted).

22. Sullivan & Gunther, "Constitutional Law" 603.

23. Thomas A. Eaton & Michael L. Wells, "Governmental Inaction as a Constitutional Tort," 66 *Wash. L. Rev.* (1991) 107, 164–65.

24. Wells, "Constitutional Torts, Common Law Torts, and Due Process of Law," 657.

25. Wells, "Available State Remedies."

26. Michael L. Wells, "Section 1983, the First Amendment, and Public Employee Speech: Shaping the Right to Fit the Remedy (and Vice Versa)," 35 *Ga. L. Rev.* (2001) 939.

27. Thomas A. Eaton & Michael L. Wells, "Government Inaction as a Constitutional Tort: *DeShaney* and Its Aftermath," 66 *Wash. U. L. Rev.* (1991) 107.

28. Id., 134.

29. Besides our article, cited above, see, for example, Jack M. Beerman, "Administrative Failure and Local Democracy: The Politics of *DeShaney*," 1990 *Duke L. J.* 1078; Steven J. Heyman, "The First Duty of Government: Protection, Liberty and the Fourteenth Amendment," 1991 *Duke L. J.* 507; Aviam Soifer, "Moral Ambition, Formalism, and the 'Free World' of *DeShaney*," 57 *Geo. Wash. L. Rev.* (1989) 1513; David A. Strauss, "Due Process, Government Inaction, and Private Wrongs," 1989 *Sup. Ct. Rev.* 53; and Lawrence H. Tribe, "The Curvature of Constitutional Space: What Lawyers Can Learn from Modern Physics," 103 *Harv. L. Rev.* (1989) 1.

30. Barbara E. Armacost, "Affirmative Duties, Systemic Harms, and the Due Process Clause," 94 *Mich. L. Rev.* (1996) 982, 990.

31. Tribe, "The Curvature of Constitutional Space," 10.

32. The most extensive defense of *DeShaney* is Armacost, "Affirmative Duties, Systemic Harms, and the Due Process Clause."

33. For discussions of common law tort cases in this area see Armacost, "Affirmative Duties, Systemic Harms, and the Due Process Clause," 997–99 (1996); and Michael L. Wells & Thomas A. Eaton, "Affirmative Duty and Constitutional Tort," 16 *Mich. J. L. Ref.* (1982) 1, 6-13.

34. Eaton & Wells, "Government Inaction as a Constitutional Tort," 164-65.

35. A more complete description of the history of state immunity may be found in Clyde E. Jacobs, *The Eleventh Amendment and Sovereign Immunity* (Westport, C.T.: Greenwood Press, 1972).

36. Richard Fallon, Daniel Meltzer & David Shapiro, *Hart & Wechsler's The Federal Courts and the Federal System* 1051 (Westbury, N.Y.: Foundation Press, 4th ed. 1996).

37. See Richard Fallon, Daniel Meltzer & David Shapiro, *Hart & Wechsler's The Federal Courts and the Federal System*, (Westbury, N.Y.: Foundation Press, 4th ed. 1996) 849–57.

38. See for a description of the "incorporation" doctrine.

39. Dan T. Coenen, "A Constitution of Collaboration: Protecting Fundamental Values With Second-Look Rules of Interbranch Dialogue," 42 *Wm. & Mary L. Rev.* (2001) 1575, 1624.

40. Peter W. Low & John C. Jeffries, Jr., *Federal Courts and the Law of Federal-State Relations* (Westbury, N.Y.: Foundation Press, 4th ed. 1998) 842.

41. Dan B. Dobbs, *The Law of Torts* (St. Paul, Minn.: West Group, 2000) §§ 9–10.

42. See, for example, John C. Jeffries, Jr., "Compensation for Constitutional Torts: Reflections on the Significance of Fault," 88 *Mich. L. Rev.* (1989) 82.

43. Nahmod et al., *Constitutional Torts* 184–85.

44. John C. Jeffries, Jr., "In Praise of the Eleventh Amendment and Section 1983," 84 *Va. L. Rev.* (1998) 47, 58 n.40.

45. Myriam E. Gilles, "Breaking the Code of Silence: Rediscovering "Custom in Section 1983 Municipal Liabilitiy," *So. B.U.L. Rev.* (2000) 17.

46. Dobbs, *The Law of Torts* § 168; Restatement (Second) Torts § 432 (1965).

47. Dobbs, *The Law of Torts.*

48. Dobbs, *The Law of Torts*. It has been suggested that a more accurate phrasing of this test would be "sufficient cause" as it refers to causal forces that are sufficient by themselves to have caused the injury; W. Page Keeton et al., *Prosser & Keeton on the Law of Torts* (St. Paul, Minn: West Pub. Co., 5th ed. 1984) §41, at 266–67.

49. This example is taken from Cook v. Minneapolis, St. P., & Ste. M. Ry., 98 *Wis.* 624, 74 N.W. 561 (1898).

50. Charles Carpenter, "Concurrent Causation," 83 *U. Pa. L. Rev.* (1935) 941, 949–52.

51. Restatement (Second) Torts § 432 (2) (1965). See Vincent v. Fairbanks Memorial Hosp., 862 P. 2d 847 (1993); Mitchell v. Gonzales, 54 Cal. 3d 1041, 819 P. 2d 872 (1991).

52. For a general discussion of proximate cause, see Dobbs, *The Law of Torts* §§ 180–197.

53. The classic treatment of this point is Leon Green, *The Rationale of Proximate Cause* (Kansas City, Mo:Vernon Law Book Co., 1927).

54. This argument was first made in Thomas A. Eaton, "Causation in Constitutional Torts," 67 *Iowa L. Rev.* (1982) 443, 456, and elaborated upon in Michael L. Wells, "Three Arguments Against Mt. Healthy: Tort Theory, Constitutional Torts, and Freedom of Speech," 51 *Mercer L. Rev.* (2001) 583, 589.

55. Thomas A. Eaton, "Causation in Constitutional Torts," 67 *Iowa L. Rev.* (1982) 443, 456.

56. Michael L. Wells, "Three Arguments Against *Mt. Healthy*: Tort Theory, Constitutional Torts, and Freedom of Speech," 51 *Mercer L. Rev.* (2001) 583, 589.

57. Restatement (Second) of Torts § 603, cmt. a (1977).

58. Wells, "Three Arguments Against *Mt. Healthy*," 589.

59. Id., 591.

60. NAACP v. Button, 371 U.S. 415, 433 (1963).

61. Sheldon H. Nahmod, "*Mt. Healthy* and Causation in Fact: The Court Still Doesn't Get It!" 51 *Mercer L. Rev.* (2001) 603, 612.

62. Christina B. Whitman, "An Essay on *Texas v. Lesage*," 51 *Mercer L. Rev.* (2001) 621, 635–36.

63. Insightful discussions of the inherent uncertainty of causation in the context of common law torts include Leon Green, "The Causal Relation Issue in Negligence Law," 60 *Mich. L. Rev.* (1962) 543; Wex Malone, "Ruminations on Cause-in-Fact," 9 *Stan. L. Rev.* (1956) 60; Strassfeld, "If . . . : Counterfactuals in the Law," 60 *Geo. Wash. L. Rev.* (1992) 340; and Richard Wright, "Causation in Tort Law," 73 *Cal. L. Rev.* (1985) 1735.

64. Another example is Owen v. City of Independence, 445 U.S. 622 (1980) in which a police chief was dismissed under allegations of wrongdoing without having been afforded a hearing. This case is discussed more fully in "Liability of Government Entities." Chief Owen was fired by the city manager following a formal motion passed by the city council. The Court assumed, without discussion, that there was a causal connection between the city council's motion and the conduct of the city manager.

65. Barbara Kritchevsky, "'Or Causes to be Subjected': The Role of Causation in Section 1983 Municipal Liability Analysis," 35 *U.C.L.A. L. Rev.* (1988) 1187, 1208 (emphasis supplied).

66. The converse of this principle is that even if the city's policy authorizes the unconstitutional use of excessive force, no claim will lie if the actual force used by the arresting officer was constitutionally permissible. City of Los Angeles v. Heller, 475 U.S. 796 (1986). In this situation, the plaintiff has not suffered a deprivation of constitutional rights.

67. The Court also expressed doubts whether the facts presented a case or controversy as required by Article 3 of the Constitution and stated that respect for state sovereignty (federalism) counseled against federal courts issuing injunctions against municipal officials.

68. Harold S. Lewis, Jr., & Elizabeth J. Norman, *Civil Rights Law and Practice* (Eagan, Minn.: West, 2001) 208 (citing to cases).

69. The lower court cases are discussed and analyzed in Lewis, Jr. & Norman, *Civil Rights Law and Practice* 211–12 and Kit Kinports, "The Buck Does Not Stop Here: Supervisory Liability in Section 1983 Cases," 1997 *U. Ill. L. Rev.* (1997) 147.

70. For a discussion of this point see Lewis & Norman, *Civil Rights Law and Practice* 212-15.

71. Dobbs, *The Law of Torts* 443.

72. Nahmod, *Constitutional Torts* 219.

73. This point was first made in Eaton, "Causation in Constitutional Torts," 472–73 n.150.

74. Cf., Commonwealth Bank & Trust v. Russell, 825 F. 2d 12 (3d Cir. 1987) (brief interval between escape and murder does not take the case out of the rule in *Martinez*).

75. Cf. Jones v. Phyfer, 761 F. 642 (11th Cir. 1985) (furloughed prisoner attacked a woman who had previously been victimized by the prisoner; *Martinez* controls; no cause of action) with Hardmon v. County of Lehigh, 613 F. Supp. 649 (E.D. Pa. 1985) (furloughed prisoner attacked a child whom correctional officials knew had been threatened by the prisoner; *Martinez* distinguished).

76. Dobbs, *The Law of Torts* §§ 186, 194. Intervening forces that relieve the defendant of liability are often referred to as "superceding causes."

77. Dobbs, *The Law of Torts* §§ 192 and 193.

78. See, for example, Barts v. Joiner, 865 F. 2d 1187 (11th Cir. 1989); Hand v. Gary, 838 F. 2d 1420 (5th Cir. 1988); and Himba v. Odengaard, 769 F. 2d 1147 (7th Cir. 1985).

79. Himba v. Odegaard, 769 F. 2d 1147 (7th Cir. 1985). But see Anderson v. Nosser, 456 F. 2d 835 (5th Cir. 1972) (en banc) (whether the police chief who violated the plaintiffs' constitutional rights in the course of an arrest was liable for subsequent mistreatment in a state prison depended on whether the prison conditions were foreseeable).

80. John C. Jeffries, Jr., "In Praise of the Eleventh Amendment and Section 1983," 84 *Va. L. Rev.* (1998) 47.

81. Nahmod, *Constitutional Torts* 234.

82. Michael L. Wells, "Constitutional Remedies, Section 1983 and the Common Law," 68 *Miss. L. J.* (1998) 157, 204–05.

83. Id. 205 nn.218–19.

84. Sheldon H. Nahmod, *Civil Rights and Civil Liberties Litigation: The Law of Section 1983* at (St. Paul, Minn: West Group, 4th ed. 1998) § 8.18.

84a. As this book was going to press, the Supreme Court decided *Hope v. Pelzer* (2002) in which it rejected the restrictive fact-specific approach to qualified immunity reflected in the decisions of the 11th Circuit Court of Appeals. The Court held that lower courts erred in requiring that the facts of previous cases be "materially similar" in order for law to be deemed "clearly established". Rather, the salient question is whether the state of the law at the time of the incident gave the defendants "fair warning" that their actions were unconstitutional.

85. John C. Jeffries, Jr., "The Right-Remedy Gap in Constitutional Law," 109 *Yale L. J.* (1999) 87.

86. Nahmod et al., *Constitutional Torts* 287.

87. Sheldon H. Nahmod, "The Restructuring of Narrative and Empathy in Section 1983 Cases," 72 *Chi.-Kent L. Rev.* (1997) 819.

88. Dobbs, *The Law of Torts* 1047–62.

89. Patrick Elsevier, note, "Out-of-Line: Federal Courts Using Comparability to Review Damage Awards," 33 *Ga. L. Rev.* (1998) 243.

90. Jean Love, "Damages: A Remedy for the Violation of Constitutional Rights," 67 *Cal. L. Rev.* (1979) 1242.

91. F. Harper & F. James, *Law of Torts* (Boston: Little, Brown, 1956) § 25.1, p. 1299.

92. Bernard P. Dauenhauer & Michael L. Wells, "Corrective Justice and Constitutional Torts," 35 *Ga. L. Rev.* (2001) 903.

93. Daryl J. Levinson, "Making Government Pay: Markets, Politics, and the Allocation of Constitutional Costs," 67 *U. Chi. L. Rev.* (2000) 345, 406–14. For a contrary view, see Dauenhauer & Wells, "Corrective Justice and Constitutional Torts."

94. See, for example, Jack Balkin, "Too Good to Be True: The Positive Economic Theory of Law," 87 *Colum. L. Rev.* (1987) 1447.

95. Wells, "Constitutional Remedies, Section 1983, and the Common Law," 68 *Miss. L. J.* (1998) 157, 218-22.

96. Levinson, "Making Government Pay," 367–73.

97. Jean Love, "Presumed General Compensatory Damages in Constitutional Tort Litigation: A Corrective Justice Perspective," 49 *Wash. & Lee L. Rev.* (1992) 67.

98. Wells, "Constitutional Remedies, Section 1983, and the Common Law," 217.

99. Dan B. Dobbs, *Law of Remedies* (St. Paul, Minn.: West Publish., 2d ed. 1993) § 7.3 at 635.

100. Michael L. Wells, "Punitive Damages for Constitutional Torts," 56 *La. L. Rev.* (1976) 841.

101. Id.

102. Richard A. Epstein, *Cases and Materials on Torts* (Gaithersburg, N.Y.: Aspen, 7th ed. 2000) 901–06.

103. See "Absolute Immunity."

104. Douglas Laycock, *Modern American Remedies* (Boston: Little, Brown, 2nd ed. 1994) 497.

105. F.W. Maitland, *Equity 1–7* (Oxford, UK: Cambridge Univ. Press, 2nd ed. 1969).

106. Laycock, *Modern American Remedies* 353–54.

107. Douglas Laycock, *The Death of the Irreparable Injury Rule* (New York: Oxford U. Press, 1991) 23.

108. Douglas Laycock, *The Death of the Irreparable Injury Rule*, 41 (1991).

109. See "Federalism and Consitutional Torts".

110. Pamela Karlan, "The Rights to Vote: Some Pessimism About Formalism," 71 *Tex. L. Rev.* (1993) 1705.

111. Richard Fallon, Daniel Meltzer & David Shapiro, supra note 36, at 187-95.

112. Id., 186.

113. Id., 249–60.

114. Richard Fallon, "Of Justiciability, Remedies, and Public Law Litigation: Notes on the Jurisprudence of Lyons," 59 *N.Y.U. L. Rev.* (1984) 1.

115. Abram Chayes, "The Role of the Judge in Public Law Litigation," 89 *Harv. L. Rev.* (1976) 1281.

116. Owen M. Fiss, The Civil Rights Injunction" (Indianapolis, Ind.: Indiana University Press, 1978) 8–12.

117. Douglas Laycock, "Injunctions and the Irreparable Injury Rule," 57 *Tex. L. Rev.* (1979) 1065, 1073-75.

118. John C. Jeffries, Jr., Pamela S. Karlan, Peter W. Low, & George A. Rutherglen, *Civil Rights Actions: Enforcing the Constitution* (Westbury, N.Y.: Foundation Press, 2000) 846–52.

119. Laycock, *Modern American Remedies* 420-22.

120. Id., 438.

121. Federal Rule of Civil Procedure 65 (b).

122. 42 U.S.C. § 1988 (b).

123. The Civil Rights Attorney's Fees Awards Act of 1976, Senate Report No. 94-1011.

124. Id.

125. Lewis, Jr. & Norman, *Civil Rights Law and Practice* 446; Jeffries et. al, *Civil Rights Actions* 335.

126. Cf. Wilcox v. City of Reno, 42 F. 3d 550 (9th Cir. 1994) (awarding $66,535 in attorney's fees to a plaintiff who recovered one dollar in compensatory damages) with Romberg v. Nichols, 48 F. 3d 453 (9th Cir. 1995) (denying attorney's fees to civil rights plaintiff who first asked for nominal damages at the end of trial). See Lewis & Norman, *Civil Rights Law and Practice* 446–49 (discussing cases).

127. Lewis & Norman, *Civil Rights Law and Practice* 447.

128. See Buckhannon Board and Care Home Inc. v. West Virginia Department of Health and Human Resources, 532 U.S. 598, n.4 (2001) (dissenting opinion) (collecting cases).

129. The Civil Rights Attorney's Fees Awards Act of 1976, Senate Report No. 94-1011.

130. See, for example, Christianburg Garment Co. v. EEOC, 434 U.S. 412, 478 (1978).

131. John Leubsdorf, "The Contingency Factor in Attorney Fee Awards," 90 *Yale L. J.* (1981) 473, 480.

132. In Pennsylvania v. Delaware Valley Citizens' Council for Clean Air, 483 U.S. 711 (1987) four justices said that contingency multipliers were inappropriate and four justices said contingency multipliers were generally available. The decisive fifth vote was cast by Justice O'Connor, who would allow for a contingency multiplier only when the plaintiff could show that absent such enhancement, he would have faced substantial difficulties in securing counsel. For citations to lower court cases, see Lewis & Norman, *Civil Rights Law and Practice* 461–62 nn.5–9.

133. The sum of the damages awarded by the jury ($60,000) plus the attorney's fees incurred at the time of the offer of judgment ($32,000) was less than the amount of the offer of judgment ($100,000).

134. See, for example, Jeffrey S. Brand, "The Second Front in the Fight for Civil Rights: The Supreme Court, Congress, and Statutory Fees," 69 *Texas L. Rev.* (1990) 291.

135. Julie Davies, "Federal Civil Rights Practice in the 1990's: The Dichotomy Between Reality and Practice," 48 *Hastings L. J.* (1997) 197.

136. Fallon, supra note 36, at 521–22.

137. Id., 351–54.

138. Seth Kreimer, "Releases, Redress, and Police Misconduct: Reflections on Agreements to Waive Civil Rights Actions in Exchange for Dismissal of Criminal Charges," 136 *U. Pa. L. Rev.* (1988) 851.

139. Nahmod et al., *Constitutional Torts* 352–53.

140. Colorado Bar Association, Ethics Opinion No. 62 (November 20, 1982), reprinted at 12 *Colorado Lawyer* (1983) 455.

141. Fallon, Meltzer, & Shapiro, *Hart & Wechsler* 6–8, 28–31.

142. Burt Neuborne, "The Myth of Parity," 90 *Harv. L. Rev.* (1977) 1105.

143. Nahmod et al. *Constitutional Torts* 377–81.

144. 28 U.S.C. § 1441(a); Nahmod et al., *Constitutional Torts* 371.

145. See "Liability of Government Entities"

146. The law on the point is now codified in 28 U.S.C. § 1367.

147. See "Reviving Section 1983: *Monroe* and Its Progeny."

148. Jeffries et al., *Civil Rights Actions* 418.

149. 42 U.S.C. § 1997e (a); Jeffries, et al., *Civil Rights Actions* 852–56.

150. 42 U.S.C. § 1997e (c).

151. Michael Wells, "'Available State Remedies' and the Fourteenth Amendment," 33 *Loyola L.A. L. Rev.* (2000) 1665.

152. Geoffrey Stone, Louis Seidman, Cass Sunstein, & Mark Tushnet, *Constitutional Law* 710–29 (4th ed. 2001).

153. 28 U.S.C. § 1341. For a detailed discussion, see Fallon, Meltzer, & Shapiro, *Hart & Wechsler*, 1216–22.

154. John Coverdale, "Remedies for Unconstitutional State Taxes," 32 *Conn. L. Rev.* (1999) 73.

155. 28 U.S.C. § 1342. Fallon, Meltzer, & Shapiro, *Hart & Wechsler*, 1215–16.

156. See "Relief" for more detailed discussion of declaratory judgments.

157. Paul M. Bator, "The State Courts and Federal Constitutional Litigation," 22 *Wm. & Mary L. Rev.* (1981) 605.

158. Fallon, Meltzer, & Shapiro, *Hart & Wechsler*, 123–47.

159. Id. 1247.

160. Michael L. Wells, "The Role of Comity in the Law of Federal Courts," 60 *N.C. L. Rev.* (1981) 59.

Part III

Conclusion

In Marbury v. Madison (1803) Chief Justice John Marshall declared that "[t]he very essence of civil liberty certainly consists in the right of every individual to claim the protection of the laws whenever he receives an injury." When the injury consists of violation of the Constitution, the case for a remedy would seem to be especially strong, for constitutional rights are the most fundamental rights we possess. Yet there are significant obstacles to obtaining certain kinds of remedies for constitutional violations. No one contests the right of a person to raise the constitution as a defense to criminal or civil charges brought against him. But many constitutional violations take place outside the courtroom. Governments and their officials may commit constitutional wrongs in the course of daily operations, for example, by firing an employee on account of protected speech, or by using excessive force in making an arrest, or by denying medical care to a prisoner. If the Constitution were conceived solely as a "shield" against civil or criminal liability, it would be of little use in any of these situations. Many of the constitutional rights that have won recognition in the past fifty years could not be adequately enforced if the Constitution could only be asserted as a defense.

Instead, the aggrieved person must become a plaintiff and wield the Constitution as a "sword." A central theme of this book is that the availability of a suitable remedy is considerably less certain when the holder of a right seeks to take the offensive side of the litigation, seeking damages or prospective relief against the violator. The Supreme Court has recognized that deterring constitutional violations and vindicating constitutional rights are compelling goals. In pursuit of these goals, it has recognized a wide array of constitutional remedies. At the same time, the Court takes the view that a variety of considerations may justify limiting the range of constitutional remedies. One obstacle is the ancient yet tenacious doctrine of sovereign immunity. Some of the difficulties relate to the choice of remedies.

In particular, the contemporary Supreme Court is reluctant to approve of broad-ranging, forward-looking relief aimed at reforming the institutions of state governments. Other limiting principles, notably the law of official immunity, are a product of the perceived need to avoid overdeterrence of beneficial actions by government officers.

The resulting body of doctrine is a rough compromise between the value of assuring that effective remedies are available to victims of constitutional violations and the array of concerns that stand in the way of a fully effective system of constitutional remedies. One cannot understand the law of constitutional rights without also learning about this complex body of remedial doctrine. Despite Chief Justice Marshall's aphorism, it would be wrong to think that there is a remedy for every violation of a constitutional right. Nor is it realistic to aspire to a system of constitutional remedies that has no gaps in its coverage, for there will always be a tension between the two sides of this debate. What one can hope for is a body of constitutional remedial law that will adequately, though not perfectly, restrain officials who may disregard constitutional rights as they pursue the ends of government.

To that end, we have suggested a number of specific doctrines that may benefit from reconsideration. Some of these relate to immunities: The sovereign immunity doctrine enjoyed by states seems anachronistic and perhaps should be abandoned. The Court's recent cases limiting the power of Congress to abrogate sovereign immunity in order to vindicate constitutional rights seem especially unwise. Some kind of official immunity is probably necessary to the functioning of government, but current formulations of the doctrine may go too far in allowing officials to escape liability even when they should know that they are violating constitutional rights. We also question the Court's reluctance to allow the award of substantial damages in the absence of proof of the kind of harm that is typical of ordinary torts. Constitutional violations produce a different, often intangible, kind of harm that is no less, and probably more deserving of an award. Some of the Court's restrictions on the availability of injunctive relief also give too little weight to the constitutional values at stake in these cases. A good example is its rule that a plaintiff who has suffered an injury must show that he or she personally is likely to be injured again in the same way in order to seek injunctive relief. Finally, the requirement of an official policy or custom to establish the liability of local governments has produced an extremely complex and confusing body of law. As has been suggested by many scholars and individual justices, perhaps it is time for the Court to reconsider whether a city can be held responsible for the constitutional violations committed by its employees.

Whatever the merit of these suggestions, the larger point of this book is that one cannot hope to understand and appreciate the real-world value of constitutional rights without also paying close attention to the statutory and judge-made remedies that are available for the violation of those rights. Many of the most difficult and consequential constitutional battles between the state and the individual have been fought not over the substantive content of constitutional rights but instead have concerned remedial matters. As government becomes bigger and more powerful, determining the appropriate scope of constitutional protection will become an ever more crucial issue. It is safe to predict that debates over constitutional remedies will continue to be a vital part of the discourse of constitutional law.

Bibliographical Essay

GENERAL WORKS

Sheldon H. Nahmod, *Civil Rights and Civil Liberties Litigation* (1997, 1998), is a heavily footnoted, comprehensive two-volume treatise that many practitioners find quite helpful. Nahmod supplements this treatise annually. Peter H. Schuck, *Suing Government: Citizen Remedies for Official Wrongs* (1983), is a wide-ranging scholarly treatment of the topic. Harold S. Lewis, Jr., & Elizabeth J. Norman, *Civil Rights Law and Practice* (2001), emphasizes legal doctrine and treats both § 1983 and other civil rights statutes. For a general introduction to § 1983, see Michael Collins, *Section 1983 Litigation in a Nutshell* (1997). There are several good casebooks on constitutional remedies, including Richard H. Fallon, Daniel J. Meltzer, & David L. Shapiro, *Hart & Wechsler's The Federal Courts and the Federal System* (4th ed. 1996); John C. Jeffries, Jr., Pamela S. Karlan, Peter W. Low, & George A. Rutherglen, *Civil Rights Actions: Enforcing the Constitution* (2000) (a book that includes excellent bibliographical notes after each block of material, from which we have borrowed in preparing this essay); Theodore Eisenberg, *Civil Rights Legislation* (4th ed. 1996); Charles F. Abernathy, *Civil Rights and Constitutional Litigation* (3d ed. 2000); and Sheldon H. Nahmod, Michael L. Wells, & Thomas A. Eaton, *Constitutional Torts* (1995). *A Section 1983 Civil Rights Anthology* (ed. Sheldon H. Nahmod, 1993) is a collection of useful law review articles on a variety of topics in the area. *Sword & Shield Revisited: A Practical Approach to Section 1983* (ed. Mary Massaron Ross, 1998) emphasizes topics of interest to litigators in trial courts. Jurisdictional issues are discussed in Erwin Chemerinsky, *Federal Jurisdiction* (3d ed. 1999). Sometimes issues of general tort law arise in constitutional tort litigation. Dan B. Dobbs, *The Law of Torts* (2000), is a good reference work.

Efforts to work out the basic theory of the law of constitutional remedies include Alfred Hill, "Constitutional Remedies," 69 *Colum. L. Rev.* (1969) 1109; Walter Dellinger, "Of Rights and Remedies: The Constitution as a Sword," 85 *Harv. L. Rev.* (1972) 1532; Al Katz, "The Jurisprudence of Remedies: Constitutional Legality and the Law of Torts in *Bell v. Hood*," 117 *U. Pa. L. Rev.* (1968) 1; John Harrison, "Jurisdiction, Congressional Power, and Constitutional Remedies," 86 *Geo. L. J.* (1998) 2513; Daniel J. Meltzer, "Congress, Courts, and Constitutional Remedies," 86 *Geo. L. J.* (1998) 2537; and Richard Fallon & Daniel J. Meltzer, "New Law, Non-Retroactivity, and Constitutional Remedies," 104 *Harv. L. Rev.* (1991) 1731. For a skeptical view of the deterrence and corrective justice goals of constitutional tort, see Daryl Levinson, "Making Government Pay: Markets, Politics, and the Allocation of Constitutional Costs," 67 *U. Chi. L. Rev.* (2000) 345. Responses to Levinson's arguments include Myriam Gilles, "In Defense of Making Government Pay: The Deterrent Effect of Constitutional Tort Remedies," 35 *Ga. L. Rev.* (2001) 845; and Bernard P. Dauenhauer & Michael L. Wells, "Corrective Justice and Constitutional Torts," 35 *Ga. L. Rev.* (2001) 903.

Discussions of the methodology of constitutional tort law include Michael L. Wells, "Constitutional Remedies, Section 1983 and the Common Law," 68 *Miss. L. J.* (1998) 157; Sheldon H. Nahmod, "Section 1983 and the Background of Tort Liability," 50 *Ind. L. J.* (1974) 5; Sheldon H. Nahmod, "Section 1983 Discourse: The Move from Constitution to Tort," 77 *Geo. L. J.* (1989) 1719; Jack M. Beermann, "A Critical Approach to Section 1983 with Special Attention to Sources of Law," 42 *Stan. L. Rev.* (1989) 51; Jack M. Beermann, "Common Law Elements of the Section 1983 Action," 72 *Chi.-Kent L. Rev.* (1997) 695; Eric H. Zagrans, "'Under Color of' What Law?: A Reconstructed Model of Section 1983 Liability," 71 *Va. L. Rev.* (1995) 499; Harry A. Blackmun, "Section 1983 and Federal Protection of Individual Rights—Will the Statute Remain Alive or Fade Away?" 60 *N.Y.U. L. Rev.* (1985) 1; and David Achtenberg, "Immunity Under 42 U.S.C. § 1983: Interpretive Approach and the Search for the Legislative Will," 86 *Nw. U. L. Rev.* (1992) 497.

On the relation between rights and remedies, see Melvyn R. Durschlag, "Federalism and Constitutional Remedies: Varying the Remedy to Save the Right," 54 *N.Y.U. L. Rev.* (1979) 723; Barry Friedman, "When Rights Encounter Reality: Enforcing Federal Remedies," 65 *S. Cal. L. Rev.* (1992) 735; John C. Jeffries, Jr., "Disaggregating Constitutional Torts," 110 *Yale L. J.* (2000) 259; John C. Jeffries, Jr., "The Right-Remedy Gap in Constitutional Law," 109 *Yale L. J.* (1999) 87; Daryl J. Levinson, "Rights Essentialism and Remedial Equilibration," 99 *Colum. L. Rev.* (1999) 857; Donald H. Zeigler, "Rights, Rights of Action, and Remedies: An Integrated Approach," 76 *Wash. L. Rev.* (2001) 67; and Harold Krent, "How to Move Beyond the Exclusionary Rule: Structuring Judicial Response to Legislative Reform Efforts," 26 *Pepp. L. Rev.* (1999) 855.

Valuable empirical studies of various aspects of constitutional remedies include Theodore Eisenberg & Stewart Schwab, "The Reality of Constitutional Tort Litigation," 72 *Corn. L. Rev.* (1987) 641; Lant B. Davis et al., "Project: Suing the Police in Federal Court," 88 *Yale L. J.* (1979) 781; Theodore Eisenberg, "Section 1983: Doctrinal Foundations and an Empirical Study," 67 *Corn. L. Rev.* (1982) 482; and Stewart Schwab & Theodore Eisenberg, "Explaining Constitutional tort Litigation: The Influence of the Attorney Fee Statutes and the Government as Defendant," 73 *Corn. L. Rev.* (1988) 719. The impact of various pieces of information on juror decision making in constitutional tort cases is examined in Jonathan D. Casper, Kennette Benedict, and Jo L. Perry, "The Tort Remedy in Search and Seizure Cases: A Case Study in Juror Decision Making, Law & Social Inquiry" (1988) 279.

Discussions of the *Bivens* doctrine include Susan Bandes, "Reinventing *Bivens*: The Self-Executing Constitution," 68 *S. Cal. L. Rev.* (1995) 289; Gene R. Nichol, "*Bivens*, *Chilicky*, and Constitutional Damages Claims," 75 *Va. L. Rev.* (1989) 1117; Note, "*Bivens* Doctrine in Flux: Statutory Preclusion of a Constitutional Cause of Action," 101 *Harv. L. Rev.* (1988) 1251; George D. Brown, "Letting Statutory Tails Wag Constitutional Dogs—Have the *Bivens* Dissenters Prevailed?" 64 *Ind. L. J.* (1989) 263; and Joan Steinman, "Backing Off Bivens and the Ramifications of This Retreat for the Vindication of First Amendment Rights," 83 *Mich. L. Rev.* (1984) 269.

HISTORY

Some of the treatments of history cited in this section are relevant to the whole of the law of constitutional remedies; others bear on specific issues but are mainly valuable for their treatment of history. Notice, too, that historical analysis has two faces. It is sometimes used as a way of defending one or another position as to what the doctrine ought to be, and on other occasions it is used as a way to undermine the notion that the answers to present-day questions can be found by looking to history. The nineteenth-century origins of constitutional remedies are examined in Ann Woolhandler, "The Common Law Origins of Constitutionally Compelled Remedies," 107 *Yale L. J.* (1997) 77. Takings of property are the focus of Robert Brauneis, "The First Constitutional Tort: The Remedial Revolution in Nineteenth-Century State Just Compensation Law," 52 *Vand. L. Rev.* (1999) 57. Various aspects of the history of federal civil rights law before *Monroe* are discussed in Eugene Gressman, "The Unhappy History of Civil Rights Legislation," 50 *Mich. L. Rev.* (1952) 1323; Louise Weinberg, "The Monroe Mystery Solved: Beyond the 'Unhappy History' Theory of Civil Rights Litigation," 1991 *BYU L. Rev.* 737; and Michael G. Collins, "'Economic Rights,' Implied Constitutional Actions, and the Scope of Section 1983," 77 *Geo. L. J.* (1989) 1493. Marshall Shapo, "Constitutional Tort: *Monroe v. Pape* and the Frontiers Beyond," 60 *Nw. U. L. Rev.*

(1965) 277, analyzes *Monroe*, its antecedents, and its immediate aftermath. The impact of the civil rights movement on the availability of federal remedies is discussed in Robert Glennon, "The Jurisdictional Legacy of the Civil Rights Movement," 61 *Tenn. L. Rev.* (1994) 869. For studies of the legislative history of § 1983, see Michael L. Wells, "The Past and the Future of Constitutional Torts," 19 *Conn. L. Rev.* (1986) 53; and David Achtenberg, "A 'Milder Measure of Villainy': The Unknown History of 42 U.S.C. § 1983 and the Meaning of 'Under Color of' Law," 1999 *Utah L. Rev.* 1. Richard Matasar, "Personal Immunities Under Section 1983: The Limits of the Court's Historical Analysis," 40 *Ark. L. Rev.* (1987) 741, is a critical look at the use of history in resolving immunity issues. Steven L. Winter, "The Meaning of 'Under Color of' Law," 91 *Mich. L. Rev.* (1992) 323, makes a historical argument for a broad reading of the phrase "under color of."

STATE ACTION

The articles cited above by Gressman, Shapo, Weinberg, Winter, and Zagrans discuss the statutory phrase "under color of." Since the "under color of" issue and the constitutional "state action" requirement generally collapse into one inquiry, the constitutional law scholarship on state action is highly relevant to § 1983 litigation. For a general introduction to the area, see Erwin Chemerinsky, *Constitutional Law: Principles and Policies* (1997) 385–414. Useful articles include Charles L. Black, Jr., "Foreword: 'State Action,' Equal Protection, and California's Proposition 14," 81 *Harv. L. Rev.* (1967) 69; William P. Marshall, "Diluting Constitutional Rights: Rethinking 'Rethinking State Action,'" 80 *Nw. U. L. Rev.* (1985) 558; Robert J. Glennon & John E. Nowak, "A Functional Analysis of the Fourteenth Amendment "State Action" Requirement," 1976 *Sup. Ct. Rev.* 221; Paul Brest, "State Action and Liberal Theory: A Casenote on *Flagg Brothers v. Brooks*," 130 *U. Pa. L. Rev.* (1982) 1296; and Henry Friendly, "The Public–Private Penumbra—Fourteen Years Later," 130 *U. Pa. L. Rev.* (1982) 1289.

SUBSTANTIVE CONSTITUTIONAL LAW AND SECTION 1983

While the main topic of this book is remedial law, one of its themes is the difficulty of separating substantive and remedial law. "Due Process and Other Constitutional Rights" and "Affirmative Constitutional Duties" discuss some of the ways in which rights and remedies are intertwined. Some of the difficulties are sorted out in Richard Fallon, "Some Confusions About Due Process, Judicial Review, and Constitutional Remedies," 93 *Colum. L. Rev.* (1993) 309; and Henry Monaghan, "State Law Wrongs, State Law Remedies, and the Fourteenth Amendment," 86 *Colum. L. Rev.* (1986) 979. The tension between *Parratt* and *Monroe* is discussed in Paul Bator, "Some Thoughts on Applied Federalism," 6 *Harv. J. L. & Pub. Policy* (1982) 51; and Leon Friedman, "*Parratt v. Taylor*: Opening and Closing the

Door on Section 1983," 9 *Hastings Con. L. Q.* (1982) 545. For discussions of the Court's efforts to reconcile federalism with Fourteenth Amendment values, see Michael L. Wells & Thomas A. Eaton, "Substantive Due Process and the Scope of Constitutional Torts," 18 *Ga. L. Rev.* (1984) 201; and Mark R. Brown, "De-Federalizing Common Law Torts: Empathy for *Parratt, Hudson*, and *Daniels*," 28 *B. C. L. Rev.* (1987) 813.

Several scholars have examined the role of state remedies in providing due process. Larry Alexander, "Constitutional Torts, the Supreme Court, and the Law of Noncontradiction: An Essay on *Zinermon v. Burch*," 87 *Nw. U. L. Rev.* (1993) 576, explores the relation between *Zinermon* and *Parratt*. Laura Oren, "Signing Into Heaven: *Zinermon v. Burch*, Federal Rights, and State Remedies Thirty Years After *Monroe v. Pape*," 40 *Emory L. J.* (1991) 1, discusses post-*Zinermon* cases in the lower courts. On the appropriate standards for distinguishing between constitutional torts and common law torts, see William Burnham, "Separating Constitutional and Common Law Torts: A Critique and a Proposed Constitutional Theory of Duty," 73 *Minn. L. Rev.* (1989) 515.

Other scholars consider the scope of constitutional protection afforded by the due process clause. A thorough analysis of *Paul* can be found in Randolph J. Haines, note, "Reputation, Stigma, and Section 1983: The Lessons of *Paul v. Davis*," 30 *Stan. L. Rev.* (1977) 191. The constitutional values at stake in *Paul* are examined in Robert C. Post, "The Social Foundations of Defamation Law: Reputation and the Constitution," 74 *Calif. L. Rev.* (1986) 691. Barbara E. Armacost, "Race and Reputation: The Real Legacy of *Paul v. Davis*," 85 *Va. L. Rev.* (1999) 569, argues that "the scholarly hand-wringing over the alleged narrowing of due process in *Paul* and the *Parratt* line of cases is misdirected." Excessive force claims are analyzed in Kathryn R. Urbonya, "Establishing a Deprivation of a Constitutional Right to Personal Security Under Section 1983: The Use of Unjustified Force by State Officials in Violation of the Fourth, Eighth, and Fourteenth Amendments," 51 *Albany L. Rev.* (1987) 171. On high-speed police chases, see Kathryn Urbonya, "The Constitutionality of High-Speed Pursuits Under the Fourth and Fourteenth Amendments," 35 St. *Louis U. L. Rev.* (1991) 205. (Note, however, that this article was written before the Supreme Court's decision in *Sacramento*) Real-world accounts of police brutality are the subject of Susan Bandes, "Tracing the Pattern of No-Pattern: Stories of Police Brutality," 2 *Loyala L. Rev.* (2001) 665. See also Susan Bandes, "Patterns of Injustice: Police Brutality in the Courts," 47 *Buff. L. Rev.* (1999) 1275.

For differing views on the role of substantive due process in constitutional tort, compare Michael L. Wells, "Constitutional Torts, Common Law Torts, and Due Process of Law," 72 *Chi.-Kent L. Rev.* (1997) 617 (arguing for constitutional protection of common law interests) with Christina Brooks Whitman, "Emphasizing the Constitutional in Constitutional Torts," 72 *Chi.-Kent L. Rev.* (1997) 661 (asserting that looking to the common law would distract attention from constitutional values).

More general discussions of "liberty" and "property" include Robert Jerome Glennon, Jr., "Constitutional Liberty and Property: Federal Common Law and § 1983," 51 *S. Cal. L. Rev.* (1978) 355; Henry Paul Monaghan, "Of 'Liberty' and 'Property,'" 62 *Corn. L. Rev.* (1977) 405; and William Van Alstyne, "The Demise of the Right–Privilege Distinction in Constitutional Law," 81 *Harv. L. Rev.* (1968) 1439.

The *DeShaney* case, analyzed in "Affirmative Constitutional Duties," gave rise to extensive commentary. A sympathetic view of *DeShaney* can be found in Barbara E. Armacost, "Affirmative Duties, Systemic Harms, and the Due Process Clause," 94 *Mich. L. Rev.* (1996) 82. Other commentators vigorously attack the decision, for example, Steven J. Heyman, "The First Duty of Government: Protection, Liberty and the Fourteenth Amendment," 41 *Duke L. J.* (1991) 507; Jack M. Beermann, "Administrative Failure and Local Democracy: The Politics of *DeShaney*," 1990 *Duke L. J.* (1990) 1078; Karen M. Blum, "*Monell*, *DeShaney*, and *Zinermon*: Official Policy, Affirmative Duty, Established State Procedure and Local Government Liability Under Section 1983," *Creighton L. Rev.* (1990) 1; and Laura Oren, "The State's Failure to Protect Children and Substantive Due Process: *DeShaney* in Context," 68 *N.C. L. Rev.* (1990) 659. Some of the commentary explores the scope of government affirmative duties and liability for state-created danger after *DeShaney*, for example, Julie Shapiro, "Snake Pits and Unseen Actors: Constitutional Liability for Indirect Harm," 62 *U. Cinn. L. Rev.* (1994) 883; Thomas A. Eaton & Michael L. Wells, "Government Inaction as a Constitutional Tort: *DeShaney* and Its Aftermath," 66 *Wash. L. Rev.* (1991) 107; Sheldon H. Nahmod, "State Constitutional Torts: *DeShaney*, Reverse-Federalisms and Community," 26 *Rutgers L. J.* (1995) 949. Advocates of broader liability look for ways to avoid the barriers set up by *DeShaney*. For an argument that *DeShaney* obstacles can sometimes be avoided by framing the case as one of supervisory liability, see Laura Oren, "Section 1983 and Sex Abuse in Schools: Making a Federal Case out of It," 72 *Chi.-Kent L. Rev.* (1997) 747. Some think that the *DeShaney* issue ought to be analyzed as a Thirteenth Amendment problem. See Akhil Amar and Daniel Widawsky, "Child Abuse as Slavery: A Thirteenth Amendment Response to *DeShaney*," 105 *Harv. L. Rev.* (1992) 1359. Michael L. Wells & Thomas A. Eaton, "Affirmative Duty and Constitutional Tort," 16 *U. Mich. J. L. Reform* (1982) 1, is a pre-*DeShaney* article, mainly of use as historical background.

First Amendment "retaliation" issues, which come up frequently in constitutional tort suits, are examined in Michael L. Wells, "Section 1983, the First Amendment, and Public Employee Speech: Shaping the Right to Fit the Remedy (and Vice Versa)," 35 *Ga. L. Rev.* (2001) 939; Cynthia L. Estlund, "Speech on Matters of Public Concern: The Perils of an Emerging First Amendment Category," 59 *Geo. Wash. L. Rev.* (1990) 1; Toni M. Massaro, "Significant Silences: Freedom of Speech in the Public Sector Workplace," 61 *S.Cal. L. Rev.* (1987) 1; and Lawrence Rosenthal, "Permissible Content Discrimination Under the First Amendment: The Strange Case of the Public Employee," 25 *Hastings Const. L. Q.* (1998) 529.

GOVERNMENTAL LIABILITY

The literature on the Eleventh Amendment is vast and growing. This bibliography makes no attempt to be comprehensive. Clyde E. Jacobs, *The Eleventh Amendment and Sovereign Immunity* (1972), is a history of sovereign immunity written before the Supreme Court's modern line of cases on the power of Congress to abrogate the immunity. Other historical treatments (most of which use history as a ground for criticizing the current Court's doctrine) include John Orth, "The Interpretation of the Eleventh Amendment, 1798–1908: A Case Study of Judicial Power," 1983 *U. Ill. L. Rev.* 423; John Orth, "The Truth About Justice Iredell's Dissent in *Chisholm v. Georgia*," 73 *N. C. L. Rev.* (1994) 255; William A. Fletcher, "A Historical Interpretation of the 11th Amendment: A Narrow Construction of an Affirmative Grant of Jurisdiction Rather Than a Prohibition Against Jurisdiction," 35 *Stan. L. Rev.* (1983) 1033; and Akhil Amar, "Of Sovereignty and Federalism," 96 *Yale L. J.* (1987) 1425. Defenders of broad immunity include William Marshall, "The Diversity Theory of the Eleventh Amendment: A Critical Evaluation," 102 *Harv. L. Rev.* (1989) 1372; and Calvin Massey, "State Sovereignty and the Tenth and Eleventh Amendments," 56 *U. Chi. L. Rev.* (1989) 61.

For early arguments that Congress may abrogate immunity in situations in which courts may not, see John Nowak, "The Scope of Congressional Power to Create Causes of Action Against State Governments and the History of the 11th and 14th Amendments," 75 *Colum. L. Rev.* (1975) 1413; and Laurence Tribe, "Intergovernmental Immunities in Litigation, Taxation, and Regulation: Separation of Powers Issues in Controversies About Federalism," 89 *Harv. L. Rev.* (1976) 682). The Supreme Court's rejection of broad congressional power is the subject of Daniel Meltzer, "The Seminole Decision and State Sovereign Immunity," 1996 *Sup. Ct. Rev.* 1. The Court's later cases limiting Congress' "section 5" power are discussed in the symposium, "Shifting the Balance of Power? The Supreme Court, Federalism, and State Sovereign Immunity," 53 *Stan. L. Rev.* (2001) 1115–1391, with contributions from Meltzer, Seth Waxman, Evan Caminker, Roderick Hills, Vicki Jackson, and Pamela Karlan. The *Alden* case, which limited congressional abrogation in state court, is the topic of "Symposium: Federalism After *Alden*," 31 *Rutgers L. Rev.* (2000) 631–831, with contributions from Ann Althouse, Vicki Jackson, Michael Dorf, David Shapiro, Earl Maltz, Michael L. Wells, William Marshall, and Robert Nagel.

Discussions of the scope of the states' obligation to provide constitutional remedies in their own courts include Carlos Manuel Vasquez, "What Is Eleventh Amendment Immunity?" 106 *Yale L. J.* (1997) 1683; Henry Monaghan, "The Sovereign Immunity 'Exception,'" 110 *Harv. L. Rev.* (1995) 102; Michael Wells, "Suing States for Money: Constitutional Remedies After *Alden* and *Florida Prepaid*," 31 *Rutgers L. J.* (2000) 771. State remedies for unconstitutional taxation are examined and found wanting in John Coverdale, "Remedies for Unconstitutional State Taxes," 32 *Conn. L. Rev.* (1999) 73.

John C. Jeffries, Jr., "In Praise of the Eleventh Amendment and Section 1983," 84 *Va. L. Rev.* (1998) 47, "analyze[s] the Eleventh Amendment and Section 1983 as an integrated package of liability rules" in an effort to show that "[t]he real role of the Eleventh Amendment is not to bar redress for constitutional violations by states but to force plaintiffs to resort to Section 1983."

Arguments for broader municipal liability under the doctrine spawned by *Monell* include Larry Kramer and Alan O. Sykes, "Municipal Liability Under § 1983: A Legal and Economic Analysis," 1987 *Sup. Ct. Rev.* 249; Brian J. Serr, "Turning Section 1983's Protection of Civil Rights Into an Attractive Nuisance: Extra-Textual Barriers to Municipal Liability Under *Monell*," 35 *Ga. L. Rev.* (2001) 881; Peter H. Schuck, "Municipal Liability Under Ssection 1983: Some Lessons from Tort Law and Organization Theory," 77 *Geo. L. J.* (1989) 1753; Christina Whitman, "Government Responsibility for Constitutional Torts," 85 *Mich. L. Rev.* (1986) 225; Mark R. Brown, "The Demise of Constitutional Prospectivity: New Life for *Owen*?" 79 *Iowa L. Rev.* (1994) 625; Harold S. Lewis, Jr., and Theodore Y. Blumoff, "Reshaping Section 1983's Asymmetry," 140 *U. Pa. L. Rev.* (1992) 755; Susanah M. Mead, "42 U.S.C. § 1983 Municipal Liability: The *Monell* Sketch Becomes a Distorted Picture," 65 *N. C. L. Rev.* (1987) 517; and Laura Oren, "Immunity and Accountability in Civil Rights Litigation: Who Should Pay?" 50 *U. Pitt. L. Rev.* (1989) 935. For an argument that fault ought to be required for liability, see John C. Jeffries, Jr., "Compensation for Constitutional Torts: Reflections on the Significance of Fault," 88 *Mich. L. Rev.* (1989) 82.

The practical question of what is and what is not "official policy" is addressed in a number of articles. See, for example, Mark R. Brown, "Accountability in Government and Section 1983," 25 *U. Mich. J. L. Ref.* (1991) 53; Steven Stein Cushman, "Municipal Liability Under Section 1983: Toward a New Definition of Municipal Policymaker," 34 *B.C. L. Rev.* (1993) 693; Michael J. Gerhardt, *The* Monell *Legacy: Balancing Federalism Concerns and Municipal Accountability Under § 1983* (1993). For discussion of supervisory liability, see Kit Kinports, "The Buck Does Not Stop Here: Supervisory Liability in Section 1983 Cases," 1997 *U. Ill. L. Rev.* 147.

CAUSATION

The *Mt. Healthy* case is discussed from a variety of perspectives in "The Burgeoning *Mt. Healthy* Mixed-Motive Defense to Civil Rights and Employment Discrimination Claims," 51 *Mercer L. Rev.* (2000) 583–760, with contributions from Michael L. Wells, Sheldon H. Nahmod, Christina B. Whitman, Joseph Z. Fleming, Robert Belton, Thomas Barnard, and George Crisci, Michael Zimmer, Lane Dennard, and Kendall Kelly, and Richard Weller. Barbara Kritchevsky, "'Or Causes to be Subjected': The Role of Causation in Section 1983 Municipal Liability Analysis," 35 *U.C.L A. L. Rev.* (1988) 1187 examines the causation issues that arise in suits against governments. A still useful, if somewhat dated, contribution is Thomas A. Eaton, "Causation in Constitutional Torts," 67 *Iowa L. Rev.* (1982) 443.

THE IMMUNITY DOCTRINES

Though we have separated immunity into two sections for clarity of exposition, most academic authors treat both absolute and qualified immunity in the same work. In general their project is either to defend the distinction the Court makes between the two, to attack it, or to urge that the whole doctrine be reformed in the direction of less immunity. The "overdeterrence" argument in favor of official immunity is made most comprehensively in Peter Schuck, Suing Government supra (also arguing in favor of broad governmental liability.) Ronald Cass, "Damage Suits Against Public Officers," 129 *U. Pa. L. Rev.* (1981) 1110 analyzes other types of arguments for immunity, which put more weight on differences in incentives faced by officers performing different functions. Barbara Armacost, "Qualified Immunity: Ignorance Excused," 51 *Vand. L. Rev.* (1998) 583, suggests that, besides the "instrumental" justification, immunity can be defended as a matter of fairness. David Achtenberg, "Immunity Under § 1983: Interpretive Approach and the Search for the Legislative Will," 86 *Nw. U. L. Rev.* (1992) 497 argues that the legislative purpose would be served by weaker immunity, while Richard Matasar, "Personal Immunities Under Section 1983: The Limits of the Court's Historical Analysis," 40 *Ark. L. Rev.* (1987) 741 calls for less emphasis on history, but agrees with Achtenberg that immunity should be a weaker defense. For broad attacks on the Court's doctrine, see, for example, Sheldon H. Nahmod, "The Restructuring of Narrative and Empathy in Section 1983 Cases," 72 *Chi.-Kent L. Rev.* (1997) 819; and David Rudovsky, "The Qualified Immunity Doctrine in the Supreme Court: Judicial Activism and the Restriction of Constitutional Rights," 138 *U. Pa. L. Rev.* (1989) 23. Alan K. Chen, "The Ultimate Standard: Qualified Immunity in the Age of Constitutional Balancing Tests," 81 *Iowa L. Rev.* (1995) 261 argues that immunity law should be formulated as rules rather than as standards. Interlocutory appeals are discussed in Kathryn R. Urbonya, "Interlocutory Appeals from Orders Denying Qualified Immunity: Determining the Proper Scope of Appellate Jurisdiction," 55 *Wash. & Lee L. Rev.* (1998) 3. A defense of the Court's approach, on the ground that it facilitates the evolution of constitutional law, is John C. Jeffries, Jr., "The Right-Remedy Gap in Constitutional Law," 109 *Yale L. J.* (1999) 87.

For more citations to the literature on immunity, see the excellent bibliography in Jeffries et al., *Civil Rights Actions* 113–15.

REMEDIES

As the leading case on damages, *Carey* is examined in Note, "Damage Awards for Constitutional Torts: A Reconsideration of Carey v. Piphus," 93 *Harv. L. Rev.*

(1980) 966. Jean Love, "Damages: A Remedy for the Violation of Constitutional Rights," 67 *Cal. L. Rev.* (1979) 1242. The same author returned to the topic some years later, arguing in favor of presumed damages. [See Jean Love, "Presumed General Compensatory Damages in Constitutional Tort Litigation: A Corrective Justice Perspective," 49 *Wash. & Lee L. Rev.* (1992) 67.] John C. Jeffries, Jr., "Damages for Constitutional Violations: The Relation of Risk to Injury in Constitutional Torts," 75 *Va. L. Rev.* (1989) 1461 argues that damages ought to be presumptively limited to harms that are reasonably foreseeable consequences of the constitutional wrong. Sheldon H. Nahmod, "Constitutional Damages and Corrective Justice: A Different View," 76 *Va. L. Rev.* (1990) 997, takes issue with Jeffries. Jon Newman, "Suing the Lawbreakers: Proposals to Strengthen the Section 1983 Damage Remedy for Law Enforcers' Misconduct," 87 *Yale L. J.* (1978) 447, argues, among other things, for liquidated damages as a way to cope with the difficulty of proving substantial monetary damages in constitutional tort cases. The special problems that arise in wrongful death cases are discussed in Steven Steinglass, "Wrongful Death Actions and Section 1983," 60 *Indiana L. J.* (1985) 559. Dorsey Ellis, "Fairness and Efficiency in the Law of Punitive Damages," 56 *S. Cal. L. Rev.* (1982) 1, is a fine analysis of the issues raised by punitive damages in general tort law. For a treatment of punitive damages in constitutional torts, see Michael L. Wells, "Punitive Damages for Constitutional Torts," 56 *La. L. Rev.* (1996) 841.

Injunctive (forward-looking) remedies have also received careful attention from scholars. The classic article on public law litigation is Abram Chayes, "The Role of the Judge in Public Law Litigation," 89 *Harv. L. Rev.* (1976) 1281. The argument for giving primacy to injunctive relief is made in Owen Fiss, *The Civil Rights Injunction* (1978). See also Owen Fiss and Doug Rendleman, *Injunctions* (2nd ed. 1984); and Owen Fiss, "The Supreme Court, 1978 Term—Foreword: The Forms of Justice," 93 *Harv. L. Rev.* (1979) 1. A good casebook on remedies in general and injunctive relief in particular is Douglas Laycock, *Modern American Remedies* (2nd ed. 1994). Christina Whitman, "Constitutional Torts," 79 *Mich. L. Rev.* (1981) 5, argues for the superiority of injunctions over damages in certain contexts. The case for broad use of injunctions to deter constitutional violations is made in Daniel J. Meltzer, "Deterring Constitutional Violations by Law Enforcement Officials: Plaintiffs and Defendants as Private Attorneys General," 88 *Colum. L. Rev.* (1988) 247. See also Myriam E. Gilles, "Reinventing Structural Reform Litigation: Deputizing Private Citizens in the Enforcement of Civil Rights," 100 *Colum. L. Rev.* (2000) 1384. Obstacles to injunctive relief based on standing and ripeness are discussed in Richard Fallon, "Of Justiciability, Remedies, and Public Law Litigation: Notes on the Jurisprudence of *Lyons*," 59 *N.Y.U. L. Rev.* (1984) 1. School desegregation is the focus of Paul Gewirtz, "Remedies and Resistance," 92 *Yale L. J.* (1983) 585, and J. Harvie Wilkinson III, *From* Brown *to* Bakke—*The Supreme Court and School Integration: 1954–78* (1979). For discussions of the implementation of judicial decrees in institutional reform litigation, see Larry W. Yackle,

Reform and Regret: The Story of Federal Judicial Involvement in the Alabama Prison System (1989); note, "The *Wyatt* Case: Implementation of a Judicial Decree Ordering Institutional Change," 84 *Yale L. J.* (1975) 1338; Robbins and Buser, "Punitive Conditions of Prison Confinement: An Analysis of *Pugh v. Locke* and Federal Court Supervision of State Penal Administration Under the Eighth Amendment," 29 *Stan. L. Rev.* (1977) 892; Note, "Implementation Problems in Institutional Reform Litigation," 91 *Harv. L. Rev.* (1977) 428. Skepticism about the role of courts in institutional reform litigation is expressed in Paul Mishkin, "Federal Courts as State Reformers," 35 *Wash. & Lee L. Rev.* (1978) 949, and in Robert Nagel, "Separation of Powers and the Scope of Federal Equitable Remedies," 30 *Stan. L. Rev.* (1978) 661. For a more sympathetic appraisal, see Malcolm M. Feeley and& Edward L. Rubin, *Judicial Policy Making and the Modern State: How the Courts Reformed America's Prisons* (1998).

ATTORNEY'S FEES

Fee shifting is not unique to constitutional litigation, and much of the literature on fee shifting in general is relevant to issues that arise in this context. The place to start any serious research on this topic is the symposium on "Attorney Fee Shifting" in 47 *Law and Contemporary Problems* (Winter 1984) 1–354, with contributions from Murray Schwartz, John Leubsdorf, Werner Pfennigstorf, Herbert Kritzer, Tom Rowe, Ronald Braeutingam, Bruce Owen and John Panzar, Frances Zemans, Bruce Fein, Robert Percival & Geoffrey Miller, Marshall Breger, A.F. Conard, and Charles Wolfram. There is also a bibliography compiled by Kathryn Christie.

The rationales for fee shifting are analyzed by Thomas Rowe in "The Legal Theory of Attorney Fee Shifting: A Critical Overview," 1982 *Duke L. J.* 651. Jeffrey Brand, "The Second Front in the Fight for Civil Rights: the Supreme Court, Congress, and Statutory Fees," 69 *Tex. L. Rev.* (1990) 291, argues that the Supreme Court has thwarted the remedial purposes of the Civil Rights Attorney Fees statute. Herbert M. Kritzer, "The Wages of Risk: The Returns of Contingency Fee Legal Practice," 47 *DePaul L. Rev.* (1998) 267 compares contingency fees to hourly rates. Peter H. Huang, "A New Options Theory for Risk Multipliers of Attorney's Fees in Federal Civil Rights Litigation," 73 *N.Y.U. L. Rev.* (1998) 1943, is an economic analysis of multipliers. *Marek* is analyzed in Roy D. Simon, Jr., "The New Meaning of Rule 68: *Marek v. Chesny* and Beyond." 4 *N.Y U. Rev. of Law & Social Change* (1986) 475. The decision is criticized in Laura Macklin, "Promoting Settlement, Foregoing the Facts," 14 *N.Y U. Rev. of Law & Social Change*, (1986) 575. Charles Silver, "Unloading the Lodestar: Toward a New Fee Award Procedure," 70 *Tex. L. Rev.* (1992) 865, argues against the lodestar approach. The catalyst theory is discussed in note, "The Catalyst Theory of Civil Rights Fee Shifting After *Farrar v. Hobby*," 80 *Va. L. Rev.* (1984) 1429.

For an assessment of the real-world impact of some of the Supreme Court's decisions restricting awards, including *Marek*, *Dague*, and *Evans, see* Julie Davies, "Federal Civil Rights Practice in the 1990's: The Dichotomy Between Reality and Theory," 48 *Hastings L. J.* (1997) 197. Emily Calhoun, "Attorney–Client Conflicts of Interest and the Concept of Non-Negotiable Fee Awards Under 42 U.S.C. § 1988," 55 *U. Colo. L. Rev.* (1984) 341, discusses ethical problems that may arise in settlement negotiations. Charles Wolfram, "The Second Set of Players: Lawyers, Fee Shifting, and the Limits of Professional Discipline," 47 *Law & Contemp. Prob.* (1984) 2393, would ban settlement terms that require waiver of fees. Support for fee waiver agreements may be found in comment, "*Evans v. Jeff D.* and the Proper Scope of State Ethics Decisions," 73 *Va. L. Rev.* (1987) 783.

Stewart Schwab and Theodore Eisenberg, "Explaining Constitutional Tort Litigation: The Influence of the Attorney Fees Statutes and the Government as Defendant," 73 Corn. L. Rev. (1988) 719, is a useful empirical study. For a study that focuses on one U.S. Circuit, see George Cochran, "Section 1988 Attorney Fee Awards in the Fifth Circuit," 15 *Tex. Tech. L. Rev.* (1984) 1.

FEDERALISM

The classic article on the disparity between federal and state courts is Burt Neuborne, "The Myth of Parity," 90 *Harv. L. Rev.* (1977) 1105. See also Erwin Chemerinsky, "Parity Reconsidered: Defining a Role for the Federal Judiciary," 36 *U.C.L.A. L. Rev.* (1988) 233; "Solimine & Walker, Constitutional Litigation in Federal and State Courts: An Empirical Analysis of Judicial Parity," 10 *Hastings Const. L. Q.* (1983) 213; Thomas B. Marvell, "The Rationales for Federal Question Jurisdiction: An Empirical Examination of Student Rights Litigation," 1984 *Wis. L. Rev.* 1315; Orley Ashenfelter et al., "Politics and the Judiciary: The Influence of Judicial Background on Case Outcomes," 24 *J. Leg. Stud.* (1995) 257; Michael L. Wells, "Is Disparity a Problem?" 22 *Ga. L. Rev.* (1988) 283; symposium: "Federalism and Parity," 71 *B. U. L. Rev.* (1991) 593–664, with contributions from Erwin Chemerinsky, Michael L. Wells, Akhil Amar, and Susan Herman. State court § 1983 suits are the topic of Steven Steinglass, *Section 1983 Litigation in State Courts* (1989) and Susan Herman, "Beyond Parity: Section 1983 and the State Courts," 54 *Brooklyn L. Rev.* (1989) 1057. Helen Hershkoff, "State Courts and the 'Passive Virtues': Rethinking the Judicial Function," 114 *Harv. L. Rev.* (2001) 1833, argues that state courts are subject to fewer "justiciability"-based restrictions on their powers than are the federal courts.

For discussion of the role of state law in § 1983 litigation, see Seth Kreimer, "The Source of Law in Civil Rights Actions: Some Old Light on § 1988," 133 *U. Pa. L. Rev.* (1985) 601, and Theodore Eisenberg, "State Law in Federal Civil Rights Cases: The Proper Scope of § 1988," 128 *U. Pa. L. Rev.* (1980) 499. Time limits on bringing suit are examined in Julie Davies, "In Search of the 'Paradigmatic

Wrong?': Selecting a Limitations Period for Section 119183," 36 *Kan. L. Rev.* (1987) 133; and John Pagan, "Virginia's Statute of Limitations for Section 1983 Claims After *Wilson v. Garcia*," 19 *U. Rich. L. Rev.* (1985) 257.

Release-dismissal agreements are discussed in Seth Kreimer, "Releases, Redress, and Police Misconduct: Reflections on Agreements to Waive Civil Rights Actions in Exchange for Dismissal of Criminal Charges," 136 *U. Pa. L. Rev.* (1988) 851, and in Michael Solimine, "Enforcement and Interpretation of Settlements of Federal Civil Rights Actions," 19 *Rutgers L. J.* (1988) 295. Treatments of issue and claim preclusion include Stephen Burbank, "Interjurisdictional Preclusion: A General Approach," 71 *Corn. L. Rev.* (1986) 733, and in Robert H. Smith, "Full Faith and Credit and § 1983: A Reappraisal," 63 *N.C. L. Rev.* (1984) 59. *Heck* is criticized in Jack M. Beermann, "Common Law Elements of the Section 1983 Cause of Action," 72 *Chi.-Kent L. Rev.* (1997) 695. A good introduction to the abstention doctrines may be found in Erwin Chemerinsky, *Federal Jurisdiction* (3d ed. 1999). See also Paul Bator, "The State Courts and Federal Constitutional Litigation," 22 *Wm. & Mary L. Rev.* (1981) 605; Owen Fiss, "*Dombrowski*," 86 *Yale L. J.* (1977) 1103; Barry Friedman, "A Revisionist Theory of Abstention," 88 *Mich. L. Rev.* (1989) 530; and Martha Field, "Abstention in Constitutional Cases: The Scope of the Pullman Abstention Doctrine," 122 *U. Pa. L. Rev.* (1974) 1071.

Table of Cases

Adickes v. S.H. Kress, 398 U.S. 144 (1970)
Albright v. Oliver, 510 U.S. 266 (1994)
Alden v. Maine, 527 U.S. 706 (1999)
Alyeska Pipeline Service Co. v. Wilderness Society, 421 U.S. (1975)
Allen v. McCurry, 449 U.S. 90 (1980)
Allen v. Wright, 468 U.S. 737 (1984)
American Manufacturers Mutual Insurance Co. v. Sullivan, 526 U.S. 40 (1999)
Anderson v. Creighton, 483 U.S. 635 (1987)
Antoine v. Byers & Anderson, Inc., 508 U.S. 429 (1993)
Archie v. Lanier, 95 F. 3d 438 (6th Cir. 1996)
Arnold v. Duchesne County, 26 F. 3d 982 (10th Cir. 1994)
Atascadero State Hospital v. Scanlon, 473 U.S. 234 (1985)
Baker v. McCollan, 443 U.S. 137 (1979)
Barney v. City of New York, 193 U.S. 430 (1904)
Barron v. Mayor and City Council of Baltimore, 32 U.S. (7 Pet.) 243 (1833)
Bates v. State Bar of Arizona, 433 U.S. 350 (1977)
Behrens v. Pelletier, 516 U.S. 299 (1996)
Bivens v. Six Unknown Named Federal Narcotics Agents, 403 U.S. 388 (1971)
Black v. Indiana Area School District, 985 F. 2d 707 (3d Cir. 1993)
Blum v. Stenson, 465 U.S. 886 (1984)
Blum v. Yaretsky, 457 U.S. 991 (1982)
BMW v. Gore, 517 U.S. 559 (1996)
Board of County Commissioners v. Umbehr, 518 U.S. 68 (1996)
Board of Education v. Dowell, 498 U.S. 237 (1991)
Board of Regents v. Roth, 400 U.S. 433 (1972)
Board of Regents v. Roth, 408 U.S. 564 (1972)
Board of Regents v. Tomanio, 446 U.S. 478 (1980)
Board of the County Commissioners of Bryan County v. Brown, 520 U.S. 397 (1997)
Board of Trustees of University of Alabama v. Garrett, 531 U.S. 356 (2001)

Boddie v. Connecticut, 401 U.S. 371 (1971)
Bogan v. Scott-Harris, 523 U.S. 44 (1998)
Bolling v. Sharpe, 347 U.S. 497 (1954)
Bowers v. DeVito, 686 F. 2d 616 (7th Cir. 1982)
Bradley v. Fisher, 80 U.S. 335 (1871)
Branti v. Finkel, 445 U.S. 507 (1980)
Brentwood Academy v. Tennessee Secondary School Athletic Association, 531 U.S. 288 (2001)
Briscoe v. LaHue, 460 U.S. 325 (1983)
Brown v. Board of Education, 349 U.S. 294 (1954)
Bryan County v. Brown, 520 U.S. 397 (1997)
Buckhannon Board and Care Home, Inc. v. West Virginia Department of Human Resources, 532 U.S. 598 (2001)
Buckley v. Fitzsimmons, 509 U.S. 259 (1993)
Burford v. Sun Oil Co., 319 U.S. 315 (1943)
Burlington v. Dague, 505 U.S. 557 (1992)
Burns v. Reed, 500 U.S. 478 (1991)
Burton v. Wilmington Parking Authority, 365 U.S. 715 (1961)
Bush v. Lucas, 462 U.S. 367 (1983)
Butz v. Economou, 438 U.S. 478 (1978)
Caine v. Hardy, 943 F. 2d 1406 (5th Cir. 1991)
California v. Grace Brethren Church, 457 U.S. 393 (1982)
Camp v. Brennan, 219 F. 3d 279 (2000)
Canton v. Harris, 489 U.S. 378 (1989)
Carey v. Piphus, 435 U.S. 247 (1978)
Carlson v. Green, 446 U.S. 14 (1980)
Carpenter v. Shaw, 280 U.S. 363 (1930)
Carroll v. President of Princess Anne, 393 U.S. 175 (1968)
Cassady v. Tackett, 938 F. 2d 693 (6th Cir. 1991)
Chappell v. Wallace, 462 U.S. 296 (1983)
Chisholm v. Georgia, 2 U.S. (2Dall.) 419 (1793)
City of Boerne v. Flores, 521 U.S. 507 (1997)
City of Canton v. Harris, 489 U.S. 378 (1989)
Cleavinger v. Saxner, 474 U.S. 193 (1985)
Cleburne v. Cleburne Living Center, 473 U.S. 42 (1985)
Clinton v. Jones, 20 U.S. 681 (1997)
Cohen v. Beneficial Industrial Loan Corp., 337 U.S. 541 (1949)
Collins v. City of Harker Heights, 503 U.S. 115 (1992)
Connick v. Myers, 461 U.S. 138 (1983)
Corfield v. Coryell, 6 F. Cas. 546 (C.C.E.D. Pa. 1823)
Craig v. Boren, 429 U.S. 190 (1976)
Crawford-El v. Britton, 523 U.S. 574 (1998)
Cushing v. City of Chicago, 3 F. 3d 115 (7th Cir. 1993)
Daniels v. Williams, 474 U.S. 327 (1986)
Davidson v. Cannon, 474 U.S. 344 (1986)
Davis v. Monroe County Board of Education, 526 U.S. 629 (1999)

Davis v. Passman, 442 U.S. 228 (1979)
Deakins v. Monaghan, 484 U.S. 193 (1988)
DeFunis v. Odegaard, 416 U.S. 312 (1974)
Delaware State College v. Ricks, 449 U.S. 250 (1980)
Delcambre v. Delcambre, 635 F. 2d 407 (5th Cir. 1981)
Dennis v. Higgins, 498 U.S. 439 (1991)
Dennis v. Sparks, 449 U.S. 24 (1980)
DeShaney v. Winnebago County Dept. of Social Services, 489 U.S. 189 (1989)
Douglas v. City of Jeannette, 319 U.S. 157 (1943)
Duncan v. Nelson, 466 F. 2d 939 (7th Cir. 1972)
Dwares v. City of New York, 985 F. 2d 94 (2d Cir. 1993)
Easter House v. Felder, 910 F. 2d 1387 (7th Cir. 1990)
Edelman v. Jordan 415 U.S. 651 (1974)
Elder v. Holloway, 510 U.S. 510 (1994)
Employment Division v. Smith, 494 U.S. 872 (1990)
England v. Louisiana State Board of Medical Examiners, 375 U.S. 411 (1964)
Erie Railroad Co. v. Tompkins, 304 U.S. 64 (1938)
Estelle v. Gamble, 429 U.S. 97 (1976)
Evans v. Jeff D., 475 U.S. 717 (1986)
Ex Parte New York, 256 U.S. 490 (1921)
Ex Parte Young 209 U.S. 123 (1908)
Fair Assessment in Real Estate Association, Inc. v. McNary, 457 U.S. 393 (1981)
Farmer v. Brennan, 511 U.S. 825 (1994)
Farrar v. Hobby, 506 U.S. 103 (1992)
FDIC v. Meyer, 510 U.S. 471 (1994)
Felder v. Casey, 487 U.S. 131 (1988)
First Evangelical Lutheran Church of Glendale v. County of Los Angeles, 482 U.S. 300 (1987)
Fitzpatrick v. Bitzer, 427 U.S. 445 (1976)
Flagg Bros., Inc. v. Brooks, 436 U.S. 149 (1978)
Flast v. Cohen, 392 U.S. 83 (1968)
Florida Prepaid Post-Secondary Education Bd. v. College Savings Bank, 527 U.S. 627 (1999)
Forrester v. White, 484 U.S. 219 (1988)
Frothingham v. Mellon, 262 U.S. 447 (1923)
Garza v. Omaha, 814 F. 2d 553 (8th Cir. 1987)
Gebser v. Lago Vista Independent School District, 524 U.S. 274 (1998)
General Oil Company v. Crain 209 U.S. 211 (1908)
Gibson v. City of Chicago, 910 F. 2d 1510 (7th Cir. 1990)
Globe Newspaper Co. v. Superior Court, 457 U.S. 596 (1982)
Goldberg v. Kelly, 397 U.S. 254 (1970)
Goss v. Lopez, 419 U.S. 565 (1975)
Governor of Georgia v. Madrazo, 26 U.S. (1 Pet.) 110 (1828)
Graham v. Connor, 490 U.S. 386 (1989)
Great Lakes Dredge & Dock Co. v. Huffman, 319 U.S. 293 (1943)
Hale v. Arizona, 993 F. 2d 1387 (9th Cir. 1993)

Hampton v. Hanrahan, 600 F. 2d 600 (7th Cir. 1979)
Hans v. Louisiana, 134 U.S. 1 (1890)
Haring v. Prosise, 462 U.S. 306 (1983)
Harlow v. Fitzgerald, 457 U.S. 800 (1982)
Harris v. McRae, 448 U.S. 297 (1980)
Hasenfus v. LaJeunesse, 175 F. 3d 68 (1st Cir. 1999)
Heck v. Humphrey, 512 U.S. 477 (1994)
Helling v. McKinney, 509 U.S. 25 (1993)
Hensley v. Eckerhart, 461 U.S. 424 (1983)
Hewitt v. Helms, 482 U.S. 755 (1987)
Hicks v. Miranda, 422 U.S. 332 (1975)
Home Telephone and Telegraph Co. v. City of Los Angeles, 227 U.S. 278 (1913)
Hope v. Peltzer. U.S. Lexis 4884 (2002)
Houston v. Hill, 482 U.S. 451 (1987)
Howlett v. Rose, 496 U.S. 356 (1990)
Hudson v. McMillian, 503 U.S. 1 (1992)
Hunter v. Bryant, 502 U.S. 224 (1991)
Hutto v. Finney, 437 U.S. 678 (1978)
Idaho v. Coeur d'Alene Tribe of Idaho, 521 U.S. 261 (1997)
Imbler v. Pachtman, 424 U.S. 409 (1976)
Ingraham v. Wright, 430 U.S. 651 (1977)
Jackson v. Metropolitan Edison Co., 419 U.S. 345 (1974)
Jett v. Dallas Independent School District, 491 U.S. 701 (1989)
Johnson v. Fankell, 520 U.S. 911 (1997)
Johnson v. Jones, 515 U.S. 304 (1995)
Juidice v. Vail, 430 U.S. 327 (1977)
Kalina v. Fletcher, 522 U.S. 118 (1997)
Kansas v. Colorado, 206 U.S. 46 (1907)
Kimel v. Florida Board of Regents, 528 U.S. 62 (2000)
Kolender v. Lawson, 461 U.S. 352 (1983)
Lake Country Estates, Inc. v. Tahoe Regional Planning Agency, 440 U.S. 391 (1979)
LaMarca v. Turner, 995 F. 2d 1526 (11th Cir. 1993)
Lassiter v. Alabama A & M University, 28 F. 3d 1146 (11th Cir. 1994)
Lincoln County v. Luning, 133 U.S. 529 (1890)
Lindsey v. Normet, 405 U.S. 56 (1972)
Lockerty v. Phillips, 319 U.S. 182 (1943)
Los Angeles v. Heller, 475 U.S. 796 (1986)
Los Angeles v. Lyons, 461 U.S. 95 (1983)
Lugar v. Edmondson Oil Co., 457 U.S. 922 (1982)
Malley v. Briggs, 475 U.S. 335 (1986)
Marbury v. Madison, 5 U.S. (1 Cranch) 137 (1803)
Marek v. Chesny, 473 U.S. 1 (1985)
Martinez v. California, 444 U.S. 277 (1980)
Matthews v. Eldridge, 424 U.S. 319 (1976)
McMillian v. Monroe County, 520 U.S. 781 (1997)
Memphis Independent School District v. Stachura, 477 U.S. 299 (1986)

Mershon v. Beasley, 994 F. 2d 449 (8th Cir. 1993)
Metzger v. Osbeck, 841 F. 2d 518 (3d Cir. 1988)
Middlesex County Ethics Commission v. Garden State Bar Association, 457 U.S. 423 (1982)
Migra v. Warren City School District City Board of Education, 465 U.S. 75 (1984)
Miller v. Kennebec County, 219 F. 3d 8 (1st Cir. 2000)
Milliken v. Bradley, 433 U.S. 267 (1977) (Milliken II)
Milliken v. Bradley, 4118 U.S. 717 (1974) (Milliken I)
Mireles v. Waco, 502 U.S. 9 (1991)
Missouri v. Jenkins, 515 U.S. 70 (1995)
Mitchell v. Forsyth, 472 U.S. 511 (1985)
Monaco v. Mississippi, 292 U.S. 313 (1934)
Monell v. Department of Social Services, 436 U.S. 658 (1978)
Monroe v. Pape, 365 U.S. 167, (1961)
Moore v. Sims, 442 U.S. 415 (1979)
Moose Lodge No. 107 v. Irvis, 407 U.S. 163 (1972)
Mount Healthy City School District v. Doyle, 429 U.S. 274 (1976)
Mt. Healthy City School District Board of Education v. Doyle 429 U.S. 274 (1976)
Murdock v. Memphis, 87 U.S. (20 Wall.) 590 (1875)
National Collegiate Athletic Association v. Tarkanian, 488 U.S. 179 (1988)
National Private Truck Council, Inc. v. Oklahoma Tax Commission, 515 U.S. 582 (1995)
Nevada v. Hall, 440 U.S. 410 (1979)
New Hampshire v. Louisiana, 108 U.S. 76 (1883)
New York Times v. Sullivan, 376 U.S. 254 (1964)
New York v. Ferber, 458 U.S. 747 (1982)
Newport v. Fact Concerts, Inc., 453 U.S. 247 (1981)
Newton v. Rumery, 480 U.S. 386 (1987)
Nicini v. Morra, 212 F. 3d 798 (3d Cir. 2000)
Nishiyama v. Dickson County, 814 F. 2d 277 (6th Cir. 1987)
Nixon v. Fitzgerald, 457 U.S. 731 (1982)
O'Connor v. Donaldson, 422 U.S. 563 (1975)
Osborn v. Bank of the United States, 22 U.S. (9 Wheat.) 738 (1824)
Owen v. City of Independence, 445 U.S. 622 (1980)
Owens v. Okure, 488 U.S. 235 (1989)
Parker v. Williams, 862 F. 2d 1471 (11th Cir. 1989)
Parratt v. Taylor, 451 U.S. 527 (1981)
Patsy v. Board of Regents, 457 U.S. 496 (1982)
Paul v. Davis, 424 U.S. 693 (1976)
Pembaur v. City of Cincinnati, 475 U.S. 469 (1986)
Pennhurst State School and Hospital v. Halderman, 465 U.S. 89 (1984)
Pennsylvania v. Union Gas, 491 U.S. 1 (1989)
Perry v. Sindermann, 408 U.S. 593 (1972)
Pickering v. Board of Education, 391 U.S. 563 (1968)
Pierson v. Ray, 386 U.S. 547 (1967)
Planned Parenthood of Southeastern Pennsylvania v. Casey, 505 U.S. 833 (1992)
Poindexter v. Greenhow, 114 U.S. 270 (1885)

Polk County v. Dodson, 454 U.S. 312 (1981)
Preiser v. Rodriguez, 411 U.S. 475 (1973)
Procunier v. Martinez, 416 U.S. 396 (1974)
Procunier v. Navarette, 434 U.S. 555 (1978)
Pulliam v. Allen, 466 U.S. 522 (1984)
Quern v. Jordan, 440 U.S. 332 (1979)
Railroad Commission v. Pullman Co., 312 U.S. 496 (1941)
Reich v. Collins, 513 U.S. 106 (1994)
Rendell-Baker v. Kohn, 457 U.S. 830 (1982)
Revere v. Massachusetts General Hospital, 463 U.S. 239 (1983)
Richardson v. McKnight, 521 U.S. 399 (1997)
Rizzo v. Goode, 220 F. 3d 8805 (7th Cir. 1976)
Rizzo v. Goode, 423 U.S. 362 (1976)
Rhodes v. Stewart, 488 U.S. 1 (1988)
Robertson v. Wegmann, 436 U.S. 584 (1978)
Rochin v. California, 342 U.S. 165 (1952)
Roe v. Wade, 410 U.S. 113 (1973)
Rosas v. Brooks, 826 F. 2d 1004 (11th Circ. 1987)
Ross v. United States, 910 F. 2d 1422 (7th Cir. 1990)
Rufo v. Inmates of the Suffolk County Jail, 502 U.S. 367 (1992)
Sacramento v. Lewis, 523 U.S. 833 (1998)
Saenz v. Heldenfels Bros., Inc., 183 F. 3d 389 (5th Cir. 1989)
Saucier v. Katz, 533 U.S. 199 (2001)
Scheuer v. Rhodes, 416 U.S. 232 (1974)
Schweiker v. Chilicky, 487 U.S. 412 (1988)
Seminole Tribe of Florida v. Florida, 519 U.S. 44 (1996)
Shields v. Utah Idaho Central R.R., 305 U.S. 177 (1938)
Shipp v. McMahon, 234 F. 3d 907 (5th Cir. 2000)
Siegert v. Gilley, 500 U.S. 226 (1991)
Singleton v. Wulff, 428 U.S. 106 (1976)
Slaughterhouse Cases 16 Wall. (83 U.S.) 36 (1873)
Smith v. Wade, 461 U.S. 30 (1983)
Sosna v. Iowa, 419 U.S. 393 (1975)
St. Louis v. Praprotnik, 485 U.S. 112 (1988)
Steagald v. United States, 451 U.S. 204 (1981)
Steffel v. Thompson, 415 U.S. 452 (1974)
Stone v. Powell, 428 U.S. 465 (1976)
Stump v. Sparkman, 435 U.S. 349 (1978)
Supreme Court of Virginia v. Consumers Union, 46 U.S. 719 (1980)
Swann v. Charlotte-Mecklenburg Board of Education, 402 U.S. 1 (1971)
Tennessee v. Garner, 471 U.S. 1 (1984)
Tenney v. Brandhove, 341 U.S. 367 (1951)
Texas v. Lesage, 528 U.S. 18 (1999)
Tinker v. Des Moines Independent Community School District, 393 U.S. 503 (1969)
Trainor v. Hernandez, 431 U.S. 434 (1977)
Truax v. Corrigan, 257 U.S. 312 (1921)

United Mine Workers of America v. Gibbs, 383 U.S. 715 (1966)
United Public Workers v. Mitchell, 330 U.S. 75 (1947)
United States v. Kubrick, 444 U.S. 111 (1979)
United States v. Lanier, 520 U.S. 259 (1997)
United States v. Mississippi, 380 U.S. 128 (1965)
United States v. Stanley, 487 U.S. 669 (1987)
University of Tennessee v. Elliot, 478 U.S. 788 (1986)
Valley Forge Christian College v. Americans United for Separation of Church and State, 454 U.S. 464 (1982)
Veronia School District 47J v. Acton, 515 U.S. 646 (1995)
Virginia v. Rives, 100 U.S. 313 (1880)
Vitek v. Jones, 445 U.S. 480 (1980)
Walker v. Birmingham, 388 U.S. 307 (1967)
Warth v. Seldin, 422 U.S. 490 (1975)
Washington v. Davis, 426 U.S. 229 (1976)
Webster v. Doe, 486 U.S. 592 (1988)
Webster v. Houston, 689 F. 2d 1220 (5th Cir. 1982)
West v. Atkins, 487 U.S. 72 (1988)
West Virginia State Board of Education v. Barnette, 319 U.S. 624 (1943)
West Virginia University Hospitals, Inc. v. Casey, 499 U.S. 83 (1991)
Westfall v. Erwin, 484 U.S. 292 (1988)
White v. Greenhow, 114 U.S. 307 (1885)
White v. Lemacks, 183 F. 3d 1253 (11th Cir. 1999)
White v. Rochford, 592 F. 2d 381 (7th Cir. 1979)
Whitley v. Albers, 475 U.S. 312 (1986)
Will v. Michigan Department of State Police, 491 U.S. 58 (1989)
Williamson County Regional Planning Commission v. Hamilton Bank, 573 U.S. 172 (1985)
Willowbrook v. Olech, 528 U.S. 562 (2000)
Wilson v. Garcia, 471 U.S. 261 (1985)
Wilson v. Layne, 526 U.S. 603 (1999)
Wisconsin v. Constantineau, 400 U.S. 433 (1971)
Wood v. Strickland, 420 U.S. 308 (1975)
Workman v. New York, 179 U.S. 552 (1900)
Wyatt v. Cole, 504 U.S. 158 (1992)
Youngberg v. Romeo, 457 U.S. 307 (1982)
Younger v. Harris, 401 U.S. 37 (1971)
Zentmyer v. Kendall County, 220 F. 3d 805 (7th Cir. 2000)
Zinermon v. Burch, 494 U.S. 113 (1990)

Index

ABOUT THE AUTHORS

MICHAEL L. WELLS is J. Alton Hosch Professor at the University of Georgia Law School. He has written a number of articles on constitutional remedies, constitutional law, and federal courts. He is co-author of the casebook *Constitutional Torts* (1995).

THOMAS A. EATON is J. Alton Hosch Professor at the University of Georgia Law School. Eaton has written numerous articles on constitutional torts and is co-author of the casebook *Constitutional Torts* (1995).

CPSIA information can be obtained at www.ICGtesting.com
Printed in the USA
LVOW10*0848180114

369937LV00002B/32/P